CASES IN
DYNAMIC FINANCE

MERGERS AND RESTRUCTURING

J. FRED WESTON

Prentice Hall
Upper Saddle River, New Jersey 07458

Editor-in-Chief: P.J. Boardman
Managing Editor (Editorial): Gladys Soto
Managing Editor (Production): John Roberts
Permissions Coordinator: Suzanne Grappi
Associate Director, Manufacturing: Vincent Scelta
Design Manager: Patricia Smythe
Manager, Print Production: Christy Mahon
Printer/Binder: Hamilton

Credits and acknowledgments borrowed from other sources and reproduced, with permission, in this textbook appear on appropriate page within text.

10 9 8 7 6 5 4 3 2 1

ISBN 0-13-060663-4

Preface

Fundamental change forces have impacted the world economy in recent decades. The pace of technological change has accelerated. The costs of communication and transportation have been so greatly reduced that markets have become global. While opportunities have expanded, the forms, sources, and intensity of competition have also grown.

The strong, new change forces have had major impacts. The technological requirements for firms have increased. As the roles of computers and the Internet have expanded, every firm has been impacted by increased requirements for information technology systems. The requirements for human capital inputs have grown relative to physical assets. The knowledge and organizational capital components of firm value have increased. Growth opportunities among product areas are unequal. New industries have been created. The pace of product introductions has accelerated. Economic activity has shifted from manufacturing to services of increasing sophistication. Distribution and marketing methods have changed, particularly by the impacts of the Internet. The value chain has deconstructed in the sense that more activities are performed by specialist firms. Forces for vertical integration have diminished in some areas, but increased in others. Changes in the organization of industries have taken place. Industry boundaries have become increasingly blurred. The forms and number of competitors have been increasing.

These new change forces have interacted with traditional ones. In an enterprise system with many independent decision units, attractive growth areas stimulate multiple firms and expanding investments. Growth and profitability areas expand and decline. Investments in plant and equipment and inventories result in overcapacity and economic adjustment periods. Business fluctuations of varying lengths and severity affect all the nations of the world economy. Financial markets continue to experience overshoots both on the upside and the downside.

The traditional models in both microeconomics and finance have been timeless or static in their orientation. But with the increased pace of change and economic turbulence, the adjustment processes that firms are required to continuously engage in need to be studied and their implications analyzed. This casebook seeks to focus on the adjustment processes of firms in increasingly dynamic environments. The cases in this compilation include firms that have succeeded and those that have floundered in the new environment. The content of the cases overlap the traditional areas of microeconomics, business finance, mergers and takeovers, restructuring, and corporate governance. The title, *Dynamic Finance*, seeks to encompass multiple areas. A convergence of disciplines is emerging.

This casebook seeks to develop material that will illuminate general concepts and principles. The cases are of unequal lengths depending on the subject matter. The longer cases lend themselves to the use of role-playing in which teams can represent different points of view and interest groups. Most of the cases involve actual companies so can be continuously updated for analysis and discussions. We find it useful to obtain multiple analyst reports with their outlook discussion to add new issues and different orientations for further discussion and analysis.

We plan to continue to add new cases as more companies adjust to the changing environment. They will be available in the Pearson Business Resources Case Series and periodically in compilations. (Please view information on this program at **www. pearsoncustom.com**). The availability of individual cases will enable users to select different compilations.

Since this will be a continuing activity, any comments or suggestions will be welcomed. Please send them to the corresponding author at:

J. Fred Weston
The Anderson School at UCLA
258 Tavistock Ave.
Los Angeles, CA 90049-3229

Tel. (310) 472-5110
Fax. (310) 472-9471
Email: jweston@anderson.ucla.edu
Web site: http://www.anderson.ucla.edu/faculty/john.weston

About the Author

J. Fred Weston is Professor Emeritus Recalled of Managerial Economics and Finance at the John E. Anderson Graduate School of Management at UCLA. He received his Ph.D. degree from the University of Chicago in 1948. He has published 31 books, 147 journal articles, and chaired 32 doctoral dissertations. Since 1968 he has been Director of the UCLA Research Program on Takeovers and Restructuring.

Dr. Weston has served as President of the American Finance Association, President of the Western Economic Association, President of the Financial Management Association, and as a member of the American Economic Association U.S. Census Advisory Committee. In 1978, he was selected as one of five outstanding teachers on the UCLA campus. In 1994, he received the Dean's Award for Outstanding Instruction in the Anderson School at UCLA. He has been an associate editor on a number of journals. He has been selected as a Fellow of the American Finance Association, of the Financial Management Association, and of the National Association of Business Economists.

Illustrative publications: Weston, Siu, and Johnson, *Takeovers, Restructuring, and Corporate Governance*, Third Edition, Prentice Hall, 2000; Weston and Copeland, *Managerial Finance*, Ninth Edition, 1998 Update; Copeland and Weston, *Financial Theory and Corporate Policy*, Third Edition, Addison Wesley, 1988; Weston, "Strategy and Business Economics," *Business Economics*, April 1989; Weston, Acquisitions Handbook, 1993; Chen, Weston, and Altman, "Financial Distress and Restructuring Models," *Financial Management*, Summer 1995; Weston and Chiu, "Growth Strategies in the Food Industry," *Business Economics*, January 1996; Weston and Siu, "Restructuring in the U.S. Oil Industry" (1996), and Weston, Johnson, and Siu, "Mergers and Restructuring in the World Oil Industry" (1999), *Journal of Energy Finance & Development*; Weston, Jawien, and Levitas, "Restructuring and Its Implications for Business Economics" (January 1998), and Weston, Johnson, and Siu, "M&As in the Evolution of the Global Chemical Industry" (October 1999) *Business Economics*.

He has been a consultant to business firms and governments on financial and economic policies since the early 1950's. Professor Weston has held professional consulting assignments with Bank of America, Lockheed, Transmerica, Boeing, Hughes Aircraft, Crocker Bank, Reading Railroad, Litton, General Electric, Westinghouse, Quaker Oats, Sun Harbor Tuna, Eli Lilly Co., Hoffman-LaRoche, 3M Company, General Motors, GAO, IRS, U.S. Department of Commerce–Bureau of the Census, Shoenfeld Industries, Chevron, Morgan Stanley & Co., and AT&T.

Contents

Case 1

The Ingersoll-Rand Acquisition of Clark Equipment

On April 9, 1995, the Ingersoll-Rand Company announced that it had reached agreement to buy the Clark Equipment Co. for $1.5 billion. This case describes the takeover process by which Ingersoll-Rand succeeded in acquiring Clark Equipment. Clark Equipment had turned down Ingersoll-Rand's initial proposal. We present a time line of the negotiation process including the defensive tactics employed by Clark Equipment.

1994   During the year Ingersoll-Rand, hereafter Ingersoll, conducted a review of the company's strategic outlook. Senior management considered potential transactions which could enhance shareholder value. An extensive list of potential acquisition candidates was developed. After successive narrowing of the list of potential acquisition candidates, in January 1995 Ingersoll began to focus on the Clark Equipment Company, hereafter Clark.

3/15/95   James E. Perrella, Chairman and CEO of Ingersoll, phoned Leo J. McKernan, Chairman and CEO of Clark. Perrella proposed to acquire Clark for cash at $75–$77. McKernan replied that Clark was not interested. The same day Perrella sent a letter to McKernan and each of Clark's directors. He expressed his disappointment that he was not given the opportunity to explain fully the Ingersoll proposal. He stated that Ingersoll had been studying Clark for some time and was impressed with its performance. He expressed the belief that the complementary aspects of the two businesses would enable the combined entity to be an even stronger competitor in the global marketplace.

3/20/95   McKernan telephoned Perrella to inform him that Clark would convene a special meeting of its Board to consider the proposal.

3/21/95   Perrella sent another letter describing the advantages of the offer to Clark.

3/23/95   McKernan phoned Perrella to report that the Board meeting would be on Monday, 3/27/95.

3/28/95   McKernan sent a letter to Perrella stating that while the Board appreciated Ingersoll's interest in Clark, it "unanimously reaffirmed its long-standing position that the Company is not for sale. We therefore decline your proposal."

3/28/95   Perrella wrote a letter to McKernan expressing surprise and disappointment. He pointed out that the acquisition proposal represented a 50% premium over the recent market price of the common stock of Clark. He said that he felt the proposed transaction was "so compelling for the stockholders of both of our companies that we feel obligated to pursue it notwithstanding your Board's rejection. Because we are confident that Clark's stockholders will enthusiastically support our proposal, we are sending this letter to you and also releasing it publicly."

Later that day Clark issued a press release reporting the Board's decision of 3/27/95 to reject the Ingersoll offer. He stated that the proposed price was "entirely inadequate." He noted that Clark's share price had reached a high of $71 only five months ago. He further stated, "I believe this is an opportunistic attempt to buy Clark during a temporary decline in the price of Clark's shares."

3/29/95   Clark filed suit against Ingersoll-Rand alleging that the proposed acquisition would violate the federal antitrust laws and requested "preliminary and permanent injunctions barring the Parent from proceeding with the acquisition."

3/30/95   Ingersoll issued a press release stating that "Clark knows as well as we do that any antitrust issues which may arise from the paver overlap between our two companies can readily be resolved. Ingersoll-Rand's 1994 domestic revenues from the relevant product line were below $10 million out of 1994 total revenues of $4.5 billion."

3/31/95   Ingersoll sent Clark a demand under Delaware law for a list of stockholders.

4/3/95   Ingersoll commenced the tender offer and delivered a notice to Clark nominating seven persons for election as directors at Clark's annual meeting scheduled for 5/9/95. In a letter of the same date Perrella stated, "We regret that we have to resort to these actions; we would have greatly preferred to enter into negotiations with you in an effort to reach agreement on a merger transaction. But even though we have commenced a tender offer, we continue to be interested in meeting with you to negotiate the terms of a transaction that can be approved by your Board. When your Board recognizes that its fiduciary duties require consideration of the sale of Clark, please call me."

4/9/95 Ingersoll announced that it had reached agreement to buy Clark with a sweetened offer at $86 per share for the 17.4 million Clark shares, representing a total of $1.5 billion. The original offer had been $77 per share for a total of $1.34 billion. A joint statement by the two companies announced that both Boards had unanimously approved the sweetened merger terms. Clark Chairman and CEO McKernan stated, "This merger delivers fair value to our shareholders and also provides our employees with excellent opportunities within the framework of a fine company like Ingersoll-Rand." Chairman and CEO Perrella said that, "this merger represents a great fit."

5/25/95 In the Ingersoll-Rand 10Q Report to the SEC dated 8/14/95, the following materials were included:

"On May 25, 1995, CEC Acquisition Corp. (CEC), a wholly-owned subsidiary of the company, acquired 16,553,617 shares of Clark Equipment Company (Clark) (which, together with shares already owned by the company, represented approximately 98.4 percent of the outstanding shares) for a cash price of $86 per share pursuant to an April 12, 1995 amended tender offer. Clark's business is the design, manufacture and sale of compact construction machinery, asphalt paving equipment, axles and transmissions for off-highway equipment, and golf cars and utility vehicles. On May 31, 1995, the company completed the merger of CEC with Clark. Upon consummation of the merger, Clark became a wholly-owned subsidiary of the company and the shareholders of Clark who did not tender their shares became entitled to receive $86 per share. The total purchase price for Clark was approximately $1.5 billion after taking into account amounts paid in respect of outstanding stock options, employment contracts and various transaction costs. The acquisition has been accounted for as a purchase. The purchase price was preliminarily allocated to the acquired assets and liabilities based on estimated fair values and is subject to final adjustment. The company has classified as goodwill, the costs in excess of the fair value of net assets acquired. Such excess costs are being amortized on a straight line basis over forty years. Intangible assets also represent costs allocated to patents and trademarks and other specifically identifiable assets arising from business acquisitions. These assets are amortized over their estimated useful lives."

SOME COMMENTS ON THE ABOVE

1. The antitrust issue was resolved by a divestiture of a product line where there was some overlap in activities.
2. When the merger transaction was completed on 4/9/95, the stock price of Ingersoll-Rand closed at $33.125. At the close of trading on 8/28/97 its stock price was $62.125.

QUESTION

Why did Clark initially reject the offer and then finally accept it?

Case 2

Acquisition of CCH by Wolters Kluwer nv

This case draws on materials filed with the SEC in connection with the acquisition of CCH by Wolters Kluwer nv. In a letter to the CCH shareholders, Mr. Oakleigh Thorne, President and CEO of CCH, requests shareholder support for the transaction.

CCH Incorporated
Riverwoods, Illinois 60015
December 1, 1995

Dear Fellow Stockholder:

I am pleased to inform you that CCH Incorporated has entered into an agreement and plan of merger with Wolters Kluwer nv pursuant to which a wholly owned subsidiary of Wolters Kluwer has commenced a tender offer to purchase all of the outstanding shares of CCH for $55.50 per share in cash. Under the agreement, consummation of the tender offer will be followed by a merger in which non-tendering stockholders will receive $55.50 per share in cash or the highest price paid per share pursuant to the tender offer and CCH will become a wholly owned subsidiary of Wolters Kluwer. Holders of shares of Class A Common Stock and holders of shares of Class B Common Stock will receive the same consideration in the tender offer and subsequent merger. Members of the Thorne family and certain trusts with Thorne family members as trustees have agreed to tender their shares (including an aggregate of approximately 58% of the outstanding shares of voting stock (i.e., Class A Common Stock) into the tender offer and to vote such shares in favor of the Merger, and have granted an option to Wolters Kluwer to purchase shares.

The Board of Directors of CCH has unanimously determined that the terms of the Wolters Kluwer tender offer and the merger are fair to, and in the best interests of, CCH and its stockholders and recommends that stockholders accept the Wolters Kluwer offer and tender their shares pursuant to it.

Enclosed are the Wolters Kluwer Offer to Purchase, dated December 1, 1995, Letter(s) of Transmittal and other related documents. These documents set forth the terms and conditions of the tender offer. Attached is a copy of the Company's Schedule 14D-9, as filed with the Securities and Exchange Commission. The Schedule 14D-9 describes in more detail the reasons for the Board's conclusions and contains other important information relating to the tender offer. We urge you to consider this information carefully.

The Board of Directors and the management and employees of CCH thank you for your support.

> Sincerely,
> Oakleigh Thorne,
> President and Chief Executive Officer

The following pages reproduce pages from the Schedule 14D-9 filed by CCH. This Schedule is required under Section 14(d)(4) in connection with any merger or tender offer.

SECURITIES AND EXCHANGE COMMISSION

WASHINGTON, D.C. 20549

SCHEDULE 14D-9

Solicitation/Recommendation Statement
Pursuant to Section 14(d) (4) of
the Securities Exchange Act of 1934

CCH INCORPORATED
(Name of Subject Company)

CCH INCORPORATED
(Name of Person(s) Filing Statement)

Class A Common Stock, $1.00 Par Value
(Title of Class of Securities)
124883109
(CUSIP Number of Class of Securities)

Class B Common Stock, $1.00 Par Value
(Title of Class of Securities)
124883208
(CUSIP Number of Class of Securities)

Oakleigh Thorne
President and Chief Executive Officer
CCH Incorporated
2700 Lake Cook Road
Riverwoods, Illinois 60015

(Name, Address, and Telephone Number of Person
Authorized to Receive Notices and Communications
on Behalf of the Person(s) Filing Statement)

Copies to:

Deirdre M. von Moltke	Douglas A. Doetsch
Sidley & Austin	Mayer, Brown & Platt
One First National Plaza	190 South LaSalle Street
Chicago, Illinois 60603	Chicago, Illinois 60603
(312) 853-7000	(312) 782-0600

Offer to Purchase for Cash

All Outstanding Shares of
Class A Common Stock and Class B Common Stock
of

CCH Incorporated

at

$55.50 Net Per Share

by

WK Acquisition Sub, Inc.
a wholly owned subsidiary
of

Wolters Kluwer nv

THE OFFER AND WITHDRAWAL RIGHTS WILL EXPIRE AT 5:00 P.M., NEW YORK CITY
TIME, ON THURSDAY, JANUARY 4, 1996, UNLESS THE OFFER IS EXTENDED.

THE OFFER IS CONDITIONED UPON, AMONG OTHER THINGS, THERE BEING VALIDLY
TENDERED BY THE EXPIRATION DATE AND NOT WITHDRAWN AT LEAST THAT
NUMBER OF SHARES OF CLASS A COMMON STOCK, PAR VALUE $1.00 PER
SHARE, OF CCH INCORPORATED WHICH WOULD CONSTITUTE A
MAJORITY OF THE OUTSTANDING SHARES OF CLASS A COMMON
STOCK ON A FULLY DILUTED BASIS. SEE SECTION 14.

THE BOARD OF DIRECTORS OF CCH INCORPORATED HAS UNANIMOUSLY APPROVED THE
MERGER AGREEMENT, THE OFFER AND THE MERGER, HAS UNANIMOUSLY
DETERMINED THAT THE MERGER IS ADVISABLE AND THAT THE TERMS OF THE
OFFER AND THE MERGER ARE FAIR TO, AND IN THE BEST INTERESTS
OF, CCH INCORPORATED'S STOCKHOLDERS AND RECOMMENDS THAT
STOCKHOLDERS ACCEPT THE OFFER AND TENDER THEIR SHARES.

IMPORTANT

*Any stockholder desiring to tender all or any portion of such stockholder's shares of Class A Common Stock
or Class B Common Stock of the Company (collectively, the "Shares") should either (a) complete and sign the
appropriate Letter of Transmittal (the Letter of Transmittal for the Class A Common Stock is BLUE and the
Letter of Transmittal for the Class B Common Stock is GREEN) or a manually signed facsimile thereof in
accordance with the instructions in the Letter of Transmittal, mail or deliver it and any other required documents
to the Depositary and either deliver the certificate(s) for such Shares to the Depositary or tender such Shares
pursuant to the procedure for book-entry transfer set forth in Section 3 or (b) request such stockholder's broker,
dealer, commercial bank, trust company or other nominee to effect the transaction. A stockholder whose Shares
are registered in the name of a broker, dealer, commercial bank, trust company or other nominee must contact
such broker, dealer, commercial bank, trust company or other nominee to tender such Shares.*

*Any stockholder who desires to tender Shares and whose certificates evidencing such Shares are not
immediately available or who cannot comply with the procedures for book-entry transfer on a timely basis may
tender such Shares by following the procedures for guaranteed delivery set forth in Section 3.*

*Questions and requests for assistance may be directed to the Information Agent or the Dealer Manager at
their respective addresses and telephone numbers set forth on the back cover of this Offer to Purchase.
Additional copies of this Offer to Purchase, the Letters of Transmittal, the Notice of Guaranteed Delivery and
other related materials may be obtained from the Information Agent or from brokers, dealers, commercial banks
and trust companies.*

The Dealer Manager for the Offer is:

CS First Boston

December 1, 1995

Item 1. Security and Subject Company.

The name of the subject company is CCH Incorporated, a Delaware corporation (the "Company"), and the address of its principal executive offices is 2700 Lake Cook Road, Riverwoods, Illinois 60015. The respective titles of the classes of equity securities to which this statement relates are: the Company's Class A Common Stock, $1.00 par value per share ("Class A Common Stock"), and the Company's Class B Common Stock, $1.00 par value per share ("Class B Common Stock," and together with the Class A Common Stock, the "Common Stock"). At the close of business on November 27, 1995 (i) 16,638,512 shares of Class A Common Stock were issued and outstanding, (ii) 16,397,122 shares of Class B Common Stock were issued and outstanding and (iii) vested options to purchase 1,217,000 shares of Class B Common Stock were issued and outstanding.

Item 2. Tender Offer of the Bidder.

This statement relates to the tender offer by WK Acquisition Sub, Inc. (the "Offeror"), a Delaware corporation and a wholly owned subsidiary of Wolters Kluwer nv, a corporation organized under the laws of The Netherlands (the "Parent"), to purchase all outstanding shares of Common Stock (collectively, the "Shares") at $55.50 per Share (the "Offer Price"), net to the seller in cash without interest, upon the terms and subject to the conditions set forth in the Offer to Purchase, dated December 1, 1995 (the "Offer to Purchase"), and the related Letters of Transmittal (which together with the Offer to Purchase and any amendments or supplements thereto constitute the "Offer"). The Offer is disclosed in the Tender Offer Statement on Schedule 14D-1 dated December 1, 1995 (the "Schedule 14D-1"), as filed by the Offeror and Parent with the Securities and Exchange Commission (the "Commission"). The Schedule 14D-1 states that the address of the principal executive offices of the Offeror and Parent is Stadhouderskade 1, 1054 ES Amsterdam, The Netherlands.

The Offer is being made pursuant to the terms of an Agreement and Plan of Merger (the "Merger Agreement"), dated as of November 27, 1995, among Parent, the Offeror and the Company, which provides that, following completion of the Offer, the Offeror will be merged with and into the Company upon the terms and subject to the conditions set forth in the Merger Agreement (the "Merger"). As a condition to signing the Merger Agreement, Parent required that the Shares owned by the Thorne family (which include, in the aggregate, approximately 58% of the voting Shares) be committed to the Offer upon the terms and subject to the conditions of the Stock Option and Tender Agreement (the "Option Agreement"), dated as of November 27, 1995, among Parent, the Offeror, and Oakleigh B. Thorne, Honore T. Wamsler, Daniel K. Thorne and certain related parties of such individuals (collectively, the "Stockholders"). Certain terms and conditions of the Merger Agreement and the Option Agreement are described below in Item 3. Copies of the Merger Agreement and the Option Agreement are filed as exhibits to this statement and are incorporated herein by reference. A copy of the press release issued by the Company on November 27, 1995 is filed as an exhibit to this statement and incorporated herein by reference.

Item 3. Identity and Background

(a) The name and business address of the Company, which is the person filing this statement, are set forth in Item 1 above, which information is incorporated herein by reference.

(b)(1) Certain contracts, agreements, arrangements and understandings between the Company and certain of its directors and executive officers are described in the Company's Information Statement dated December 1, 1995 under Directors and Executive Officers of the Company, Executive Compensation, Options/SAR Grants, Pension Plan, Supplemental Retirement Plan, Shareholder Return Performance Information, and Stock Ownership of Principal Stockholders, Nominee Directors, and Management. The Information Statement is attached hereto as Schedule I, filed as Exhibit 3 to this Schedule 14D-9 and incorporated herein by reference. In addition, certain contracts, agreements, arrangements and understandings relating to the Company and/or the Company's directors and executive officers are contained in the Merger Agreement and are described below under "Merger Agreement."

(b)(2) Certain Background Information.

In 1991, in response to declining levels of customer satisfaction, eroding profit margins and a weakening competitive position, the Company developed a new strategic direction focused on re-engineering the processes required to create value for customers, building new capabilities and returning the Company to a position of financial strength. The Company has invested approximately $314.7 million in the re-engineering of its business units, focusing first on CCH Legal Information Services ("CCH LIS"), which offers a variety of services to assist attorneys in handling corporate, securities, credit and intellectual property matters, second on Computax, which offers software and computer services for the processing of tax returns, and last on U.S. Publishing, a provider of legal and tax information products delivered in print, CD-ROM and on-line formats. The re-engineering of CCH LIS has resulted in increased customer satisfaction, sales growth and profitability. The Company's re-engineering initiative has transformed Computax from a provider of mainframe-based services to a provider of software-based services and dramatically improved the operating profits of Computax. The investment program at U.S. Publishing, which involves the re-engineering of the content creation, operations, customer management and product management processes as well as the development of an electronic product development capability, is nearing completion.

All references to time in the following summary are to New York City time.

In the late spring of 1995, the Chief Executive Officer ("CEO") of the Company met with the Chairman of the Executive Board ("Chairman") of Parent to discuss the Company's and Parent's respective businesses and recent developments in the publishing industry.

In mid-summer, the CEO of the Company was contacted by a senior executive (the "Senior Executive") of another multi-national publisher ("Entity Two") to set up a meeting. During the meeting, the Entity Two Senior Executive and the CEO of the Company discussed a possible business combination and arranged a meeting for mid-September.

In August, the CEO of the Company discussed with the Board of Directors of the Company at their regularly scheduled teleconference meeting the contacts the CEO had had with Parent and Entity Two. The CEO of the Company, in August, also contacted Goldman, Sachs & Co. ("Goldman Sachs") to discuss an engagement wherein Goldman Sachs would conduct a study of the Company's strategic alternatives. Goldman Sachs was asked to present its findings at the Company's regularly scheduled Board of Directors meeting in mid-September.

In mid-September, Goldman Sachs made a presentation to the Company's Board of Directors. The presentation included a review of a range of alternatives, including, but not limited to, operating the business on a stand alone basis and implementing the Company's re-engineering plans, possible business combinations, acquisitions and dispositions and a recapitalization. In addition, legal counsel briefed the Company's Board of Directors about their duties in considering the alternatives. The Board of Directors of the Company authorized management to continue discussions with Entity Two and to engage in discussions with other potential parties.

Following the meeting of the Board of Directors of the Company in mid-September, the CEO of the Company, another member of the Company's senior management and a Company consultant met with the Senior Executive and the Chief Financial Officer ("CFO") of Entity Two to discuss the merits of a potential business combination. Entity Two indicated that it had an interest in pursuing a possible acquisition of the Company and that it expected to provide a preliminary indication of its valuation for the Company.

In October, the CEO of the Company and a representative of Goldman Sachs met with the Senior Executive and CFO of Entity Two to discuss Entity Two's valuation of a business combination of the two companies.

Subsequent to the meeting, the CFO and another member of management of Entity Two arranged to meet a representative of Goldman Sachs to determine how a business combination between the Company and Entity Two could move forward and scheduled meetings with the Company for November 7 and 8 to discuss the Company's business activities and its financial performance.

At the regularly scheduled meeting of the Board of Directors of the Company on October 19, the CEO of the Company updated the Company's Board of Directors on the discussions with Entity Two.

In late October, the Chairman of Parent contacted the CEO of the Company to invite the CEO of the Company to meet with the Chairman of Parent at Parent's headquarters to discuss strategic opportunities for the two companies in light of the current activity in the legal publishing industry.

On October 30, the CEO of the Company, another member of the Company's senior management and a representative of Goldman Sachs met with members of the Executive Board and the CFO of Parent. Parent expressed an interest in pursuing a possible acquisition of the Company and meetings were scheduled with the Company for November 16 and 17 to discuss the Company's business activities and its financial performance.

On November 7 and 8, the senior management of the Company conducted the scheduled meetings with members of senior management of Entity Two and its financial advisors. A further meeting was planned to review Entity Two's evaluation of the matters discussed on November 7 and 8.

On November 16 and 17, the senior management of the Company conducted the scheduled meetings with members of senior management of Parent. A further meeting was planned to review Parent's evaluation of the matters discussed on November 16 and 17.

On November 21 and 22, the CEO of the Company, another member of the Company's senior management and a representative of Goldman Sachs met with the Senior Executive and the CFO of Entity Two. In the late afternoon of November 21, the CFO of Entity Two presented to a member of the Company's senior management and a representative of Goldman Sachs a letter preliminarily outlining the terms of a cash offer for the purchase of the Company.

On the morning of November 22, the parties met again to discuss Entity Two's offer. Following a discussion of the economic value that a business combination would create, the Senior Executive of Entity Two agreed to convene the Executive Board of Entity Two to reconsider its offer. After meeting with the Executive Board of Entity Two, the Chairman made an increased cash offer for the purchase of the Company.

In the afternoon of November 22, the CEO of the Company contacted the Chairman of Parent and indicated that their planned meeting should occur soon and the Chairman of Parent agreed to give the Company an indication of Parent's ability to make an offer for the Company following a meeting of Parent's Supervisory Board on November 23. They tentatively agreed to meet, if appropriate, on November 24.

In the afternoon of November 23, after Parent's Supervisory Board Meeting, the Chairman of Parent made a verbal offer of $1.9 billion. Following that conversation, the CEO of the Company contacted the Senior Executive of Entity Two to discuss the status of the Entity Two offer. The CEO of the Company then consulted with the Company's legal and financial advisors and established a formal process through which written offers would be submitted for evaluation by the Company's Board of Directors. The process required that offer letters be sent by Entity Two and Parent to the offices of the Company's legal advisors by 5pm on November 24. The offers would be presented to the Company's Board of Directors at a special meeting to be held on November 25.

In the afternoon of November 24, the Chairman of Parent, other members of Parent's senior management and representatives of Parent's legal and financial advisors met with the CEO of the Company, a member of Company's senior management and representatives of Goldman Sachs to discuss the instructions for submitting an offer.

The Company received offer letters from Parent and Entity Two in the early evening on November 24.

On November 25, the Company's legal and financial advisors met with the Board of Directors of the Company by teleconference to discuss the Parent and Entity Two offers. Both offers were conditioned on the binding agreement of members of the Thorne family to sell their Shares. The Board of Directors reviewed the two offers and discussed the terms of the offers and Goldman Sachs discussed a preliminary financial analysis of the offers. During the meeting of the Board of Directors, a financial advisor to Entity Two called and indicated to the CEO of the Company and a representative of Goldman Sachs that Entity Two was in a position to make an improvement to its offer, but could make only a modest increase. Entity Two was not informed of the amount of Parent's offer. The Board of Directors authorized senior management to enter into discussions with Parent regarding a possible transaction. Parent's offer was conditioned on negotiations being conducted on an exclusive basis.

The CEO of the Company contacted other members of the Thorne family to discuss a possible transaction involving the sale of their Shares and to solicit their views of such a transaction.

On November 25 and November 26, the legal and financial advisors to the Company met with those of Parent to negotiate the Merger Agreement and legal advisors to the Thorne family met with those of Parent to negotiate the Option Agreement. In the evening of November 26, the Board of Directors met with its financial and legal advisors. Representatives of Goldman Sachs provided a fairness opinion orally to the Board of Directors. The Company's legal advisors briefed the Board of Directors on the terms of the Merger Agreement and Option Agreement. Based on the factors described below in Item 4, the Board of Directors approved the transaction.

In the late morning of November 27, the trustees with voting power over the Thorne family shares executed the Option Agreement. The Merger Agreement was finalized and executed in the early afternoon of November 27. Goldman Sachs confirmed its oral fairness opinion in writing. Public announcements were made in the United States and The Netherlands immediately after the execution of the Merger Agreement.

(b)(3) Merger Agreement.

The following summary of the Merger Agreement, a copy of which is filed as an Exhibit hereto and incorporated by reference herein, is qualified by reference to the text of the Merger Agreement.

The Offer. Pursuant to the terms of the Merger Agreement, the Offeror is required to commence the Offer no later than December 1, 1995 and to keep the Offer open until 5:00 p.m. (EDT) January 4, 1996. The obligations of the Offeror to accept for payment, and pay for, any Shares tendered pursuant to the Offer are subject to the conditions that (i) all waiting periods under the Hart-Scott-Rodino Antitrust Improvements Act of 1976, as amended (the ''HSR Act''), applicable to the purchase of Shares pursuant to the Offer shall have expired or been terminated, (ii) there shall have been validly tendered and not withdrawn prior to the expiration of the Offer such number of Shares that would constitute a majority of the voting power of the outstanding shares (determined on a fully diluted basis) of Class A Common Stock (the ''Minimum Condition''), and (iii) on or after the date of the Merger Agreement none of the following conditions, exist or shall occur and remain in effect:

(a) there shall have been any action taken, or any statute, rule, regulation, judgment, order or injunction promulgated, entered, enforced, enacted or issued, by any domestic (federal or state) court, commission, governmental body, regulatory agency, authority or tribunal which (i) prohibits or limits or seeks to prohibit or materially limit Parent's or Offeror's (x) ownership, or seeks to impose material limitations on the ability of Parent or Offeror to acquire or hold, or exercise full rights of ownership of, any Shares accepted for payment pursuant to the Offer, including, without limitation, the right to vote such Shares or (y) operation of all or a material portion of the Company's business or assets, or compels Parent to dispose of or hold separate all or a material portion of the Company's business or assets as a result of the Offer or the Merger, or (ii) prohibits, or limits or seeks to prohibit or materially limit, or makes illegal, the acceptance for payment, purchase or payment for Shares or the consummation of the Offer or the Merger and such statute, rule, regulation, judgment, order or injunction shall remain in effect for a period of fifteen business days after the issuance thereof; *provided, however,* that in order to invoke this condition with respect to any such statute, rule, regulation, judgment, order or injunction Parent shall have used its reasonable best efforts to prevent such statute, rule, regulation, judgment, order or injunction or ameliorate the effects thereof; *provided, further,* that if any such order or injunction is a temporary restraining order or preliminary injunction, Parent may not, for a period of 30 days, by virtue of this condition alone, amend or terminate the Offer, but may only extend the Offer and thereby postpone acceptance for payment or purchase of Shares;

(b) the Merger Agreement shall have been terminated in accordance with its terms;

(c) the Company shall have breached any of its representations and warranties set forth in the Merger Agreement (other than any matters that, in the aggregate, would not have a material adverse effect on the Company);

(d) the Company shall have failed in any material respect to perform any material obligation or covenant required by the Merger Agreement to be performed or complied with by it;

(e) the Board of Directors of the Company shall have withdrawn or modified in a manner adverse to Parent or Offeror its approval or recommendation of the Offer, the Merger or the Merger Agreement, or approved or recommended any Takeover Proposal (as hereinafter defined); or

(f) there shall have occurred and continued to exist for at least three business days (i) any general suspension of trading in, or limitation on prices for, securities on a national securities exchange in the United States or (ii) a declaration of a banking moratorium or any suspension of payments in respect of banks in the United States or The Netherlands;

which, in the reasonable judgment of Offeror, makes it inadvisable to proceed with the Offer or with such acceptance for payment or payment.

The foregoing conditions may be waived by Offeror, in whole or part, at any time and from time to time, in the sole discretion of Offeror. The failure by Offeror at any time to exercise any of the foregoing rights will not be deemed a waiver of any right and each right will be deemed an ongoing right which may be asserted at any time and from time to time.

Company Actions.   Pursuant to the Merger Agreement, the Company has agreed that on the date of the commencement of the Offer, subject to the fiduciary duties of the Board of Directors of the Company under applicable law as determined by the Board of Directors of the Company in good faith after consultation with the Company's outside counsel, it will file with the Commission and mail to its stockholders, a Solicitation/Recommendation Statement on Schedule 14D-9 containing the recommendation of the Board of Directors that the Company's stockholders accept the Offer and that the holders of shares of Class A Common Stock approve the Merger.

The Merger.   The Merger Agreement provides that, upon the terms and subject to the conditions of the Merger Agreement, and in accordance with the General Corporation Law of the State of Delaware, as amended (the "DGCL"), the Offeror shall be merged with and into the Company at the effective time of the Merger (the "Effective Time"). Following the Merger, the separate corporate existence of the Offeror shall cease and the Company shall continue as the surviving corporation (the "Surviving Corporation") and shall succeed to and assume all the rights and obligations of the Offeror in accordance with the DGCL. The Certificate of Incorporation and Bylaws of the Offeror shall become the Certificate of Incorporation and Bylaws of the Surviving Corporation. The directors of the Offeror shall become the initial directors of the Surviving Corporation and the officers of the Company shall become the initial officers of the Surviving Corporation.

Conversion of Securities.   At the Effective Time, each Share issued and outstanding immediately prior thereto shall be cancelled and extinguished and each Share (other than Shares held by the Company as treasury shares, Shares owned by any wholly owned subsidiary of the Company, Shares owned by Parent, the Offeror or any wholly owned subsidiary of Parent, and Dissenting Shares (as defined below)) shall, by virtue of the Merger and without any action on the part of the Offeror, Parent, the Company or the holders of the Shares, be converted into and represent the right to receive in cash, without interest, the per Share consideration paid in the Offer (the "Merger Consideration"). Each share of common stock of the Offeror issued and outstanding immediately prior to the Effective Time shall, at the Effective Time, by virtue of the Merger and without any action on the part of the Offeror, Parent, the Company or the holders of Shares, be converted into and shall thereafter evidence one validly issued and outstanding share of common stock of the Surviving Corporation.

Dissenting Shares.   If required by the DGCL, Shares which are held by holders who have properly exercised appraisal rights with respect thereto in accordance with Section 262 of the DGCL ("Dissenting

Shares'') will not be exchangeable for the right to receive the Merger Consideration, and holders of such Shares will be entitled to receive payment of the appraisal value of such Shares unless such holders fail to perfect or withdraw or lose their right to appraisal and payment under the DGCL.

Merger Without a Meeting of Stockholders.   In the event that the Offeror, or any other direct or indirect subsidiary of Parent, shall acquire at least 90% of the outstanding Shares, the parties agree to take all necessary and appropriate actions to cause the Merger to become effective without a meeting of stockholders of the Company, in accordance with Section 253 of the DGCL, as soon as practicable after the expiration of the Offer, but in no event later than six business days thereafter.

Representations and Warranties.   In the Merger Agreement, the Company has made customary representations and warranties to Parent and the Offeror, including, but not limited to, representations and warranties relating to the Company's organization and qualification, capitalization, its authority to enter into the Merger Agreement and carry out the related transactions, filings made by the Company with the Commission under the Securities Act of 1933, as amended (the ''Securities Act''), or the Securities Exchange Act of 1934, as amended (the ''Exchange Act'') (including financial statements included in the documents filed by the Company under the Securities Act and the Exchange Act), required consents and approvals, the absence of certain material adverse changes or events, approval by the Board of Directors of the Merger Agreement and the Option Agreement for all purposes under Section 203 of the DGCL, payment of taxes, compliance with applicable laws, litigation, material liabilities of the Company and its subsidiaries, employee benefit plans, intellectual property and environmental matters.

The Offeror and Parent have also made customary representations and warranties to the Company, including, but not limited to, representations and warranties relating to the Offeror's and Parent's organization and qualification, capitalization, authority to enter into the Merger Agreement and carry out the related transactions, required consents and approvals and the availability of sufficient funds to consummate the Offer.

Items for discussion in the above CCH Schedule D and Proxy Statement to shareholders:

1. Note that page 1–8 is simply the covering page for filing the Schedule 14D.

2. The next page is a copy of the summary offer by the WK Acquisition Sub, Inc. of Wolters Kluwer nv to buy CCH for cash at $55.50 Net Per Share. The premerger price of CCH had been relatively flat for months at about $30 per share. The price represented a substantial premium.

3. The bulk of the Schedule D that we have reproduced is "Item 3" which describes the merger negotiating process. In 1991 CCH suffered some reversals. CCH (referred to in Schedule D as "the Company") developed a new strategic direction. Apparently in connection with its restructuring, CCH began a relationship with Wolters Kluwer which received representation on the CCH Board of Directors. In Schedule D Wolters Kluwer is referred to as "Parent."

Schedule D then lists a sequence of negotiations on the sale of CCH. These will be summarized in a time line.

a. Spring, 1995. The CEO of CCH met with the Chairman of Wolters Kluwer to discuss their respective businesses and trends in the publishing industry.

b. Mid-summer, 1995. The CEO of CCH was contacted by a senior executive of another multi-national publisher (Entity Two). They met and discussed a possible business combination.

c. August, 1995. The Board of CCH discussed the negotiations that CCH had had with Parent and Entity Two. Goldman Sachs was hired to conduct a study of the stratetgic alternatives available to CCH.

d. Mid-September, 1995. Goldman Sachs made a presentation to the Board. The Board authorized management to continue discussions with existing and other potential partners.

e. October, 1995. The CEO of CCH and Goldman Sachs met with Entity Two to discuss the valuation of CCH in a combination of the two companies.

f. October 30, 1995. Parent (Wolters Kluwer) met with CCH and Goldman Sachs to discuss a possible acquisition.

g. November 7–8, 1995. More meetings between CCH and Entity Two about an acquisition.

h. November 21–22, 1995. Entity Two makes a cash offer for the purchase of CCH.

i. November 23, 1995. Parent makes a verbal offer of $1.9 billion to buy CCH.

j. November 24, 1995. CCH received offer letters from the two bidders.

k. November 25, 1995. CCH and its advisors reviewed the two offers. The Thorne family was contacted to solicit their views with respect to an acquisition.

l. November 26, 1995. CCH and its advisors met with Wolters Kluwer and its advisors to negotiate an Option Agreement to purchase. The CCH Board approved the transaction.

m. November 27, 1995. The trustees with voting power over the Thorne family shares executed the Option Agreement. The Merger Agreement was finalized. Goldman Sachs confirmed its oral fairness opinion in writing.

The above time table of the merger negotiations is a good illustration of a concept emphasized in chapter 2 of our Text. The Board of Directors is obligated to test the market to get the best possible price for shareholders. Since CCH and Wolters Kluwer already had a relationship, Wolters Kluwer was in an advantageous position.

Nevertheless, the Board seriously considered the proposal from Entity Two and opened the bidding to other parties as well. Although Wolters Kluwer won the bidding contest, the Board demonstrated due diligence by considering competitive offers.

The remainder of the above materials describes some aspects of the technical, procedural processes involved in completing a merger transaction. They provide information on the procedural aspects of completing a merger transaction.

QUESTION

How did the long time relationship between CCH and Wolters Kluwer affect the transaction?

Case 3

Growth Opportunities and the Dynamic Financial Strategies of MCI

The story of MCI represents the origins and development of the modern telecommunications industry. Before MCI, the telecommunications industry and particularly the long-distance market were dominated by AT&T. MCI challenged that dominance. MCI initiated competition in the telecommunications industry, it introduced a series of new technologies to provide telephone services at lower prices, it introduced new types of telephone services, and in so doing set in motion a series of developments that transformed the telecommunications industry and laid important foundations for the emergence of the broader information industry.

The story of MCI is a classic case. It is a classic because it treats the fundamental issues that face every firm whether it is in the early or late stages of its development and growth. The story of MCI is the story of how a new firm can enter an industry with high entry barriers to become a significant competitor in one of the major industries of the economy. It charged lower prices; it applied new technologies and provided new services. In so doing, it introduced competition into the telecommunications industry, setting in motion forces ultimately leading to the Telecommunications Act of 1996. There is, therefore, much to learn from the MCI history.

This history of MCI is both instructive and inspirational. It started with a concept. At each stage along the way it faced the normal problems of establishing a new company in an industry with a formidable dominant competitor, AT&T. At each major step regulatory and/or congressional approval was required. In addition, the obstacles thrown up by its dominant competitor and the hurdles and reversals in the regulatory process repeatedly threatened the ability of the company to raise financing and, therefore, its very existence. The story of MCI is an exciting history because there were successive new impacts on MCI that had to be overcome. It is an inspirational story because if a small growing company could overcome the formidable obstacles that impacted MCI, it offers hope to every company as it faces reversals in its development.

The history of MCI also demonstrates the vital role that the art of finance performs in the growth and development of a business firm. Growth requires financing. The expansion of sales and services for growth to attain the critical mass required for low cost operations requires a solid foundation of a healthy financial organization. Finance and operations are not separate parts of a business firm. They are inseparable and interacting parts of one organization. Finance provides the score cards to evaluate past operations. Finance puts numbers on the visions of the future. Business plans, sales forecasts, and finance forecasts are intertwined. Financing decisions have implications for what can be attempted in the product-market operations of the firm. Decisions in the product-market operations have direct implications for what balance sheets, income statements, cash flow statements, and financial forecasts will be.

The central core of the MCI story is the acquisition and development of its human capital. Its founders and the personnel subsequently added to the company were the human capital that made all other things possible. Its executive leadership demonstrated the qualities of entrepreneurship, vision, creativity, determination, courage, and above all, an indomitable spirit that refused to be discouraged or quit or to seek more comfortable environments when the going became really tough. In the beginning, MCI's existence depended upon dealing with its legislative, regulatory, and legal environments. Eleven of the 15 top executives of MCI in its early years were lawyers. The headquarters of the company were established in Washington, D.C. because of the continued need to work on the legislative, regulatory, and legal challenges that continuously were crucial to the existence and growth of MCI. The early group of pioneers included the names of John D. Goeken, William G. McGowan, Bert Roberts, Michael H. Bader, Thomas L. Leming, V. Orville Wright, and Wayne G. English. This group was augmented with entrepreneurial and managerial skills needed to continuously renew its vision and widen the breadth of capabilities to embrace technological change to support the momentum of MCI's growth.

In early 1982, during court proceedings, AT&T had agreed to the divestiture of the local operating phone companies to become effective in 1984. This was a watershed for MCI. Its significance for MCI was expressed eloquently in the "Letter to Shareholders" by William G. McGowan, Chairman and CEO, and V. Orville Wright, President and COO, in MCI's "Report to Stockholders for the Twelve Months Ended December 31, 1984," stating,[1] "Divestiture has changed our world. This is no longer just the telephone industry, perhaps not merely the telecommunications industry, but a new emerging worldwide information industry. MCI intends to be right in the thick of it." (MCI Communications Corporation, Annual Report, 1994, p. 4)

Thus, the leadership of MCI already had a vision of the worldwide information industry of the 1990's and into the 21st century. To provide perspective as a basis for understanding strategic aspects of MCI's growth strategies and financing decisions, it is necessary to understand the background of MCI's previous history and how it was interwoven with the changing characteristics of the economic, financial, regulatory, and competitive environments in which MCI operated.

These materials will be covered in two sections: (1) MCI Timeline 1963–September 1998, and (2) Financing and M&As.

MCI TIMELINE 1963–9/14/98

The history of MCI and the critical role of its financing policies and decisions is presented first. This history describes the interaction of business vision, competitor reactions, regulatory changes, financing decisions, and the transformation of a major industry.

10/63
Microwave Communications, Inc. (MCI) organized by five mobile-radio salesmen with John D. (Jack) Goeken as leader. The business concept was to establish a private microwave communications system between Chicago and St. Louis shared by many small commercial users.

12/63
MCI filed its construction applications with the SEC. AT&T responded that the system was unnecessary and that MCI was unqualified to operate a microwave system.

10/67
The FCC ruled that MCI was technically qualified to build the system and had customers. MCI had planned to use vendor financing from General Electric in connection with the purchase of equipment to build the system. But GE cancelled the contract. An offering of stock to its current owners raised only $30,000.

2/68
William (Bill) G. McGowan, financially successful in turning around failing companies, invested in MCI stock. McGowan aimed to develop a nation-wide network of regional microwave companies under a new company called Micom. Allen & Company provided $1 million venture capital. Bechtel Corporation provided $1 million in vendor financing. Business firms such as hotel operators invested, hoping to reduce phone expenses.

8/13/69
The FCC by a margin of 4-3 approved the MCI construction applications.

3/8/71
MCI formed a joint venture with Lockheed to build a $168 million satellite system to bounce signals to relay systems on the ground in areas where building microwave towers would be unprofitable. Later the Communication Satellite Corporation (COMSAT) was added to the joint venture to provide experience as well as additional funds.

5/25/71
The FCC approved general competition in private line and specialized common carrier markets.

6/22/72

MCI's IPO raised $30 million with a market equity valuation of $120 million. This was related to a $64 million line of credit agreement signed with a group of banks. Vendors of network equipment guaranteed 50% of the amount borrowed by MCI. MCI would pay an interest rate of 3.75% above prime plus 0.5% on any unused portion of the loan.

10/9/72

Bert C. Roberts, Jr., with a background in electrical engineering and the computer industry, joined MCI.

3/7/74

MCI filed an antitrust civil suit against AT&T for refusing access to interconnection with local telephone networks. While the litigation dragged on, AT&T's cooperation continued erratic. This uncertainty clouded MCI's outlook and limited its access to financing working capital requirements. The common stock of MCI was 77.5% below its IPO price.

7/3/74

MCI sold its interest in the satellite joint venture to realize $2.5 million.

7/12/74

Jack Goeken resigned. Goeken's strategy was to seek niches in the private line market. McGowan's strategy was to become a full competitor to AT&T.

8/74

MCI developed a new service aimed at executives of businesses not large enough to have their own private lines. The service represented an executive's network whose name was shortened to Execunet.

7/2/75

AT&T complained that Execunet would not represent the kind of private wire services that MCI had been authorized to perform. The FCC ordered MCI to stop its Execunet service, but MCI obtained a stay of the order from the U.S. Court of Appeals. The ensuing litigation created uncertainties which caused the banks to limit their loan commitments. The bankers proposed that McGowan find a merger partner or sell MCI outright.

11/18/75

MCI, desperate for financing, sold equity under onerous conditions. Common stock was sold which carried warrants for further purchases and, if exercised, would have represented the sale of about 40% of MCI for $21.6 million. McGowan hated the deal, calling it atrocious.

5/25/76
After a court-ordered review of Execunet, the FCC again rejected the service. The earlier Court of Appeals stay of the order remained in place pending further litigation.

4/7/77
The banks extended the debt payment schedule to enable MCI to complete construction of its network.

7/28/77
The U.S. Court of Appeals ruled that MCI could offer Execunet without restrictions. Appeals by the FCC and AT&T to the Supreme Court failed.

4/78
Negotiation on rates for local interconnections initiated with AT&T.

6/1/78
MCI purchased key Microwave groups to California from Western Communications for $6.5 million.

9/78
New negotiated rates with AT&T agreed upon.

12/78
MCI customers reached 15,000 and new installations were 1,000 per month. Revenue and profitability of MCI were rising.

12/12/78
MCI made a public offering of convertible preferred stock at a premium of 16.7% over the price of the common, netting $28.6 million. Bank debt reduced by $11.5 million and $4 million was used to cancel purchase warrants on 32 million shares of common stock.

4/30/79
MCI filed a second antitrust suit against AT&T seeking $3 billion in damages.

9/21/79
Rising revenues enabled MCI to complete a public offering of senior cumulative convertible preferred stock of $69.5 million. Remaining bank loans were paid off. More than 1/2 of the proceeds were used for net work exchange.

7/29/80
MCI sold $52.5 million 20-year notes.

10/1/80
MCI raised $51.4 million using cumulative convertible preferred stock, its third convertible preferred stock financing in less than one year.

3/3/80

With its improved financing base, MCI entered the residential market with 80 million households as potential customers.

6/13/80

A jury awarded MCI $18 billion related to its 1975 suit against AT&T.

4/2/81

With its improved financial position and revenue outlook, MCI was able to shift from preferred stock to subordinated debenture financing. MCI sold $125 million 20-year subordinated debentures at original issue discount (OID) of 15.29%. This was the first MCI financing handled by Drexel Burnham Lambert.

12/15/81

MCI purchased Western Union International (WUI) from Xerox for $185 million. WUI's overseas customer base provided MCI entry into the international communications industry with a 20% per annum growth potential.

5/18/82

MCI sold $246 million convertible subordinated debentures with a conversion premium of 21% and a coupon of 10% when 30-year treasuries were yielding 13.24%.

9/30/82

Another financing milestone was reached when MCI sold straight subordinated 20-year debentures with an OID yield to maturity of 15.18% when U.S. 30-year treasuries were yielding 12.07%.

1/83

MCI placed large orders for fiberoptics regarded as superior to either wire or microwave. Using railroad right-of-ways across the entire country, MCI began a series of deals to put in place fiberoptic cables covering the entire country.

2/3/83

MCI purchased 24 satellite transponders to be used as radio relays to supplement the use of fiberoptics.

3/11/83

MCI sold $400 million convertible subordinated debentures with a conversion premium of 20% and a coupon of 7.75%. The convertible feature enabled MCI to cut the coupon by almost ½. Moody's upgraded MCI's ratings to an investment grade status.

4/1/83

MCI opened direct dial service to Canada with rates 30% lower than AT&T. MCI shortly thereafter continued its international expansion into Europe and Australia.

7/29/83

MCI sold 10-year bonds with a coupon of 9.5% with 72 warrants (five-year) per bond with call protection for five years. The exercise price of the warrants was $13.75 per share. After three years, MCI had the option to redeem its warrants at $213 per warrant. The warrants were originally priced at $2.84 representing a 31% premium in relationship to the common stock then trading at $10.47. The bonds were priced at $797.57 for a yield-to-maturity of 13.25%. One month following the offering it was widely rumored that local interconnection fees would be increased. MCI's common stock dropped by 26% to $7.75. Because of the continued uncertainty about local interconnection fees, MCI's stock price would not recover until after 1988 when the warrants expired virtually unexercised.

9/30/84

MCI formed an alliance with British Telecom to support its European exchange.

4/7/86

MCI sold $575 million 10% subordinated debentures.

12/4/89

MCI raised $502 million (issued at $1.305 billion) Lyon (liquid yield option note) which is a zero coupon callable, convertible note with a put option attached.

6/4/93, 8/4/93

British Telecommunications invests $4.33 billion for 20% of MCI common stock.

1993

During the year, MCI's stock price reaches a high of $29.63.

3/29/96

BT resumes talks to buy Cable & Wireless.

5/3/96

BT and Cable & Wireless end discussions.

6/10/96

MCI and BT plan expansion of corporate internet services.

6/12/96

Intel and MCI announce network computer.

8/27/96

MCI joins Nextwave in wireless communications venture.

9/12/96

MCI projects growth for data and network consulting business.

9/28/96
MCI seeks okay to offer lower rates.

10/28/96
Cable & Wireless, Bell Canada to merge with Nynex, UK.

11/4/96
BT and MCI announce $20.88 billion merger. BT offered $6 in cash and 0.54 share of each BT American depository receipt for each MCI share. BT also agreed to assume about $4 billion of MCI's debt.

11/14/96
Microsoft joins MCI-BT to sell intranet services.

11/15/96
BT announces fall in earnings.

12/10/96
MCI begins offering local phone service in California.

4/2/97
MCI shareholders approve BT takeover.

4/21/97
BT-MCI detail pact with Telefonica.

5/14/97
BT-MCI deal cleared by European Union.

7/8/97
BT purchase of MCI cleared by Justice Department.

7/12/97
Report of local phone loss sends shares of MCI lower, upsets BT.

8/21/97
BT receives FCC approval for MCI takeover.

8/22/97
BT-MCI to revise merger terms.

8/23/97
BT slices $5 billion from MCI bid. BT offered $7.75 cash and 0.375 of a BT American depository receipt for each share of MCI.

10/1/97
MCI posts $182 million loss from restructuring charges.

10/1/97
WorldCom launches $30 billion MCI bid. This represented $41.50 per share, all stock.

10/16/97
GTE bids $28 billion for MCI, representing $40 per share, all cash.

11/10/97
WorldCom increases offer to $36 billion, representing $50 per share, all cash.

9/14/98
After having received approvals from U.S. and European regulatory authorities, the acquisition of MCI by WorldCom was completed. The new company is named MCI WorldCom with Bernard J. Ebbers as President and Chief Executive Officer, and Bert C. Roberts appointed Chairman of MCI WorldCom.

We have traced the key events in the history of MCI. We started with the organization of the company in October 1963 to its sale to WorldCom effective 10/8/98. We now develop some implications from the history of MCI.

FINANCING AND M&As

MCI's history records the dynamic interactions between the financial markets, regulatory policies, competitor reactions, and company innovations and initiatives for survival, growth, and profitability, in uncertain, changing environments.

Reflecting the long history of the interaction of market opportunity, inconsistent regulation, aggressive competitive reactions by AT&T, the operating income and net income of MCI, required some years to develop some momentum. The early years reflected these factors plus the usual startup costs of a new firm. Its net operating income and net income were negative in 1975 and 1976 as shown in Table 1 which presents the income statements of MCI. When net income turned positive, it remained flat at slightly over $5 million for the years 1978 through 1980.

The balance sheet patterns of MCI also reflected influences similar to those impacting the income statements. As shown in Table 2, the book value of shareholders' equity was a substantial negative figure through 1978 and had reached only $5.8 million by 1979 when revenues were almost $100 million. As revenues grew to the $1 billion level by 1983, shareholders' equity with conversions of preferred and debt instruments with options plus retained earnings moved equity at book to $766 million.

Needs to finance investments in communications systems were in the $20–$30 million per year range for the years 1975 through 1978. These requirements jumped to over $50 million in 1979 and, on average, almost doubled every year thereafter through 1983. Net working capital investments also increased with revenue growth.

An overview of MCI financing from its initial public offering on June 22, 1972 through the July 29, 1983 financing, which established MCI's financial strength, is summarized in Table 3. When MCI was organized in October 1963, it was financed

TABLE 1 Summary Income Statement for MCI Communications (All Amounts Are in Millions of Dollars)

	1978	1979	1980	1981	1982	1983	1984	1985	1986	1987	1988	1989	1990	1991	1992	1993	1994	1995	1996	1997
Sales (Net)	95	144	234	506	1073	1665	1959	2542	3592	3939	5137	6471	7680	9491	10562	11921	13338	15265	18494	19653
Cost of Goods Sold	52	90	157	284	674	1172	1519	1989	3000	3233	4004	4799	5767	7654	8461	9551	10574	12103	14517	16253
Selling, General, and Administrative Expenses	C	C	C	C	C	C	C	C	C	C	C	C	C	C	C	C	C	C	C	C
Operating Income Before Depreciation	43	54	77	223	399	492	440	553	592	706	1133	1672	1913	1837	2101	2370	2764	3162	3977	3400
Depreciation and Amortization	12	17	26	56	104	183	265	347	451	471	549	655	743	746	843	952	1160	1308	1664	2022
Operating Income After Depreciation	31	37	51	167	295	309	175	206	141	235	584	1017	1170	1091	1258	1418	1604	1854	2313	1378
Interest Expense	-23	-26	-31	-57	-88	-186	-223	-240	-231	-279	-286	-282	-262	-270	-270	-239	-231	-242	-349	-448
Nonoperating Income (Expense)	0	2	3	19	33	126	148	337	147	147	124	104	82	27	22	16	55	116	-9	12
Special Income (Expense) Items	0	0	0	0	0	-50	-50	-136	-520	3	0	-35	-550	0	-47	-150	-148	-831	0	-703
Pretax Income	7	13	24	129	241	200	51	168	-463	106	422	804	440	848	963	1045	1280	897	1955	239
Income Taxes—Total	4	6	5	43	70	44	-9	28	-32	21	66	201	141	297	354	418	485	349	753	90
Minority Interest	0	0	0	0	0	0	0	0	0	0	0	0	C	C	C	C	C	C	C	C
Income Before Extraordinary Items	4	7	19	86	171	156	59	140	-431	85	356	603	299	551	609	627	795	548	1202	149
Dividends—Preferred	2	8	12	4	0	0	0	0	0	0	12	29	29	29	20	1	1	0	0	0
Income Before Extraordinary Items—Available for Common	2	-1	7	82	171	156	59	140	-431	85	344	574	270	522	589	626	794	548	1202	149
Common Stock Equivalents—Dollar Savings	0	0	0	0	0	0	0	0	0	0	0	0	0	0	0	1	1	0	0	0
Income Before Extraordinary Items—Adjusted for Common Stock Equivalents	2	-1	7	82	171	156	59	140	-431	85	344	574	270	522	589	627	795	548	1202	149
Extraordinary items	4	6	2	0	0	0	0	-26	-17	3	-10	-45	0	0	0	-45	0	0	0	0
Extraordinary Items and Discontinued Operations	4	6	2	0	0	0	0	-26	-17	3	-10	-45	0	0	0	-45	0	0	0	0
Net Income Adjusted for Common Stock Equivalents	6	6	9	82	171	156	59	113	-448	88	334	529	270	522	589	582	795	548	1202	149
Net Income (Loss)	7	13	21	86	171	156	59	113	-448	88	346	558	299	551	609	582	795	548	1202	149

TABLE 2 Summary Balance Sheet for MCI Communications (All Amounts Are in Millions of Dollars)

	1978	1979	1980	1981	1982	1983	1984	1985	1986	1987	1988	1989	1990	1991	1992	1993	1994	1995	1996	1997
Assets																				
Cash and Short Term Investments	10	8	13	144	542	1133	865	853	778	725	453	197	231	51	232	165	2268	844	348	261
Receivables—Total	6	14	32	78	162	302	305	422	567	581	823	1171	1447	1615	1764	2250	2376	3127	3671	4514
Inventories—Total	0	0	0	0	0	0	0	0	0	0	0	0	0	0	0	0	0	0	0	0
Current Assets—Other	1	3	4	5	10	53	63	87	54	50	45	53	133	92	185	186	244	576	697	485
Current Assets—Total	18	24	49	228	713	1488	1233	1362	1399	1356	1321	1421	1811	1758	2181	2601	4888	4547	4716	5260
Property, Plant, and Equipment—Total (Net)	189	282	410	619	1324	1971	2614	3045	3710	3854	4363	4753	5033	5697	6165	7321	9059	10309	12174	13868
Investments and Advances—Equity Method	0	0	0	0	0	0	0	0	0	0	0	C	C	C	C	C	199	495	690	653
Investments and Advances—Other	0	0	0	0	0	0	0	0	0	0	0	C	C	C	C	C	824	1000	2301	NA
Intangibles	0	0	0	0	0	0	0	0	0	0	0	C	C	C	C	C	C	C	C	C
Assets—Other	3	4	8	12	33	49	46	103	149	170	159	164	1405	1379	1332	1354	1396	2950	3097	5729
Assets—Total	209	310	467	860	2070	3507	3894	4510	5258	5380	5843	6338	8249	8834	9678	11276	16366	19301	22978	25510
Liabilities and Net Worth																				
Debt in Current Liabilities	27	32	40	40	48	49	61	456	108	184	134	184	244	318	215	215	130	500	203	2111
Accounts Payable	6	13	17	96	203	363	501	766	505	530	781	828	1388	1402	467	742	609	706	992	1321
Income Tax Payable	0	0	0	8	22	23	13	18	19	0	0	0	0	0	0	0	0	0	0	0
Current Liabilities—Other	12	13	17	40	49	45	66	67	505	492	607	705	790	580	1782	2244	2398	3664	3851	4664
Current Liabilities—Total	45	58	74	186	321	481	641	1308	1137	1206	1522	1717	2422	2300	2464	3201	3137	4870	5046	8096
Long Term Debt—Total	153	173	243	400	896	1722	1821	1696	2676	2663	2677	2241	3147	3104	3432	2366	2997	3444	5548	4026
Liabilities—Other	0	0	0	0	0	169	233	188	183	158	140	145	180	126	74	69	36	28	26	211
Deferred Taxes and Investment Tax Credit	0	0	2	34	88	0	0	0	0	0	145	240	160	345	558	927	1192	1357	1697	1866
Minority Interest	0	0	0	0	0	0	0	0	0	0	0	C	C	C	C	C	C	C	C	C
Liabilities—Total	198	231	319	620	1305	2372	2695	3192	3996	4027	4484	4343	5909	5875	6528	6563	7362	9699	12317	14199
Preferred Stock—Carrying Value	1	1	1	0	0	0	0	0	0	0	1	1	1	1	0	0	0	0	0	0
Common Equity—Total	11	78	147	241	766	1136	1199	1318	1262	1353	1358	1994	2339	2958	3150	4712	9004	9602	10661	11311
Stockholders' Equity—Total	11	79	148	241	766	1136	1199	1318	1262	1353	1359	1995	2340	2959	3150	4713	9004	9602	10661	11311
Liabilities and Stockholders' Equity—Total	209	310	467	860	2070	3507	3894	4510	5258	5380	5843	6338	8249	8834	9678	11276	16366	19301	22978	25510

TABLE 3 MCI Securities Issuances

Description	Date	Common Stock Price Issue Date Adjusted	NetProceeds (In Millions)
Common stock initial public offering 26,400,000 shares at $1.25 per share.	6/22/72	$0.317	$30.2
1.2 million units consisting of 32 shares of common stock and 32 five-year warrants, each to purchase one share of MCI common at $0.3125 per share.	11/18/75	$0.219	$8.5
Issued 1,469,050 shares of $2.64 cumulative convertible preferred stock (conversion price $0.547 per share of common). 1,229,050 shares in an underwritten public offering and 120,000 shares each to Bechtel and North American Corp.	12/5/78	$0.469	$28.6
Issued 4,950,000 shares of $1.80 senior cumulative convertible preferred stock at $15 per share (conversion price $1.25 per share of common).	9/21/79	$0.813	$69.5
Sold $52.5 million (of which $5 million was issued in January 1981) of 15% subordinated debentures, due 8/1/00.	7/29/80	$1.240	$50.5
Issued 3,630,000 shares of $1.84 cumulative convertible preferred stock at $15 per share (conversion price $2.25 per share of common).	10/1/80	$1.516	$51.4
Sold $125 million of 14.125% subordinated debentures, due 4/1/01. The debenture sold at an original issue discount of 84.71% of par.	4/2/81	$1.703	$102.1
Sold $100 million of 10.25% convertible subordinated debentures, due 8/15/01 (conversion price $3.21 per share of common).	8/27/81	$2.719	$98.2
Sold $250 million of 10% convertible subordinated debentures, due 5/15/02 (conversion price $5.625 per share of common).	5/18/82	$4.656	$246
Sold $250 million of 12.875% subordinated debentures, due 10/1/02. The debenture sold at an original discount of 85.62% of par.	9/30/82	$5.844	$214
Sold $400 million of 7.75% convertible subordinated debentures, due 3/15/03 (conversion price of $13.03 per share of common).	3/11/83	$10.844	$393.7
Sold $1 billion in units of 9.5% subordinated notes, due 8/1/93, priced at $795.57 plus 72 warrants priced at $2.84 each or $204.48 for the 72 warrants per $1,000 bond (each warrant could buy one share of MCI common for $13.75).	7/24/83	$11.000	$1,000

from the personal savings of the five mobile-radio salesmen who started the company. In February of 1968, the company brought in Bill McGowan, who had a track record of turning around troubled companies. McGowan invested in MCI stock. Based on McGowan's own investment and his compelling vision and plans for MCI, other outside financing became available. Allen and Company was a source of $1 million of venture capital. Vendors such as Bechtel and General Electric provided some vendor financing. Even customers such as hotel operators invested in MCI hoping to reduce phone expenses. In mid-1971 the FCC ruled in principle that private line and specialized common carrier markets would be open to general competition. This improved the outlook for MCI which made possible its initial public offering on June 22, 1972, as summarized in Table 3. Subsequent securities issuances are discussed below.

In parallel with its financing activities, MCI was active in forming alliances, joint ventures, and other forms of M&A activities, as summarized in Table 4. These activities helped MCI expand its operations and revenues, which increased its financing needs. These activities also conserved financing by bringing in partners.

The Convertible Preferred Stock Financing

The previous section on the MCI company history described the FCC ruling of 7/2/75 which ordered MCI to stop offering its new Execunet service. The ensuing three years of litigation slowed the expansion of MCI. These uncertainties were not resolved until the decision of the U.S. Court of Appeals of 7/28/77 permitting MCI to offer Execunet without restrictions. The appeals by AT&T and the FCC were turned down so that by the beginning of 1978 Wayne English, the Chief Financial Officer of MCI, could plan

---

TABLE 4 MCI Alliances and M&A Activities

- CML Joint Venture
    Formed on 3/8/71
    Sold interest in CML 7/3/74
- Purchased Western Union International (WUI) from Xerox, 12/15/81
- Alliance with British Telecom, 9/30/84
- Alliance with AVANTEL in Mexico added to Alliance with Stentor in Canada to complete MCI's North American network, October 1984
- MCI agrees to invest up to $2 billion in News Corp. to form a global joint venture, May 1995
- MCI develops program to resell cellular services, August 1995
- MCI acquires SHL Systemhouse Inc., a computer services provider for about $1 billion, September 1995
- MCI with News Corp. win with $682 million bid for remaining satellite to develop a direct-broadcast TV service, 1/25/96
- MCI and Microsoft form a partnership to sell each others products, including the on-line Microsoft network, 1/29/96
- The Telecommunications Act of 1996 was signed by President Clinton on 2/8/96 with implications for new realignments in the Information Industry
- Discussions with AT&T on joint efforts to access the local telephone markets, 2/12/96

for the resumption of new financing from the public markets. Three successive issues of cumulative convertible preferred stock were sold. The net proceeds of the 12/5/78 offering were about $29 million. The 9/21/79 offering netted about $70 million. The 10/1/80 offering netted about $51 million. The conversion price on each preferred stock offering approximately doubled from one to the next.

Table 1, MCI's Income Statement History, shows that MCI had incurred losses through 1977 and carried these losses forward so that no income taxes were paid until 1981 and then only at a relatively small rate. Thus, there was no tax cost to MCI for providing an instrument whose dividend was 85% tax deductible to corporate purchasers. This helped achieve relatively favorable terms to MCI.

In addition, these preferred issues carried a call provision which provided MCI with the ability to force their conversion into common stock. MCI did not begin paying dividends on the common until 1988. Thus, as the legal uncertainty surrounding the Execunet service was resolved by the end of 1977, MCI was enabled to expand its markets and revenues. The resulting improvements in profitability were associated with rising levels of the market price of MCI's common stock. The call provisions provided that when the market price of the MCI common exceeded the conversion price by a factor such as 20% for 30 consecutive trading days, MCI could purchase (call) the outstanding preferred stock shares at 110% of their issue value. The strong price performance of the common stock made conversion into common stock at a higher market value than accepting the MCI call. Thus, MCI was able to force conversion of the preferred stock. By 11/18/81, virtually all of these three preferred stock issues had been converted into common stock.

Thus, the first phase of MCI's history of financing were two issues of common stock. The second phase during which MCI had no income tax payments, three issues of cumulative convertible preferred were the method of financing. These were all converted into common by the end of 1981. Thus, in effect, MCI had been able to sell common stock in future stages to capture portions of the future increase in common stock prices. This reduced the dilution to the earlier common stock investors to lower levels than it otherwise would have been.

Shift in Financing Policy to Debt Financing

As shown in Table 1, during 1980, MCI's revenues had grown to $234 million, an increase of almost $100 million over 1979 revenues. In 1981, revenues more than doubled to over $506 million. As shown in Table 2, investment requirements as shown by net fixed assets grew at even higher rates reaching $619 million in 1981 and $1,324 million in 1982. With the strong growth in revenues and profitability, moving MCI into a positive corporate tax rate, the use of preferred stock would have involved the loss of the tax benefits of debt. Accordingly, MCI moved from preferred financing to debt financing.

Six debt offerings totaling over $1.1 billion were made through 3/11/83. The first issue of $50 million on 7/29/80 was straight subordinated debentures with a 15%

coupon. This was in an environment of high and rising interest rates. The second debt financing on 4/02/81 of $102.1 million was also sold in an environment of a rising interest rate economy. Between 1980 and 1981, the yield on 10-year U.S. treasury securities had risen by about 250 basis points.

The July 29, 1983 Financing

Beginning with the April 2, 1981 financing, Drexel Burnham Lambert began to participate as a comanager of the underwriting group. Innovative features were introduced in this and subsequent MCI financings by Michael Milken. Milken introduced an original issue discount (OID) feature to the subordinated debenture issue. The OID was set at 84.71% of par, reducing the coupon substantially. After selling two additional subordinated debentures with convertibility rights, MCI was brought back to the market in September 1982 with a straight subordinated debenture issue sold at an original issue discount at 85.62% of par with a coupon of 12.875%, relatively low for the capital market conditions of that period.

Convertible subordinated debentures were sold in three successive offerings. The approximately $100 million sold on 8/27/81 carried a 10.25% coupon and called for redemption which forced conversion into common stock on 2/16/83. The $246 million convertible subordinated debentures sold 5/18/82 carried a coupon of 10%. Only one interest payment was made on this debenture. A call for redemption on 5/18/82 forced conversion into common stock. The net proceeds of $394 million convertible subordinated debentures sold on 3/11/83 carried a substantially lower coupon of 7.75%.

This lower coupon rate reflected an improvement in the economy-wide interest rate environment as well as in MCI's prospects. The realized returns on high-yield bonds were over 32% for 1982 and almost 22% for 1983. This reflected the sharp drop in the required returns to high-yield debt. The spreads between the yields on U.S. treasuries and high-rated corporate in relation to MCI's high-yield debt were relatively narrow. Thus, the market was favorable for the sale of further high-yield debt (junk bonds).

Revenues in the fiscal year ending 3/31/83 for MCI had risen to over $1 billion for the first time and net income after actual income taxes paid had risen to $224 million. The MCI common stock price (adjusted) at the 3/11/83 offering was $10.84 per share. This represented a quadrupling of the stock price (adjusted) over the $2.72 price per share at the time of the 8/27/81 convertible subordinated debenture financing. Reflecting the higher stock prices as well as forced conversions, the common stock market value of MCI had risen from $808 million on 8/27/81 to over $5 billion on 3/11/83, representing a 621% increase over the 18 months.

As it considered its second 1983 financing, MCI management, in consultation with their investment banker, projected that financing needs would be in the rage of $3 to $4 billion in the next five years. Hence, another financing appeared desirable given the improving capital market conditions. A wide range of financing alternatives was assembled and analyzed by Michael Milken, who had been handling the MCI financing for Drexel Burnham Lambert since April 1981. The possibilities were narrowed to six alternatives summarized in Table 5.

TABLE 5 Terms of Financing Alternatives

Straight Bonds

Maturity	10
Call Protection: 5 Years Minimum then at a Premium	
Annual Interest Rate	14%
Par Value, Gross Proceeds	$1,000,000,000
Issue Cost as % of Gross Proceeds	1.25%

Vendor Financing

Maturity	10
Annual Interest Rate	12.75%
Par Value, Gross Proceeds	$1,000,000,000
Issue Cost as % of Gross Proceeds	0.75%

Zero Coupon Bonds

Maturity	10
Callable Any Time at Par (100%)	
Annual Interest Rate	14.50%
Gross Proceeds	$1,000,000,000
Issue Cost as % of Gross Proceeds	2.60%

Convertible Bonds

Maturity	20
Call Protection: 3 Years, Then at a Premium Equal to 1 Year's Interest	
Conversion Price	$12.50
Annual Interest Rate	10.00%
Par Value, Gross Proceeds	$1,000,000,000
Issue Cost as % of Gross Proceeds	1.50%

Bond/Warrant Units

Maturity	10
Call Protection: 5 Years, then at a Premium Equal to 1 Year's Interest	
Warrants Per Bond (Exercise Price $13.75 per share)	72
Coupon	9.50%
Gross Proceeds	$1,000,000,000
Issue Cost as % of Gross Proceeds	1.40%

Note: After 3 years, MCI can redeem warrants at its option at $2.13 per warrant if the last reported sale price for MCI stock has averaged at least 150% of the exercise price of the warrants for the immediately preceding 20 consecutive days.

Common Stock

Gross Proceeds	$1,000,000,000
Issue Cost as % of Gross Products	3.50%

NOTE

1. On June 19, 1984, MCI changed its fiscal year from March 31 to December 31. Thus, MCI's report for the 12 months ending 12/31/84 was the first Annual Report following its Annual Report for the fiscal year ending 3/31/82.

QUESTIONS

1. Discuss the role of convertible debt or convertible preferred stock financing.

2. Describe the logic behind each form of financing at each phase during MCI's early life cycle. Your discussion should include vendor financing, venture capital financing, the IPO, commercial bank financing, subordinated debt, convertible preferred, convertible debt, debt with warrants.

3. Discuss the pros and cons of the six alternatives under consideration for MCI's July 1983 financing.

Case 4

Office Depot and Staples

On July 1, 1997, a federal judge granted an injunction enabling the Federal Trade Commission to block a proposed merger between Office Depot and Staples. The two companies are the largest office supply superstore chains. Office Depot operates 576 stores with 550 for Staples. Judge Thomas Hogan was quoted in the *Wall Street Journal* on July 1, 1997 saying that the companies had created an entirely new market. He observed also that the two companies had brought "undeniable benefits to consumers."

Staples and Office Depot had argued that combining the two companies would help them achieve further economies of scale and scope. With regard to economies of scale, Office Depot had spent $25 million on its computers to improve its information systems for tracking inventory, for selling products through its catalogs, and for servicing large corporate clients.

Both companies sell a wide range of office stationery, office furniture, and personal computers. Other competitors in the business include number three OfficeMax. In addition, individual office supply stores as well as office supply departments of department stores (Wal-Mart, for example) are competitors. The three largest chains operate about 1,700 stores and have about 10% of the office supply market. Market studies show a potential for 3,500 stores in the next few years.

Other competitors include catalog suppliers and large contract stationers who deal directly with big companies. For example, U.S. Products Company, a contract stationer was expected to have a sales volume of $3.5 billion in 1997. It announced on July 1, 1997 the takeover of 12 smaller suppliers in deals totaling $175 million. The contract business of Office Depot and Staples was about $1 billion each. Thus, the two combined in the contract stationers segment had about 57% of the volume of one large contract stationer.

Size provides economies for bargaining power in dealing with suppliers. Lower prices from suppliers have helped Office Depot and Staples to charge lower prices to consumers. The larger size of the combined company would make it possible to automate further their inventory and sales systems as well as reduce prices from suppliers. Blocking the merger, the two chains argued, would prevent economies that would have translated into further lower prices for consumers. The Federal Trade Commission argued in response that it was the competition between Office Depot and Staples that caused prices to be lower and that without an independent Staples, prices to consumers would rise.

QUESTION

Summarize the arguments for and against the FTC decision to block the merger.

Case 5

WorldCom/Sprint1

On October 5, 1999, MCI WorldCom and Sprint announced what at that time was the largest merger in history. The firms were the two leading long distance telephone service competitors to AT&T. WorldCom and Sprint were also leading providers of Internet backbone services. To consummate the deal, WorldCom had to win a bidding war with Bell South, and negotiate a deal with Deutsche Telekom to buy out that firm's 10% stake in Sprint. Even after the deal was worked out, WorldCom and Sprint had to work together to try to convince regulators at the Department of Justice, Federal Communications Commission, European Commission, and even in Brazil and other countries to permit the merger to occur. The industry characteristics are important to strategy and valuation; they are also critical to antitrust concerns involved in any merger.

CHARACTERISTICS OF THE TELECOMMUNICATIONS INDUSTRY

Beginning in the mid-1990s, the telecom industry has undergone a significant wave of consolidation. The Telecommunications Act of 1996 brought a degree of deregulation to the industry. The booming popularity of the Internet and wireless communications changed the needs of many consumers. With such rapid and dramatic changes in the industry, firms are finding it necessary to merge in order to be able to provide customers with all the services they require.

Prior to its 1984 breakup, AT&T was virtually synonymous with telecommunications in the United States. Almost all calls originated within the area covered by AT&T's local service, and almost all long distance calling services were provided by AT&T. On January 1, 1984, as part of a settlement with the Department of Justice, AT&T was broken up into seven local phone companies and one long distance company. The seven local companies, "Baby Bells" or regional bell operating companies (RBOCs), continued to maintain a virtual monopoly over local phone service. This forced them to remain closely regulated by the Federal Communications Commission

[1]Tables and figures obtained from FCC Web site (www.fcc.gov),
"First 2000 Trends in Telephone Service Report", released 3/00.

(FCC). AT&T itself continued to exist as the long distance company. It also retained most of the equipment making assets and Bell Labs, the research and development division. As part of the settlement, AT&T was prohibited from providing local telephone service, and the RBOCs were prohibited from providing long distance service. The resulting structure of the telecom industry has been described as that of a sandwich, with distinct separate levels.

The "sandwich" structure of the industry was maintained until the approval of the Telecommunications Act of 1996. The Act eliminated or established the means for elimination of many governmental restrictions on the telecom industry. The RBOCs would be allowed to provide long distance phone service provided they could demonstrate that competition existed in their own markets. Similarly, long distance providers could provide local service after proving there was competition in their markets. This forced all telecom companies to consider means of bundling all telecom services. These services can be loosely grouped into four categories: local, long distance, broadband data, and wireless. There is some speculation that the emergence of a few very large telecom companies will cause all of these services to converge, giving customers one bill to pay for all of their telecom services. Table 1 shows household telecom expenditures by provider. Table 2 shows telecom revenues by type of service.

Local

Local telephone service has been and still is dominated by the RBOCs. Created in the breakup of AT&T, they have had the advantage of being the incumbent carriers for most households and businesses. However, deregulation brought on by the Telecommunications Act of 1996 has forced the Baby Bells to deal with more serious competition.

Competing local exchange carriers (CLECs) have emerged as rivals to the RBOCs. The CLECs are new companies that have established the lines to reach primarily businesses, but also residences, in areas that once were a monopoly for the Baby Bells.

TABLE 1 Household Telecommunications Expenditures by Type of Provider

	Local Exchange Carriers		Long Distance Carriers		Wireless Carriers		Total Expenditures	
	Average	Median	Average	Median	Average	Median	Average	Median
1995	$358	$305	$250	$136	$ 62	$0	$670	$515
1996	359	309	250	132	83	0	692	531
1997	379	323	305	183	100	0	784	610
1998	398	336	270	150	119	0	787	616

Source: Calculated by IAD staff with data provided by PNR and Associates Inc., *TLC MarketShare Monitor.*
Annual expenditures are based on monthly household bills for those with wireline telephone service.
The sample does not include households from Alaska and Hawaii.

TABLE 2 Telecommunications Revenue Reported by Type of Service (Dollar Amounts Shown

			TRS Data			Universal Service & TRS Data	
	1992	**1993**	**1994**	**1995**	**1996**	**1997**	**1998**
Local Exchange	$39,235	$40,176	$42,245	$45,194	$48,717	$53,771	$59,245
Pay Telephone*						2,182	2,536
Local Private Line**	1,049	1,088	1,138	1,226	1,616	8,282	10,403
Other Local***	7,687	8,002	8,302	10,428	10,543	2,847	2,179
Subscriber Line Charges**						8,327	11,052
Access**	29,353	30,832	32,759	33,911	35,641	21,423	18,449
Universal Service Surcharges on Local Service Bills****							103
Additional revenue from TRS Worksheets						595	595
Total Local Service	77,324	80,098	84,443	90,759	96,516	97,426	104,563
Wireless Service	7,285	10,237	14,293	18,759	26,049	32,760	36,240
Universal Service Surcharges on Wireless Service Bills****							345
Additional revenue from TRS Worksheets						189	189
Total Wireless Service	7,285	10,237	14,293	18,759	26,049	32,950	36,775
Operator*	9,465	10,772	10,539	11,170	10,975	12,002	12,205
Non-Operator Switched Toll	54,448	60,591	61,468	65,217	73,751	72,059	74,168
Long Distance Private Line	7,783	8,067	9,043	9,719	10,665	10,504	11,952
Other Long Distance	4,048	3,095	3,428	3,523	4,299	4,695	3,386
Universal Service Surcharges on Toll Service Bills****							1,810
Additional revenue from TRS Worksheets						1,532	1,532
Total Toll Service	75,744	82,525	84,478	89,629	99,691	100,793	105,055
Non-Telecommunications Formerly Reported as Other Local and Wireless***	(6,944)	(7,518)	(8,324)	(9,071)	(10,474)		
Total Telecommunications***	153,409	165,342	174,890	190,076	211,782	231,168	246,392
Non-Telecommunications***						25,633	27,944
Total Reported Revenue	$160,353	$172,860	$183,214	$199,147	$222,256	$256,801	$272,019
Service Reported as:							
Intrastate	89,323	96,927	102,603	112,923	127,849	133,654	142,108
Interstate	71,030	75,933	80,611	86,224	94,407	97,514	104,284

Source: Industry Analysis Division, Telecommunications Industry Revenue.

Note: Some data for prior years have been revisited. Detail may not add to totals due to rounding.

* TRS filers generally reported pay telephone revenue as local service revenue, access revenue or operator toll revenue. The Universal Service Worksheet contains a separate category for pay telephone revenue.

TABLE 2 (Continued)

** TRS Worksheet filers generally reported special access revenue as access revenue. Using Universal Service Worksheet data as the primary source instead of TRS worksheet data explains the jump in local private line revenue and the fall in access revenues.

Universal Service Worksheet filers report subscriber line charges in a separate category. The jump from 1997 to 1998 represents PICC charges levied by ILECs as well as $1.2 billion of PICC pass-through charges levied by toll carriers.

*** Significant amounts of enhanced service, billing and collection, CPE and other non-telecommunications revenues were reported in the TRS mobile and other local service categories through 1996. Universal Service Worksheet filers report these revenues in the reported as mobile and other local revenue were estimated as 70% of the amounts that Tier 1 LECs reported in ARMIS as miscellaneous and nonregulated revenues (currently Account 5200 + Account 5280) and 10% of amounts reported as mobile service revenue.

**** Charges on end-user bills identified as recovering state or federal universal service contributions are reported separately from local, wireless and toll revenue.

Figure 1 shows that since 1994, local markets have grown from having virtually no competitors for the RBOCs to having at least one competitor in 92% of markets. Figure 2 demonstrates that these competing firms have begun laying extensive fiber networks. While not yet on the scale of the Bells, these CLECs have shown the potential to be serious competitors. Some combinations among these firms have also increased the challenge to the RBOCs. For example, AT&T bought Teleport, a leading RBOC, to establish its initial foothold in local phone service.

New technologies are also providing new means of entry into the local market. AT&T bought TCI and MediaOne to gain cable access to homes. AT&T envisioned

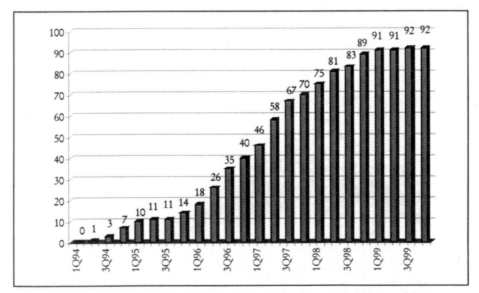

FIGURE 1 Percentage of LATAS with One or More Local Service Competitors Holding Numbering Codes

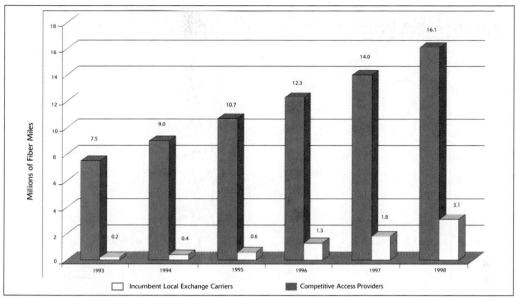

FIGURE 2 Fiber Miles

upgrading the existing television cable systems to be able to offer television, Internet, and telephone service through the same pipeline. While this has not been fully implemented, it presents serious challenges to AT&T's competitors throughout the telecom industry. Another technological challenge is the possibility of wireless technology providing local access to homes. Firms such as Sprint have the goal of implementing multichannel multipoint distribution services (MMDS). These services are a fixed wireless system, which could offer broadband and telephone access even to remote areas.

Long Distance

Historically, long distance telephone calling has been dominated by AT&T. Until it was broken up in 1984, AT&T was virtually the only choice in long distance for most customers. While competitors emerged after the breakup, AT&T was still by far the dominant firm. Even today, it has the largest share of the long distance market, but that share has been eroded over the years. This is shown in Figure 3.

During the 1980s and 1990s, the largest competitors to emerge in the long distance arena were MCI and Sprint. These firms established the necessary infrastructure to provide long distance, and also used extensive advertising campaigns to take some market share from AT&T. MCI was acquired by WorldCom in 1998. A comparison of the combined MCI, WorldCom and Sprint revenues to those of AT&T is presented in Figure 4.

In addition to the three largest long distance providers, new firms are emerging. Table 3 shows the revenues of long distance service firms. These firms have been able to establish smaller market shares, but have increasing growth prospects due to the

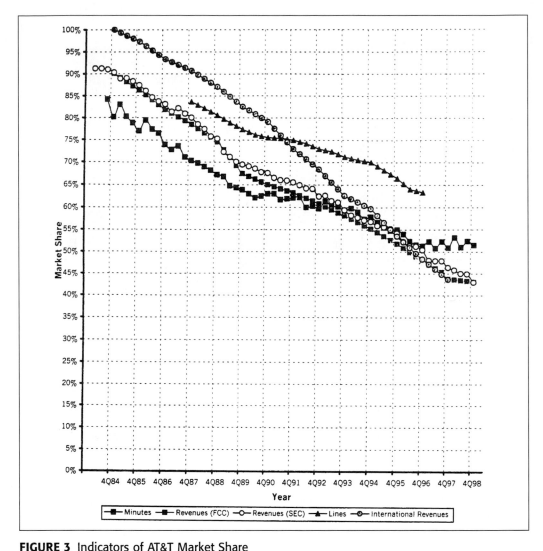

FIGURE 3 Indicators of AT&T Market Share

Source: Industry Analysis Division, *Long Distance Market Shares.*

increased competition from the Telecom Act of 1996. The other source of potential competitive firms is the Baby Bells. Studies have shown that local firms that package long distance service have been able to capture significant market share. When the RBOCs are able to do this, it will cause the industry to become even more competitive.

New technologies are bound to change the long distance market. Voice over IP (VoIP) utilizes the Internet to transmit conversations, entirely circumventing the

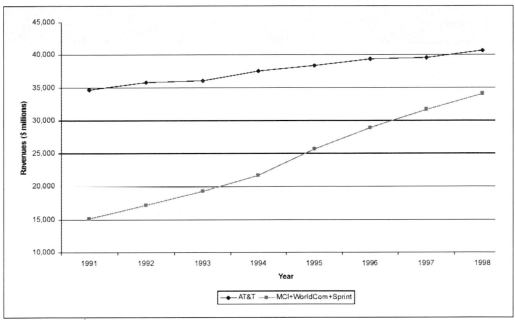

FIGURE 4 Long Distance Revenues of the Big Two

phone lines. This could become a viable alternative to conventional phone lines. Another technological factor that could make long distance cheaper is the possibility of the very large phone companies being able to implement "all distance" calling, in which the distinctions of long distance will be eliminated.

Broadband

In a matter of a few years, the Internet has greatly transformed American businesses. Figure 5 shows that the Internet has expanded from being in virtually no households in 1994 to being in greater than 1 of 4 by 1998. This expansion has continued since 1998.

The Internet has become a powerful form of communication. Firms like Dell have essentially built supplier and customer relations through computer networking. E-commerce firms have made thousands of products available to customers without needing to leave their homes. The Internet is also a powerful conduit of information, and perhaps more importantly, entertainment.

As the Internet is used for entertainment purposes, the need for bandwidth increases. Downloading video and audio files is extremely time consuming over the conventional modem. As more users of the Internet seek to obtain large files such as these, the capabilities of their connection to the Internet will need to increase. Some

TABLE 3 Total Operating Revenues of Long Distance Service Providers (Dollar Amounts Shown in Millions)

Company	1997	1996	1995	1994	1993	1992	1991
AT&T Companies 1/							
AT&T Communications Inc.	$39,470	$39,264	$38,069	$37,166	$35,731	$35,495	$34,384
Alascom, Inc.			325	329	320	333	338
MCI Companies 2/							
MCI Communications Corp.	17,150	16,372	14,617	11,715	10,947	9,719	8,266
Telecom*USA							
Sprint Companies 3/							
Sprint Communications Co.	8,595	7,944	7,277	6,805	6,139	5,658	5,378
GTE Sprint							
US Telecom							
Worldcom Companies 4/							
Worldcom, Inc.	5,897	4,485	3,640	2,221	1,145	801	263
Advanced Telecommunications Corp.							356
Metromedia Communications Corp.					297	369	369
ITT Communication Services, Inc.							
Comsystems Network Services					116	135	131
Wiltel, Inc.				917	664	494	405
MFS Intelenet, Inc.		122	118				
Excel Companies 5/							
Excel Telecommunications, Inc.	1,180	1,091	363	156			
Telco Holdings, Inc.	379	429	215				
Long Distance Wholesale Group	176						
Frontier Companies 6/							
Allnet Comm. SVCS.							
dba Frontier Comm. SVCS.	775	1,119	827	568	436	376	347
Lexitel							
Frontier Communications Int'l. Inc.	223	323	309	306	213	168	155
Frontier Communications							
of the West, Inc.	324		127	144			
Frontier Comm. of the							
North Central Region		121	133	123			
LCI Companies 7/							
LCI International Telecom Corp.	1,001	1,103	671	453	317	243	208
USLD Communications Corp.	241	188	155	136	100		
Cable & Wireless, Inc.	1,066	919	700	654	557	495	406
Vartec Telecom, Inc.	820	470	125	107			
Star Telecommunications, Inc.	376	208					
PT-1 Communications, Inc.	358	117					
Communication Telesystems Int'l.	345	196	115				
GTE Communications Corp.	340						
Telegroup, Inc.	337	213	129				
Tel-Save, Inc.	305	232	180				
Pacific Gateway Exchange, Inc.	299	162					

Company	1997	1996	1995	1994	1993	1992	1991
IXC Long Distance, Inc.	258						
Williams Communications, Inc.	227						
Business Telecom, Inc. 8/	195	149	115				
RSL Communications, Ltd.	192						
Cherry Communications, Inc. 9/	180	354					
General Communication, Inc.	158	143	120	106	92		
Trescom International Inc.	158	140					
SNET America, Iinc.	142						
Total-Tel USA Communications, Inc.	123						
ACC Long Distance Corp.	122	118					
One Call Communications, Inc.	118	114					
Midcom Communications, Inc. 10/		149	204	109			
GE Capital Communications Services Corp.			120				
Oncor Communications, Inc.			111	172	140	159	181
The Furst Group, Inc.			109				
American Network Exchange, Inc.			101	109			
Telesphere Network, Inc. 11/ National, Telephone Services, Inc.							308
Others 12/	7,097	5,788	5,168	5,055	4,319	3,923	2,948
Total Long Distance Carriers Toll Service Revenues:	88,627	82,033	74,143	67,351	61,533	58,368	54,443
Bell Operating Companies	7,138	7,950	8,189	9,527	9,849	9,718	10,066
Other Local Telephone Companies 12/	2,804	3,298	3,143	3,848	3,908	3,897	4,049
Total Local Exchange Companies	9,942	11,248	11,332	13,375	13,757	13,615	14,115
Total Revenues of Long Distance Service Providers	$98,569	$93,281	$85,475	$80,726	$75,290	$71,983	$68,558

proponents envision a time where even television will arrive in the house through the same data pipeline as the phone and Internet.

Currently, there are two common residential high-speed Internet options. DSL runs through the existing local phone lines. Cable utilizes television cable to access the homes. There has been talk that a widely implemented wireless service may be another alternative to gain fast Internet access. Because data transmission is essentially the same business as telephone service, telecom companies are the leaders in implementing internet access and high-speed lines.

Wireless

Wireless telecommunications is one of the booming segments of the telecom market. Table 4 shows the rapid growth of the U.S. wireless market. Between June of 1996 and June 1999, the number of subscribers about doubled. Wireless has also been seen as a

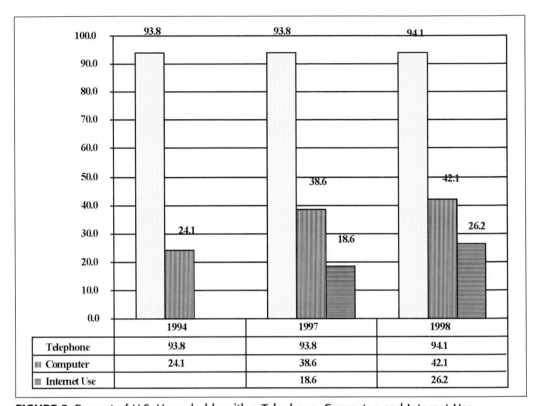

FIGURE 5 Percent of U.S. Households with a Telephone, Computer, and Internet Use

Source: National Telecommunications and Information Administration (NTIA) and U.S. Census Bureau, Current Population Surveys.

possible alternative to conventional wireline local telephone service, such as that offered by the RBOCs.

This potential continuing growth is attractive to many telecom firms. AT&T, whose Bell Labs essentially invented cellular technology, ignored the cellular market for many years, but eventually bought McCaw Cellular in the early 1990s. More recently, AT&T has issued a tracking stock of its wireless unit, the sale of which provided capital for implementing its cable strategy. As of first quarter 2000, AT&T was the 3rd largest wireless carrier, with 14% of the market. The first was Verizon Wireless, a joint venture between Vodafone Airtouch, Bell Atlantic, and GTE (29%). The second largest, with 19%, was a joint venture between SBC and Bell South. The involvement of Bell Atlantic, SBC, and Bell South (all RBOCs) illustrates the growth of the "Baby Bells" to include services outside of their conventional local duties. The fourth largest wireless service is Sprint's PCS, which is unique in that it is digital, while most services of the other firms are analog.

TABLE 4 Cellular Telephone Subscribers		
	Number of Systems	**Subscribers**
1984 December	32	91,600
1985 June	65	203,600
December	102	340,213
1986 June	129	500,000
December	166	681,825
1987 June	206	883,778
December	312	1,230,855
1988 June	420	1,608,697
December	517	2,069,441
1989 June	559	2,691,793
December	584	3,508,944
1990 June	592	4,368,686
December	751	5,283,055
1991 June	1,029	6,390,053
December	1,252	7,557,148
1992 June	1,483	8,892,535
December	1,506	11,032,753
1993 June	1,523	13,067,318
December	1,529	16,009,461
1994 June	1,550	19,283,506
December	1,581	24,134,421
1995 June	1,581	28,154,415
December	1,627	33,785,661
1996 June	1,629	38,195,466
December	1,740	44,042,992
1997 June	2,005	48,705,553
December	2,228	55,312,293
1998 June	2,300	60,831,431
December	3,073	69,209,321
1999 June	3,447	76,284,753

Source: Cellular Telecommunications Industry Association.

The potential of wireless has driven many telecom firms to invest heavily in such services. The ultimate goal for many firms is to offer "one-stop shopping" for all telecom needs for businesses and for residential customers. These firms envision packaging local, long distance, Internet, and wireless services in order to capture maximum revenue from each customer.

DEAL TERMS

Under the terms of the agreement between WorldCom and Sprint, WorldCom agreed to pay $76.00 of its stock for each share of Sprint. If WorldCom stock traded above

$53.90 as an average closing price, Sprint would receive more than $76. If WorldCom's average trading was below $41.44, Sprint would receive a smaller amount of WorldCom shares. In addition, WorldCom would issue a new WorldCom PCS tracking stock to the holders of Sprint's PCS wireless tracking stock. Sprint PCS holders would also receive 0.116025 shares of regular WorldCom common stock.

ANTITRUST PROCEEDINGS

The potential combination of WorldCom and Sprint drew a large amount of antitrust scrutiny. Because the deal involved the telecommunications industry, the companies needed to get approval from the Federal Communications Commission (FCC) as well as the Department of Justice (DOJ). The deal also needed to gain international approval from the European Commission. Regulators in other countries, such as

---

THE COMPANIES

MCI WorldCom

MCI WorldCom is one of the largest telecommunications companies in the United States, serving local, long distance and Internet customers domestically and internationally. Organized in 1983, MCI WorldCom provides telecommunications services to businesses, governments, telecommunications companies and consumer customers through its networks of primarily fiber optic cables, digital microwave and fixed and transportable satellite earth stations. Prior to September 15, 1998, MCI WorldCom was named WorldCom, Inc.

MCI WorldCom is one of the first major telecommunications companies with the capability to provide consumers and businesses with high quality local, long distance, Internet, data and international communications services over its global networks. With service to points throughout the nation and the world, MCI WorldCom provides telecommunications products and services that include:

- switched and dedicated long distance and local products
- dedicated and dial-up Internet access
- wireless services
- 800 services
- calling cards
- private lines
- broadband data services
- debit cards
- conference calling
- messaging and mobility services

- advanced billing systems
- enhanced fax and data connections
- high speed data communications
- facilities management
- local access to long distance companies
- local access to asynchronous transfer mode-based backbone service
- web server hosting and integration services
- dial-up networking services and
- interconnection via network access points to Internet service providers.

MCI WorldCom's core business is communications services, which include voice, data, Internet and international services. During each of the last three years, more than 90% of MCI WorldCom's operating revenues were derived from communications services. MCI WorldCom is a holding company for its subsidiaries' operations.

Sprint

Sprint is a diversified telecommunications company, providing long distance, local and wireless communications services. Sprint's business is organized in two groups: the Sprint PCS group and the Sprint FON group.

The Sprint PCS Group

The Sprint PCS group markets its wireless PCS telephony products and services under the Sprint® and Sprint PCS® brand names. The Sprint PCS group operates the only 100% digital PCS wireless network in the United States with licenses to provide service nationwide utilizing a single frequency band and a single technology. The Sprint PCS group owns licenses to provide service to the entire United States population, including Puerto Rico and the U.S. Virgin Islands. As of December 31, 1999, the Sprint PCS group, together with its affiliates, operated PCS systems in more than 280 metropolitan markets within the United States, including all of the 50 largest metropolitan areas. The services offered by the Sprint PCS group and its affiliates reach areas with a total population of approximately 190 million.

The Sprint FON Group

The Sprint FON group consists of all of Sprint's businesses and assets not included in the Sprint PCS group.

Sprint's long distance division is the nation's third-largest provider of long distance telephone services. In this division, Sprint operates a nationwide, all-digital long distance telecommunications network that uses fiber optic and electronic technology. This division primarily provides domestic and international voice, video and data communications services.

Sprint's local telecommunications division consists primarily of regulated local telephone companies serving approximately 8 million access lines in 18 states. This division provides local services and access for telephone customers and other carriers to Sprint's local telephone facilities and sells telecommunications equipment and long distance services within specified geographical areas.

Sprint's product distribution and directory publishing businesses consist of wholesale distribution of telecommunications equipment and publishing and marketing white and yellow page telephone directories.

Sprint is developing and deploying new integrated communications services, referred to as Sprint ION ℠, Integrated On-Demand Network. Sprint ION extends Sprint's existing advanced network capabilities to the customer and enables Sprint to provide the network infrastructure to meet customers' demands for data, Internet and video communications services. It is also expected to be the foundation for Sprint to provide new competitive local services.

Other activities of the Sprint FON group include Sprint's investments in EarthLink Network, Inc., an Internet service provider, Call-Net, a long distance provider in Canada, and other telecommunications investments and ventures.

Recent Results

MCI WorldCom

The following information reflects selected information for MCI WorldCom's quarter and year ended December 31, 1999.

For the fourth quarter of 1999, MCI WorldCom's net income was $1.3 billion, or $0.44 per common share. On a full year basis, net income was $3.9 billion, or $1.35 per common share.

Revenues for the fourth quarter of 1999 were $9.6 billion, and for all of 1999, total revenues were $37.1 billion. MCI WorldCom now receives 40 percent of communications services revenues and more than 80 percent of its incremental communications services revenues from high growth areas such as data, Internet and international revenues.

Sprint

The following information reflects selected results for the quarter and year ended December 31, 1999 for the Sprint FON group, the Sprint PCS group and Sprint as a whole.

For the fourth quarter of 1999, the Sprint FON group's revenues increased 8 percent to $4.41 billion from $4.08 billion in the fourth quarter of 1998. For 1999, revenues grew 8 percent to $17.02 billion from $15.76 billion in 1998. Net income was $416 million in the fourth quarter of 1999, an increase of 3 percent from $404 million in the fourth quarter of 1998. Net income for 1999 rose 2 percent to $1.57 billion from $1.54 billion for 1998.

The Sprint FON group's long-distance division reported an increase in quarterly revenues of over 7 percent to $2.71 billion from $2.52 billion in the fourth quarter of 1998. For 1999, revenues increased 9 percent to $10.57 billion from $9.66 billion in 1998. Operating income was $431 million for the fourth quarter of 1999, a 13 percent improvement from $382 million in the fourth quarter of 1998. Operating income for 1999 increased 20 percent to $1.63 billion from $1.37 billion for 1998. Calling volumes rose 20 percent for the fourth quarter of 1999 and 22 percent for the year compared to the same periods in 1998.

The Sprint FON group's local telecommunications division reported an increase in revenues in the fourth quarter of 1999 of 7 percent to $1.48 billion compared to $1.38 billion in the fourth quarter of 1998. For 1999, revenues grew by 6 percent to $5.65 billion from $5.33 billion in 1998. Operating income rose 18 percent in the fourth quarter of 1999 to $384 million from $325 million in the fourth quarter of 1998. Operating income for 1999 was $1.50 billion, up 8 percent from $1.38 billion in 1998. Access lines increased 4.9 percent from the fourth quarter of 1998.

The Sprint FON group's product distribution and directory publishing division reported an increase in revenues of 3 percent in the fourth quarter of 1999 to $422 million from $411 million in the fourth quarter of 1998. Annual revenues were up 3 percent to $1.73 billion from $1.68 billion in 1998. Non-affiliate revenues increased 15 percent in the fourth quarter of 1999 compared to the fourth quarter of 1998 and 12 percent during 1999 compared to 1998. Operating income increased 17 percent to $63 million in the fourth quarter of 1999 from $54 million in the fourth quarter of 1998. Annual operating income was $242 million, an increase of 5 percent from $231 million for 1998.

The Sprint PCS group's subscriber growth for the fourth quarter of 1999 represented a 24 percent increase over the fourth quarter of 1998. The Sprint PCS group added 1.04 million new subscribers in the fourth quarter of 1999 compared to 836 thousand new subscribers for the fourth quarter of 1998. For 1999, the Sprint PCS group added 3.14 million subscribers to end the year with a total of more than 5.7 million subscribers, a 121 percent increase from 1998. Total net operating revenues were $996 million in the fourth quarter of 1999 compared to $437 million in the fourth quarter of 1998. Annual revenues were $3.18 billion for the year compared to $1.23 billion in 1998. Average monthly revenue per user remained steady at $54 for the fourth quarter of 1999 and the twelve months ended December 31, 1999. Capital expenditures were $1.0 billion for the fourth quarter of 1999 and $2.65 billion for all of 1999, reflecting the continued expansion of the Sprint PCS group's nationwide wireless network.

Consolidated net operating revenues for Sprint for 1999 increased 18 percent to $19.93 billion from $16.88 billion in 1998. Revenues for the fourth quarter of 1999 increased 19 percent to $5.32 billion from $4.47 billion in the fourth quarter of 1998.

Regulatory Matters

Federal Communications Commission

Under the Communications Act of 1934, the Federal Communications Commission must approve, before the completion of the merger, the transfer of control to MCI WorldCom of Sprint and those subsidiaries of Sprint that hold FCC licenses and authorizations. The FCC must determine whether MCI WorldCom is qualified to control such licenses and authorizations and whether the transfer is consistent with the public interest, convenience and necessity. MCI WorldCom and Sprint filed transfer of control applications with the FCC in November 1999.

United States Antitrust

Under the Hart-Scott-Rodino Act, and the rules promulgated thereunder by the Federal Trade Commission, the merger may not be completed until notifications have been given and information furnished to the FTC and to the Antitrust Division of the U.S. Department of Justice and the specified waiting period has been terminated or has expired. MCI WorldCom and Sprint each filed notification and report forms under the Hart-Scott-Rodino Act with the FTC and the Antitrust Division. On November 10, 1999, the Antitrust Division requested additional information from MCI WorldCom and Sprint. MCI WorldCom and Sprint are currently working to respond to this request as promptly as practicable. The waiting period under the Hart-Scott-Rodino-Act will expire twenty days after MCI WorldCom and Sprint have complied with the request, unless such waiting period is terminated earlier. At any time before or after completion of the merger, the Antitrust Division could take such action under the antitrust laws as it deems necessary or desirable in the public interest, including seeking to enjoin completion of the merger or seeking divestiture of substantial assets of MCI WorldCom or Sprint. The merger also is subject to review under state antitrust laws and could be the subject of challenges by private parties under the antitrust laws.

State Regulatory Approvals

Various subsidiaries of Sprint hold licenses and service authorizations issued by state public utility commissions. Approximately 26 state commissions must review the transfer of control of these licenses and authorizations to MCI WorldCom. MCI WorldCom and Sprint believe that the merger complies with applicable state standards for approval.

Foreign Regulatory Reviews

MCI WorldCom and Sprint each conduct business in member states of the European Union. Member state competition authorities exercise jurisdiction over transactions that fall below the thresholds set forth in European merger regulation 4064/89 (which grants exclusive jurisdiction to the European Commission), but above thresholds set forth in their individual national laws. Such national thresholds are typically based on worldwide sales and sales in the individual member states. The national authorities will review the merger to determine whether it is compatible with their national laws on merger control. If a national authority concludes that the transaction is incompatible with applicable law, it could withhold its approval or condition its approval upon the receipt of undertakings by the parties, including the divestiture of assets or businesses.

Transactions which exceed the thresholds set forth in European merger regulation 4064/89 fall within the exclusive jurisdiction of the European Commission and will be assessed to determine if they create a position of dominance which is restrictive of competition. Similar to the position that prevails in the member states, the European Commission can withhold its approval or condition its approval on undertakings of the parties including the divestiture of assets or businesses.

The merger is currently being reviewed by the European Commission, which is investigating the effects of the merger on competition in the European Union. The European Commission has announced that its review is focusing on issues related to the Internet, international voice telecommunications services and global telecommunications services. The European Commission's review is expected to be completed in early July 2000.

MCI WorldCom and Sprint each conduct business in Brazil. MCI WorldCom owns an indirect controlling interest in Empresa Brasileira de Telecomunicações S.A.—Embratel, which holds a concession to provide fixed long-distance telephony services and authorizations to provide additional telecommunications services in Brazil. Sprint has an ownership interest in Intelig Telecomunicações Ltda., which holds an authorization to provide fixed long-distance telephony services in competition with Embratel. In these circumstances, the merger is notifiable to the Brazilian telecommunications and antitrust authorities, ANATEL and CADE, pursuant to Articles 2 and 54, § 3 of Law No. 8,884/94. The authorities will review the transaction to determine whether it is compatible with the Brazilian antitrust law as well as the General Telecommunications Law (GTL)—Law 9.472/97 and the General Grant Plan (GGP)—Decree 2.534/98. If ANATEL and/or CADE conclude that the transaction is incompatible with applicable law, they could withhold their approval or condition approval on undertakings by the parties, including the divestiture of overlapping assets or operations in Brazil. On October 26, 1999, the required notifications were filed with ANATEL/CADE. A decision is anticipated within several months.

MCI WorldCom and Sprint are not aware of any other foreign governmental approvals or actions that would be required for completion of the merger. However, MCI WorldCom and Sprint conduct business in a number of other foreign countries, some of which have voluntary and/or post-merger notification procedures. If any other approval or action is required, MCI WorldCom and Sprint currently contemplate that such approval or action will be sought.

Brazil, also vowed to investigate, but probably would not have had the political clout to block the merger.

After being announced in October 1999, the deal immediately came under investigation. By November, Bernard Ebbers, CEO of WorldCom, and William Esrey, CEO of Sprint, were testifying before the Senate Judiciary Committee, explaining the logic of the deal. In the following few months, regulators were largely silent on the deal. At one point in January 2000, when asked about the regulatory process, Ebbers said, "There's been a lot of speculation about the scrutiny, but the DOJ hasn't taken up the case yet, the FCC hasn't taken up the case yet. Where's the scrutiny? There's been some public commentary or something like that, but that doesn't really deal with the facts of the case." However, by May 2000 it was clear that Justice Department officials were urging antitrust chief Joel Klein to oppose the merger. On June 27, 2000, the DOJ filed a complaint to block the merger of WorldCom and Sprint. In the immediate aftermath, the two firms attempted to work out some compromise. Ultimately, they decided to cancel their merger agreement on July 13, 2000. If U.S. regulators had not blocked the merger, it is likely that European Commission regulators would have.

Shortly after the merger was announced, FCC Chairman William Kennard released a statement: "American consumers are enjoying the lowest long distance rates in history and the lowest Internet rates in the world for one reason: competition. Competition has produced a price war in the long distance market. This merger appears to be a surrender. How can this be good for consumers? The parties will bear a heavy burden to show how consumers would be better off." In essence, this was a key issue in the evaluation of the merger. Antitrust regulators were concerned that price reductions would be reversed. WorldCom and Sprint executives argued that the changing landscape of the industry required the merger to keep ahead of the competition.

Regulators' Arguments

Following are some excerpts from the complaint filed by the Department of Justice:

The United States of America, acting under the direction of the Attorney General of the United States, brings this civil action to enjoin WorldCom, Inc. from acquiring Sprint Corporation and alleges as follows:

1. For most of the twentieth century, the provision of long distance telecommunications services and many other telecommunications services in the United States was monopolized by AT&T. In the 1970s, this monopoly was challenged by new entrants, supported by changes in Federal Communications Commission ("FCC") regulations designed to promote competition and by the government's antitrust case challenging AT&T's actions to preserve its monopoly. These efforts ultimately succeeded in bringing competition to long distance services.

2. In the 1980s and 1990s, two companies—and only two companies—emerged as major competitors to AT&T, and to each other. MCI (which merged with WorldCom in 1998) and Sprint each constructed national and international fiber optic networks, developed sophisticated systems for handling many millions of customer accounts, hired and trained large workforces capable of providing a wide range of high-quality telecommunications services to customers throughout the nation, and invested billions of dollars over many years to establish widely known and trusted brands.

3. Many other carriers have entered on a much smaller scale, but none has produced beneficial effects on competition comparable in magnitude to the effects produced by competition between WorldCom and Sprint, and between those companies and AT&T. Those two companies, together with AT&T, dominate the provision of long distance services to residential and small/home office consumers, the provision of international services between the United States and many countries throughout the world for customers in the United States, and the provision of key data network services and custom network services used by many large business customers. In addition, WorldCom has attained (primarily through a series of acquisitions) a commanding position in the ownership and operation of the "backbone" networks that connect the thousands of smaller networks that constitute the Internet, and Sprint is WorldCom's largest competitor in that market.

4. In particular, the Defendants are:
   - the largest and second largest of a small group of top-tier providers of Internet "backbone" network services in the United States and the world;
   - the second- and third-largest of three providers who collectively dominate long distance telecommunications within the United States, and between the United States and numerous overseas destinations;

- the largest and third-largest of three providers who collectively dominate international private line services to business customers;

- two of three providers who collectively dominate various data network services to large business customers; and

- two of three providers who collectively dominate custom network telecommunications services to large business customers.

5. The proposed merger of WorldCom and Sprint will cause significant harm to competition in many of the nation's most important telecommunications markets. By combining two of the largest telecommunications firms in these markets, the proposed acquisition would substantially lessen competition in violation of Section 7 of the Clayton Act, as amended, 15 U.S.C. § 18. For millions of residential and business consumers throughout the nation, the merger will lead to higher prices, lower service quality, and less innovation than would be the case absent its consummation. The United States therefore seeks an order permanently enjoining the merger.

Market Concentration and Anticompetitive Effects in Internet Backbone Services Market

32. WorldCom's wholly owned subsidiary, UUNET, is by far the largest Tier 1 IBP (Internet Backbone Provider) by any relevant measure and is already approaching a dominant position in the Internet backbone market. Based upon a study conducted in February 2000, UUNET's share of all Internet traffic sent to or received from the customers of the 15 largest Internet backbones in the United States was 37%, more than twice the share of Sprint, the next-largest Tier 1 IBP, which had a 16% share. These 15 backbones represent approximately 95% of all U.S. dedicated Internet access revenues. UUNET's and Sprint's 53% combined share of Internet traffic is at least five times larger than that of the next-largest IBP. The Herfindahl-Hirschman Index ("HHI"), the standard measure of market concentration (defined and explained in Appendix A), indicates that this market is highly concentrated. The HHI in terms of traffic is approximately 1850; post-merger, the HHI will rise approximately 1150 points to approximately 3000. (Note: Throughout the Complaint, market share percentages have been rounded to the nearest whole number, but HHIs have been estimated using unrounded percentages in order to accurately reflect the concentration of the various markets.)

33. The proposed merger threatens to destroy the competitive environment that has created a vibrant, innovative Internet by forming an entity that is larger than all other IBPs combined, and thereby has an overwhelmingly disproportionate size advantage over any other IBP.

34. The proposed transaction would produce anticompetitive harm in at least two ways. First, it would substantially lessen competition by eliminating Sprint, the second-largest IBP in an already concentrated market, as a competitive con-

straint on the Internet backbone market. The elimination of this constraint will provide the combined entity with the incentive and ability to charge higher prices and provide lower quality of service for customers.

35. Second, the combined entity ("UUNET/Sprint") will have the incentive and ability to impair the ability of its rivals to compete by, among other things, raising its rivals' costs and/or degrading the quality of its interconnections to its rivals. As a result of the merger, UUNET/Sprint's rivals will become increasingly dependent upon being connected to the combined entity, and the combined entity will exploit that advantage. Such behavior will likely enhance the market power of the combined firm, and ultimately facilitate a "tipping" of the Internet backbone market that will result in a monopoly.

• • •

41. When a single network grows to a point at which it controls a substantial share of the total Internet end user base and its size greatly exceeds that of any other network, network externalities may cause a reversal of its previous incentives to achieve efficient interconnection arrangements with its rival networks. In this context, degrading the quality or increasing the price of interconnection with smaller networks can create advantages for the largest network in attracting customers to its network. Customers recognize that they can communicate more effectively with a larger number of other end users if they are on the largest network, and this effect feeds upon itself and becomes more powerful as larger numbers of customers choose the largest network. This effect has been described as "tipping" the market. Once the market begins to "tip," connecting to the dominant network becomes even more important to competitors. This, in turn, enables the dominant network to further raise its rivals' costs, thereby accelerating the tipping effect. As a result of an increase in their costs, rivals may not be able to compete on a long-term basis and may exit the market. If rivals decide to pass on these costs, users of connectivity will respond by selecting the dominant network as their provider. Ultimately, once rivals have been eliminated or reduced to "customer status," the dominant network can raise prices to users of its own network beyond competitive levels. Once this occurs, restoring the market to a competitive state often requires extraordinary means, including some form of government regulation.

Entry into Internet Backbone Services

47. Entry into the Tier 1 Internet backbone services market would not be timely, likely, or sufficient to remedy the proposed merger's likely anticompetitive harm. In the current market environment, entry barriers are already high, and the proposed transaction will substantially raise barriers to entry. An entrant into the Tier 1 Internet backbone market must establish and maintain adequate peering interconnections to provide Internet connectivity. Entry into the Tier 1 Internet backbone market requires that an IBP peer privately, on a settlement-free basis, with all other Tier 1 IBPs, as well as interconnect with other IBPs

without having to purchase any significant amount of Internet connectivity. Incumbent Tier 1 IBPs only grudgingly grant private peering to another IBP when it has a sufficiently large customer base such that other Tier 1 IBPs will be able to derive sufficient positive network externalities from interconnection with it. In a classic "Catch-22," without adequate peering interconnections a rival cannot gain customer traffic and without sufficient customer traffic a rival cannot gain peering connections.

48. UUNET/Sprint would be able to control and inhibit successful entry by refusing to interconnect with new entrants or by limiting those connections in order to control the growth of its rivals. By degrading the quality of interconnection and raising its rivals' costs, UUNET/Sprint would further prevent entry and expansion by other IBPs. Moreover, through its control of public interconnection facilities (e.g., MAE-East, MAE-West, New York NAP) and its refusal to upgrade these facilities, UUNET/Sprint would be able to limit opportunities for existing rivals and new entrants to build their traffic volumes through public peering.

49. Entry into the Tier 1 Internet backbone services market also requires substantial time and enormous sums of capital to build a network of sufficient size and capacity, and to attract and retain the scarce, highly skilled technical personnel required for its operations.

Market Concentration and Anticompetitive Effects of Long Distance Telecom Service

62. The market for the provision of mass-market long distance services is highly concentrated, and will become substantially more concentrated as a result of the proposed combination of WorldCom and Sprint. AT&T, WorldCom, and Sprint each provide long distance telephone services by carrying voice and data communications over their broad national and international fiber optic networks, and collectively the Big 3 have continuously dominated mass market long distance for many years. For example, in 1999 more than 80% of residential lines in the United States that are presubscribed to one of the Big 3 as their long distance carrier, with approximately 19% of residential lines subscribing to WorldCom and approximately 8% subscribing to Sprint. In Sprint's local exchange territories, substantially more than 8% of the lines subscribe to Sprint; outside of its local exchange territories approximately 7% of the lines subscribe to Sprint. The Big 3 in 1999 also accounted for approximately 80% of interLATA revenue, including dial-1 and dial-around, with WorldCom accounting for approximately 21% and Sprint for approximately 9%. Again, Sprint has captured substantially more than 9% in its local exchange territories, and slightly less outside of its local exchange territories. According to the HHI, the standard measure of market concentration (defined and explained in Appendix A), this market is highly concentrated. The HHI for this market measured in terms of residential lines is approximately 3500; post-merger, the HHI will rise approximately 300 points to approximately 3800, and the combined company will have

a share of approximately 27%. Measured in terms of revenue, including dial-1 and dial-around, the HHI is approximately 3500; post-merger, the HHI will rise approximately 400 points to 3900, and the combined company will have a share of approximately 30%.

63. The Big 3 each have substantial competitive advantages in serving the mass market because of their respective powerful brand equity and recognition, as well as the scale and scope of their respective operations, including near ubiquitous facilities-based networks, broad customer bases, storehouses of technological expertise and service experience, and corps of highly skilled, experienced personnel.

64. Over the years, the Defendants and AT&T have collectively invested billions of dollars to market their long distance services and to establish, maintain, and enhance their brand images with mass-market consumers. Brand recognition is often a deciding factor in mass-market consumers' choices when they face complex price decisions such as those often presented by competing long distance plans.

65. The Defendants and AT&T are the only telecommunications providers whose broad networks and operations reach virtually every corner of the United States without significant reliance upon the facilities of other long distance carriers, and who benefit from widely recognized and firmly established brand names. Both WorldCom's and Sprint's fiber optic networks have local interconnection points of presence ("POPs") in LATAs reaching more than 99% of U.S. households.

66. Apart from the Big 3, there are many smaller competitive "fringe" long distance carriers that offer services to mass-market consumers. A large number of these smaller domestic carriers have few or no network facilities of their own and purchase capacity from the Defendants and AT&T to provide them with access to network facilities on a wholesale basis. As a result, "resellers" and other fringe carriers are handicapped in any competitive response, not only by their little-known brands, but also because their networks are often dependent upon the provision of wholesale services by the Big 3 and others. In addition, many of the competitive fringe carriers confine their marketing activities to local or regional areas, or to targeted ethnic or other niche groups. The Defendants and AT&T have been the only mass-market long distance carriers since AT&T's divestiture of the regional BOCs in the mid-1980s to garner more than a two to three percent nationwide market share.

• • •

69. The merger will also facilitate coordinated or collusive pricing or other anticompetitive behavior by the merged entity and AT&T. If the merger is consummated, AT&T and WorldCom/Sprint will collectively control approximately 80% of the market, while their next largest competitor will have a market share of no more than 3%.

70. The merged entity would be able to raise prices without losing sufficient sales to the "competitive fringe" carriers to cause the price increase to be unprofitable. Despite the fact that for many years a large number of long distance carriers have been competing and, in many cases, have offered materially lower prices than the Big 3, none has ever successfully attracted a substantial share of the nationwide mass market.

71. Competition from the fringe carriers will be insufficient to prevent coordinated pricing or other anticompetitive behavior based on the strength of the Big 3's brand names and to some extent on the superior capacity and coverage of their networks.

72. Allowing the Defendants to merge will remove the competitive pressure directly exerted by the merging Defendants on each other, and on AT&T. This will harm consumers through higher prices.

Market Concentration and Anticompetitive Effects of International Long Distance Service

89. The relevant markets for the provision of mass-market international long distance telecommunications services between the United States and each of the countries listed in Appendix B are highly concentrated according to the HHI, the standard measure of market concentration (defined and explained in Appendix A). The merger would substantially increase concentration in each of these markets. On seven of these U.S.-foreign country routes, the combined market share of WorldCom and Sprint would be 50% or greater. See Appendix B.

90. For mass market international long distance services, the best publicly available data is the FCC's report on international message telecommunication service ("IMTS") revenues, which includes data on outbound voice services to both businesses and mass market consumers. Based on FCC data for 1998, the most recent year for which the data is available, the merger will substantially increase concentration in many markets. For example, WorldCom had a 26% share of the IMTS revenues of carriers that had their own facilities on the U.S.-Brazil route, and Sprint had an 8% share. The Big 3 combined accounted for 98% of revenues on the U.S.-Brazil route. The pre-merger HHI is 4868; post-merger, it will increase by 389 points to 5257. Similarly, on the U.S.-India route in 1998, WorldCom had a 39% market share and Sprint's share was 7%. The Big 3's combined share was 89%. The pre-merger HHI is 3481; post-merger, it will increase by 533 points to 4014. On the U.S.-Israel route, WorldCom had a 22% market share, and Sprint had a 14% share. The Big 3's combined market share was 99%. The pre-merger HHI is 4580; post-merger, it will increase 625 points to 5205. On the U.S.-Vietnam route, WorldCom and Sprint accounted for 34% and 13% of the 1998 U.S.-billed IMTS revenues, respectively. The Big 3's combined market share was 92%. The pre-merger HHI is 3379; post-merger, it will increase 913 points to 4292.

In essence, the critical arguments of the Justice Department center around the Internet backbone and long distance services of the two companies. Although the combined companies were willing to divest the Internet service (and even expected to), they anticipated that long distance would not become a stumbling block. In fact, one of the reasons that Sprint cited for selecting WorldCom over Bell South was the fact that Bell South was seen as having a more difficult time gaining approval to offer Sprint's long distance services. This reflects the somewhat unpredictable nature of antitrust investigations.

Another factor illustrated by the DOJ actions against WorldCom is the potential importance of a good track record with regulators. Shortly before the antitrust suit was filed, WorldCom was forced to settle "slamming" charges with the FCC. Slamming is the practice of long distance companies switching customers to their services without gaining the proper consent. WorldCom was ordered to pay $3 million to settle the charges, one of the largest slamming settlements in the history of the FCC.

A potential concern may have arisen from WorldCom's MCI acquisition. As a part of that acquisition, WorldCom was required to sell off MCI's Internet assets. This was executed in an agreement with Cable & Wireless, a British company. However, Cable & Wireless later filed a suit that charged that WorldCom had failed to deliver fully on the deal. Cable & Wireless said WorldCom did not provide the full amount of customer information and technological know-how that was expected. Cable & Wireless kept European regulators informed of WorldCom's resistance, and eventually WorldCom had to settle by paying $200 million to Cable & Wireless to settle the dispute. Such a historical track record likely made dealings with regulators difficult.

WorldCom and Sprint Arguments

WorldCom and Sprint used a variety of arguments to defend their merger. Most of the points of contention settled on the long distance business. The firms essentially conceded that they would have to divest the Internet assets of Sprint. They made some argument about the increasing number of competitors in the Internet Backbone market, but the firms knew that combining Internet assets was not likely to be approved. However, rumors said that European regulators wanted the firms to divest WorldCom's UUNet Internet services, which likely would have effectively forced the companies to reconsider the deal.

The central disagreement between regulators and WorldCom/Sprint officials centered on their visions of the telecommunications future. The companies argued that regulators should not be concerned about the market shares of the firms (2nd and 3rd). WorldCom and Sprint tried to demonstrate that even after the merger 90% of Americans would be served by four or more facilities based long distance companies. Emerging long distance carriers such as Qwest, Broadwing, Level 3, Williams, and Frontier have built their networks to the point where they are legitimate competitors to AT&T, WorldCom, and Sprint. The firms argued that consumers and business carriers looked for the best deal and service, regardless of the company that provided it.

WorldCom and Sprint also pointed to the imminent entry of the "Baby Bells" (RBOCs) into the long distance arena. In December 1999, Bell Atlantic was approved to offer long distance service in New York, and SBC was approved to offer long distance to customers in Texas shortly after the rejection of the WorldCom/Sprint merger. WorldCom and Sprint argued that the entry of these local firms would further increase competition. The RBOCs were seen as moving to an "all distance" model of telecommunications, much like AT&T and WorldCom, in which one firm could offer local and long distance phone service, Internet, and wireless services. This type of firm would be able to bundle the individual services at a cost saving to consumers. However, the Justice Department felt that since the RBOCs had not yet entered the long distance market, it was not appropriate to approve the WorldCom/Sprint merger.

WorldCom and Sprint also argued that they could become a viable local competitor as a combined company. Through a combination of Sprint's already existing local services and the implementation of a "fixed wireless" system (in which wireless is used as an entry to homes instead of existing telephone lines) the companies believed they could become a viable local alternative to the RBOCs and AT&T. However, the firms would need to retain the cash flows from Sprint's long distance service to be able to deploy the technology involved in the fixed wireless system.

AFTERMATH

In the immediate aftermath of the abandonment of the deal, speculation about the future of WorldCom and Sprint abounded. There were rumors that Sprint would again become the subject of bidding between Bell South and Deutsche Telekom. However, both firms would face serious regulatory challenges as well. Bell South had not yet gained FCC approval to offer long distance. Deutsche Telekom's regulatory problems were different. Because the German government owned 56% of the firm, American politicians were against allowing it to purchase any telecom properties.

WorldCom was seen as suffering a crucial loss by not gaining Sprint's wireless assets. Some overzealous analysts were speculating that it could be worth it for WorldCom to buy Sprint and sell off everything but its wireless properties. On the other hand, Jack Grubman of Salomon Smith Barney pointed out that in many ways wireless did not fit that well into the WorldCom business model. Since most firms reimburse their employees for their wireless phone service, wireless is very consumer oriented. WorldCom was structured around providing telecom services to business. Since businesses do not generally provide wireless phones, it may not be such a critical segment for the future success of WorldCom.

QUESTIONS

1. Describe the major provisions of the 1984 divestiture of AT&T.
2. What are the main segments of the household telecom market and the key players in it?
3. What is the role of wireless in the telecom industry?
4. What were the main arguments of the DOJ against the merger?
5. What were the WorldCom and Sprint arguments?

Case 6

Purchase Accounting: Time Warner, AOL, WorldCom

Three examples of the use of purchase accounting are provided by the Time Warner merger with Turner Broadcasting in 1996, the merger between AOL and Time Warner announced in 2000, and the WorldCom purchase of MCI in 1998.

TIME WARNER PURCHASE OF THE TURNER BROADCASTING SYSTEM

In a letter dated September 6, 1996 addressed to stockholders, Gerald M. Levin, the Chairman of the Board and Chief Executive Officer of Time Warner Inc. (TW), announced a special meeting of stockholders to approve and adopt a plan to purchase the Turner Broadcasting System (TBS) for $7.6 billion in new TW common stock. This letter was accompanied by a two-page Notice of the Special Meeting to be held on October 10, 1996, plus a Joint Proxy Statement addressed to stockholders of 191 pages with schedules, glossary of terms, and appendix materials of about 200 additional pages. The proxy materials included the merger agreement and detailed terms of the transaction. The materials also stated that, "The transaction will be accounted for by the purchase method of accounting for combinations. . . ." An exact copy for the resulting Pro Forma Consolidated Condensed Balance Sheet is reproduced as Table 1. While many adjustments in addition to the merger transactions were made, the major entries for purchase accounting were:

TABLE 1 New Time Warner Pro Forma Consolidated Condensed Balance Sheet
June 30, 1996 (millions, unaudited)

	Time Warner Historical	TBS Transaction		New Time Warner Pro Forma
		TBS Historical(a)	Pro Forma Adjustments(b)	
ASSETS				
Cash and equivalents	$ 482	$ 119	$ --	$ 601
Other current assets	2,742	1,292	(174)	3,860
Total current assets	3,224	1,411	(174)	4,461
Investments in and amounts due to and from Entertainment Group	5,945	—	—	5,945
Other investments	2,507	—	(539)	1,968
Noncurrent inventories	—	2,042	—	2,042
Property, plant and equipment	1,481	368	—	1,849
Cable television franchises	3,970	—	—	3,970
Goodwill	5,825	260	6,428	12,513
Other assets	1,556	407	—	1,963
Total assets	$24,508	$4,488	$5,715	$34,711
LIABILITIES AND SHAREHOLDERS' EQUITY				
Total current liabilities	$ 2,762	$ 822	$ —	$ 3,584
Long-term debt	9,928	2,600	162	12,690
Borrowings against future stock option proceeds	225	—	—	225
Deferred income taxes	3,983	421	—	4,404
Other long-term liabilities	1,232	174	—	1,406
Time Warner-obligated mandatorily redeemable preferred securities of subsidiaries holding solely subordinated notes and debentures of Time Warner(1)	949	—	—	949
Series K exchangeable preferred stock	1,586	—	—	1,586
Shareholders' equity:				
Preferred stock	36	—	(32)	4
Common stock	387	—	(381)	6
Paid-in capital	5,866	—	6,437	12,303
Unrealized gains on certain marketable securities	177	—	—	177
TBS shareholders' equity	—	471	(471)	—
Accumulated deficit	(2,623)	—	—	(2,623)
Total shareholders' equity	3,843	471	5,553	9,867
Total liabilities and shareholders' equity	$24,508	$4,488	$5,715	$34,711

(1) Includes $374 million of preferred securities that are redeemable for cash or, at Time Warner's option, approximately 12.1 million shares of Hasbro, Inc. common stock owned by Time Warner.

Source: Time Warner and TBS Joint Proxy Statement/Prospectus dated September 6, 1996, p. 113.

Debit ($ billion)

Goodwill	$6.4
TBS shareholders' equity	0.5
Other misc. adjustments	<u>0.7</u>
	$7.6

Credit ($billion)

TWX common stock at par issued to pay for TBS	$1.2
Addition to Time Warner Paid-in Capital	<u>6.4</u>
	$7.6

Among the adjustments Time Warner made was to change the par value of its stock from $1.00 to $0.01 so the credit to the common stock account of Time Warner to record the new series issued to buy TBS would be multiplied by $0.01 instead of $1.00. The balance sheet in Table 1 shows that the common stock of "Time Warner Historical" was $387 million. The common stock account of the "New Time Warner Pro Forma" was $6 million. Note that the combined goodwill account was adjusted upward by $6,428 million and the Paid-in capital account was adjusted upward by $6,437 million.

The effect of these adjustments on the book value measures of leverage of Time Warner were quite substantial, as shown in Table 2.

AOL MERGER WITH TIME WARNER (TWX)

The merger was announced on January 10, 2000. Before the merger announcement, AOL had been trading at about $74 per share and TWX at $65. The detailed pro forma consolidated balance sheet for the new AOL Time Warner Inc. is shown in Table 3. The basic purchase accounting entries without other adjustments made would have been:

TABLE 2 Effect on Book Leverage of Time Warner Purchase of Turner Broadcasting

	TWX		TBS		Combined	
	Amount	%	Amount	%	Amount	%
Total Liabilities	$20,665		$4,017		$24,844	
Shareholders' Equity	$3,843		$471		$9,867	
Total Claims	$24,508	100.0%	$4,488	100.0%	$34,711	100.0%
Liabilities/Equity						

TABLE 3 AOL Time Warner Inc. Pro Forma Consolidated Balance Sheet
March 31, 2000 (in millions, unaudited)

	AOL(a)	Time Warner(b)	Pro Forma Adjustments(c)	AOL Time Warner Pro Forma
ASSETS				
Cash and equivalents	$ 2,655	$ 848	$ —	$ 3,503
Other current assets	1,545	8,028	—	9,573
Total current assets	4,200	8,876	—	13,076
Noncurrent inventories	—	4,233	—	4,233
Investments	4,791	2,134	—	6,925
Property, plant and equipment, net	991	8,933	—	9,924
Goodwill and other intangibles, net	432	24,507	174,386	199,325
Other assets	375	1,530	—	1,905
Total assets	$10,789	$50,213	$174,386	$235,388
LIABILITIES AND SHAREHOLDERS' EQUITY				
Total current liabilities	$ 2,323	$ 8,649	$ 300	$ 11,272
Long-term debt and other obligations(1)	1,625	19,554	—	21,179
Deferred income taxes	—	4,033	34,476	38,509
Other long-term liabilities	422	4,548	—	4,970
Minority interests	—	3,165	—	3,165
Shareholders' Equity				
Preferred stock	—	1	—	1
Series LMCN-V common stock	—	1	—	1
Common stock	23	12	6	41
Paid-in capital	4,283	14,745	135,109	154,137
Accumulated earnings (deficit)	1,051	(4,553)	4,553	1,051
Accumulated other comprehensive income	1,062	58	(58)	1,062
Total shareholders' equity	6,419	10,264	139,610	156,293
Total liabilities and shareholders' equity	$10,789	$50,213	$174,386	$235,388

(1) For Time Warner, includes $1.245 billion of borrowings against future stock option proceeds and $575 million of mandatorily redeemable preferred securities of subsidiaries.

Debit ($ billion)

Goodwill	$132.5
Time Warner book equity	10.3
	$142.8

Credit ($billion)

AOL common stock issued to pay for TWX (1.93B times $.01 par)	$0.0193
Paid-in Capital ($142.8-$0.0193)	142.78
	$ 142.8

The main effect was to create goodwill of $132.5 billion and to increase the shareholders' equity account of the new company by $142.78 billion. The pro forma numbers in Table 3 included numerous other adjustments. The effects of the asset structures on AOL and TWX are shown in Table 4. The effects on leverage are summarized are in Table 5.

WORLDCOM PURCHASE OF MCI

The third illustration of purchase accounting is provided by the acquisition of MCI by WorldCom on 3/11/98. The major entries for purchase accounting were:

Debit ($ billion)

Goodwil	$28.6
MCI shareholders' equity	11.3
Other misc. adjustments	(14.0)
	$25.9

Credit ($billion)

WorldCom common stock at par issued to pay for MCI	$0.2
Addition to WorldCom Paid-in Capital	25.7
	$25.9

The effect on book leverage of the WorldCom purchase of MCI is shown in Table 6.

TABLE 4 Effects of Asset Structures, AOL/TWX

	AOL		TWX		Combined	
	Amount	%	Amount	%	Amount	%
Total Assets	$10,789	100.0%	$50,213	100.0%	$235,388	100.0%
Goodwill+other intangibles	$432		$24,507		$199,325	
Tangible assets	$10,357		$25,706		$36,063	

TABLE 5 Leverage Changes in the AOL and TWX Merger

	AOL		TWX		Combined	
	Amount	%	Amount	%	Amount	%
Total Liabilities	$4,370		$39,949		$79,095	
Shareholders' Equity	$6,419		$10,264		$156,293	
Total Claims	$10,789	100.0%	$50,213	100.0%	$235,388	100.0%
Liabilities/Equity						

TABLE 6 Effect on Book Leverage of WorldCom Purchase of MCI

	WorldCom		MCI		Combined	
	Amount	%	Amount	%	Amount	%
Total Liabilities	$7,447		$13,396		$27,274	
Shareholders' Equity	$13,366		$11,321		$44,177	
Total Claims	$20,813	100.0%	$24,717	100.0%	$71,451	100.0%
Liabilities/Equity						

QUESTIONS

1. Complete Table 2 and discuss how Time Warner's liabilities/equity ratio was reduced as a result of its merger with Turner.

2. Discuss the change in the asset structures of AOL and TWX as a combined company.

3. Discuss the leverage changes as a result of the AOL/TWX merger.

4. How did the effects on leverage in the WorldCom purchase of MCI differ from the previous two examples?

5. Discuss the implications of these examples for the FASB proposal to eliminate pooling of interests accounting so that only purchase accounting for business combinations would remain. Include in your discussion the proposal that goodwill created in purchase accounting would be written off in 20 years, would be non tax-deductible, and cause a further divergence between cash accounting and GAAP accounting.

Case 7

Compaq Computer Corp.
Acquisition of Digital Equipment Corp.

On January 26, 1998, the two companies announced a merger agreement. The deal terms are summarized in Table 1. On the day before the merger announcement, Compaq Computer Corporation (CPQ) had a total market value of $49.7 billion. Digital Equipment Corporation (DEC) had a total market value of $6.8 billion. Whether measured on a per share basis or total market values, the premium paid by CPQ was 32.1%. First some background on the companies will be presented, then more financial information will be set forth.

TABLE 1 Deal Terms Between CPQ and DEC			
Premerger	**CPQ**	**DEC**	**Total**
Number of Shares (million)	1,564.0	149.7	
Market Value per Share	$31.75	$45.44	
Total Market Value (million)	$49,657	$6,802	$56,459
Percentage	88.0%	12.0%	100.0%
Merger Consideration			
Cash $30 x 149.7			$4,491
Shares 0.945 CPQ X 149.7 x 31.75			$4,492
			$8,983
			-6802
			$2,180
			32.1% premium
Postmerger	**CPQ**	**DEC**	**Total**
Number of Shares	1,564.0	141.5	1,705.5
Percentage	91.7%	8.3%	100.0%

BACKGROUND OF THE MERGER

During the summer of 1995, Mr. Robert Palmer, Digital's Chairman of the Board, President and Chief Executive Officer, contacted Mr. Ben Rosen, Compaq's Chairman of the Board, to discuss a variety of collaboration opportunities, including a potential business combination. These discussions were terminated in the fall of that year. In late 1996, a financial adviser to Compaq met with certain Digital representatives to discuss a possible business combination. This meeting did not lead to further merger discussions at that time.

During May 1997, representatives of Compaq, including Mr. Eckhard Pfeiffer, Compaq's President and Chief Executive Officer, Mr. Earl Mason, Compaq's Senior Vice President, Finance and Chief Financial Officer, and Mr. John Rose, Senior Vice President for Compaq's Enterprise Computing Group, met on two occasions with representatives of Digital, including Mr. Palmer, Mr. Vincent Mullarkey, Digital's Senior Vice President, Finance and Chief Financial Officer, and Mr. Frank Doyle, one of Digital's directors, to discuss pursuing a closer business relationship. After preliminary discussions, the parties decided not to pursue a transaction at that time.

In December 1997, Mr. Robert Greenhill of Greenhill & Co., LLC met with Mr. Doyle and Mr. Palmer to discuss again the possibility of a business combination.

In early January 1998, Mr. Pfeiffer indicated to Mr. Doyle Compaq's interest in pursuing a business combination. On behalf of Digital, Mr. Doyle sought advice from Skadden, Arps, Slate, Meagher & Flom LLP and Lehman Brothers, and then met with Mr. Pfeiffer on January 15, 1998.

On January 19, Mr. Mason met with Mr. Mullarkey and Ms. Ilene Jacobs, Digital's Senior Vice President, Human Resources. After initial discussions regarding a possible transaction, the parties agreed to continue preliminary discussions throughout that week.

On January 22, the Compaq Board of Directors (the "Compaq Board") met in New York and considered the possibility of a transaction and approved further discussions. After the Compaq Board meeting on January 22, Mr. Pfeiffer called Mr. Doyle to advise Mr. Doyle of Compaq's interest in pursuing a business combination on an expedited basis. Management representatives of Compaq traveled to New York later the same day.

At a special meeting held on January 23, the Digital Board met to discuss the communications and discussions which had taken place to date between Mr. Palmer, Mr. Doyle and representatives of Compaq. Following discussions, the Digital Board authorized Mr. Doyle and Mr. Palmer to proceed with formal merger negotiations.

Also on January 23, the parties began their formal due diligence reviews.

On the evening of January 23, Messrs. Pfeiffer, Mason and Rose met with Messrs. Palmer, Doyle and Mullarkey. They discussed several issues, including a possible structure of a combination and other fundamental aspects of a potential combination.

Over the next two days, the parties, together with their legal and financial advisors, finalized their due diligence reviews and negotiated the terms and conditions of the proposed merger. The parties continued to meet, and on January 25 Messrs. Pfeiffer and Mason met with Messrs. Palmer and Doyle and the parties' respective financial advisors and reached agreement on the form and amount of the consideration to be paid in the merger. Drafts of the Merger Agreement were delivered to the Compaq and Digital Boards on January 25.

The Compaq Board held a special meeting on January 25 to discuss the proposed transaction. At the meeting, Mr. Pfeiffer reviewed the status of the transaction; the results of Compaq's due diligence review were presented; representatives of Greenhill & Co., LLC and Morgan Stanley & Co. Incorporated, Compaq's financial advisors, presented an analysis of the financial terms of the proposed transaction; representatives of Davis Polk & Wardwell, Compaq's legal counsel, outlined the terms of the proposed transaction and the Compaq Board's legal duties and responsibilities; and representatives of Price Waterhouse LLP discussed accounting matters regarding the proposed transaction. At the conclusion of the meeting, the Compaq Board unanimously approved entering into the proposed Merger Agreement.

The Digital Board held a special meeting on January 25 to discuss the proposed transaction and the terms of the Merger Agreement. At the meeting, Mr. Doyle and Mr. Palmer reviewed the status of the transaction; the results of Digital's due diligence review were presented; representatives of Lehman Brothers, Digital's financial advisor, presented an analysis of the financial terms of the proposed transaction and presented an opinion as to the fairness of the Merger Consideration, from a financial point of view, to the holders of Digital Common Stock; and representatives of Skadden, Arps, Slate, Meagher & Flom LLP, Digital's legal counsel, outlined the terms of the proposed transaction and the Merger Agreement and the Digital Board's legal duties and responsibilities. At the conclusion of the meeting, the Digital Board unanimously approved and adopted the Merger Agreement and the consummation of the transactions contemplated thereby and recommended that the Merger Agreement be presented to and approved and adopted by the holders of Digital Common Stock.

Final agreement on terms was reached on January 25, and both parties signed the Merger Agreement. A press release announcing the proposed Merger was issued on January 26.

As originally signed, the Merger Agreement contemplated the conversion of the Digital Preferred Stock into a new series of Compaq preferred stock with substantially the same terms. This conversion transaction would have required the approval of the holders of Digital Preferred Stock and, if consummated, would have caused such holders to recognize gain or loss for federal income tax purposes even though they would not have received any cash upon the conversion. A consequence of the conversion transaction would have been the elimination of Digital's reporting obligations under the securities laws. After the signing, Compaq and Digital reassessed this approach and determined not to proceed with the conversion transaction. The Merger Agreement was then amended and restated to delete the provisions relating to the conversion transaction. After considering actions that it could take to permit Digital to cease its separate reporting obligations under the securities laws that would not have adverse tax consequences to the holders of Digital Preferred Stock, Compaq intends, upon receipt of regulatory approval, to guarantee (including dividends, redemption price and liquidation preference) the Digital Preferred Stock. In addition, Compaq may cause the redemption of the Digital Preferred Stock after April 1, 1999.

Digital's Reasons for the Merger; Recommendation of the Digital Board

At its special meeting held on January 25, the Digital Board, by unanimous vote, (i) determined that the terms of the Merger Agreement and the transactions contemplated thereby, including the Merger, are fair to and in the best interest of Digital and its stockholders, (ii) approved the Merger Agreement and the Merger and (iii) recommended that holders of Digital Common Stock approve and adopt the Merger Agreement.

The decision of the Digital Board to approve the Merger and the Merger Agreement and to recommend approval and adoption of the Merger Agreement by the holders of Digital Common Stock was based upon a number of factors. The following are the material factors considered by the Digital Board, certain of which factors contained both positive and negative elements:

i. the Digital Board's understanding of the present and anticipated environment in the computer industry, and how possible consolidation within the computer industry could affect Digital's competitive position on a stand-alone basis;

ii. the Digital Board's consideration of information concerning the financial condition, results of operations, prospects and businesses of Digital and Compaq, including the revenues of the companies, their complementary businesses, the recent stock price performance of Digital Common Stock and Compaq Common Stock and the ratio of the price of Digital Common Stock to the price of Compaq Common Stock over various periods, and the percentage of the combined company to be owned by Digital common stockholders following the Merger;

iii. current industry, economic market conditions;

iv. an analysis of how access to Compaq's significant resources would enable Digital to better implement its plans;

v. the financial and business prospects for the combined business, including general information relating to possible synergies, cost reductions, and operating efficiencies and consolidations.

vi. the fact that the Merger Consideration represented, as of the signing of the Merger Agreement, approximately $60.00 per share of Digital Common Stock in value and a premium of approximately 32% over the $45-7/16 closing price of Digital Common Stock on the NYSE Composite Transactions Tape of January 23, 1998, the last trading day prior to the announcement of the execution of the Merger Agreement;

vii. the opportunity for the holders of Digital Common Stock to benefit from ownership in a higher growth, higher price-to-earnings ratio business and to participate in the enhanced prospects of the combined company through ownership of Compaq Common Stock;

viii. presentations from, and discussions with, senior executives of Digital, representatives of its outside legal counsel and representatives of Lehman Brothers regarding the business, financial, accounting and legal due diligence with respect to Compaq and the terms and conditions of the Merger Agreement, and discussions with its advisors of the possible reactions of the United States antitrust authorities, the European Commission and other governmental entities to the proposed Merger;

ix. the Digital Board's understanding of the risks involved in successfully integrating the businesses and managements of the two companies;

x.   the corporate governance aspects of the Merger, including the fact that Compaq will cause a candidate recommended by Digital's Board to be elected as a member of the Compaq Board. The Digital Board, while recognizing that these arrangements presented certain potential conflicts of interests to the persons involved, and considering these interests in connection with its approval and adoption of the Merger Agreement, believed that these would be beneficial in integrating the two companies and in achieving the potential benefits of the combination;

xi. the financial and other analysis presented by Lehman Brothers, including the oral opinion of Lehman Brothers (subsequently confirmed in writing) that the consideration to be offered to Digital common stockholders in the Merger was fair to such stockholders from a financial point of view as of the date of such opinion (a copy of the Lehman Brothers opinion, dated as of January 25, 1998, setting forth the assumptions and qualifications made, facts considered and the scope of the review undertaken is attached hereto as Annex B and is incorporated by reference herein. Common stockholders of Digital are encouraged to read the opinion of Lehman Brothers carefully and in its entirety); and

xii. the Digital Board's recognition that certain members of the Digital Board and of Digital's management have interests in the Merger that are in addition to and not necessarily aligned with the interests of holders of Digital

Common Stock, which interests were considered in connection with its approval and adoption of the Merger Agreement. See "Interests of Certain Person in the Merger and Related Matters" on page 41.

The January 25, 1998 meeting of the Digital Board was attended by Digital's Senior Vice President and General Counsel and its outside law counsel who regularly advises Digital on Massachusetts corporation law issues. Massachusetts is the state of Digital's incorporation. Before making its decision, the Digital Board was advised by counsel of the standards of conduct for directors of a Massachusetts corporation, including a director's duty to act in good faith and without self-interest. The directors were also given the opportunity and encouraged to discuss with legal counsel any questions they might have on their duties.

The Digital Board also considered (i) the risk that the benefits sought in the Merger would not be obtained, (ii) the risk that the Merger would not be consummated, (iii) the effect of the public announcement of the Merger on Digital's sales, customer and supplier relationships, operating results and ability to retain employees, and on the trading price of Digital's Common Stock, (iv) the substantial management time and effort that will be required to consummate the Merger and integrate the operations of the two companies, (v) the impact of the Merger on Digital and Compaq employees, (vi) the possibility that certain provisions of the Merger Agreement might have the effect of discouraging other persons potentially interested in merging with or acquiring Digital from pursuing such an opportunity and (vii) other matters described under "Risk Factors" and "—Forward Looking Statements May Prove Inaccurate". In the judgment of the Digital Board, the potential benefits of the Merger outweighed these considerations.

The foregoing discussion of the information and factors considered by the Digital Board is not intended to be exhaustive. In view of the wide variety of factors considered, the Digital Board did not assign relative weights to the factors discussed above or determined that any factor was of particular importance. Rather, the Digital Board viewed its positions and recommendation as being based upon the totality of the information presented.

Compaq's Reasons for the Merger

Through its acquisition of Digital, Compaq will accelerate its momentum toward enterprise solutions leadership. The combination will achieve Compaq's stated goal of becoming one of the top three global information technology companies. More importantly, it will create a new breed of enterprise leader committed to delivering high customer value through standards-based, partner-leveraged computing that features world-class services and support and market-segment focused solutions, particularly in communications, manufacturing and finance. The Merger will also strengthen Compaq's customer focus, positioning Compaq as a strategic information technology partner to customers of all sizes. After the Merger, Compaq's product offerings will span from $649 handheld computers to powerful $2 million failsafe computer servers. In addition, Compaq will add over 20,000 service and consulting employees to its staff.

Opinion of Digital's Financial Advisor

Lehman Brothers has acted as financial advisor to Digital in connection with the Merger. As part of its role as financial advisor to Digital, Lehman Brothers was engaged to render its opinion as to the fairness, from a financial point of view, to the holders of Digital Common Stock of the consideration to be offered to such stockholders pursuant to the Merger Agreement.

The full text of the written opinion of Lehman Brothers, dated as of January 25, 1998, is attached as Annex B and is incorporated herein by reference. Stockholders should read such opinion for a discussion of assumptions made, factors considered and limitations on the review undertaken by Lehman Brothers in rendering its opinion. The summary of the Lehman Brothers opinion set forth in this Proxy Statement/ Prospectus is qualified in its entirety by reference to the full text of such opinion.

In connection with the evaluation of the Merger Agreement by the Digital Board, Lehman Brothers rendered a written opinion as of January 25, 1998 that, as of the date of such opinion, and subject to certain assumptions, factors and limitations set forth in such opinion described below, the consideration to be offered to the holders of Digital Common Stock in the Merger was fair, from a financial point of view, to such stockholder.

COMPARATIVE PER COMMON SHARE MARKET PRICE AND DIVIDEND INFORMATION

Compaq Common Stock is listed on the New York Stock Exchange (the "NYSE"). The Compaq symbol on the NYSE is CPQ. Digital Common Stock is listed on the NYSE, the Pacific Stock Exchange, the Chicago Stock Exchange, Swiss Exchange, and the German Stock Exchanges of Frankfurt, Munich and Berlin. The Digital ticker symbol is DEC.

SOME HISTORICAL FINANCIAL DATA

The merger was treated as a purchase for accounting and was a taxable transaction. Table 2 shows that DEC had operating revenues that had declined over $1 billion between 1993 and 1997. Its cumulative loss for the five-year period was $2.3 billion, causing an erosion in its stockholders' equity from $4.9 billion to $3.5 billion. During the same five-year period, Table 3 shows that revenues and income of CPQ had shown a strong upward trend. It was the second largest computer firm in the industry after IBM.

The table below sets forth, for the calendar quarters indicated, the reported high and low closing prices of Compaq Common Stock and Digital Common Stock as reported on the NYSE Composite Transaction Tape, in each case based on published financial sources, and the dividends declared on such stock.

| | Compaq Common Stock | | | Digital Common Stock | |
| | Market Price | | Cash Dividends Declared | Market Price | |
	High	Low		High	Low
1995					
First Quarter	8.775	6.400	—	37.875	31.625
Second Quarter	9.075	6.350	—	49.125	38.625
Third Quarter	10.850	9.000	—	45.625	36.000
Fourth Quarter	11.300	8.975	—	64.625	43.000
1996					
First Quarter	10.600	7.300	—	75.625	50.250
Second Quarter	9.950	7.525	—	61.625	41.875
Third Quarter	12.950	8.300	—	45.875	31.875
Fourth Quarter	17.150	12.875	—	41.375	28.750
1997					
First Quarter	17.350	14.400	—	38.375	27.375
Second Quarter	21.625	14.400	—	37.750	27.375
Third Quarter	39.125	20.375	—	46.875	35.500
Fourth Quarter	38.625	26.656	.015	53.438	36.250
1998					
First Quarter	36.438	23.250	.015	62.000	35.125
Second Quarter	29.500	24.063		56.875	51.063

On January 23, 1998, the last full trading day prior to the public announcement of the proposed Merger, the closing price on the NYSE Composite Transaction Tape was $31¾ per share of Compaq Common Stock and $45⁷⁄₁₆ per share of Digital Common Stock. On May 1, 1998, the most recent practicable date prior to the printing of this Proxy Statement/Prospectus, the closing price on the NYSE Composite Transaction Tape was $29½ per share of Compaq Common Stock and $56⅞ per share of Common Stock.

Table 1 showed that DEC's premerger market value was 12% of the combined market values of the two firms. Table 4 shows that DEC's revenues, total assets, and book equity averaged about one-third of CPQ. However, DEC's net income was only 7.1% of the combined total. Table 5 shows that total liabilities in relation to total assets was 61.4%; it was 35.6% for CPQ. Thus, DEC's debt position had become excessive.

TABLE 2 Selected Digital Historical Financial Data

	1997	1996	1995	1994	1993
Income Statement:					
Operating Revenues	$13,047	$14,563	$13,813	$13,451	$14,371
Income (Loss)	$141	($112)	$57	($2,105)	($251)
Balance Sheet					
Total Assets	$9,693	$10,075	$9,947	$10,580	$10,950
Stockholders' Equity	$3,545	$3,606	$3,528	$3,280	$4,885
Total Liabilities	$6,148	$6,469	$6,419	$7,300	$6,065

TABLE 3 Selected Compaq Historical Financial Data

	1997	1996	1995	1994	1993	
Income Statement:						**Growth Rate**
Operating Revenues	$24,584	$20,009	$16,675	$12,605	$8,873	20.0%
Income (Loss)	$1,855	$1,318	$893	$988	$19	214.3%
Balance Sheet						
Total Assets	$14,631	$12,331	$9,637	$7,862	$5,752	26.3%
Stockholders' Equity	$9,429	$7,290	$5,757	$4,644	$3,468	28.4%
Total Liabilities	$5,202	$5,041	$3,880	$3,218	$2,284	22.8%

TABLE 4 Financial Relations in CPQ and DEC ($ millions)

	CPQ		DEC		Combined	
	Amount	**%**	**Amount**	**%**	**Amount**	**%**
Revenues	$24,584	65.3%	$13,047	34.7%	$37,631	100.0%
Net Income	$1,855	92.9%	$141	7.1%	$1,996	100.0%
Total Assets	$14,631	60.2%	$9,693	39.8%	$24,324	100.0%
Book Equity	$9,429	72.7%	$3,545	27.3%	$12,974	100.0%

TABLE 5 Balance Sheet Structure in CPQ and DEC ($ millions)

	CPQ		DEC		Combined	
	Amount	**%**	**Amount**	**%**	**Amount**	**%**
Total Claims	14,631	100.0%	8,793	100.0%	$22,848	100.0%
Shareholders' Equity	9,429	64.4%	3,396	38.6%	$10,574	46.3%
Total Liabilities	5,202	35.6%	5,397	61.4%	$12,274	53.7%

QUESTIONS

1. In view of the deteriorating financial position of DEC, what were the reasons for its acquisition by CPQ and the 32.1% premium?

2. From the background information presented, what are some of the problems that might be encountered in the attempt to integrate the two companies?

3. How might these problems be solved?

Case 8

Alcoa/Reynolds Metals

The aluminum industry has become a scene of high levels of competition. Since the mid 1980s, aluminum prices have fallen close to 30%, hurting the profitability of aluminum producing companies. Beginning in the early 1990s, aluminum companies began to pursue massive restructuring and cost cutting. More recently, these firms have turned to mergers. This was clear in August 1999, when Alcoa announced a takeover of Reynolds Metals Company shortly after Alcan, Pechiney, and Alusuisse Lonza Group (Algroup) disclosed talks of a three way merger deal.

ALUMINUM PRODUCTION

Aluminum is the most abundant metallic element in the earth's crust, and one of the most difficult to extract. It is found locked in combination with other elements such as oxygen or sulfur as various common aluminum-bearing minerals. The one most often used in aluminum production is bauxite.

Bauxite ore is mined and then taken to a refining plant. At a bauxite refinery, the mineral is subjected to pressure and heat, and certain chemical processes to yield alumina. About four tons of bauxite yield about two tons of alumina. Alumina is a powdery oxide of aluminum. The alumina must subsequently be smelted. This smelting process was invented by Charles Martin Hall, who was the founder of Alcoa. The smelting of two tons of alumina yields about a ton of aluminum.

Aluminum has many advantages which have enabled the industry to grow. Before alumina smelting was invented, it is estimated that the aluminum production of the United States in 1884 was about 125 pounds. In contrast, in 1998 Alcoa produces over 2.8 million tons of aluminum. Aluminum is lighter than many competing metals. It is resistant to corrosion and is a good conductor of heat and electricity. It also has unusual recycling properties. Making aluminum from recycled scrap takes 5% of the energy it would take to make new metal from ore.

Once it is processed, aluminum is put to many uses. Aluminum has been used in packaging since the early 1900s, when foil was first used in cigarette packaging. In the following years, food companies began to use foil, and aluminum foil was marketed to the American public as a means of wrapping foodstuffs in the kitchen. Aluminum is also used in the construction industry. Many buildings contain at least some aluminum due to its light weight and relative strength. The metal has also become a standard in window framing. Some machinery and parts of machines are made of aluminum. In addition, aluminum has made some inroads in the transportation industry. Since the earliest metal airplanes, it has been critical to the aerospace industry due to its light weight.

THE CHARACTERISTICS OF THE ALUMINUM INDUSTRY

Most of the leading aluminum producers have integrated all the steps of aluminum production into their organizations. From bauxite mining, to alumina smelting, and finally to the production of finished aluminum and aluminum products, these organizations require large size. Each individual step of the process takes large amounts of capital and requires large scale to yield sufficient efficiencies to justify the integration. It is these large integrated firms that have an advantage in the industry. They must be lean and efficient at all levels. This was vividly illustrated in the late 1990s, when aluminum prices were generally low. The largest and most efficient producer was Alcoa, which had engaged in many restructuring efforts in the early 1990s. These made it well positioned to turn a profit despite lagging aluminum prices. Firms that were less efficient during the 1990s became takeover targets at the end of the decade.

TABLE 1 Large Aluminum Producers (Aug. 1999) (Thousands of Tons)		
	Avg. Capacity/Year	**Production (1999 est.)**
Alcoa	3,138	2,735
Alcan	1,661	1,490
Reynolds	1,118	1,065
Billiton	886	890
Pechiney	828	827
Hydro	745	749
Comalco	659	654
Aluminum Bahrain	537	515
CVG	520	482
Kaiser	510	413
Dubal	424	433
VAW	421	421
Ormet	256	256
Algroup	254	254

Source: CRU International, *Wall Street Journal.*

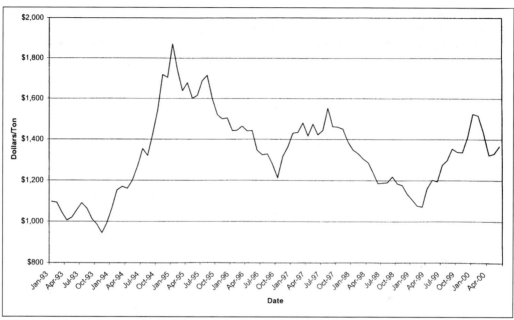

FIGURE 1 Average Monthly Aluminum Price on the London Metal Exchange

The aluminum industry is highly dependent upon the price of aluminum. Prices were relatively high during the late 1980s, and aluminum firms thrived. During the 1990s, aluminum prices have been relatively unstable. Figure 1 shows the average monthly price of aluminum on the London Metals Exchange since 1993. Between March 1999 and January 2000, aluminum ranged from as low as $1,150 per ton to over $1,600 per ton.

As the generally low prices of the 1990s indicate, the aluminum industry is highly competitive, with a large capacity spread among many producers. Before recent merger announcements, the industry was structured as illustrated in Table 1. Alcoa was the clear market leader. After the largest firms, there are many smaller producers, most located in Europe.

One force that has contributed to the drastic aluminum price changes has been the uncertain production levels of Russia's aluminum firms. Russia has the natural resources to be a major aluminum supplier, but its economic difficulties have complicated the efforts of its firms to become effective. Some aluminum firms have tried to move into the region with little success. Rampant corruption and a depressed economy have kept many firms from considering investments in Russia.

Another significant factor in the aluminum industry is the existence of competing materials. Since it was first mass produced, aluminum has been a competitor of steel.

Many of today's uses of aluminum exist because aluminum was recognized as a light-weight alternative to steel. Primarily in the 1970s, aluminum experienced great growth as a substitute for steel in beverage cans. High growth rates of aluminum cans continued into the 1980s, but have slowed and even reversed in the 1990s. The aerospace industry was one of the first industries where the lightweight advantages of aluminum became critical. Because steel was too heavy for flight, aerospace firms required large amounts of aluminum. This was a major contributor to the boom in the aluminum industry during World War II. In the auto industry, aluminum continues to slowly replace steel throughout the market. Projections show that the average North American car consisted of 253 pounds of aluminum in 1999, up from 191 pounds in 1991 (see Figure 2). This figure is projected to increase to 281 pounds in 2000, and 290 pounds in 2001. Some auto firms, such as Audi, have led the way by introducing models with frames made entirely of aluminum. However, the steel industry is entrenched in automobiles, and is constantly working on means of making steel lighter and stronger to compete with aluminum and other alternative metals.

Just as aluminum became popularized as an alternative to steel, plastic is replacing aluminum in some uses. The decreasing use of aluminum cans has been attributed to cheap plastic prices during the 1990s (see Figure 3). Plastic beverage bottles have become a cost effective alternative to aluminum cans. In aerospace and autos, plastic is preferable to aluminum when weight is the primary concern. As plastics become stronger, aluminum itself may be replaced in auto and plane bodies.

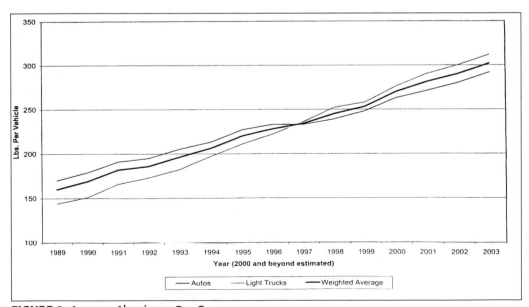

FIGURE 2 Average Aluminum Per Car

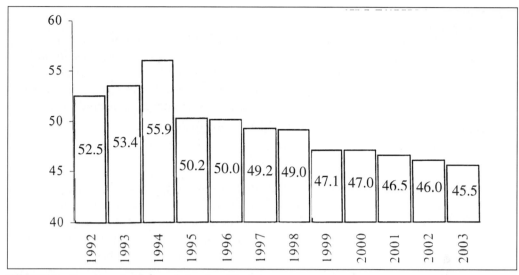

FIGURE 3 Aluminum's Share of the Can Market

Source: The O'Carroll Aluminum Bulletin.

THE ALCAN, PECHINEY, ALUSUISSE LONZA THREE-WAY DEAL

On August 10, 1999, Alcan, Pechiney and Algroup (APA) publicly announced that they were in advanced merger talks. The following day they announced that they had reached a merger agreement. The combined company would present a significant rival to Alcoa. In terms of revenues, the combined company would become the largest aluminum firm, surpassing Alcoa.

Alcan

Headquartered in Montreal, Canada, Alcan is one of the most international aluminum companies in the world. It has operations and sales offices in more than thirty countries, and employs approximately 39,000 people. Alcan is involved in nearly every stage of the aluminum industry from mining to recycling. It has eight bauxite mines in six countries; its smelter system is among the lowest cost in the world; it is a leading producer of flat rolled products used in beverage cans, automotive, and other sectors; it has annual recycling capacity of 772,000 tons.

During the past five years, the company has refocused its activities on its core business of primary aluminum and world class fabrication. It has divested more than 55 businesses, using the proceeds to strengthen its balance sheet and invest in its high quality, low-cost smelting and fabrication system.

Pechiney

Pechiney is a worldwide industrial company based in France with two core businesses, aluminum (production and fabricated products) and packaging materials, in both of which it holds leading positions. It is the fourth largest producer of primary aluminum in the world and the second largest producer of technical flat products for the aerospace and transportation industries. It is also a global leader in electrolysis technique. Pechiney is among the world's foremost packaging manufacturers.

Algroup

Based in Switzerland, Algroup's core businesses focus on aluminum, packaging, and chemicals, encompassing a wide reach of technologies from the mining of bauxite to the manufacture of active ingredients for some of today's most innovative pharmaceutical drugs. The aluminum business of Algroup reaches from bauxite to finished products. In packaging, Algroup is a world leading supplier for the pharmaceutical and cosmetic industries, and it also is a major supplier for the food and beverage markets.

Algroup holds a position in fine chemicals and biotechnology with advanced intermediates and active ingredients for the pharmaceutical and agro industry, as well as intermediates and additives for a variety of industrial applications. In view of the merger, the chemicals and energy business of Algroup will be demerged.

The deal was considered to be the first major three-way intercontinental merger agreement. The combined APA would have its headquarters in Montreal and a regional headquarters in Europe. The CEO's office would be in New York City. The firm would become a leading aluminum firm, and it would be particularly strong in the

TABLE 2 Alcan/Pechiney/Algroup Deal Terms							
Pre-Merger							
	Dollar Amounts				**Percentage**		
	Alcan	Pechiney	Algroup	Total	Alcan	Pechiney	Algroup
Share Price (8/9/99)	$33.63	$56.50	$1,210.06				
Shares Outstanding (million)	222	83	6.6				
Total Market Value (billion)	$7.5	$4.7	$8.0	20.1	37.1	23.3%	39.7%
Exchange Terms	1	to 1.7816	to 20.6291				
Post-Merger							
Number of Shares (million)	222	148	136	506	43.9	29.2%	26.9%
Premium Analysis		**Pechiney**	**Algroup**				
Total Offered (billion)		$5.0	$4.6				
Premium Over Market							
Amount (billion)		$0.3	-$3.4				
Percent		6.0%	−42.7%				

packaging segment. Table 2 depicts the terms of the deal. Alcan would hold 44% of the combined company and Pechiney and Algroup would hold 29% and 27% respectively. Although Table 2 shows small or negative premiums for Pechiney and Algroup, these numbers are a bit misleading. Alcan increased about 10% upon the announcement of the merger. So the merger consideration was actually higher than the table shows (the table uses prices from the day before the announcement). Furthermore, both stocks had increased significantly in the preceding month, which is not reflected in these estimates of the premium paid.

On August 11, 1999 Algroup announced that it would spin off its chemicals and energy business to shareholders. The firms projected $600 million of cost savings from reducing selling, general, and administrative expenses (corporate functions, purchasing synergies, sales, distribution) as well as optimization of R&D and streamlining of plant operations.

The merger was seen to have broad ramifications. The combined firms were depicted as an attempt to create a serious rival for Alcoa, which had clearly been the industry leader. While Alcoa was clearly primarily an American company, the combined APA made a point of emphasizing their global reach. Another side effect of the deal was that many analysts felt it put pressure on European firms in declining industries. Investors would be looking for maximization of shareholder value, forcing these firms to find partners or sell out, without worrying about typical European nationalistic sentiments.

THE ALCOA / REYNOLDS MERGER

Alcoa

Alcoa Inc., a Pennsylvania corporation, is the world's leading producer of primary aluminum, fabricated aluminum and alumina, and a major participant in all segments of the industry: mining, refining, smelting, fabricating, and recycling. Alcoa serves customers worldwide primarily in packaging, transportation (including aerospace, automotive, rail, and shipping), building and industrial markets with a great variety of fabricated and finished products. Alcoa is organized into 24 business units and has over 215 operating locations in 31 countries.

Reynolds

Reynolds Metals Company, a Delaware corporation, is the world's third-largest aluminum producer and the world's leading aluminum foil producer. Reynolds serves customers in growing world markets including the alumina and primary aluminum, packaging and consumer, commercial construction, distribution, and automotive markets, with a wide variety of aluminum, plastic and other products. Reynolds employs approximately 18,000 people. Reynolds has operations or interests in operations at more than 100 locations in 24 countries. Reynolds' operations are organized into four market-based, global business units: Base Materials; Packaging and Consumer; Construction and Distribution; and Transportation. The packaging and consumer business, which included Reynolds Wrap, was perceived by many to be the company's crown jewel.

Reynolds began a restructuring process in 1996 to improve the focus and profitability of the company and thereby increase shareholder value. The first three phases of that process were substantially completed by December 31, 1998. As part of that process, Reynolds raised $1.7 billion in proceeds from asset sales, achieved its $900 million debt reduction goal in the third quarter of 1998, reduced interest expense $80 million annualized, executed a stock repurchase plan, reduced corporate expenses by $44 million annually, reorganized into market-focused global business units and initiated enhanced segment reporting. At the end of 1998, the effects of this restructuring were beginning to be realized. Earnings per share from operations improved 144% comparing 1998 results with 1996 results. In 1999, Reynolds began the first phase of an aggressive growth plan designed to increase long-term profitable growth. However, in late 1998 and early 1999 Reynolds' business was adversely affected by a downturn in the aluminum market resulting in a sharp fall in the price of Reynolds shares.

In February 1999, Highfields Capital Management notified Reynolds of its intention to take a stake in the firm and present a proposal at the annual meeting to ask the board of Reynolds to retain an investment bank to explore strategic alternatives. This was publicly disclosed on March 17, 1999, when Highfields filed the requisite Schedule 13D with the SEC.

On March 22, 1999, Alcoa officials met with Reynolds executives and offered to purchase Reynolds for $56 per share in cash and Alcoa stock. During the discussions, Alcoa raised its offer as high as $60 per share. In connection with the meeting, Alcoa's CEO, Paul O'Neill, sent a letter to Jeremiah Sheehan, Reynolds' CEO, encouraging the board to accept Alcoa's offer. In the letter, O'Neill wrote, "As I explained on the subject of 'premium' this morning – $60 per share is, in fact, a 50% premium to the prices at which Reynolds shares were trading prior to the Highfields Schedule 13D public filing and the takeover speculation it generated. We think our $60 proposal (or 1.42 Alcoa shares) represents a full and fair price for the Reynolds stockholders, especially when we consider the impact on our ability to maintain attractive returns on equity for your shareholders who elect to take Alcoa shares." Despite these overtures, the Alcoa offer was refused. Merger negotiations were broken off.

Alcoa launched a hostile bid for Reynolds Metals on August 11, 1999. The bid began with a bear-hug letter, sent to Reynolds and released to the press. Alcoa offered $65 in cash for half of the outstanding Reynolds shares, and an equivalent value of Alcoa shares (0.9784 Alcoa shares for each Reynolds share) for the remaining half. In the letter, Alcoa revealed that the firms had had previous discussions about a merger. Alcoa emphasized its desire for a friendly strategic merger as opposed to a hostile takeover fight.

The Reynolds board met on August 15, 1999 and determined the offer from Alcoa to be inadequate. In response, Alcoa announced that it would commence a cash tender offer within a week. Reynolds had limited options to resist the bid. The only competing offer Reynolds had was from Michigan Avenue Partners, a Chicago investment firm, who never specified a price, timing, or means of financing a bid. The lack of alternatives forced Reynolds to bargain with Alcoa.

On August 18, 1999, the terms of a deal were agreed upon by both parties. The details of the deal are shown in Table 3. Alcoa agreed to exchange 1.06 of its shares for each share of Reynolds. These terms valued Reynolds at about $70.43 per share ($4.4 billion). This represented a premium of 26% from the day before Alcoa's offer was announced. The deal allowed Reynolds flexibility to seek competing bids for 30 days, and there was a relatively light $100 million breakup fee. Even with a seemingly easy path to find a different merger partner, Reynolds was not able to find a better offer. Alcoa was able to get a friendly deal with Reynolds by raising its bid by 0.0816 shares, or $5.42 per share.

Tables 4 through 7 present historical financial information on Alcoa and Reynolds. Tables 4 and 5 are the income statement and balance sheets, respectively, of Alcoa. Tables 6 and 7 present the same data for Reynolds Metals.

THE AFTERMATH: ANTITRUST CONSIDERATIONS

Antitrust issues became a significant factor in both of these large mergers. The three-way APA merger was blocked by the European Commission. In a decision in early March 2000, the commission refused to accept the merger between Alcan and Pechiney. The companies were not able to come up with any alterations to the merger

TABLE 3 Alcoa/Reynolds Deal Terms

Pre-Merger

| | Dollar Amounts | | | Percentage | |
	Alcan	Reynolds	Total	Alcoa	Reynolds
Share Price (8/10/99)	$66.44	$55.88			
Shares Outstanding (million)	364	62			
Total Market Value (billion)	$24.2	$3.5	$27.6	87.5%	12.5%
Exchange Terms	1.06	for	1		
Post-Merger					
Number of Shares (million)	364	66	430	84.7%	15.3%
Premium Analysis					
Total Paid (billions)	$4.4				
Premium Over Market					
Amount (billion)	$0.9				
Percent	26.0%				

TABLE 4 Summary Income Statement for Alcoa Inc. (All Amounts Are in Millions of Dollars)

	1994	1995	1996	1997	1998
Sales (Net)	9904.3	12499.7	13061	13319.2	15339.8
Cost of Goods Sold	7952.8	9486.9	10092.6	10285.9	11947.1
Selling, General, and Administrative Expense	758.5	848.9	874.3	813.8	897.2
Operating Income Before Depreciation	1193	2163.9	2094.1	2219.5	2495.5
Depreciation and Amortization	671.3	712.9	747.2	734.9	842.4
Operating Income After Depreciation	521.7	1451	1346.9	1484.6	1653.1
Interest Expense	-108.2	-121.7	-139	-149.9	-211.1
Nonoperating Income (Expense)	88.5	157.1	72.7	171.5	162.8
Special Income (Expense) Items	320.5	-16.2	-198.9	95.5	0
Pretax Income	822.5	1470.2	1081.7	1601.7	1604.8
Income Taxes - Total	219.2	445.9	360.7	528.7	513.5
Minority Interest	160.2	233.8	206.1	267.9	238.3
Income Before Extraordinary Items	443.1	790.5	514.9	805.1	853
Dividends - Preferred	2.1	2.1	2.1	2.1	2
Inc. Before Extraordinary Items - Available for Common	441	788.4	512.8	803	851
Common Stock Equivalents - Dollar Savings	0	0	0	0	0
Inc. Before Extraordinary Items - Adj. for CS Equiv.	441	788.4	512.8	803	851
Extraordinary Items	-67.9	0	0	0	0
Extraordinary Items and Discontinued Operations	-67.9	0	0	0	0
Net Income Adjusted for Common Stock Equivalents	373.1	788.4	512.8	803	851
Net Income (Loss)	375.2	790.5	514.9	805.1	853

TABLE 5 Summary Balance Sheet for Alcoa Inc. (All Amounts Are in Millions of Dollars)

	1994	1995	1996	1997	1998
Assets					
Cash and Short-Term Investments	624.7	1062.4	616.6	906.4	381.6
Receivables - Total	1990	1843.3	1828.9	1797.6	2334.2
Inventories - Total	1144.2	1418.4	1461.4	1312.6	1880.5
Current Assets - Other	394.3	417.6	374.3	400.3	428.8
Current Assets - Total	4153.2	4741.7	4281.2	4416.9	5025.1
Property, Plant, and Equipment - Total (Net)	6689.4	6929.7	7077.5	6666.5	9133.5
Investments and Advances - Equity Method	423.5	491.8	573.2	548.6	586.2
Intangibles	396.6	600	571.1	607.4	1541.4
Assets - Other	690.5	880.2	946.9	831.2	1176.3
Assets - Total	12353.2	13643.4	13449.9	13070.6	17462.5
Liabilities and Net Worth					
Debt in Current Liabilities	415.9	693.2	385	494.9	612.1
Accounts Payable	739.3	861.7	799.2	811.7	1044.3
Income Taxes Payable	393	304.7	407.9	334.2	431.3
Current Liabilities - Other	1005.3	792.6	781.3	811.7	1180.6
Current Liabilities - Total	2553.5	2652.2	2373.4	2452.5	3268.3
Long-Term Debt - Total	1029.8	1215.5	1689.8	1457.2	2877
Liabilities - Other	2862.3	3413	2996.7	3020.8	3427.2
Deferred Taxes and Investment Tax Credit	220.6	308.6	317.1	281	358.1
Minority Interest	1687.8	1609.4	1610.5	1439.7	1476
Liabilities - Total	8354	9198.7	8987.5	8651.2	11406.6
Preferred Stock - Carrying Value	55.8	55.8	55.8	55.8	55.8
Common Equity - Total	3943.4	4388.9	4406.6	4363.6	6000.1
Stockholders' Equity - Total	3999.2	4444.7	4462.4	4419.4	6055.9
Liabilities and Stockholders' Equity - Total	12353.2	13643.4	13449.9	13070.6	17462.5

TABLE 6 Summary Income Statement for Reynolds Metals Co.
(All Amounts Are in Millions of Dollars)

	1994	1995	1996	1997	1998
Sales (Net)	5879.1	7213	6972	6881	5859
Cost of Goods Sold	4983.7	5772	5886	5658	4774
Selling, General, and Administrative Expense	389	449	445	406	378
Operating Income Before Depreciation	506.4	992	641	817	707
Depreciation and Amortization	294.8	311	365	368	252
Operating Income After Depreciation	211.6	681	276	449	455
Interest Expense	-155.6	-172	-173	-161	-126
Nonoperating Income (Expense)	45.9	39	57	27	12
Special Income (Expense) Items	88.2	0	-7	-75	-144
Pretax Income	190.1	548	153	240	197
Income Taxes - Total	68.4	159	49	104	45
Minority Interest	Combined	Combined	Combined	Combined	Combined
Income Before Extraordinary Items	121.7	389	104	136	152
Dividends - Preferred	34.1	36	36	0	0
Inc. Before Extraordinary Items - Available for Common	87.6	353	68	136	152
Common Stock Equivalents - Dollar Savings	0	36	0	0	0
Inc. Before Extraordinary Items - Adj. for CS Equiv.	87.6	389	68	136	152
Extraordinary Items	0	0	-15	0	-86
Extraordinary Items and Discontinued Operations	0	0	-15	0	-86
Net Income Adjusted for Common Stock Equivalents	87.6	389	53	136	66
Net Income (Loss)	121.7	389	89	136	66

TABLE 7 Summary Balance Sheet for Reynolds Metals Co.
(All Amounts Are in Millions of Dollars)

	1994	1995	1996	1997	1998
Assets					
Cash and Short-Term Investments	433.7	39	38	70	94
Receivables - Total	962.2	1043	961	1015	894
Inventories - Total	873.1	891	787	744	500
Current Assets - Other	53.1	41	87	165	114
Current Assets - Total	2322.1	2014	1873	1994	1602
Property, Plant, and Equipment - Total (Net)	3108.4	3223	3237	2954	2024
Investments and Advances - Equity Method	856.1	1286	1337	1381	1478
Intangibles	63.8	Combined	Combined	0	0
Assets - Other	1110.9	1217	1069	897	1030
Assets - Total	7461.3	7740	7516	7226	6134
Liabilities and Net Worth					
Debt in Current Liabilities	138.3	212	313	209	312
Accounts Payable	657.7	527	499	512	401
Income Taxes Payable	0	0	0	0	0
Current Liabilities - Other	628.5	628	521	562	528
Current Liabilities - Total	1424.5	1367	1333	1283	1241
Long-Term Debt - Total	1848.4	1853	1793	1501	1035
Liabilities - Other	1733.5	1667	1494	1434	1392
Deferred Taxes and Investment Tax Credit	183.2	236	262	269	272
Liabilities - Total	5189.6	5123	4882	4487	3940
Preferred Stock - Carrying Value	505.1	505	0	0	0
Common Equity - Total	1766.6	2112	2634	2739	2194
Stockholders' Equity - Total	2271.7	2617	2634	2739	2194
Liabilities and Stockholders' Equity - Total	7461.3	7740	7516	7226	6134

agreement that would satisfy the regulators. The Commission did approve the merger between Alcan and Algroup. In the month following the decision, the three companies tried to devise some combination that would be approved by the European regulators, but concerns were that Alcan and Pechiney had too much overlapping capacity, much of it located in Europe. The companies attempted to convince the regulators that steel is a viable competitor to aluminum, but the argument was not accepted. As a result, in mid-April 2000 Pechiney elected to abandon the deal. On June 1, 2000, Alcan and Algroup announced that they had reached a revised merger agreement.

Many analysts felt that the Alcoa combination with Reynolds would face the same kind of scrutiny that the APA merger underwent. The United States Department of Justice issued a second request for more materials on the merger. The European Commission blocked the APA merger. Despite these factors seemingly working against the Alcoa/Reynolds merger, the deal was approved, requiring only some upstream production divestitures. The combined company had to sell off certain Reynolds interests in alumina refineries and aluminum smelters. However, Alcoa was able to retain Reynolds' packaging, transportation, and construction divisions. Following the approval of U.S. and European regulators, Alcoa and Reynolds announced the completion of their deal on May 4, 2000.

QUESTIONS

1. What forces were behind these major aluminum mergers?
2. What were the advantages of the timing of Alcoa's bid for Reynolds?
3. Why did the Reynolds board reject Alcoa's offers? What led the board to accept?
4. Do you agree with the antitrust decisions regarding the mergers?

Case 9

Masco's Acquisition and Diversification Strategy

For nearly 30 years into 1987, Masco Corp. had achieved outstanding growth and profitability. This growth was achieved in its core activities of building and home improvement products. Between 1986 and 1989 acquisitions of unrelated businesses such as auto parts businesses were made. Masco's operating margins, net income, and share values declined between 1990 and 1992. In 1992 it made the decision to spin off its auto parts divisions and acquired some home furnishing businesses. Masco viewed the furniture industry as one to which it could bring financial resources and marketing capabilities. Earnings and share values continued to lag. In August of 1996 the home furnishing businesses were sold. On 3/13/97, Masco acquired LaGard Inc., a manufacturer of electronic locks with sales of $15 million. On 4/15/97, Masco acquired Liberty Hardware Manufacturing Corporation, a producer of quality cabinet and builders' hardware and drawer slides for residential and commercial applications with annual sales of $30 million.

QUESTION

Evaluate the diversification and acquisition strategy of the Masco Corp.

Case 10

Clark's Purchase of Club Car

On February 5, 1995, Clark Equipment, a maker of industrial equipment such as highway paving machines, announced its purchase of Club Car, a manufacturer of golf carts. According to Club Car's CEO, the purchase would allow Club Car to benefit from Clark's expertise in manufacturing, distribution, and overseas marketing. Clark's management touted the purchase as a move away from the cyclical industrial machinery industry.

Analysts described Clark's offer as being at "full price," implying that Clark paid a significant premium for Club Car. On the day of the announcement, Clark's stock rose 5.1%. On the same day, Clark also announced its intention to repurchase as much as 17% of its outstanding common stock.

In April of 1995 Clark Equipment was taken over as a result of a hostile tender offer from Ingersoll-Rand, another large construction equipment manufacturer.

QUESTION: BRIEFLY DISCUSS THE FOLLOWING:

A. Clark's justification for the acquisition of Club Car.

B. The stock market reaction to the acquisition. Was the increase in Clark's stock price an unambiguous endorsement of the merger?

C. The takeover of Clark by Ingersoll-Rand. Could Clark's acquisition of Club Car have been a factor in its subsequently being taken over?

Case 11

The World Defense Business

The announcement on 7/9/97 of Lockheed Martin's (LM) proposed acquisition of the Northrop Grumman Corp. (NG) for $8.26 billion was seen as the last major deal in the aerospace/defense industry consolidation movement. Between 1992 and 1996, 32 U.S. defense businesses have been consolidated into nine companies with LM and Boeing emerging as the largest.

This world industry is divided into two major sectors: Commercial and defense. In the world commercial market, Airbus has a 40% share and with the acquisition of McDonnell Douglas (MD) (10%), Boeing's share is somewhat less than 60%. Other smaller producers include Bombardier of Canada whose revenues in 1996 were $8.5 billion. Bombardier is a successful niche player in the commuter and business-jet aviation markets with 65% of the regional-jetliner sector. In the world defense industry the top ten with their 1995 defense revenues in billion dollars were:

1. Lockheed Martin (US)	$19
2. Boeing (with MD) (US)	$18
3. British Aerospace (UK)	$6
4. Hughes Electronics (US)	$6
5. Northrop Grumman (US)	$6
6. Thomson (FR)	$5
7. General Electric Co. (UK)	$4
8. Raytheon (US)	$4
9. United Technologies (US)	$4
10. Lagardere Groupe (FR)	$3

In assessing future developments in the aerospace-defense industry it is important to recognize that the biggest military contractors in the United States have different mixes in their major business lines. This is shown below:

Company	Main Business Lines	New Military Contracts, 1995
1. Lockheed Martin	Aeronautics, electronics, information and technology services, and missiles	$12 billion
2. Boeing/MD	Commercial and military transportation, missiles and space products	$10
3. Tenneco	Automotive products and packaging design	$4
4. G.M.'s Hughes Electronics unit	Weapons, radar, communications, and auto electronics	$3
5. Northrop Grumman	Military and commercial aircraft and electronic systems	$3
6. Raytheon	Electronics, aircraft products, energy services, and appliances	$3
7. General Electric	Appliances, broadcasting, communications, and transportation	$2
8. United Technologies	Products and services in aerospace, building, and automotive	$2

The above demonstrates that each company has a different mix of commercial and military businesses. The companies are in different varieties of businesses outside aerospace/defense. The nondefense businesses of the companies also represent diverse patterns of activities.

Finally, we note the 10 largest U.S. transactions that have taken place since 1992:

	Acquirer	Acquired	Date	Price
1.	Boeing	McDonnell Douglas	12/15/96	$14.0 billion
2.	Lockheed Martin	Loral	1/9/96	9.0
3.	Raytheon	Hughes Electronics Defense Unit	1/16/97	9.0
4.	Lockheed Martin	Northrop Grumman	7/9/97	8.3
5.	Lockheed	Martin Marietta	8/8/94	5.0
6.	Boeing	Rockwell Defense Unit	12/5/96	3.2
7.	Martin Marietta	GE Aerospace Unit	11/23/92	3.1
8.	Northrop Grumman	Westinghouse Defense Unit	1/4/96	3.0
9.	Raytheon	Texas Instruments Defense Unit	1/6/97	3.0
10.	Northrop	Grumman	4/4/94	2.2

QUESTION

Discuss the underlying business economics factors that have produced the consolidation and transformation of the aerospace/defense industry.

Case 12

Glaxo Acquisition of Wellcome

In early 1995 Glaxo made a hostile bid of $15 billion for the Wellcome drug company, the largest takeover in the history of the drug industry. The combination took place and the revenues of Glaxo-Wellcome in 1997 were over $13 billion. Glaxo-Wellcome faces new generic competition with the end of patent protection on Ventolin, an asthma medication, on Zovirax, an antiviral agent, and on Zantac, an ulcer medicine. In contrast to Merck, Lilly, and SmithKline Beecham which acquired drug distributors, Glaxo appeared to follow a different strategy in seeking to achieve competitive advantage. Glaxo's aim appeared to be to add new products to its portfolio to seek to influence HMOs through its large presence in the marketplace in selling cost effective pharmaceutical products. Another aim may be to develop strength in particular therapeutic product areas.

The combined Glaxo Wellcome became a significant force in the pharmaceutical industry, but the industry continued to undergo consolidation. In early 1998, Glaxo Wellcome began discussions with SmithKline Beecham about a possible combination. At the time the talks collapsed because of tension among the top executives. However, investors held out hope that the firms would come to an agreement. The pressure was increased in late 1999 when Warner-Lambert became the subject of a takeover battle between Pfizer and American Home Products. Furthermore, Monsanto and Pharmacia announced a merger of equals in December 1999.

Such combinations led to Glaxo Wellcome and SmithKline Beecham finally reaching an agreement. On January 17, 2000, the firms announced a deal valued at over $70 billion. Glaxo Wellcome would control about 59% of the combined company, and SmithKline Beecham would control the remaining 41%. The companies believed that increased scale would ease the burden of R&D, and would make the company a more balanced global firm. The firms also believed they had a complementary mix of drugs. The deal is scheduled to be completed in October 2000.

QUESTION

Discuss the strategic implications of these acquisitions.

Case 13

Dow Chemical/Union Carbide

The chemical industry has a long history of M&A activity. In the 1920s, Imperial Chemical was formed in England, and Germany's largest chemical firms combined to form IG Farben. Following World War II, IG Farben was broken up into Bayer, BASF, and Hoechst. These and other large firms, such as Dow and DuPont, have long dominated the chemical industry. New developments in the chemical industry and the changing nature of the economy have contributed to the resurgence of M&A activity within the industry. This case studies the Dow Chemical Company's merger with Union Carbide announced on August 4, 1999.

THE CHARACTERISTICS OF THE CHEMICAL INDUSTRY

Sound analysis of any merger transaction requires knowledge of the economic characteristics of the industry(ies) of the companies involved. The nature of the industry is key to explaining the economic and business logic of the transaction.

Like most industries, the chemical industry has been affected by the powerful change forces of globalization and technological innovations. The industry consists of many large international competitors. In *Fortune*'s 1999 list of the global 500 firms, 8 countries were represented by the top 12 chemical firms. The chemical industry is crucial because chemicals are a "keystone" industry. They are involved in many manufactured products. Innovations in the chemical industry have effects on other industries, including textiles, petroleum refining, agriculture, rubber, autos, metals, and pharmaceuticals, to name a few.

Chemicals require firms to be high tech and R&D oriented in order to maintain relatively high margins of profitability. Even innovative firms are threatened by the relative ease with which new technology diffuses through the industry. This has led to a distinction between specialty and commodity chemicals. Commodity chemicals have been established for a period of time and many firms compete to distribute high volumes. The margins on such chemicals are low. Specialty chemicals result from firm innovation and provide firms with high margins during a period of competitive advantage. However, as more firms enter the market segment, the margins will be reduced by the increasing industry capacity. Specialized engineering firms have aided the rapid dispersal of technology. These firms install turnkey chemical production plants, making it difficult for firms to maintain a competitive advantage based on production procedures.

Another source of increasing competition is the expansion of other industries into chemicals. Because chemicals are important in many industries, some firms find it effective to move into the production of chemicals. This proved to be particularly true in the oil industry. Since oil byproducts have become important in the chemical industry following the widespread applications of petrochemicals, oil companies have found it to be profitable to expand into the chemical industry. Among the leaders in chemical sales in recent years have been such companies as Exxon and British Petroleum.

One factor that has a negative effect on the chemical industry is the changing nature of the economy. Although the chemical industry represents 2% of U.S. GDP, this figure has been greatly reduced in the last 30 years. As the growth of the service sector of the economy outpaces the growth in the production sector (which is a major consumer of chemicals), chemicals are growing at a slower rate than the economy as a whole. Because this dynamic is most pronounced in the United States, it is increasingly important for chemical firms to have a global scope of operations and sales.

As a response to the highly competitive nature of the industry, as well as the changing nature of the economy, the chemical industry has been an active participant in M&A activity. Though the narrowly defined chemical industry rarely emerges on lists of the most active industries, there has been much activity involving firms which produce chemicals. The consolidation of firms in oil and other industries has created large potential competitors. These potential sources of competition have helped spur the mergers in the chemical industry.

THE COMPANIES

Dow Chemical Company

Dow manufactures and sells chemicals, plastic materials, agricultural and other specialized products and services. Dow is a global science and technology-based company that develops and manufactures a portfolio of chemicals, plastics and agricultural products and services for customers in 168 countries around the world. Dow conducts its operations through subsidiaries and 14 global businesses, including 121 manufacturing sites in 32 countries, and supplies more than 3,500 products through the efforts of its 39,000 employees.

Union Carbide Corporation

Union Carbide operates in two business segments of the chemicals and plastics industry. The specialties and intermediates segment converts basic and intermediate chemicals into a diverse portfolio of chemicals and polymers serving industrial customers in many markets. This segment also provides technology services including licensing, to the oil and gas and petrochemicals industries. The basic chemicals and polymers segment converts hydrocarbon feedstocks, principally liquefied petroleum gas and naphtha, into ethylene or propylene used to manufacture polyethylene, polypropylene, ethylene oxide and ethylene glycol for sale to third parties, as well as for consumption by Union Carbide's specialties and intermediates segment. Union Carbide, with nearly 12,000 employees worldwide, operates 32 principal manufacturing facilities in 13 countries to provide products to customers in over 100 countries. In addition to these operations, Union Carbide participates in the global market through 10 principal corporate joint ventures and partnerships.

DOW'S STRATEGIC DEALS

In the 1990s, Dow has made an effort to restructure the portfolio of companies and divisions it owns. Even prior to its merger with Union Carbide, Dow had made over $10 billion of acquisitions between 1994 and 2000. Over the same period, Dow had divested over $10 billion. Dow's deals demonstrate a focus on technology and globalization that is necessitated by the nature of the chemical industry.

Dow has made joint ventures that allow it to develop technology that may not have been available to the chemical company alone. Dow Corning, Dow's joint venture with Corning, Inc., was established in 1943 (when Corning was known as Corning Glass Works). Dow Corning demonstrates the long-term potential of a well developed joint venture relationship. Dow brought chemical know-how to the deal, and Corning brought its knowledge of silicon. Together the firms developed silicone. Although this led to a subsequent large lawsuit over silicone in breast implants, the joint venture created a means for the companies to combine their technological capabilities.

More recently, in 1997 Dow formed Cargill Dow Polymers, a joint venture with Cargill, Inc. Cargill is a leading processor and distributor of agricultural products. Cargill Dow Polymers combines the chemical technology of Dow with the agricultural expertise of Cargill. As a result, the Cargill Dow joint venture has announced plans to begin producing plastic made from starches, which can result from agricultural products such as corn, wheat, and rice. This plastic is known as polyactic acid (PLA). PLA has gained attention because it will be a viable source of plastic that will not require the use of petroleum. As a result, the plastic can be made to be biodegradable. The joint venture is building a plant to mass produce PLA scheduled to open in 2001.

In addition to technology developing ventures, Dow has formed many ventures to gain access to various regions of the world. As chemicals become less important to the

U.S. economy, it is crucial for chemical firms to develop global capabilities. Dow has forged relationships throughout the world, allowing it to make 60% of its 1999 sales outside the United States. Dow owns 80% of BSL, a joint venture with the German government to refurbish old East German chemical plants. Dow did not have to contribute much capital, and primarily had the job of overseeing the design and construction of the plants. Dow is scheduled to take sole control of the venture in June 2000.

Furthermore, Dow has formed joint ventures with local firms in foreign countries to allow easier access to certain local markets. Sumitomo-Dow Ltd. is a joint venture with Sumitomo to sell CALIBRE brand polycarbonate resins in Japan, a market notoriously difficult for American firms to penetrate. Polisur SA is a joint venture with Yacimientos Petroliferos Fiscales (YPF) to manufacture polyethylene in South America. Siam Polystyrene Co. Ltd. is a joint venture with Cementhai Chemicals Company to produce polystyrene in Thailand. These are just a few of the deals that Dow has formed throughout the world.

UNION CARBIDE'S STRATEGIC DEALS

Union Carbide's deals have been similar to Dow's in that both firms have sought joint ventures and alliances to penetrate new markets and to try to take advantage of new technologies. However, Union Carbide's deals seem to have less emphasis on technological capabilities. This is appropriate, given Union Carbide's reputation as primarily a commodity chemical producer. Univation Technologies, a joint venture with Exxon Chemical Company, is Union Carbide's most notable technology oriented deal. The firm focuses on the technology and licensing of polyethylene.

Most of Union Carbide's other large deals are international. Equate is a joint venture with Petrochemical Industries of Kuwait, with the goal of producing polyethylene and other products for the Asian market. Union Carbide has formed a venture with PETRONAS, the national oil company of Malaysia to produce chemicals for that region. In Europe, Union Carbide has ventures with Enichem of Italy and France's Elf Atochem to produce various chemicals for the European market. Union Carbide's partnerships have drawn criticism from analysts. They are cited as a primary reason that the firm's earnings underperformed in the late 1990s. If this analysis is correct, it is possible that these ineffective joint ventures led to Union Carbide's sale to Dow.

GENERAL DESCRIPTION OF THE MERGER

The merger agreement provides that, at the effective time of the merger, Transition Sub Inc., a wholly owned subsidiary of Dow, will merge with and into Union Carbide, with Union Carbide continuing in existence as the surviving corporation. Each share of Union Carbide common stock issued and outstanding at the effective time of the merger, other than shares owned by Dow, Union Carbide or any direct or indirect subsidiary of Dow or Union Carbide, which will be canceled in the merger, will be converted into 0.537 of a share of Dow common stock. At the effective time of the merger, Union Carbide will become a wholly owned subsidiary of Dow and market trading of Union Carbide common stock will cease.

Background of the Merger

Following some informal contacts between the senior management of Union Carbide and Dow, on October 19, 1998, Union Carbide and Dow entered into a confidentiality agreement with the intention of exploring a business combination between the two companies. After executing the confidentiality agreement, Union Carbide and Dow exchanged data in order to permit the two companies to make estimates of synergies with respect to a potential business combination.

At various times between December 1998 and June 1999, Dow made proposals to Union Carbide for a stock-for-stock merger. Union Carbide rejected these proposals, concluding that in each case the proposal was inadequate in light of the circumstances existing at the time the proposal was made.

At the regularly scheduled meeting of Union Carbide's board of directors on June 23, 1000, Dr. William H. Joyce, Chairman, President and Chief Executive Officer of Union Carbide, comprehensively reviewed the Dow discussions. Union Carbide's board of directors reiterated its dissatisfaction with respect to the Dow proposals received to date and expressed its confidence with respect to Union Carbide's independent course. It also reinforced its position on maximizing stockholder value and authorized Dr. Joyce to respond to unsolicited overtures. Dr. Joyce reported that an updated long-range financial forecast with respect to Union Carbide was nearing completion. Union Carbide's board of directors agreed that the forecast and related valuations would be presented at the next regularly scheduled meeting of Union Carbide's board of directors. It was also agreed that Union Carbide should retain financial advisors to aid in the evaluation of the long-range forecast and subsequently engaged Credit Suisse First Boston to assist Union Carbide in this evaluation and related matters.

On July 22, 1999, Dr. Joyce and Dr. William S. Stavropoulos, President and Chief Executive Officer of Dow, met and Dow made a revised proposal for a stock-for-stock merger. Dr. Joyce agreed to consider the new proposal and to discuss it with Union Carbide's advisors.

From July 23 through July 25, 1999, Dr. Joyce met with Union Carbide's senior management, as well as Credit Suisse First Boston and Union Carbide's legal advisors, Sullivan & Cromwell. After extensive discussions regarding the strategic benefits of the merger, the potential cost savings, technology leveraging and other financial and operating benefits that could be obtained through a merger between the two companies, Union Carbide decided to meet again with Dow to discuss its proposal.

On July 25, 1999, Dr. Joyce and Dr. Stavopoulos and their respective senior managements met to negotiate pricing and terms of due diligence with respect to a potential transaction. As a result of those negotiations, the parties, subject to the approval of each company's board of directors, agreed that an exchange ratio of 0.537 of a share of Dow common stock per share of Union Carbide's common stock would be acceptable if other aspects of a merger agreement could be worked out. Subject to the favorable reactions of their respective boards of directors, Dr. Joyce and Dr. Stavropoulos proposed a tentative schedule for merger agreement negotiations, including the start of due diligence on July 30, 1999.

On July 27, 1999, Union Carbide's board of directors met, together with Union Carbide's legal and financial advisors, to review the status of discussions with Dow. At this meeting, Dr. Joyce summarized the proposed combination, and John K. Wulff, Union Carbide's Chief Financial Officer, presented management's long-range financial forecast with respect to Union Carbide.

Also on July 27, 1999, Dow's board of directors, which had previously been advised of the discussions between Dow and Union Carbide, met to discuss the proposed transaction with Union Carbide. At that meeting, Dow's board of directors authorized Dow's senior management to continue negotiations with respect to the proposed transaction, subject to approval by the board of any agreements that might be reached in those discussions.

On July 28, 1999, Union Carbide's board of directors met again. Representatives of Union Carbide's financial advisors, Credit Suisse First Boston, reviewed with Union Carbide's board of directors the financial aspects of the proposed transaction. Representatives from Sullivan & Cromwell provided advice as to the responsibilities and duties of the board of directors and the legal standards that would govern Union Carbide's board of director's consideration of any proposed transaction. Union Carbide's management recommended proceeding to detailed negotiations of a definitive merger agreement. The Union Carbide board of directors, after discussing the matter, unanimously voted to authorize management to commence detailed negotiations of a definitive merger agreement.

From July 30 to August 3, 1999, senior management of both companies and their respective legal and financial advisors met in New York City, performing due diligence and negotiating definitive terms of the merger agreement. At Dow's insistence and subject to the approval of Union Carbide's board of directors, Union Carbide agreed to enter into a stock option agreement at the same time it entered into a definitive merger agreement. The stock option agreement would grant Dow the right to purchase up to 19.9% of Union Carbide's stock at a specified price and upon specified events. See "The Merger Agreement and the Merger—The Stock Option Agreement."

On August 3, 1999, Union Carbide's board of directors met to consider the merger agreement. Representatives of Sullivan & Cromwell reviewed the merger agreement. Representatives of Credit Suisse First Boston presented a financial analysis of the proposed exchange ratio, and rendered to Union Carbide's board of directors its oral opinion, which opinion was confirmed by delivery of a written opinion dated August 3, 1999, to the effect that, as of that date and based on and subject to the matters described in its opinion, the exchange ratio was fair, from a financial point of view, to the holders of Union Carbide's common stock. After questions by and discussion among Union Carbide's board of directors, Union Carbide's board of directors, by a unanimous vote of the directors present and voting, adopted the merger agreement and approved entering into the merger agreement and stock option agreement and the transactions contemplated by those agreements.

Also on August 3, 1999, Dow's board of directors met to consider the merger agreement and the stock option agreement. After hearing presentations from its legal and financial advisors and discussing the matter, Dow's board of directors unanimously approved entering into the merger agreement and the stock option agreement and the transactions contemplated by those agreements.

Union Carbide and Dow entered into the merger agreement and stock option agreement on August 3, 1999, and the transaction was publicly announced on August 4, 1999.

Merger-Related Litigation

Union Carbide, its board of directors and Dow have been named as defendants in three purported class actions recently filed in New York Supreme Court on behalf of Union Carbide's common stock. The complaints allege that the merger consideration is inadequate because, among other things, it did not result from an appropriate consideration of the value of Union Carbide and, therefore, the approval of the merger did not reflect an informed decision of Union Carbide's board of directors. The complaints, which seek injunctive relief and damages, assert that the directors of Union Carbide thereby violated their fiduciary duties to Union Carbide's stockholders and that Dow aided and abetted these violations. One of the complaints also alleges that one of the Union Carbide directors had a conflict of interest with respect to the approval of the transaction. It is expected that an amended complaint will be filed that will consolidate the three actions.

Recommendations of Union Carbide's Board of Directors and Reasons for the Merger

Union Carbide's board of directors has adopted, by a unanimous vote of all of the directors present and voting at a meeting at which a quorum of directors was present, the merger agreement, and recommends that Union Carbide stockholders vote to adopt the merger agreement.

In reaching its decision to adopt the merger agreement, Union Carbide's board of directors consulted with Union Carbide's management, as well as its financial and legal advisors, and considered a variety of factors, including the following:

- the structure of the transaction as a stock-for-stock merger and that Union Carbide's stockholders will continue to benefit from future appreciation in the value of the combined company;

- the premium of approximately 37% to be received by the stockholders of Union Carbide based on the exchange ratio provided for in the merger agreement and the closing stock prices of Union Carbide and Dow on August 3, 1999, the last trading day before the announcement of the merger, and the premium of approximately 41% based on the average closing stock prices of Union Carbide and Dow during the one-month period before the announcement of the merger;

- that during recent years Union Carbide has periodically reviewed its strategic alternatives and that Union Carbide's board of directors believed the merger with Dow to be the most favorable alternative for Union Carbide's stockholders;

- the anticipated benefit to Union Carbide's stockholders of the anticipated reduced earnings cyclicality of the combined company's business portfolio;

- Union Carbide's board of directors' belief that the increased scale of the combined company will:

  —strengthen Union Carbide's operations as the chemicals industry continues to consolidate and build mass;

  —provide greater flexibility to pursue acquisitions and other strategic options; and

  —provide the combined company with greater access to capital than available to Union Carbide on a stand-alone basis;

- the business, operations, financial conditions, earnings and prospects of each of Union Carbide and Dow—in making its determination, Union Carbide's board of directors took into account Union Carbide's long-range financial forecasts and the results of Union Carbide's due diligence review of Dow's business plan;

- the scale, scope and diversity of operations and product lines that could be achieved by combining Union Carbide and Dow, as illustrated by the fact that, based on information available as of the date of the merger agreement, the combined company would have a market capitalization of approximately $35 billion and annual revenue of approximately $24 billion and would be the second largest chemical company in the world;

- the opportunity to capitalize on numerous opportunities for revenue growth by offering more products to existing customers more quickly on a global basis;

- the complementary nature of the businesses of Union Carbide and Dow and the anticipated improved stability of the combined company's businesses and earnings in varying economic and industry climates relative to Union Carbide on a stand-alone basis made possible by the merger as a result of greater geographic and product line diversification;

- the expectation that the merger will result in synergies for the combined company estimated at $250 million in the first year following the merger and $500 million per year thereafter;

- the structure of the merger, which is intended to qualify as a tax-free "reorganization" for U.S. federal income tax purposes and a "pooling-of-interests" for accounting purposes;

- the proposed arrangements with respect to employees and the management of the combined company, including the fact that Dr. Joyce and one other director serving on Union Carbide's board of directors will serve on Dow's board of directors and that Dr. Joyce will serve as Vice Chairman of the board of directors of Dow—see "The Merger Agreement and the Merger—Interests of Union Carbide Directors and Officers in the Merger that are Different from Your Interests;"

- the likelihood of the merger being approved by the applicable regulatory authorities, including the parties' obligations to use their respective best efforts to obtain all required antitrust approvals, although Dow is not required to, and Union Carbide may not, divest, license or hold separate any assets if doing so would have a material adverse effect on the combined company—see "The Merger Agreement and the Merger—Regulatory Requirements;"

- the opinion of Credit Suisse First Boston to Union Carbide's board of directors as to the fairness, from a financial point of view, of the exchange ratio to the holders of Union Carbide common stock and the related financial analyses performed by Credit Suisse First Boston, as described below under "The Merger Agreement and the Merger—Opinion of Union Carbide's Financial Advisor;"

- that the merger agreement must be adopted by the holders of two-thirds of the outstanding shares of Union Carbide;

- the terms of the merger agreement, including the term that permits Union Carbide's board of directors to take the steps necessary to accept a superior proposal in compliance with its fiduciary duties to stockholders;

- that the termination payment provisions of the merger agreement could have the effect of deterring alternative business combination proposals and that the stock option agreement, which would have the effect of precluding any alternative business combination from being accounted for as a pooling-of-interests, might deter certain provisions, which it regarded as customary for transactions of this nature, was required for Dow to enter into the merger agreement; and

- the possibility that the market value of the merger consideration received by Union Carbide's stockholders upon completion of the merger (which is determined by a fixed exchange ratio) may be higher or lower than the value that would have been received if the merger had been consummated on the date the merger agreement was executed.

Dow's Reasons for the Merger

The merger is part of Dow's overall business strategy for growth through increased sales of existing products, product development, and strategic mergers and acquisitions. Dow's board of directors believes that Dow and its stockholders will benefit from the merger because the merger:

- will continue two predominantly complementary chemical producers to achieve a broader product line and geographic scope than either of them individually possesses;
- is expected to enhance the ability of the combined company to maintain its competitiveness through efficiency and reduced costs in the face of marketplace pressures for lower cost and higher quality chemical products;
- is expected to produce an estimated $250 million in synergies in the first year following the merger and $500 million in synergies per year thereafter, which should translate into increased cash flow and earnings per share for the combined company;
- is expected to provide the combined company with greater technological resources required to meet increasing and evolving customer demands for higher performance chemical products;
- is expected to increase the combined company's array of chemical products, permitting multinational customers to achieve purchasing efficiencies through one-stop shopping;
- is expected to strengthen Dow's product offerings to customers in such industries as automotive, pharmaceuticals, coating and personal care products; and
- is expected to strengthen the combined company's balance sheet, which will permit the combined company to fund strategic investments.

Opinion of Union Carbide's Financial Advisor

Credit Suisse First Boston has acted as Union Carbide's financial advisor in connection with the merger. Union Carbide selected Credit Suisse First Boston based on Credit Suisse First Boston's experience, expertise and reputation and familiarity with Union Carbide's business. Credit Suisse First Boston is an internationally recognized investment banking firm and is regularly engaged in the valuation of businesses and securities in connection with mergers and acquisitions, leveraged buyouts, negotiated underwritings, competitive biddings, secondary distributions of listed and unlisted securities, private placements and valuations for corporate and other purposes.

In connection with Credit Suisse First Boston's engagement, Union Carbide requested that Credit Suisse First Boston evaluate the fairness, from a financial point of view, to the holders of Union Carbide common stock of the exchange ratio provided for in the merger. On August 3, 1999, at a meeting of Union Carbide's board of directors held to consider the merger, Credit Suisse First Boston rendered to Union Carbide's board of directors an oral opinion, which opinion was confirmed by delivery of a written opinion dated August 3, 1999, to the effect that, as of that date and based on and subject to the matters described in its opinion, the exchange ratio was fair, from a financial point of view, to the holders of Union Carbide common stock.

In arriving at its opinion, Credit Suisse First Boston reviewed the merger agreement and related documents, as well as publicly available business and financial information relating to Union Carbide and Dow. Credit Suisse First Boston also reviewed other information relating to Union Carbide and Dow, including financial forecasts, which Union Carbide and Dow provided to or discussed with Credit Suisse First Boston, and met with the managements of Union Carbide and Dow to discuss the businesses and prospects of Union Carbide and Dow.

Credit Suisse First Boston also considered financial and stock market data of Union Carbide and Dow and compared those data with similar data for other publicly held companies in businesses similar to Union Carbide and Dow and considered, to the extent publicly available, the financial terms of other business combinations and other transactions recently effected. Credit Suisse First Boston also considered other information, financial studies, analyses and investigations and financial, economic and market criteria that it deemed relevant.

In connection with its review, Credit Suisse First Boston did not assume any responsibility for independent verification of any of the information that was provided to or otherwise reviewed by it and relied on that information being complete and accurate in all material respects. With respect to financial forecasts, Credit Suisse First Boston was advised, and assumed, that the forecasts were reasonably prepared on bases reflecting the best currently available estimates and judgments of the management of Union Carbide and Dow as to the future financial performance of Union Carbide and Dow and the potential synergies and strategic benefits anticipated to result from the merger, including the amount, timing and achievability of those synergies and benefits. Credit Suisse First Boston also assumed that the merger will be treated as a pooling-of-interests in accordance with generally accepted accounting principles and as a tax-free reorganization for U.S. federal income tax purposes. In addition, Credit Suisse First Boston assumed that in the course of obtaining the necessary regulatory and third party consents for the proposed merger and related transactions, no delay or restriction will be imposed that will have a material adverse effect on the contemplated benefits of the proposed merger or related transactions.

Credit Suisse First Boston was not requested to, and did not, make an independent evaluation or appraisal of the assets or liabilities, contingent or otherwise, of Union Carbide or Dow, and was not furnished with any evaluations or appraisals. Credit Suisse First Boston's opinion was based on information available to, and financial, economic, market and other conditions as they existed and could be evaluated by, Credit Suisse First Boston on the date of its opinion. Credit Suisse First Boston did not express any opinion as to the actual value of Dow common stock when issued in the merger or the prices at which shares of Dow common stock will trade after the merger. In connection with its engagement, Credit Suisse First Boston was not requested to, and did not, solicit third party indications of interest in the possible acquisition of all or a part of Union Carbide. Although Credit Suisse First Boston evaluated the exchange ratio from a financial point of view, Credit Suisse First Boston was not requested to, and did not, recommend the specific consideration payable in the merger, which consideration was determined by Union Carbide and Dow. No other limitations were imposed on Credit Suisse First Boston with respect to the investigations made or procedures followed in rendering its opinion.

In preparing its opinion to Union Carbide's board of directors, Credit Suisse First Boston performed a variety of financial and comparative analyses, including those described below. This summary of Credit Suisse First Boston's analyses is not a complete description of the analyses underlying Credit Suisse First Boston's opinion. The preparation of a fairness opinion is a complex analytical process involving various determinations as to the most appropriate and relevant methods of financial analysis and the application of those methods to the particular circumstances, and, therefore, a fairness option is not readily susceptible to summary description. In arriving at its opinion, Credit Suisse First Boston made qualitative judgments as to the significance and relevance of each analysis and factor that it considered. Accordingly, Credit Suisse First Boston believes that its analyses must be considered as a whole and that selecting portions of its analyses and factors or focusing on information presented in tabular format, without considering all analyses and factors or the narrative description of the analyses, could create a misleading or incomplete view of the processes underlying its analyses and opinion.

In its analyses, Credit Suisse First Boston considered industry performance, regulatory, general business, economic, market and financial conditions and other matters, many of which are beyond the control of Union Carbide and Dow. No company, transaction or business used in Credit Suisse First Boston's analyses as a comparison is identical to Union Carbide or Dow or the proposed merger, and an evaluation of the results of those analyses is not entirely mathematical. Rather, the analyses involve complex considerations and judgments concerning financial and operating characteristics and other factors that could affect the acquisition, public trading or other values of the companies, business segments or transactions analyzed.

The estimates contained in Credit Suisse First Boston's analyses and the ranges of valuations resulting from any particular analysis are not necessarily indicative of actual values or predictive of future results or values, which may be significantly more or less favorable than those suggested by the analyses. In addition, analyses relating to the value of businesses or securities do not purport to be appraisals or to reflect the prices at which businesses or securities actually may be sold. Accordingly, Credit Suisse First Boston's analyses and estimates are inherently subject to substantial uncertainty.

Credit Suisse First Boston's opinion and financial analyses were not the only factors considered by Union Carbide's board of directors in its evaluation of the proposed merger and should not be viewed as necessarily determinative of the views of Union Carbide's board of directors with respect to the merger or the exchange ratio.

The following is a summary of the material analyses underlying Credit Suisse First Boston's opinion to Union Carbide's board of directors in connection with the merger. The financial analyses summarized below include information presented in tabular format. In order to fully understand Credit Suisse First Boston's financial analyses, the tables must be read together with the text of each summary. The tables alone do not constitute a complete description of the financial analyses. Considering the data set forth in the tables below without considering the full narrative description of the financial analyses, including the methodologies and assumptions underlying the analyses, could create a misleading or incomplete view of Credit Suisse First Boston's financial analyses.

Discounted Cash Flow Analysis

Credit Suisse First Boston estimated the present value of the stand-alone, unlevered, after-tax cash flows that Union Carbide could produce over calendar years 1999 through 2008, and that Dow could produce over calendar years 1999 through 2003, based on two scenarios. The first scenario, the management case, was based on estimates of the managements of Union Carbide and Dow. The second scenario, the adjusted management case, was based on adjustments to the management case developed by, or discussed with and reviewed by, Union Carbide management to reflect, among other things, the potential for lower variable margins, and in the case of Union Carbide higher capital expenditures, than the management case.

Ranges of estimated terminal values were calculated by multiplying the average of estimated calendar year 1999 to estimated calendar year 2008 earning before interest, taxes, depreciation and amortization, commonly referred to as EBITDA, by terminal EBITDA multiples of 6.0x to 7.0x in the case of Union Carbide and by multiplying the average of estimated calendar year 1999 to estimated calendar year 2003 EBITDA by terminal EBITDA multiples of 7.0x to 8.0x in the case of Dow. Ranges of estimated terminal values were also calculated using the average of estimated unlevered, after-tax free cash flows over the same periods for Union Carbide and Dow as above and perpetuity growth rates of 1.5% to 2.5% in the case of Union Carbide and 4.0% to 4.5% in the case of Dow. The estimated unlevered after-tax free cash flows and estimated terminal values were then discounted to present value using discount rates of 10.0% to 11.0%. This analysis indicated an implied exchange ratio reference range of 0.43x to 0.68x.

Selected Companies Analysis

Credit Suisse First Boston compared financial, operating and stock market data of Union Carbide and Dow to corresponding data of the following publicly traded companies in the commodity chemicals business:

- The Geon Company
- Georgia Gulf Corp.
- Lyondell Chemical Co.
- Millenium Chemicals Inc.
- NOVA Chemicals Corp,

In addition, Credit Suisse First Boston compared financial, operating and stock market data of Union Carbide to corresponding data of the following publicly traded companies in the commodity and specialty chemicals businesses:

- Cyrec Industries Inc.
- E.I. du Pont de Nemours and Company
- Eastman Chemical Co.
- PPG Industries, Inc.
- Rohm and Haas Co.
- Solutia Inc.

Credit Suisse First Boston reviewed equity values as a multiple of estimated calendar years 1999 and 2000 earnings per share, commonly referred to as EPS, and enterprise values, calculated as equity value, plus debt and minority interest, less cash and options proceeds, as multiples of estimated calendar years 1999 and 2000 EBITDA and latest 12 months revenues. All multiples were based on closing stock prices on August 2, 1999. Estimated financial data for the selected companies were based on publicly available research analysts' estimates, and estimated financial data for Union Carbide and Dow were based on internal estimates of the managements of Union Carbide and Dow, respectively. Credit Suisse First Boston then applied a range of selected multiples for the selected companies of estimated calendar years 1999 and 2000 EPS, estimated calendar years 1999 and 2000 EBITDA, and the latest 12 months revenues to corresponding financial data of Union Carbide and Dow, utilizing adjusted management case estimates for Union Carbide and Dow. This analysis indicated an implied exchange ratio reference range of 0.30x to 0.47x.

Selected Mergers and Acquisitions Analysis

Credit Suisse First Boston analyzed the implied transaction multiples paid in the following selected mergers and acquisition transactions in the commodity chemicals industry announced since April 1998:

Acquiror	Acquired Company
• OMV/International Petroleum Investment Co.	• Borealis Technology Corp.
• Lyondell Chemical Co.	• ARCO Chemical Co.
• Huntsman Polymers Corp.	• Rexene Corp.
• Huntsman Polymers Corp.	• Texaco Chemical Company
• Hanson America Inc.	• Quantum Chemical Corp.
• Shell Oil Co.	• Goodyear Tire & Rubber Co. (Polyester division)
• Occidental Petroleum Corp.	• Cain Chemical Inc.
• The Sterling Group, Inc./The Unicorn Group, LLC	• Sterling Chemicals, Inc.
• Gordon Cain (The Sterling Group, Inc.)	• Texas Petrochemicals Corp.
• Dow/YPF S.A./Itochu Corp.	• Petroquimica Bahia Blanca/ Indupa
• Lyondell Chemical Co.	• Occidental Chemical Co. (Alathon product line)
• RWE-DEA	• Vista Chemical Co.
• Management	• Aristech Chemical Corp.
• Montedison SPA	• Himont Inc.
• Lyondell Chemical Co.	• Rexene Products Co. (Bayport product lines)

Credit Suisse First Boston compared enterprise values in the selected transactions as multiples of, among other things, latest 12 months revenues and EBITDA. All multiples were based on publicly available financial information. Credit Suisse First Boston then applied a range of selected multiples for the selected transactions of latest 12 months revenues and EBITDA to corresponding financial data of Union Carbide and Dow. This analysis indicated an implied exchange ratio reference range of 0.31x to 0.54x.

Aggregate Reference Range

Based on the valuation methodologies described above, Credit Suisse First Boston derived an aggregate reference range of 0.43x to 0.60x, as compared to the exchange ratio in the merger of 0.537x.

Relative Analyses

Credit Suisse First Boston also conducted the following relative analyses and compared the exchange ratio in the merger of 0.537x with the exchange ratios implied by these analyses, based on closing stock prices of Union Carbide common stock and Dow common stock on August 2, 1999.

Relative Contribution Analysis

Credit Suisse First Boston performed an exchange ratio analysis, based on adjusted management case estimates of Union Carbide and Dow, comparing the relative contributions of Union Carbide and Dow to calendar year 1998 and estimated calendar years 1999 and 2000 net income and cash flows of the combined company. This analysis yielded, after adjustment for extraordinary items, an implied exchange ratio reference range of 0.293x to 0.433x and an implied percentage contribution reference range for Union Carbide of 16% to 21%, as indicated in the following table:

	Union Carbide Percentage Contribution	Dow Percentage Contribution	Implied Exchange Ratios
Net Income:			
1998	18%	82%	0.344x
1999	19%	81%	0.383x
2000	16%	84%	0.293x
Cash Flow:			
1998	21%	79%	0.433x
1999	21%	79%	0.423x
2000	20%	80%	0.394x

Historical Stock Trading Analysis

Credit Suisse First Boston performed an exchange ratio analysis comparing the average daily closing stock prices for Union Carbide common stock and Dow common stock on August 2, 1999, and during the one-week, one-month, three-month, six-month, one-year and two-year periods preceding August 2, 1999, and the premiums over those periods implied by the exchange ratios in the merger. This comparison yielded an implied exchange ratio reference range of 0.377x to 0.483x and an implied premium reference range of 11.2% to 42.6%, as indicated in the following table:

Period	Implied Exchange Ratio	Implied Premium at Merger Exchange Ratio
August 2, 1999	0.385x	39.3%
One week preceding	0.386x	39.2%
One month preceding	0.377x	42.6%
Three months preceding	0.396x	35.5%
Six months preceding	0.422x	27.1%
One year preceding	0.450x	19.3%
Two years preceding	0.483x	11.2%

Pro Forma Merger Analysis

Credit Suisse First Boston analyzed the potential pro forma effect of the merger on Dow's estimated EPS and cash flows for calendar year 2000 and 2001, based on publicly available research analysts' estimates, both before and after giving effect to potential cost savings and other synergies anticipated by the management of Union Carbide to result from the merger. Based on the exchange ratio in the merger of 0.537x, this analysis indicated that the merger would be accretive with synergies and dilutive without synergies on an EPS basis, and accretive both with and without synergies on a cash flow basis, in each of the years analyzed. The actual results achieved by the combined company may vary from projected results and the variations may be material.

Other Factors

In the course of preparing its opinion, Credit Suisse First Boston also reviewed and considered other information and data, including:

- the trading characteristics of Union Carbide common stock and Dow common stock;

- the earnings performance of Dow and price-to-earnings and EBITDA multiples of Dow relative to selected companies in the chemical industry;

- equity research coverage of Dow;

- the pro forma capitalization of Union Carbide and Dow; and

- selected market premium date in selected transactions announced in 1998 and 1999 with transaction values of $5.0 billion to $15.0 billion.

DEAL TERMS

The deal was announced on August 4, 1999. Dow, which closed at $124.68 on August 3, offered .537 shares of its stock for each Union Carbide stock. This represented a premium of 37% for Union Carbide shareholders, which had been trading at $48.81. Union Carbide's market capitalization had been $6.5 billion, but under the terms of the deal, Dow was paying $8.9 billion. Following the merger, Dow will hold 75% of the shares, and Union Carbide will hold 25%. Tables 1 and 2 present this background of the merger.

HISTORICAL DATA ON DOW AND UNION CARBIDE

Historical data for Dow for the years 1979–1998 are presented in Table 3 for the income statement and Table 4 for the balance sheet. Related regression data are shown in Table 5 with some related regressions in Figure I. Historical data for Union Carbide for the years 1979–1998 are presented in Table 6 for the income statement and Table 7 for the balance sheet. Related regression data are shown in Table 8 with some related regressions in Figure II.

A summary of a partial pro forma balance sheet for the combined companies using the pooling of interests accounting method is presented in Table 9.

TABLE 1 Dow/Union Carbide Deal Terms

Pre-Merger

	Dollar Amounts			Percentage	
	Dow	Union Carbide	Total	Dow	Union Carbide
Share Price	$124.68	$48.81			
Shares Outstanding (million)	217	133			
Total Market Value (billion)	$27.1	$6.5	$33.5	80.6%	19.4%
Exchange Terms	0.537 for	1			
Post-Merger					
Number of Shares (million)	217	71	288	75.2%	24.8%

TABLE 2 Dow/Union Carbide Financial Relations

	Dow	Union Carbide
Market Value (billion)	$27.1	$6.5
Book Value (billion)	$7.6	$2.6
Market Value/Book Value	3.6	2.5
LTM Net Income (million)	$1,243	$272
PE Ratio	21.8	23.9
Total Paid (billion)	$8.9	
Premium Over Market		
Amount (billion)	$2.4	
Percent	37.2%	
Premium Over Book		
Amount (billion)	$6.3	
Percent	245.1%	

TABLE 3 Dow Chemical Summary Income Statement for (All Amounts Are in Millions of Dollars)

	1979	1980	1981	1982	1983	1984	1985	1986	1987	1988	1989	1990	1991	1992	1993	1994	1995	1996	1997	1998
Sales (Net)	9,255	10,626	11,873	10,618	10,951	11,418	11,537	11,128	13,397	16,703	17,625	19,804	18,527	18,992	18,006	20,040	20,223	20,079	20,065	18,473
Cost of Goods Sold	(6,597)	(7,921)	(9,213)	(8,440)	(8,605)	(8,608)	(8,638)	(7,568)	(7,846)	(9,611)	(9,488)	(11,865)	(11,355)	(11,362)	(10,652)	(11,698)	(11,908)	(12,849)	(13,471)	(12,491)
Selling, General, and Administrative Expenses	(690)	(765)	(938)	(952)	(989)	(1,054)	(1,265)	(1,496)	(2,405)	(2,725)	(3,125)	(3,859)	(4,061)	(4,412)	(4,164)	(4,322)	(2,995)	(2,897)	(2,665)	(2,473)
Operating Income Before Depreciation	1,968	1,940	1,722	1,226	1,357	1,756	1,614	2,044	3,146	5,167	5,012	4,080	3,411	3,218	3,070	3,820	5,280	4,333	3,929	3,509
Depreciation and Amortization	(634)	(728)	(806)	(870)	(841)	(908)	(977)	(771)	(841)	(976)	(1,036)	(1,296)	(1,435)	(1,489)	(1,522)	(1,490)	(1,407)	(1,298)	(1,269)	(1,276)
Operating Income After Depreciation	1,334	1,212	916	356	516	848	637	1,273	2,305	4,191	3,976	2,784	1,976	1,729	1,548	2,330	3,853	3,035	2,660	2,233
Interest Expense	(359)	(456)	(605)	(579)	(478)	(465)	(413)	(383)	(397)	(400)	(513)	(740)	(704)	(773)	(666)	(603)	(462)	(529)	(502)	(540)
Nonoperating Income (Expense)	256	412	421	631	466	449	398	346	223	225	472	519	573	349	823	325	138	782	790	430
Special Items	82	70	12	(94)	(58)	(157)	(592)	0	0	(149)	0	0	(157)	(433)	(190)	0	0	0	0	(111)
Pretax Income	1,313	1,238	744	314	446	675	30	1,236	2,131	3,867	3,935	2,563	1,688	872	1,525	2,052	3,529	3,288	2,948	2,012
Income Taxes - Total	(515)	(424)	(176)	29	(153)	(126)	28	(495)	(886)	(1,457)	(1,436)	(978)	(510)	(274)	(606)	(779)	(1,442)	(1,167)	(1,041)	(685)
Income Taxes - Federal	106	169	218	(57)	21	(109)	(163)	130	111	34	(32)	143	177	(299)	24	34	288	308	150	(19)
Income Taxes - Foreign	251	125	(103)	(104)	(19)	145	(25)	308	311	528	701	442	429	381	404	457	535	499	478	329
Income Taxes - State	144	117	62	129	148	2	175	7	425	855	684	364	243	149	115	285	507	347	402	348
Income Taxes - Other	15	13	NA	NA	NA	38	NA	39	0	42	83	15	15	83	63	23	132	35	13	23
Minority Interest	(14)	(9)	(4)	(1)	NA	0	0	0	0	0	(12)	(201)	(236)	(322)	(275)	(335)	(196)	(194)	(99)	(17)
Income Before Extraordinary Items	784	805	564	342	293	549	58	741	1,245	2,410	2,487	1,384	942	276	644	938	1,891	1,907	1,808	1,310
Dividends - Preferred	0	0	0	0	0	0	0	0	0	0	(1)	(6)	(7)	(7)	(7)	(7)	(7)	(7)	(6)	(8)
Income Before Extraordinary Items - Available for Common	784	805	564	342	293	549	58	741	1,245	2,410	2,486	1,378	935	269	637	931	1,884	1,900	1,802	1,304
Common Stock Equivalents - Dollar Savings	0	0	0	0	0	0	0	0	0	0	0	0	0	0	0	0	0	0	0	0
Income Before Extraordinary Items - Adjusted for Common Stock Equivalents	784	805	564	342	293	549	58	741	1,245	2,410	2,486	1,378	935	269	637	931	1,884	1,900	1,802	1,304
Extraordinary Items and Discontinued Operations	0	0	0	57	41	36	0	(9)	(5)	(12)	0	0	0	(765)	0	0	187	0	0	0
Net Income Adjusted for Common Stock Equivalents	784	805	564	399	334	585	58	732	1,240	2,398	2,486	1,378	935	(496)	637	931	2,071	1,900	1,802	1,304
Net Income (Loss)	784	805	564	399	334	585	58	732	1,240	2,398	2,487	1,384	942	(489)	644	938	2,078	1,907	1,808	1,310
EPS (Primary) - Excluding Extra Items	4.33	4.42	3.00	1.77	1.50	2.83	0.31	3.87	6.50	12.82	9.20	5.10	3.46	0.99	2.33	3.37	7.03	7.71	7.81	5.83
EPS (Primary) - Including Extra Items	4.33	4.42	3.00	2.07	1.71	3.02	0.31	3.82	6.47	12.76	9.20	5.10	3.46	(1.83)	2.33	3.37	7.72	7.71	7.81	5.83
EPS (Fully Diluted) - Excluding Extra Items	4.33	4.42	3.00	1.77	1.51	2.83	0.31	3.87	6.50	12.82	9.20	4.98	3.35	0.99	2.29	3.31	NA	7.56	7.70	5.76
EPS (Fully Diluted) - Including Extra Items	4.33	4.42	3.00	2.07	1.71	3.02	0.31	3.82	6.47	12.76	9.20	4.98	3.35	(1.77)	2.29	3.31	7.58	7.56	7.70	5.76
Dividends per Share by Ex-Date	1.500	1.650	1.800	1.800	1.800	1.800	1.800	1.900	2.150	2.600	2.367	2.600	2.600	2.600	2.600	2.600	2.900	3.000	3.360	3.490
Common Shares Outstanding (millions)	181.181	182.702	189.393	194.170	195.846	190.092	190.160	191.258	189.380	183.533	269.301	269.990	270.708	272.589	274.486	277.123	250.957	241.139	225.468	220.377
Price - High	34.875	39.250	39.000	28.875	38.375	34.500	41.875	61.750	109.625	94.000	72.250	75.750	58.000	62.875	62.000	79.250	78.000	92.500	102.625	101.437
Price - Low	24.375	28.250	23.375	19.625	25.000	25.750	27.000	39.875	56.125	76.750	76.750	37.000	44.125	55.500	49.000	56.500	61.375	68.250	76.375	74.688
Price - Close	32.125	32.125	26.250	25.875	33.375	27.500	41.000	58.500	90.000	87.750	71.375	47.500	53.750	57.250	56.750	67.250	70.250	78.375	101.500	90.938
Price - Average High-Low	29.625	31.188	31.188	24.250	31.688	30.125	34.438	50.813	84.188	85.375	63.875	56.375	51.063	56.938	55.500	67.875	69.588	80.375	89.500	88.063
Adjustment Factor (Cumulative) by Ex-Date	1.500	1.500	1.500	1.500	1.500	1.500	1.500	1.500	1.500	1.500	1.000	1.000	1.000	1.000	1.000	1.000	1.000	1.000	1.000	1.000
Price - Average High-Low (Adjusted)	19.750	22.500	20.792	16.167	21.125	20.083	22.958	33.875	56.125	56.917	63.875	56.375	51.063	56.938	55.500	67.875	69.588	80.375	89.500	88.063
Price - Close (Adjusted)	21.417	21.417	17.500	17.250	22.250	18.333	27.333	39.000	60.000	58.500	71.375	47.500	53.750	57.250	56.750	67.250	70.250	78.375	101.500	90.938
Common Shares Outstanding (Adjusted)	271.772	274.053	284.090	291.255	293.769	285.138	285.240	286.887	284.070	275.300	269.301	269.990	270.708	272.589	274.486	277.123	250.957	241.139	225.468	220.377

TABLE 4 Dow Chemical Summary Balance Sheet for (All Amounts Are in Millions of Dollars)

	1979	1980	1981	1982	1983	1984	1985	1986	1987	1988	1989	1990	1991	1992	1993	1994	1995	1996	1997	1998
ASSETS																				
Cash and Short-Term Investments	252	168	93	183	178	121	114	261	418	225	289	299	536	606	837	1,134	3,450	2,302	537	390
Cash	42	25	28	22	12	19	11	16	21	225	117	204	238	375	407	569	2,839	1,903	235	123
Short-Term Investments	209	143	67	161	165	102	103	245	397	0	172	95	300	231	430	565	611	399	302	267
Receivables - Total	2,053	2,159	2,279	2,034	2,266	1,883	2,187	2,368	3,229	3,768	4,219	4,538	4,215	3,730	3,832	4,458	4,109	4,398	4,956	4,537
Inventories - Total	1,313	1,934	2,113	1,748	1,961	1,927	2,023	1,940	2,105	2,370	2,832	3,182	2,968	2,692	2,526	2,712	2,748	2,815	2,921	2,810
Current Assets - Other	135	129	26	0	0	0	0	0	0	0	0	0	0	415	457	389	247	317	224	303
Current Assets - Total	3,753	4,390	4,511	3,963	4,405	3,931	4,324	4,560	5,752	6,363	7,340	8,019	7,719	7,443	7,852	8,693	10,554	9,830	8,640	8,040
Property, Plant, and Equipment - Total (Net)	5,236	5,672	6,174	5,961	5,695	5,173	5,127	5,347	5,551	6,576	7,642	8,249	8,775	8,801	8,580	8,726	8,113	8,484	8,052	8,447
Property, Plant, and Equipment - Total (Gross)	8,909	9,873	10,984	11,199	11,524	11,256	11,875	12,715	13,502	15,300	17,334	19,149	20,853	21,444	21,608	23,210	23,218	23,737	23,345	24,435
Depreciation, Depletion, Amortization (Accumulated)	(3,673)	(4,201)	(4,810)	(5,238)	(5,829)	(6,083)	(6,748)	(7,368)	(7,951)	(8,784)	(8,692)	(10,900)	(11,888)	(12,643)	(13,028)	(14,484)	(15,105)	(15,253)	(15,293)	(15,988)
Investment and Advances - Equity Method	856	966	1,095	1,160	1,031	1,152	1,250	1,111	1,064	1,053	1,111	1,156	1,248	1,417	1,019	931	848	1,387	1,206	1,311
Investment and Advances - Other	166	261	332	386	484	797	470	518	1,083	1,170	1,576	1,755	2,020	1,923	2,095	1,859	1,872	2,497	2,929	2,615
Intangibles	107	109	228	195	196	202	265	303	485	C	3,997	4,190	4,310	4,395	4,442	4,414	723	899	1,762	1,641
Assets - Other	133	140	156	162	170	164	394	394	421	1,077	500	584	655	1,381	1,717	1,922	1,472	1,576	1,451	1,778
Assets - Total	10,252	11,538	12,496	11,807	11,981	11,419	11,830	12,242	14,356	16,239	22,166	23,953	24,727	25,360	25,505	26,545	23,582	24,673	24,040	23,830
LIABILITIES AND NET WORTH																				
Debt in Current Liabilities	601	736	496	276	764	484	463	279	179	432	2,266	1,433	1,573	1,278	1,042	1,275	698	1,272	2,062	1,826
Notes Payable	529	617	448	213	694	250	289	221	129	328	2,208	1,194	1,222	687	877	741	323	645	466	1,526
Debt - Due in One Year	73	119	48	63	70	234	174	58	50	104	80	239	351	591	165	534	375	607	406	300
Account Payable	1,011	974	983	804	1,056	947	1,028	901	1,085	1,320	1,767	1,874	1,653	1,500	1,479	1,928	1,529	1,596	1,731	1,862
Income Taxes Payable	267	215	69	95	226	235	207	310	508	619	263	275	324	218	245	664	791	567	521	290
Current Liabilities - Other	737	878	1,140	1,066	1,092	1,010	1,277	1,318	1,683	1,804	2,168	2,172	2,585	2,645	2,885	2,751	2,583	2,569	3,028	3,044
Current Liabilities - Total	2,615	2,803	2,688	2,241	3,138	2,676	2,975	2,808	3,455	4,175	6,484	5,754	6,135	5,641	5,851	6,616	5,601	6,004	7,340	6,842
Long-Term Debt - Total	3,055	3,438	3,968	3,502	2,803	2,745	3,198	3,404	3,779	3,338	3,855	5,209	6,079	6,191	5,902	5,303	4,705	4,196	4,196	4,051
Liabilities - Other	64	68	65	253	277	339	508	391	790	857	2,633	2,838	1,539	3,204	3,091	3,240	3,140	3,369	3,504	4,166
Deferred Taxes and Investment Tax Credit	582	745	840	733	683	576	331	441	527	567	642	698	529	214	372	659	644	1,005	649	747
Minority Interest	40	44	44	38	33	21	26	30	36	47	595	726	1,000	2,036	2,439	2,506	1,775	2,091	676	532
Liabilities - Total	6,355	7,098	7,605	6,767	6,934	6,357	7,038	7,074	8,597	8,984	14,209	15,225	15,282	17,286	17,455	18,311	15,880	16,685	16,385	16,358
Preferred Stock - Carrying Value	0	0	0	0	0	0	0	0	0	0	0	0	4	10	16	22	28	34	49	43
Common Equity - Total	3,897	4,440	4,891	5,040	5,047	5,062	4,792	5,168	5,769	7,255	7,957	8,728	9,441	8,064	8,034	8,212	7,674	7,954	7,626	7,429
Stockholders' Equity - Total	3,897	4,440	4,891	5,040	5,047	5,062	4,792	5,168	5,769	7,255	7,957	8,728	9,445	8,074	8,050	8,234	7,702	7,988	7,675	7,472
Liabilities and Stockholders' Equity - Total	10,252	11,538	12,496	11,807	11,981	11,419	11,830	12,242	14,356	16,239	22,166	23,953	24,727	25,360	25,505	26,545	23,582	24,673	24,040	23,830
Net Working Capital	1,530	2,180	2,252	1,837	1,865	1,637	1,709	1,795	2,079	2,620	2,970	3,603	2,857	2,849	2,613	2,785	5,040	4,699	3,060	2,757
Total Capital	6,766	7,852	8,426	7,798	7,560	6,810	6,836	7,142	7,630	9,196	10,612	11,852	11,632	11,650	11,193	11,511	13,153	13,183	11,112	11,204
Investment	719	1,086	574	(628)	(238)	(750)	26	306	488	1,566	1,416	1,240	(220)	18	(457)	318	1,642	30	(2,071)	92

TABLE 5 Growth Rates and Value Driver Relations, Dow Chemical, 1979–1998

| | Annual Growth Rate | | | Regression Against Revenues 1979–1998 | | | |
	1979 1989	1989 1998	1979 1998	Intercept	t-stat*	Coefficient	t-stat*
Revenues	5.0%	0.7%	4.4%	—	—	—	—
Cost of Goods Sold	1.4%	2.6%	3.1%	3,044.431	**3.992**	0.449	**9.415**
SG&A	15.1%	−4.6%	9.1%	−1,972.363	**−3.632**	0.283	**8.346**
Depreciation	3.3%	0.6%	4.1%	96.341	0.858	0.064	**9.171**
Interest Expenses	−0.9%	−3.2%	1.5%	279.771	**2.994**	0.016	2.748
EBITDA	10.5%	−0.4%	6.0%	−1,072.068	−1.665	0.268	**6.662**
NOI	14.5%	−0.3%	7.8%	−1,168.409	−1.598	0.204	**4.456**
EBIT	9.9%	0.3%	6.4%	−974.227	−1.317	0.215	**4.641**
EBT	12.0%	1.7%	9.5%	−1,253.998	−1.560	0.199	**3.951**
Net Income (Loss)	10.9%	—	—	372.987	−0.597	0.092	2.345
Net Income + (1-T)*							
Interest Expense*	8.8%	8.6%	3.1%	−187.419	0.322	0.102	2.810
#Average Tax Rate Used	32.6%	35.0%	33.7%				
Cash and Short-Term Investments	6.0%	11.9%	12.5%	−1,128.203	−1.783	0.113	2.854
Receivables—Total	6.5%	1.2%	5.2%	−529.494	−2.048	0.251	**15.545**
Inventories—Total	4.4%	−0.5%	3.2%	597.074	**4.016**	0.115	**12.405**
Current Assets—Total	5.3%	2.3%	5.4%	−1,282.181	−2.378	0.502	**14.906**
Property, Plant, and Equipment—							
Total (Net)	1.7%	0.2%	3.1%	1,855.105	**4.127**	0.333	**11.869**
Assets—Total	**5.2%**	**0.3%**	**5.6%**	**−4,596.309**	**−3.280**	**1.487**	**16.979**
Debt in Current Liabilities	0.9%	−1.3%	7.6%	−678.810	−1.678	0.107	**4.219**
Account Payable	4.1%	−0.5%	4.0%	52.388	0.439	0.083	**11.178**
Current Liabilities—Total	6.6%	1.3%	6.3%	−1,634.329	**−3.108**	0.401	**12.214**
Long-Term Debt—Total	0.9%	−2.3%	2.7%	1,146.392	1.744	0.194	**4.714**
Liabilities—Total	4.9%	1.2%	6.6%	−5,146.637	**−3.914**	1.094	**13.309**
Stockholders' Equity—Total	5.5%	−1.5%	3.9%	550.341	1.184	0.393	**13.523**
New Working Capital	3.3%	1.5%	4.3%	−255.434	−0.508	0.187	**5.943**
Total Capital	2.1%	0.6%	3.4%	1,599.671	2.623	0.520	**13.650**
Price—Average High-Low (Adjusted)	12.8%	5.6%	9.1%				
Price—Close (Adjusted)	14.2%	6.2%	9.3%				

*t-stats in bold font are significant at the 1% level.

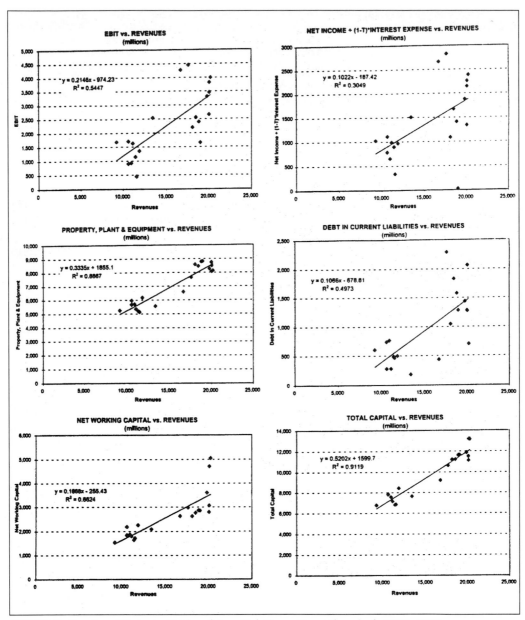

FIGURE 1 Graphs of Selected Value Driver Relations, Dow Chemical, 1979–1998

TABLE 6 Union Carbide Corp. Summary Income Statement for (All Amounts Are in Millions of Dollars)

	1979	1980	1981	1982	1983	1984	1985	1986	1987	1988	1989	1990	1991	1992	1993	1994	1995	1996	1997	1998
Sales (Net)	9,176	9,994	10,168	9,061	9,001	9,508	9,003	6,343	6,914	8,324	8,744	7,621	4,877	4,872	4,640	4,865	5,888	3,106	6,502	5,659
Cost of Goods Sold	(6,691)	(7,186)	(7,431)	(6,587)	(6,561)	(6,702)	(6,252)	(4,343)	(4,773)	(5,485)	(5,875)	(5,121)	(3,770)	(3,750)	(3,589)	(3,589)	(4,100)	(1,568)	(4,608)	(4,204)
Selling, General, and Administrative Expense	(1,213)	(1,318)	(1,428)	(1,469)	(1,468)	(1,485)	(1,564)	(888)	(938)	(961)	(1,105)	(1,050)	(565)	(538)	(479)	(426)	(463)	(460)	(481)	(447)
Operating Income Before Depreciation	1,472	1,490	1,309	885	932	1,320	1,187	1,112	1,203	1,878	1,764	1,450	542	584	572	766	1,325	1,058	1,215	916
Depreciation and Amortization	(470)	(326)	(386)	(426)	(477)	(507)	(596)	(453)	(463)	(473)	(498)	(476)	(287)	(293)	(276)	(274)	(294)	(312)	(340)	(389)
Operating Income After Depreciation	1,003	1,164	923	459	455	813	591	659	740	1,405	1,266	974	255	291	296	492	1,031	746	875	528
Interest Expense	(178)	(217)	(249)	(330)	(358)	(373)	(318)	(554)	(395)	(419)	(432)	(467)	(245)	(164)	(84)	(80)	(89)	(121)	(130)	(157)
Nonoperating Income (Expense)	(3)	135	270	222	245	167	125	121	111	250	159	231	68	30	33	60	253	204	224	62
Special Items	11	0	10	53	(241)	0	(1,411)	0	(51)	(71)	(77)	(112)	(244)	7	(2)	2	110	0	C	180
Pretax Income	833	1,082	954	404	101	607	(1,013)	226	405	1,185	916	626	168	164	243	528	1,305	828	966	623
Income Taxes - Total	(251)	(360)	(258)	(58)	10	(227)	441	(64)	(133)	(439)	(284)	(279)	50	(45)	(78)	(137)	(380)	(236)	(279)	(217)
Deferred Taxes	104	185	185	(34)	(100)	(80)	(909)	(64)	(47)	127	127	219	(52)	(44)	(34)	(29)	(39)	80	80	118
Income Taxes - Federal	31	11	11	18	7	48	33	67	104	127	80	53	(24)	40	31	57	315	80	140	73
Income Taxes - Foreign	105	151	105	4	3	49	36	61	14	185	127	170	(7)	31	31	35	18	34	40	20
Income Taxes - State	12	13	4	NA	NA	11	27	7	3	30	24	24	0	0	0	0	0	0	0	6
Income Taxes - Other	NA	NA	NA	NA	NA	0	0	0	0	0	0	0	2	0	0	C	0	0	0	0
Minority Interest	(25)	(49)	(47)	(36)	(32)	(39)	(27)	(32)	(40)	(64)	(59)	(39)	2	0	0	0	0	0	(14)	(3)
Income Before Extraordinary Items	556	673	649	310	79	341	(599)	130	232	662	573	308	(118)	118	165	389	925	593	676	403
Dividends - Preferred	0	0	0	0	0	0	0	0	0	0	0	0	(19)	(17)	(13)	(13)	(13)	(13)	(9)	0
Income Before Extraordinary Items Available for Common	556	673	649	310	79	341	(599)	130	232	662	573	308	(135)	102	152	376	912	580	667	403
Common Stock Equivalents - Dollar Savings	0	217	0	0	0	0	0	366	0	0	0	0	107	(294)	(97)	0	0	0	(17)	0
Income Before Extraordinary Items Adjusted for Common Stock Equivalents	556	673	649	310	79	341	(599)	130	232	662	573	308	(135)	102	152	376	912	580	644	403
Extraordinary Items and Discontinued Operations	0	217	0	0	0	(18)	18	366	0	0	0	0	107	(294)	(97)	0	0	0	(17)	0
Net Income Adjusted for Common Stock Equivalents	556	890	649	310	79	323	(581)	496	232	662	573	308	(28)	(192)	55	376	912	580	627	403
Net Income (Loss)	556	890	649	310	79	323	(581)	496	232	662	573	308	(9)	(175)	68	389	925	593	650	403
EPS (Primary) - Excluding Extra Items	8.47	10.08	9.56	4.47	1.13	4.84	(8.58)	1.25	1.76	4.88	4.07	2.19	(1.06)	0.76	1.00	2.44	6.44	4.28	5.02	2.96
EPS (Primary) - Including Extra Items	8.47	13.36	9.56	4.47	1.13	4.59	(8.34)	4.78	1.76	4.88	4.07	2.19	(0.22)	(1.45)	0.36	2.44	6.44	4.28	4.69	2.96
EPS (Fully Diluted) - Excluding Extra Items	8.47	10.08	9.56	4.47	1.13	4.84	(8.58)	1.24	1.75	4.66	3.92	2.13	(1.06)	0.78	0.97	2.27	5.83	3.90	4.53	2.91
EPS (Fully Diluted) - Including Extra Items	8.47	13.36	9.56	4.47	1.13	4.59	(8.34)	4.75	1.75	4.66	3.92	2.13	(0.22)	(1.01)	0.41	2.27	5.83	3.90	4.41	2.91
Dividends per Share by Ex-Date	2.900	3.100	3.300	3.400	3.400	3.400	3.400	1.500	1.500	1.150	1.000	1.000	1.000	0.875	0.750	0.750	0.750	0.750	0.787	0.900
Common Shares Outstanding	66.206	67.367	68.582	70.153	70.465	70.450	67.607	127.695	132.248	137.602	141.578	125.674	127.607	132.865	150.547	144.412	135.108	128.440	136.944	132.686
Price - High	44.500	52.500	62.125	61.000	73.875	65.250	74.250	33.187	32.500	28.375	33.250	24.875	22.625	29.625	23.125	35.875	42.750	49.875	58.812	55.750
Price - Low	34.000	35.250	45.250	40.125	51.000	32.750	36.000	18.750	15.500	17.000	17.000	14.125	15.375	10.875	16.000	21.500	25.500	38.375	40.500	38.750
Price - Close	42.000	50.250	51.375	52.675	62.750	36.750	70.875	22.500	21.750	22.750	23.750	16.375	16.625	16.625	22.375	29.375	37.500	40.875	42.937	42.500
Price - Average High-Low	39.250	43.875	53.688	50.563	62.438	49.000	55.125	25.969	24.000	22.688	25.625	19.500	19.000	20.250	19.563	28.688	34.125	43.125	48.656	46.250
Adjustment Factor (Cumulative) by Ex-Date	3.000	3.000	3.000	3.000	3.000	3.000	3.000	1.000	1.000	1.000	1.000	1.000	1.000	1.000	1.000	1.000	1.000	1.000	1.000	1.000
Price - Average High-Low (Adjusted)	13.083	14.625	17.896	16.854	20.813	16.333	18.375	25.959	24.000	22.688	28.000	19.500	19.000	20.250	19.563	28.688	34.125	43.125	48.656	46.250
Price - Close (Adjusted)	14.000	16.750	17.125	17.625	20.917	12.250	23.625	22.500	21.750	25.625	23.750	16.375	20.250	16.625	22.375	29.375	37.500	40.875	42.937	42.500
Common Shares Outstanding (Adjusted)	198.618	202.101	205.746	210.459	211.395	211.350	202.821	127.695	132.248	137.602	141.578	125.674	127.607	132.865	150.547	144.412	135.108	128.440	136.944	132.686

TABLE 7 Union Carbide Corp. Summary Balance Sheet for (All Amounts Are in Millions of Dollars)

	1979	1980	1981	1982	1983	1984	1985	1986	1987	1988	1989	1990	1991	1992	1993	1994	1995	1996	1997	1998
ASSETS																				
Cash and Short-Term Investments	449	243	253	154	118	96	459	299	201	146	142	127	64	171	108	109	449	94	68	49
Cash	*116*	*69*	*93*	*34*	*46*	*28*	*31*	*38*	*25*	*146*	*142*	*127*	*64*	*171*	*108*	*109*	*449*	*94*	*68*	*49*
Short-Term Investments	*333*	*174*	*160*	*120*	*72*	*68*	*428*	*261*	*176*	*0*	*0*	*0*	*0*	*0*	*0*	*0*	*0*	*0*	*0*	*0*
Receivables - Total	1,433	1,598	1,513	1,420	1,460	1,512	1,644	1,085	1,294	1,413	1,474	1,639	1,884	748	689	898	996	1,047	993	933
Inventories - Total	1,774	1,887	1,902	1,740	1,510	1,546	1,422	746	827	1,032	932	724	529	456	385	390	544	541	604	667
Current Assets - Other	155	191	208	187	157	152	353	284	233	292	239	440	164	204	247	217	207	191	201	257
Current Assets - Total	*3,811*	*3,919*	*3,876*	*3,501*	*3,245*	*3,306*	*3,878*	*2,414*	*2,555*	*2,883*	*2,787*	*2,930*	*2,641*	*1,579*	*1,429*	*1,614*	*2,196*	*1,873*	*1,866*	*1,906*
Property, Plant, and Equipment - Total (Net)	4,458	5,207	5,794	6,356	6,282	6,383	5,780	4,379	4,344	4,416	4,584	4,325	2,499	2,539	2,420	2,542	2,808	3,409	3,780	4,181
Property, Plant and Equipment - Total (Gross)	*8,729*	*9,636*	*10,047*	*10,793*	*10,708*	*11,131*	*10,674*	*8,558*	*8,639*	*9,009*	*9,530*	*8,923*	*5,542*	*5,730*	*5,626*	*5,889*	*6,357*	*7,159*	*7,707*	*8,409*
Depreciation, Depletion, Amortization (Accumulated)	*(4,271)*	*(4,429)*	*(4,253)*	*(4,437)*	*(4,426)*	*(4,748)*	*(4,894)*	*(4,179)*	*(4,295)*	*(4,593)*	*(4,946)*	*(4,598)*	*(3,043)*	*(3,191)*	*(3,206)*	*(3,347)*	*(3,549)*	*(3,750)*	*(3,927)*	*(4,228)*
Investment and Advances - Equity Method	213	307	239	293	300	288	303	272	387	680	727	836	479	475	437	418	739	695	690	624
Investment and Advances - Other	155	239	298	319	301	306	372	358	374	238	211	283	232	144	233	288	284	263	305	272
Intangibles	93	59	57	64	69	116	178	75	72	52	63	146	121	85	44	37	66	133	96	80
Assets - Other	73	61	91	83	98	119	70	73	160	172	174	213	854	119	126	129	163	193	227	228
Assets - Total	**8,803**	**9,659**	**10,423**	**10,616**	**10,295**	**10,518**	**10,581**	**7,571**	**7,892**	**8,441**	**8,546**	**8,733**	**6,826**	**4,941**	**4,689**	**5,028**	**6,256**	**6,546**	**6,964**	**7,291**
LIABILITIES AND NET WORTH																				
Debt in Current Liabilities	208	317	325	387	331	321	1,067	459	317	462	655	896	1,282	358	35	47	38	112	429	426
Notes Payable	*156*	*266*	*217*	*328*	*240*	*217*	*847*	*388*	*264*	*270*	*445*	*502*	*606*	*324*	*24*	*28*	*24*	*102*	*424*	*408*
Debt - Due in One Year	*52*	*51*	*108*	*59*	*91*	*104*	*220*	*71*	*53*	*192*	*210*	*394*	*676*	*34*	*11*	*14*	*14*	*10*	*5*	*18*
Account Payable	528	432	440	415	492	470	473	414	559	756	689	637	496	375	310	326	316	268	273	264
Income Taxes Payable	178	227	173	155	114	82	244	280	188	193	146	175	12	162	189	179	259	133	75	110
Current Liabilities - Other	827	819	791	797	825	885	1,271	728	747	1,044	838	831	642	582	662	733	725	765	727	670
Current Liabilities - Total	*1,741*	*1,795*	*1,729*	*1,754*	*1,762*	*1,758*	*3,055*	*1,881*	*1,811*	*2,455*	*2,328*	*2,539*	*2,432*	*1,477*	*1,196*	*1,285*	*1,338*	*1,278*	*1,504*	*1,470*
Long-Term Debt - Total	1,773	1,859	2,101	2,428	2,387	2,362	1,750	3,057	2,863	2,295	2,080	2,340	1,160	1,113	931	899	1,285	1,487	1,458	1,796
Liabilities - Other	244	226	191	179	203	355	1,062	742	804	538	515	527	593	976	1,019	1,176	1,453	1,443	1,358	1,193
Deferred Taxes and Investment Tax Credit	709	673	810	765	662	764	333	530	596	732	634	616	365	107	78	91	62	142	263	347
Minority Interest	294	330	329	331	352	355	362	356	571	585	606	338	13	1	1	24	29	33	33	36
Liabilities - Total	4,760	4,883	5,160	5,457	5,366	5,594	6,562	6,566	6,645	6,605	6,163	6,360	4,563	3,674	3,225	3,475	4,162	4,379	4,616	4,842
Preferred Stock - Carrying Value	0	0	0	0	0	0	0	0	0	0	0	0	24	29	36	44	49	53	0	0
Common Equity - Total	4,043	4,776	5,263	5,159	4,929	4,924	4,019	1,005	1,247	1,836	2,383	2,373	2,239	1,238	1,428	1,509	2,045	2,114	2,348	2,449
Stockholders' Equity - Total	4,043	4,776	5,263	5,159	4,929	4,924	4,019	1,005	1,247	1,836	2,383	2,373	2,263	1,267	1,464	1,553	2,094	2,167	2,348	2,449
Liabilities and Stockholders' Equity - Tot	8,803	9,659	10,423	10,616	10,295	10,518	10,581	7,571	7,892	8,441	8,546	8,733	6,826	4,941	4,689	5,028	6,256	6,546	6,964	7,291
Net Working Capital	1,945	2,267	2,312	2,014	1,742	1,801	1,462	731	885	890	1,114	1,287	1,491	460	268	376	896	707	791	862
Total Capital	6,403	7,474	8,106	8,370	8,024	8,184	7,242	5,110	5,229	5,306	5,698	5,612	3,990	2,999	2,688	2,918	3,704	4,116	4,571	5,043
Investment	446	1,071	632	264	(346)	160	(942)	(2,132)	119	77	392	(86)	(1,622)	(991)	(311)	230	786	412	455	472

TABLE 8 Growth Rates and Value Driver Relations, Union Carbide, 1979–1998

	Annual Growth Rate			Regression Against Revenues 1979–1998			
	1979 1989	1989 1998	1979 1998	Intercept	t-stat*	Coefficient	t-stat*
Revenues	−2.6%	−2.0%	−3.6%	—	—	—	—
Cost of Goods Sold	−3.5%	−1.2%	−3.3%	387.746	1.879	0.663	**24.411**
SG&A	−3.5%	−9.1%	−7.6%	−587.172	**−3.811**	0.208	**10.229**
Depreciation	2.4%	−2.5%	−2.2%	154.069	2.304	0.034	**3.805**
Interest Expenses	8.5%	−14.2%	−5.8%	17.866	0.148	0.034	2.142
EBITDA	2.1%	−0.6%	−2.1%	199.426	0.747	0.129	**3.671**
NOI	2.0%	0.6%	−2.0%	45.356	0.173	0.095	2.768
EBIT	—	7.7%	—	254.030	0.529	0.075	1.190
EBT	—	—	—	236.164	0.474	0.041	0.629
Net Income (Loss)	—	—	—	109.746	0.325	0.035	0.788
Net Income + (1−T)* Interest Expense*	—	—	—	122.540	0.372	0.059	1.367
#Average Tax Rate Used	29.1%	27.3%	28.4%				
Cash and Short-Term Investments	−5.3%	−5.5%	−6.1%	31.377	0.269	0.022	1.403
Receivables—Total	−1.1%	−5.7%	−3.1%	422.439	1.797	0.117	**3.777**
Inventories—Total	−9.0%	−2.2%	−8.2%	−959.516	**−5.227**	0.267	**11.052**
Current Assets—Total	−4.2%	−4.4%	−4.8%	−364.778	0.840	0.404	**9.735**
Property, Plant, and Equipment— Total (Net)	−2.0%	0.1%	−3.9%	−323.982	−0.574	0.631	**8.486**
Assets—Total	−2.0%	−1.5%	−3.3%	961.238	1.428	0.960	**10.832**
Debt in Current Liabilities	7.9%	−16.8%	−5.1%	300.794	0.971	0.017	0.409
Account Payable	3.9%	−11.0%	−3.1%	180.620	1.581	0.036	2.400
Current Liabilities—Total	3.2%	−6.8%	−1.8%	1,046.046	2.459	0.106	1.898
Long-Term Debt—Total	2.5%	−1.8%	−3.4%	504.457	1.049	0.186	**2.932**
Liabilities—Total	3.5%	−2.5%	−1.7%	2,817.720	3.311	0.317	2.829
Stockholders' Equity—Total	−13.0%	0.9%	−5.4%	−1,817.720	−2.356	0.643	**6.195**
New Working Capital	−10.6%	−4.3%	−7.4%	−848.739	−2.674	0.280	**6.703**
Total Capital	−4.0%	−1.0%	−4.7%	−1,172.721	−1.806	0.912	**10.657**
Price—Average High- Low (Adjusted)	6.5%	10.3%	5.3%				
Price—Close (Adjusted)	5.1%	11.2%	4.9%				

*t-stats in bold font are significant at the 1% level.

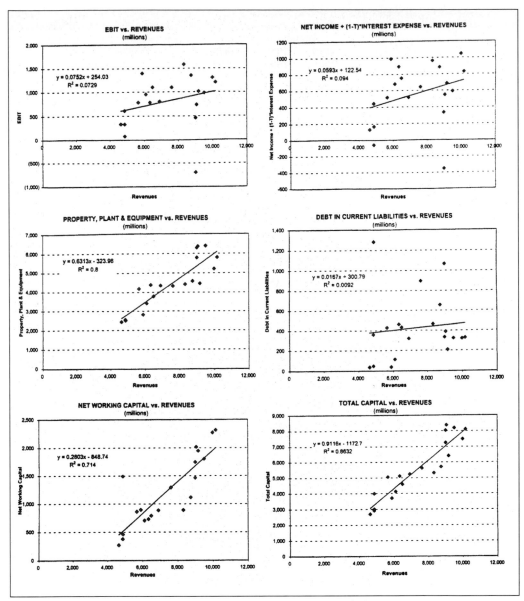

FIGURE 2 Graphs of Selected Value Driver Relations, Union Carbide Corp., 1979–1998

TABLE 9 Partial Pro Forma Balance Sheet for Dow/Union Carbide Combination

	Dow Chemical	Union Carbide	Pro Forma Adjustments	Combined Pro Forma
Total Assets	$23,105	$7,465		_____
Total Liabilities	$15,411	$5,024		_____
Stockholders' Equity:				
Common stock (Dow par value = $2.50)	818	157		
Additional paid-in capital	891	114		
Retained earnings	13,242	3,404		
Unearned employee compensation–ESOP and other equity adjustments		(58)		(58)
Accumulated other comprehensive loss	(300)	(157)		(457)
Treasury stock, at cost	(6,957)	(1,019)		
Net stockholders' equity	7,694	2,441		_____
Total Liabilities and Stockholders' Equity	$23,105	$7,465		_____

QUESTIONS

1. Complete the pro forma balance sheet for the combined companies, based on Table 9.

2. In calculating the terminal value of Union Carbide, Credit Suisse First Boston (CSFB) said that they applied terminal EBITDA multiples of 6.0x to 7.0x. For Dow, the EBITDA multiples used were 7.0x to 8.0x. For the period of supernormal growth, CSFB used discount rates ranging from 10% to 11%. Using a tax rate of 35% for Dow and 30% for Union Carbide, what is the implied discount rate that CSFB is using for the after-tax EBIT numbers for the two companies? (Hint: use a numerical example assuming that the terminal EBITDA of each company is $100 and that DA is $20, so that EBIT is $80 for each company. Now you can calculate the after-tax EBIT.)

3. Based on the nature of the chemical industry and the outlook for each of the two companies, calculate your best judgment of the value of Dow and Union Carbide as independent companies.

4. Based on the nature of the chemical industry and the outlook for each of the two companies, calculate your best judgment of the combined company.

5. Comparing the results in the previous questions, how much value does the merger add to the premerger intrinsic values of the individual companies? Compare your combined intrinsic value to the market values of the companies before the merger. What portion of the value created (or destroyed) is allocated to Dow and Union Carbide shareholders?

Case 14

Fashion, Inc.*

TRANSACTION OVERVIEW

Fashion, Inc. ("Fashion" or the "Company") was originally seeking to raise $10 million to finance its future growth. To determine the percentage ownership that the source of financing should be allocated, a valuation of Fashion was required. In comparing proposals from financial buyers and industry buyers, it was clear that the latter placed a substantially higher valuation on Fashion. The ultimate buyer perceived a good fit between Fashion and its own product line. In addition by taking over some of the administrative functions of Fashion the two top executives of Fashion who possessed creative design capabilities could spend more time in developing new fashion ideas.

Management financial projections are contained in the income statements, balance sheets and cash flow statements for the years 1998 through 2002 in Tables 1, 2 and 3 at the end of the case.

Company Background

Fashion Inc. is a rapidly growing women's sportswear company that is currently generating over $60 million in sales pro forma primarily through the internally developed Fashion

*This case was originally presented by Trenwith Securities, Inc. to the Anderson School at UCLA's Mergers & Acquisition Program. Trenwith is an investment banking firm that provides Corporate Finance and M&A Advisory Services to private and public middle-market companies. Trenwith's West Coast Office is at 450 Newport Center Drive, Suite 550, Newport Beach, California 92660. Telephone number (949) 792-3200. This case study has been adapted from an actual M&A transaction completed by Trenwith in 1998. The names of participating companies have been changed to protect the confidentiality of the client. This case is used with permission of Mr. Ron E. Ainsworth, Managing Partner. We are using this case because it provides an example of the circumstances under which a strategic buyer in a related business can place a higher valuation on a seller than could a financial buyer without synergies. The case is also of interest because it illustrates our emphasis in our Textbook that valuation depends heavily upon the business economics of the industry in the place of the buying and selling firms in the competitive framework of that industry. The case also demonstrates that the valuation concepts set forth in our textbook are actually used in practice.

brand. With its recent strategic acquisition full year sales for 1999 will exceed $80 million. The Company is comprised of the following two "companies": Sportswear Inc. & Casual Inc.

Fashion, Inc. operates as a holding company with the following division subsidiary structure. Sportswear Inc., the core business, is a division of Fashion, Inc. Casual, Inc. is a wholly owned subsidiary formed in June 1998 to acquire the XXX brand in an asset sale.

Beginning in 1994, with the addition of Byron M. Smith, a well respected apparel industry executive, Fashion has successfully implemented a major company and brand development strategy that has resulted in a 32% compound annual growth rate (CAGR) (1994–1997). This dramatic and profitable growth was achieved by:

- Focusing on the large and growing Better-Bridge women's sportswear market
- Capitalizing on the high demand for fresh designs as an alternative to "megabrand" saturation
- Developing a strong brand with a focused lifestyle concept, brand image, and advertising
- Developing a steady and profitable private label business
- Investing in the Company's infrastructure

The result has been the creation of a solid platform and a strong brand that is capable of sustained and profitable growth. The Company has grown from $19 million in 1994 to $44 million in 1997 with $57 million projected for 1998.

The Company is positioned to leverage this platform and continue its growth momentum by:

- Continuing to increase distribution into the department store channel
- Capturing the untapped potential of its recently launched and well-received brand and product extensions, particularly 000.
- Replicating its proven brand and company development strategy for its recent acquisition of XXX.

The Company expects to grow to over $100 million in annual sales within two to three years. The result will be a high value company with critical mass, high growth, and strong brands that will be ideally positioned for an IPO or suitable business combination.

A brief background description of the Company follows.

Fashion Inc. was founded in 1984 by (founders), to produce an art-driven clothing line for sale to small outdoor and resort retailers. Known over the years by the (various labels), the line eventually grew into a sportswear collection that could be found in specialty stores and in the classic and country departments of major department stores, hanging with such resources as Marisa Christina, Cambridge Dry Goods, and Susan Bristol.

In 1993, as a response to changing market conditions and with an eye on future growth, the label was changed to (Fashion label) to reflect a commitment to a single lifestyle identity. Refocused, with a new aesthetic, the product was then redeveloped in order to reposition the brand in the Less Traditional, Upper Better market. The line now can be found hanging with other Better to Bridge resources such as Karen Kane, David Dart, and Eileen Fisher in both specialty stores and department stores including Nordstroms, Parisian, and Bloomingdales.

Fashion label is comprised of three separate collections, each of which has a unique and forward point of view. These different collections, (various labels) address specific segments of a woman's wardrobe and define a complete 'World of Fashion.' A commitment to major consumer advertising also reinforces this image nationally and places the label in the mainstream of notable fashion resources.

In 1998, as part of its brand portfolio strategy, the Company formed XXX and acquired the 000 brand. The brand is positioned in the Lower to Mid Bridge market with contemporary styling and design. The Company has excellent relations with top bridge retailers such as Saks Fifth Avenue and Neiman Marcus, which is its primary channel of distribution.

Investment Highlights

Positioned in a Large Market with Strong Brands

Fashion has created a portfolio of strong brands, each with a fresh alternative look that is in high demand in the growing Upper Better to Bridge market.

- Large Market
  - The Better-Bridge women's sportswear market represents over $10 billion (20% to 30%) of the $41.9B women's sportswear market (1997 annual domestic sales at the retail level)
- Strong Underlying Growth Trends
  - Increased casual wear in the workplace
  - Increased casual lifestyle trends
  - "Baby Boomer" population and income growth
  - Compression of the fashion pyramid toward Upper Better-Bridge price points
- High Demand for "Fresh" Brands
  - Consumers seek alternative or fresh lifestyle concepts with a focused brand image
  - Retailers seek differentiation from "megabrand" saturation or sameness

Solid Platform Established

Fashion has made significant investments and improvements creating a strong platform capable of significant growth and profitability.

- Strong Management Team
  - Led by Byron M. Smith, a well respected and well known industry executive with significant brand, image, and company building expertise

- Proven "Brand" Strategy
- Fashion brand successfully refocused and redefined
- Grew at 32% CAGR since 1994
- Strong Multi Channel Position
  - Continued growth of specialty store base
  - Profitable expansion via department store partnerships
  - Currently in all doors of Nordstroms, Parisian, and Jacobson's
  - Established in 14 doors of Bloomingdales (Federated) and growing significantly
- Improved Business Systems
- Expanded Distribution Center
- New product line extensions leveraging the Fashion brand
  - (various labels)
- Initiating licensing program

Brand Portfolio/Acquisition Strategy
Leveraging its proven brand building capabilities and solid platform the Company has initiated an acquisition strategy to significantly enhance its growth prospects with the addition of complementary brands, new channels, and new product lines.

- Targeted acquisition criteria
  - Established management
  - Good product fundamentals
  - Readily accretive
  - Established distribution channels
- Synergies will be developed through the application of the proven Fashion "model"
  - Brand and image development
  - Distribution channel expansion
  - Management refocus
  - Improved business systems and infrastructure

Fashion has applied a brand development strategy to the Fashion brand that capitalizes on the driving factors in the women's sportswear industry, namely strong brand image with unique design as an alternative to "megabrand" sameness. The Fashion brand was refocused and redefined as a unique and fresh lifestyle concept in the casual women's sportswear market and reinforced by strong brand building and promotion. As a result the Company has realized a 32% compound annual growth rate (CAGR) since 1994, while maintaining gross margins at 32.5% and EBITDA margin at 6.5% (including investments).

The Company is expected to continue its strong, profitable growth. The Fashion brand has significant untapped potential in department store channels and new product line extensions. The XXX acquisition will also experience significant growth through the application of the proven Fashion brand strategy. The result will be a high growth company with critical mass and a diversified portfolio of strong brands that will be well positioned for an IPO or suitable business combination.

Financial Summary

The resultant sales and profits from the implementation of Fashion brand and company development strategy are presented below. It should be noted that EBITDA includes these significant brand and company infrastructure investments.

Selected Historical Financials: Fashion. Inc.

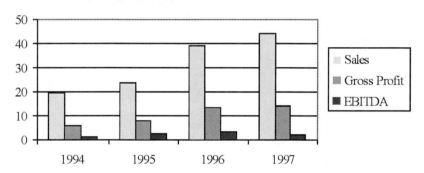

	1994	1995	1996	1997	Average
Sales	$19,400	$23,780	$39,015	$44,084	
Sales Growth	5.6%	22.6%	64.1%	13.0%	31.4%
Gross Profit	$5.846	$8,074	$13,357	$14,011	
Gross Margin	30.1%	34.0%	34.2%	31.8%	32.7%
EBITDA	$1,440	$2,446	$3,464	$1,964	
EBITDA Margin	7.4%	10.4%	8.9%	4.5%	6.5%

$ in thousands, includes investments in advertising, brand building, and infrastructure

Fashions formed its XXX subsidiary and acquired the XXX brand in June 1998. The Company will implement its proven brand development strategy for this acquisition and continue to grow the Fashion business allowing the Company to achieve over $100 million in sales within two years as presented below.

Selected Forecasted Financials: Fashion, Inc.

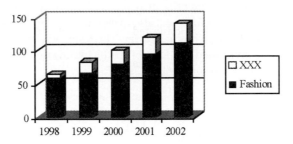

	1998	**1999**	**2000**	**2001**	**2002**
Fashion	$57,561	$65,747	$79,144	$93,706	$110,188
XXX	$6,148	$16,561	$20,612	$25,696	$30,032
Total Sales	$63,709	$82,308	$99,756	$119,402	$140,220
Sales Growth	45%	29%	21%	20%	17%
Fashion	$3,673	$4,647	$7,293	$9,979	$13,288
XXX	($30)	$1,237	$1,718	$2,940	$3,924
EBITDA	$3,643	$5,884	$9,011	$12,919	$17,212
Fashion	6.40%	7.10%	9.20%	10.7%	12.1%
XXX	0%	7.50%	8.30%	11.4%	13.1%
EBITDA Margin	5.70%	7.10%	9.00%	10.8%	12.3%

$ in thousands, includes partial year 1998 acquisitions

Industry Overview

Introduction

Beginning in 1994, Fashion refocused and repositioned its Fashion brand in the Upper Better-Lower Bridge women's sportswear segment, the largest and strongest segment of the overall women's apparel market. With its investment in the Fashion brand and the Company's infrastructure in place, the Company has developed and is now implementing a brand portfolio strategy. Seeking to capitalize on the solid platform it has built in this dominant market segment, the Company is adding the complimentary XXX brand. The Company is now positioned with a portfolio of brands each with excellent design teams, product lines, and distribution channels.

An overview of the industry structure is presented below, followed by the current trends that are impacting the industry and Fashion.

Composition of the Apparel Industry

Market Segmentation

The overall US apparel market accounted for $169 billion in retail sales in 1997 representing 2% of US GDP. The women's apparel segment is the largest segment within the overall apparel market accounting for $89 billion or 50%. This segment has been growing at a 5% annual growth rate.[1]

Within the overall women's apparel market is the $41.9 billion (1997, US Retail) women's sportswear market segment, which is the largest and most influential segment with a 47% share.[1]

1997 US Women's Apparel Share by Product

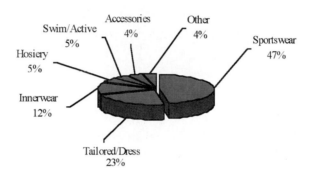

Industry Structure

The structure of the women's apparel market can be described as a pyramid consisting of four tiers. "Designer" emphasizes fashion and quality, and sells at high price points to a narrow customer base. Donna Karan, Ralph Lauren, Calvin Klein, Gucci, and Versace are examples of the top players in the Designer market. The "Bridge" market, whose players include CK by Calvin Klein, DKNY, Ralph, Ellen Tracy, and St. John Knits focuses on offering less expensive versions of Designer styles. The third segment is "Better" which delivers sportswear and casual work clothes at medium price points. Large branded names in the Better market include Liz Claiborne, Lauren by Ralph Lauren, and Jones New York. Finally, "Moderate" emphasizes low price points over style and aims towards broad mass appeal. Players in this segment include Gitano, Guess, and Chaus and overlaps into the mass merchandising channel including Sears, Target, Kmart, and JC Penney. The structure of the industry can be summarized by the following graphic:

---

[1]*Fairchild.*

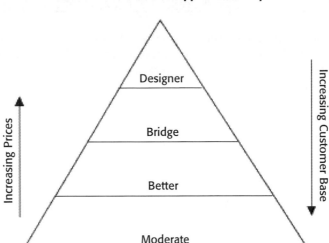

Structure of Women's Apparel Industry

The Better and Bridge/Designer segments of the pyramid have been gaining segment share at the expense of the Moderate segment. Moderate sportswear lost 2.5 points of sportswear market share in 1997, mostly to Better. Bridge/Designer increased share by over a half point. The trends behind this shift are described later in this section.

Favorable Demographics

Trends indicate that women between the ages of 35 and 54, which encompasses the heart of the "Baby Boomer" population, are becoming a dominant consumer group in the women's apparel market. This segment of the population is growing, becoming more affluent, and is purchasing more. These women are the target audience for each of the Fashion brands.

1997 Women's Sportswear % Share by Age

Age Group	1997 Sales	%
25–34	$7.1B	17%
35–44	$7.9B	19%
45–54	$7.9B	19%

Source: Fairchild.

As the chart indicates, women 35 to 54 have become the dominant age group for women's apparel spending within the 45 to 54 age group actually gaining in share approximately 1.5 points.

The growth in the upper middle income to lower affluent population is another factor driving the growth in the Better and Bridge tiers of the fashion pyramid. The middle income bracket ($25,000 to $60,000 annual income) accounts for approximately 50% of the women's apparel market according to NPD. The affluent segment of the population segment grew from 20% to 22% of the women's apparel market in 1997 according to Mendelsohn Research.

Overview of Middle Income and Affluent Buyer Segment

	Household Income	Percent of Women's Apparel Market	Average Women's Apparel Purchase
Middle Income*	$25,000–$59,999	50%	
Lower Tier Affluent**	$60,000–$99,999	12%	$839/year
Mid Tier Affluent**	$100,000–$199,000	8%	$1,361/year
Top Tier Affluent**	$200,000 or more	2%	$3,041/year

Source: NDP   **Source:* Mendelsohn Research

Distribution Channels

The women's apparel market, which grew $4.5 billion (5%) in 1997 to $89 billion was led by growth in the specialty and department store segments, both key Fashion channels. A summary of retail sales by distribution channel is presented below.[2]

Overview of Women's Apparel Distribution Channels

	1996	1997	Growth
Specialty Stores	$21.2	$22.8	7.1%
Department Stores	$18.1	$19.2	6.0%
Major Chains	$12.1	$13.0	7.0%
Discounters	$13.8	$14.1	2.4%
Off-pricers	$5.6	$5.8	3.2%
Direct-mail	$6.5	$6.7	2.5%
Factory Outlets	$3.2	$3.0	(5.2%)

$ in billions

In the women's sportswear market, specialty chains were the top sellers of with $9.2 billion (22%), followed by department stores selling $8.4 billion (20%).

Another significant trend in the women's apparel market is the consolidation of retail stores, and in particular, of department stores. This consolidation trend has flattened out. The result is that the buyer is capable of exerting more power in the negotiation of terms and the overall relationship. In order to counter this trend the sellers must have a product with sufficient consumer interest or "pull," or provide a unique product that allows the retailer to differentiate itself from competitors. Fashion has implemented a strategy with strong brand and fresh unique designs, which creates strong customer pull and provides retailers with an alternative to "megabrand" sameness.

---

[2]*Women's Wear Daily/American Shoppers Panel.*

Brand Positioning

The Fashion brand is positioned in the mid to upper Better market of the sportswear/casualwear market, with the designs tending toward "classic" and "updated contemporary" as opposed to "traditional." The XXX brand is positioned in the lower to mid Bridge segment. Its designs tend toward contemporary. The following chart identifies the key competitors and their respective retail positioning.

Retail Positioning

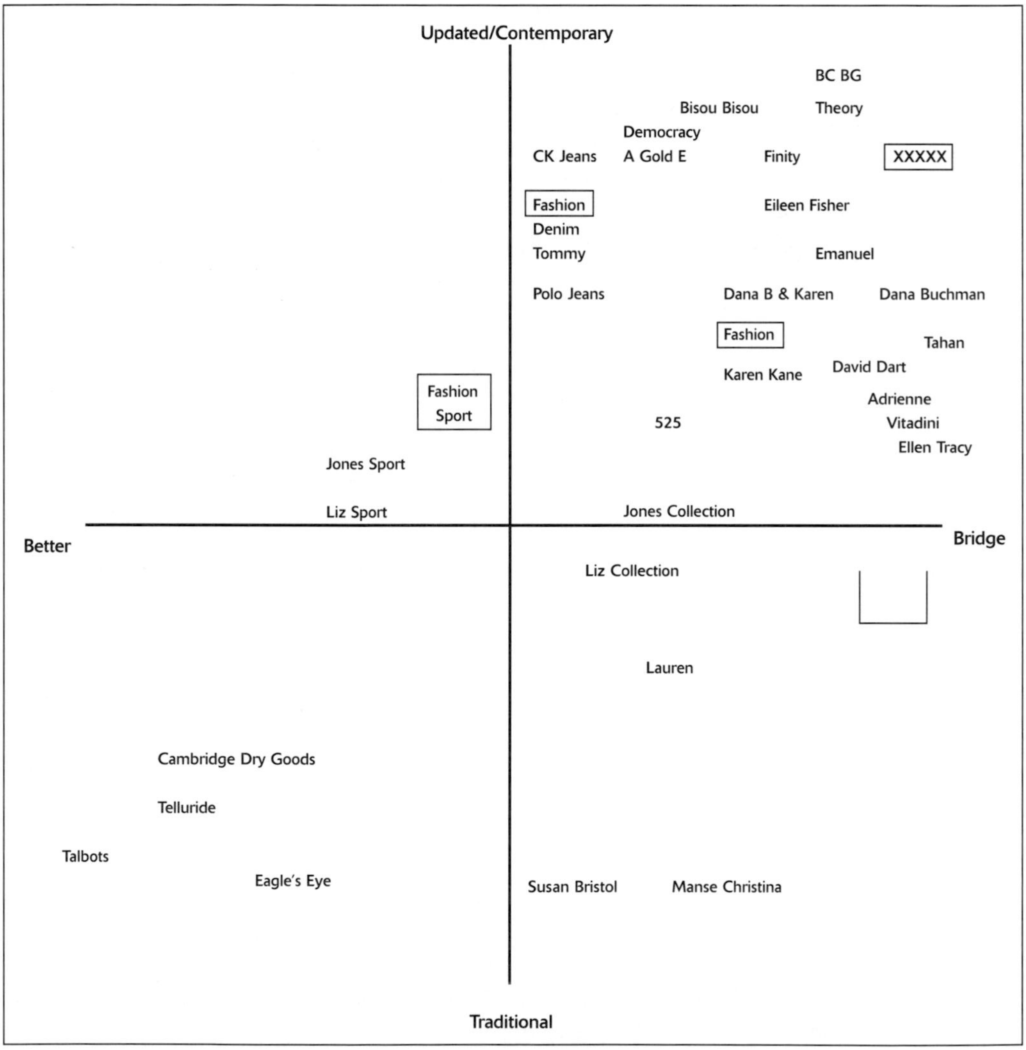

Chart content — axes: vertical top "Updated/Contemporary", vertical bottom "Traditional", horizontal left "Better", horizontal right "Bridge".

Brands plotted:
BC BG, Theory, Bisou Bisou, Democracy, CK Jeans, A Gold E, Finity, XXXXX, Fashion, Eileen Fisher, Denim, Tommy, Emanuel, Polo Jeans, Dana B & Karen, Dana Buchman, Fashion, Tahan, Karen Kane, David Dart, Adrienne, Fashion Sport, 525, Vitadini, Ellen Tracy, Jones Sport, Liz Sport, Jones Collection, Liz Collection, Lauren, Cambridge Dry Goods, Telluride, Talbots, Eagle's Eye, Susan Bristol, Manse Christina.

Together this portfolio of brands creates a constellation of complementary product lines that capture the full spectrum of the strong Upper Better to Bridge market.

Each of the Fashion product lines are also competitively priced within each product category, and offer more design elements such as embroidery, creative prints, and higher quality materials, differences that further distinguish Fashion from its competitors. This competitive differentiation allows the Company to achieve greater sell through and thereby maintain its gross margin and sales growth. The table below presents the retail price points for each of the Fashion collections and the primary competitors.

Fall/Winter 1998 Retail Analysis

	Shorts	Skirts Pants	Knit Tops	Woven Tops	Sweaters	Jackets Outerwear	Dresses
Collection							
Karen Kane	N/A	$106–$140	$78–$118	$68–$138	N/A	$198–$338	$140–$158
Eileen Fisher	$64–$72	$58–$160	$38–$68	$58–$168	$76–$184	$110–$138	$90–$250
David Dart	$98–$118	$98–$138	$58–$118	$59–$158	$88–$168	$158–$358	$128–$178
Lauren	$78–$84	$98–$158	$29–$89	$60–$98	$88–$158	$198–$358	$128–$160
Fashion	$68–$78	$68–$158	$39–$78	$58–$138	$64–$198	$138–$358	$94–$198
Sport							
Karen Kane	$52–$78	$48–$140	$20–$118	$64–$138	$34–$128	$74–$278	$49–$146
Lauren	$58–$64	$48–$158	$26–$124	$28–$80	$84–$188	$99–$168	$84–$160
Jones Co. & Sport	$29–$49	$54–$89	$24–$89	$34–$80	$49–$149	$79–$238	$69–$120
Liz Sport	$30–$44	$38–$79	$20–$72	$40–$72	$49–$130	$69–$140	$59–$120
Fashion Sport	$38–$58	$42–$138	$24–$78	$48–$138	$64–$198	$74–$238	$58–$118
Denim							
Tommy	$39–$69	$48–$82	$24–$94	$44–$79	$69–$92	$68–$175	$68–$78
Polo Jeans	$39–$64	$48–$115	$24–$68	$38–$58	$68–$110	$78–$225	$78–$120
Democracy	$49–$84	$88–$128	$39–$48	$80–$136	$128–$164	$124–$179	$124–$136
CK Jeans	$39–$72	$48–$98	$24–$60	$50–$98	$72–$92	$82–$100	$68–$78
Easel	N/A	N/A	N/A	N/A	$54–$128	N/A	N/A
A. Gold E.	$44–$78	$52–$178	$24–$112	$49–$106	N/A	$102–$240	$94–$128
Fashion Denim	$48–$98	$44–$148	$24–$88	$48–$118	$74–$118	$78–$238	$48–$148

The value proposition of competitive pricing strategies in combination with a focused brand image and a quality product have driven the increase in the Fashion brand awareness and the correspondingly strong sales growth.

Primary Competitors

As shown above, the Company considers its primary competitors to be Jones Apparel Group, Liz Claiborne, Karen Kane, and Eileen Fisher, as well as Tommy Hilfiger, Polo Jeans, and CK Jeans in the jeanswear market. As shown above, the Company competes head to head on price and product design (as reflected by retail positioning). In the specialty store market, the Company does not, in general, compete against the Liz Claiborne and Jones New York brands. The Company is, however, beginning to compete in the department store channels by offering a fresh, colorful, art-driven alternative to the mega-brands.

Sales for each of these top competitors are presented below.

Sales of Selected Competitors

	1994	1995	1996	1997
Liz Claiborne	$2,162	$2,082	$2,217	$2,410
Jones Apparel	$642	$787	$1,034	$1,387
Karen Kane	n/a	n/a	n/a	$70
Eileen Fisher	n/a	n/a	$66	$95

$ in millions

Industry Trends

The following are trends affecting the women's apparel industry and Fashion Inc.

Compression of the Fashion Pyramid

Increasing consumer demand for Designer styles at Better price points has resulted in a compression of the fashion pyramid, with Designer and Bridge fashion trends migrating to mass market price points, and Better apparel designers seeking to incorporate trendier fashions into their offerings. As a result, a new niche, known as Upper Better or Lower Bridge has emerged in response to the pyramids compression of the Bridge market.

Designs in the Upper Better segment provide fashionable yet value-conscious consumers Bridge styling at price points, which are 20% above the Better category and 25% below Bridge.[3] Upper Better sportswear firms competing in this market have upgraded their fabrics to include wool, cashmere, silk, wool tricotene, crepes, and velvet, with styles now including easy dressing coordinated elements. Target customers are women aged 30 to 45 who are in the middle to upper middle income brackets.

The Fashion collections are designed for the Better to Upper Better segments. The target consumer group is the "Fashion Woman"— a middle to upper income woman between the ages of 30 and 55.

The XXX brand is positioned in the Lower to Mid Bridge market. The target consumer group is the more contemporary woman between the ages of 25 to 50.

Demand for Better-Bridge Apparel Expanding Rapidly

Within the women's sportswear apparel industry, the Better-Bridge market is estimated to represent approximately twenty to thirty percent. Better sportswear sales grew 20% from 1995 to 1997 while Bridge sportswear sales grew 15% over the same period. Industry experts predict continued expansion of this market segment at a rate exceeding that of apparel expenditures overall over the next few years.[4]

---

[3] *Women's Wear Daily*, 8/95.
[4] *Fairchild*.

The growth in Better market sales stems primarily from five trends: increased casual wear in the workplace; increased casual lifestyle trends; compression of the fashion pyramid toward better; demographic growth and income trends; and affordable fashion.

Office wear guidelines have become increasingly casual and relaxed. According to a study by KSA, an Atlanta-based consulting firm, 84% of women and 92% of men consider comfort important.[5] The trade publication *Women's Wear Daily* concluded that roughly 37% of the respondents wear casual apparel to work everyday while an additional 23% dress casually on Fridays.[6]

Increasing demand for Better casual wear also results from broader lifestyle trends, as consumers are becoming more focused on the family and the home. As a result the demand for sportswear and quality casual wear is also increasing.

As discussed above, the trends behind the compression of the fashion pyramid toward Designer fashion at Better price points creating the Upper Better segment are further enhancing the segments growth prospects.

Finally, the demand for affordable fashion is increasing, which is a key attribute of the Better segment and its growth. This is a primary competitive advantage for the Company, which offers competitively priced products with more design elements. For example, a sweater may be priced at $53, the middle of the $50 to $55 targeted price range. However, the Fashion sweater will have design element details that larger firms simply don't have the ability to effectively focus on, such as embroidery and a mixture of different yarns.

Brands Increasingly Important

Brands have become an increasingly important factor in the apparel market. Consumers are demanding brands. Many consumers have less time to shop and are spending their disposable income more carefully. According to KSA, 53% of those surveyed were shopping less than they used to in order to save time. As more women have entered the work force over the years, less time remains for shopping. The rush of women into the workforce in the 1970s and 1980s, which fueled increases in demand and drove the growth of firms such as Liz Claiborne and The Limited, is no longer there.

Despite the overall market's fragmentation, national brands, according to Standard & Poors, are produced by about 20 sizable companies and account for 30% of overall U.S. wholesale apparel sales.[7] The remaining 70% consists of smaller brands and private labels. In the women.s apparel market, however. the top three companies account for only about 5% of the $89 billion retail market.

Nevertheless, the "mega-brands," such as Liz Claiborne, Tommy Hilfiger, and Jones New York have successfully leveraged their brand positioning by significantly increasing the retail space in department stores as well as through licensing and new product line extensions.

The trend toward more branded shops in department stores ("shop in shops") builds traffic for the department stores and helps to heighten brand awareness. The strong brands also ensure strong sales for the department store. If a smaller brand has an off season it could lose its foothold unless it has a loyal base or the financial strength to support its

---

[5]*KSA.*
[6]*Women's Wear Daily.*
[7]*Standard & Poors' Apparel Industry Report,* 1997.

brand. In addition any increase in retail space is that much less space for a competitor. Thus, it has become difficult for a smaller brand to rapidly enter the department store channels.

In response to these market conditions the Company has adopted a "Brand Strategy" in order to effectively compete in this marketplace. The initial investment in building the Fashion brand, including advertising and showrooms, has been made and is a continuing part of the Company's strategy. The product is fresh and unique enough, such that key department store chains have initiated retail partnerships with the Company. These partnerships include shop in shops in several chains, including Bloomingdale's, which is the gateway to the much larger Federated Department Stores. This strategy will be further leveraged with the XXX brand.

Retailer and Consumer Focus On Fresh Alternative Products
The trend toward "mega-brands," however, is beginning to show signs of discontent in the public and in the trade press. Several industry experts have expressed concern that the trend leads to "saturation" and "sameness." Sameness, they warn, will lead to customer boredom, markdowns, and discounts. Department stores are becoming top heavy in the same looks. They must therefore either offer incentives or new fresh looks to differentiate themselves and keep the customer excited.

Because of the highly competitive nature of the retail industry, department stores must identify high demand niches. An increasing number of sportswear firms are now enjoying the attention of department store giants who are making strategic moves in response to updated Better-Bridge apparel trends. The Upper Better-Bridge segment fits in extremely well with the needs of moderate and upscale department stores, such as Neiman Marcus, Bloomingdale's, Nordstrom, and Parisians, who have lost customers to specialty retailers such as The Gap and Banana Republic. As specialty retailers began to offer trendy versions of their casual wear to capture a portion of the upscale market whose tastes had shifted towards casual fashions, department stores have been forced to adopt new career and casual merchandising strategies in response. The Upper Better segment of apparel meshes well with this strategy of offering slightly more casual versions of trendy designer wear without excessive dilution of the retailers' upscale images.

More importantly, as a result of these industry dynamics, companies that offer fresh alternatives to megabrand sameness are experiencing rapid growth in response to this high demand. Retailers seek a new product offering to differentiate themselves. Consumers seek a fresh new look, balanced with a focused brand or image. Companies with a strong brand and fresh product can generate greater sell through and improve their bargaining position with retailers.

Other Industry Issues
For small to medium sized firms the issue of economies of scale are very important. Critical mass creates a competitive advantage in this fragmented market. Larger apparel makers gain leverage in negotiating discounts with suppliers, realize savings in distribution, enhance service towards retail customers, gain leverage in establishing retail partnerships, and achieve cost efficiencies in corporate areas. If apparel makers maintain efficient cost

structures, they are able to pass these savings to their retail customers. Fashion is rapidly growing and financially strong. Fortunately it is perceived as a company that has already achieved critical mass. As volume increases further, particularly with its recent acquisitions, the Company expects additional discounts from its offshore sourcing, and increased leverage with the retailers.

TABLE 1 Fashion, Inc. Income Statements ($000)					
	Info: 1998 Full Year	**1999**	**2000**	**2001**	**2002**
Sales	$ 63,709	$ 82,308	$ 99,756	$ 119,402	$ 140,220
Cost of Sales	$ (43,415)	$ (55,286)	$ (66,254)	$ (78,193)	$ (90,859)
Gross Profit	$ 20,294	$ 27,022	$ 33,501	$ 41,210	$ 49,361
SG&A	$ (17,498)	$ (22,196)	$ (25,802)	$ (29,803)	$ (33,811)
Operating Income (EBIT)	$ 2,797	$ 4,826	$ 7,699	$ 11,407	$ 15,549
Interest Expense	$ (1,302)	$ (377)	$ (293)	$ —	$ —
Earnings Before Taxes	$ 1,494	$ 4,449	$ 7,406	$ 11,406	$ 15,549
Tax	$(598)	$ (1,780)	$ (2,962)	$ (4,563)	$ (6,220)
Net Income	$ 896	$ 2,669	$ 4,444	$ 6,844	$ 9,329
Amortization	$ 6	$ 11	$ 11	$ 11	$ 11
Depreciation	$840	$ 1,407	$ 1,302	$ 1,502	$ 1,652
EBITDA	$ 3,643	$ 5,884	$ 9,011	$ 12,919	$ 17,212
Key Ratios					
Sales Growth (%)		29%	21%	20%	17%
Gross Margin (%)	32%	33%	34%	35%	35%
SG&A % of Sales	−28%	−27%	−26%	−25%	−24%
Operating Margin (%)	4%	6%	8%	10%	11%
EBITDA Margin (%)	6%	7%	9%	11%	12%

TABLE 2 Fashion, Inc. Balance Sheets ($000)

	Opening 10/01/1998	1998	1999	2000	2001	2002
Holding Company						
Excess Cash	$ —	$ —	$ —	$ —	$ 165.6	$ 5,438.3
Cash	$ 300.0	$ 300.0	$ —	$ —	$ —	$ —
Accounts Receivable	$ 10,811.0	$ 6,559.9	$ 7,053.4	$ 8,558.3	$10,262.2	$ 12,048.8
Inventory	$ 11,518.0	$15,425.3	$ 16,691.6	$ 20,375.0	$24,291.8	$ 28,592.7
Other Notes Receivable	$ 25.0	$ 25.0	$ 24.9	$ 24.9	$ 24.9	$ 24.9
Other Current Assets	$ 1,757.0	$ 1,911.0	$ 2,173.7	$ 2,223.5	$ 2,273.2	$ 2,320.0
Current Assets	$ 24,411.0	$24,221.1	$25,943.7	$ 31,181.7	$37,017.7	$48,424.7
Gross PP&E	$ 5,305.0	$ 5,640.4	$ 7,228.5	$ 8,658.5	$10,226.2	$11,892.4
Accumulated Depreciation	$ (1,825.0)	$ (2,074.9)	$ (3,122.3)	$ (4,424.0)	$(5,925.7)	$ (7,577.5)
Net PP&E	$ 3,480.0	$ 3,565.5	$ 4,106.2	$ 4,234.5	$ 4,300.5	$ 4,315.0
Other Assets	$ 150.0	$ 150.0	$ 150.0	$ 150.0	$ 150.0	$ 150.0
Goodwill	$ 421.7	$ 419.1	$ 408.5	$ 398.0	$ 387.4	$ 376.9
Total Assets	$ 28,462.7	$28,355.6	$30,608.3	$35,964.2	$41,855.6	$53,266.5
Accounts Payable	$ 3,628.0	$ 6,146.1	$ 6,976.1	$ 8,455.0	$10,120.6	$11,885.0
Accrued Liabilities	$ 1,037.0	$ 1,074.3	$ 1,452.6	$ 1,760.8	$ 2,108.0	$ 2,475.4
Debt	$ 8,202.7	$ 5,373.2	$ 3,770.1	$ 2,924.8	$ —	$ —
Current Liabilities	$ 12,867.7	$12,593.6	$ 12,198.8	$ 13,140.6	$12,228.6	$ 14,360.4
Preferred Stock	$ 10,000.0	$10,000.0	$ 10,000.0	$ 10,000.0	$10,000.0	$ 10,000.0
Common Stock	$ 5,095.0	$ 5,095.0	$ 5,095.0	$ 5,095.0	$ 5,095.0	$ 5,095.0
Retained Earnings	$ 1,040.1	$ 666.6	$ 3,314.1	$ 7,728.2	$14,532.1	$ 23,810.7
Dividends	$ (540.1)	$ —	$ —	$ —	$ —	$ —
Total Equity	$ 15,595.0	$15,761.6	$ 18,409.1	$ 22,823.2	$29,627.1	$ 38,905.7
Total Liabilities & Equity	$ 28,462.7	$28,355.2	$ 30,607.9	$ 35,963.8	$41,855.6	$ 53,266.1

TABLE 3 Fashion, Inc. Cash Flow Statements ($000)					
	1998 10/1-12/31	**1999**	**2000**	**2001**	**2002**
Net Income	$ 166.6	$ 2,647.5	$ 4,414.1	$ 6,803.9	$ 9,278.6
Depreciation/Amortization	$ 252.5	$ 1,058.0	$ 1,312.2	$ 1,512.2	$ 1,662.3
Decrease (Increase) in:					
Accounts Receivable	$ 4,251.1	$ (493.6)	$ (1,504.9)	$ (1,703.9)	$(1,786.6)
Inventory	$(3,907.3)	$(1,266.4)	$ (3,683.4)	$ (3,916.8)	$(4,300.9)
Other Notes Receivable	$ —	$ 0.1	$ —	$ —	$ —
Other Current Assets	$ (154.0)	$ 37.3	$ (49.7)	$ (49.7)	$ (46.8)
Increase (Decrease) in:					
Accounts Payable	$ 2,518.1	$ 830.0	$ 1,479.0	$ 1,665.5	$ 1,764.4
Accrued Liabilities	$ 37.3	$ 378.3	$ 308.2	$ 347.2	$ 367.4
Change in Working Capital	$ 2,745.2	$ (514.2)	$ (3,450.9)	$ (3,657.7)	$(4,002.4)
Cash From Operations	$ 3,164.4	$ 3,191.2	$ 2,275.4	$ 4,658.4	$ 6,938.5
Capital Expenditures	$ (335.4)	$(1,588.1)	$ (1,430.0)	$ (1,567.6)	$(1,666.3)
Decrease (Increase) in Other Assets	$ —	$ —	$ —	$ —	$ —
Cash From Investing	$ (335.4)	$(1,588.1)	$ (1,430.0)	$ (1,567.6)$	$(1,666.3)
Dividends	$ —	$ —	$ —	$ —	$ —
Increase (Decrease) in:					
Revolver	$(2,829.5)	$(1,603.1)	$ (845.4)	$ (2,924.8)	$ —
Preferred Stock	$ —	$ —	$ —	$ —	$ —
Common Stock	$ —	$ —	$ —	$ —	$ —
Cash From Financing	$(2,829.5)	$(1,603.1)	$ (845.4)	$ (2,924.8)	$ —
Excess Cash at Beginning	—	—	—	—	166
Cash Generated (Used)	(0)	(0)	(0)	166	5,272
Excess Cash at Ending	(0)	(0)	(0)	166	5,438

Case 15

TECH.com

I. EXECUTIVE SUMMARY

Company Overview

Annual worldwide retailing revenues on the Internet are projected to grow from $1.8 billion in 1997 to $35.3 billion in 2002 (eStats, 1998). TECH.com (or the "Company"), a market leader in providing merchant accounts and facilitating end-to-end transaction processing services to small and medium size on-line businesses, is well-positioned to capitalize upon this compelling growth opportunity.

This industry segment typically requires a more hands on customer service orientation; is less price sensitive, allowing for more attractive margins; and has largely been ignored by other market participants (i.e., conventional banks and other credit card processors) that lack the infrastructure and operational capabilities which TECH.com possesses, and which enables it to service this market segment in a low cost and efficient manner.

TECH.com has attained its existing position of market leadership by providing its customers with a superior end-to-end solution compared to that offered by competitors—one that features a bundled merchant account number, quick turnaround, a high approval rate, customer-friendly sign-up procedures, and easy-to-implement and secure on-line processing capabilities which can have a new merchant accepting credit card and electronic check payments via the Internet within 5 days of submitting an application.

Since inception in 1989, TECH.com has grown to be one of the largest independently owned providers in the country focusing on small and medium size on-line merchants (as well as home-based businesses, new merchants, business owners with credit problems, and high risk or non-conventional businesses that banks or other credit card processors won't service), as measured by the number of new merchant accounts, (i.e., customers with sales between $100,000 and $10,000,000 per annum).

It currently has over 14,000 active customers, which are served by over 200 affiliated employees in 12 offices nationwide. TECH.com presently processes over 1,500 new on-line merchant accounts each month, a number that is expected to grow to 4,250 by 2003.

TECH.com had revenues and EBITDA of $20.3 million and $4.4 million, respectively, for the last twelve months ended December 31, 1998. The Company projects revenues and EBITDA of $31.8 million and $7.6 million in 1999, respectively, increasing to $92.4 million and $34.4 million, respectively, in 2003.

This rapid growth is attributable to a number of key strengths which TECH.com possesses including its sales and marketing prowess, the superiority of its end-to-end solution, and its specialized concentration and expertise in providing quick and easy setup of merchant accounts for on-line merchants.

TECH.com differentiates itself in the marketplace in several ways. First, it offers its customers a user-friendly application and set-up process backed by responsive customer service. A new merchant processing account can be setup within 5 days, compared to 15 to 45 days for most banks. Representatives are on call 24 hours a day, 7 days a week to handle customer inquiries regarding their merchant accounts.

Second, TECH.com offers a complete bundled solution by providing merchants with all three of the critical elements of an e-commerce solution: a) merchant account number, b) payment processing software for Internet or retail store front, and c) a secure server link for web transactions. Most of its competitors do not provide a merchant number.

Finally, and consistent with acceptable credit risk parameters, TECH.com affords a 95 percent application to approval rate, compared to 60 to 70 percent by most banks. This high approval rate is the result of the Company's select banking and underwriting relationships, and capital commitments from companies that have reliable access to securitization markets.

Market Opportunity

The buying and selling of merchandise (both consumer and business-to-business) over the Internet is projected to be one of the fastest growing market segments in the world. Annual number of purchases and revenue are expected to grow by 2002 to 128 million and $35.3 billion, respectively.

A recent study conducted by Keenan Vision (March 1999), estimates that there are now 5,000,000 small, 10,000 medium to large, and 1,000 global businesses in the United States. With the growing clout of the Internet, many of these small businesses now feel that a web presence is no longer a luxury but a vital necessity for their survival.

According to International Data Corporation, in 1998 44% of small businesses with less that than 100 employees had access to the Internet. This number is expected to grow by 2001 to 54%, or over 4 million businesses. In addition, the small business market accounts for 98% of all U.S. companies and 34% of all sales. Small firms spent $39 billion on technology in 1998, with expenditures projected to more than double to $87 billion by 2002.

Based on surveys of major Internet merchant service providers, it is estimated that between 20,000 and 30,000 Internet merchants (defined as "companies who have a merchant account linked to a web site") were able to collect payments via the Internet in January 1999. By 2003, the number of U.S. Internet merchants is expected to explode to 400,000, representing a CAGR of 75%. Additionally, the need by traditional merchants to reduce costs, expand marketing reach through strategic alliances, and exploit lower cost distribution channels is also expected to accelerate the growth of the market TECH.com addresses. Such large e-commerce infrastructure companies as Microsoft, IBM, and AOL have readjusted their business strategies to capitalize on the compelling market opportunity that this segment affords.

TECH.com's core strengths, including its track record of profitability, industry leadership, marketing prowess, brand name recognition, and organizational and infrastructure capabilities well position it to capitalize upon this fast growing market opportunity.

Transaction Summary

In order to enable it to better address and capitalize on its future growth opportunities, the Company is currently seeking a strategic acquiror or financial recapitalization. As part of a successful transaction, the Company's Management team has agreed to remain in its current capacity on a negotiated basis.

Financial Summary

For the twelve months ending December 31, 1998, the Company generated revenues of $20.3 million and EBITDA of $4.4 million. The following Table sets forth the consolidated operating results of the Company for the 1998 fiscal year.

TECH.com	
Statement or Income, Fiscal Year Ending December 31,1998 (in thousands)	
Net Revenue	$20,387
COGS	8,158
Gross Profit	12,229
Expenses	7,867
Income Before Taxes	$4,362
EBITDA	**$4,420**
EBITDA % of Sales	21.7%

The following Table summarizes the Company's projected operations for the five-year period, 1999 to 2003.

TECH.com					
Projected Statement of Income, Fiscal Year Ending December 31 (in thousands)					
	1999	**2000**	**2001**	**2002**	**2003**
Revenues	$28,941	$42,156	$49,778	$62,223	$74,667
COGS	17,924	24,479	28,614	35,493	42,365
Gross Profit	11,017	17,678	21,165	26,730	32,302
Residual Income	2,846	6,387	9,826	13,419	17,700
Operating Expenses	6,430	8,645	10,855	13,482	16,102
Operating Income	7,433	15,420	20,136	26,667	33,900
Depreciation	(170)	(297)	(340)	(398)	(466)
Other Income	404	594	1,180	1,625	2,303
Income Before Taxes	$7,667	$15,717	$20,976	$27,894	$35,737
EBITDA	**$7,603**	**$15,717**	**$20,476**	**$27,065**	**$34,366**
EBITDA % of Sales	26.3%	37.3%	41.1%	43.5%	46.0%

TECH.com	
Revenue & EBITDA Growth ($ in thousands)	

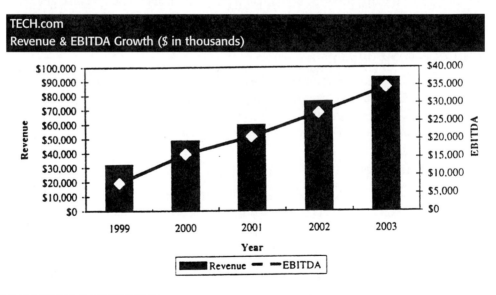

II. INDUSTRY OVERVIEW

The growth of e-Commerce is expected to create opportunities which have been compared to those of the California Gold Rush of 150 years ago. With an estimated 20,000 to 30,000 e-merchants on-line right now—and over five million off-line merchants in the U.S. who currently use credit cards to process e-commerce payments—there will be significant competition from merchants to "mine" or capture market share.

However, like the gold rush miners who needed the "picks, shovels and supplies," so today's e-commerce merchants will also require the necessary infrastructure to conduct business on-line. TECH.com provides a key required part of this infrastructure, i.e., end-to-end transaction processing services for small and medium size businesses, bundled with a merchant number, which features customer-friendly sign-up and ease of use capabilities.

The following Figure illustrates what has been termed the "E-merchant stack," which represents those services that will be required for selling on the Internet.

Yahoo	Sales & Marketing	Excite
UPS	Distribution	FedEx
Microsoft	User Interface	PalmPilot
Mercantec	E-Commerce Apps	Open Market
IBM	Intermediary Software	WebMethods
Microsoft	Application Servers	Sun Microsystems
Visa	The New Money	American Express
MCI Worldcom	The Internet	

Source: Keenan Vision

TECH.com's business model is targeted to that element which has been termed "The New Money," which addresses the flow of money back and forth between buyers and sellers. E-merchants need a bank account and services to accept and offer payment for goods and services purchased over the Internet. The E-merchant needs to create a merchant account, process credit cards, and gain financial leverage to buy goods on credit.

Both banks and a newer generation of payment processors are expected to play key roles addressing these needs. As the total amount of commerce that represents e-Commerce approaches $100 billion, the market that TECH.com addresses will provide significant growth opportunities.

For example, financial services companies will need to offer complete solutions to their e-merchant customers, not just accounts and money services. The e-Commerce solutions TECH.com provides will be required to do business under this new paradigm.

Market Segmentation

The e-Commerce market in the U.S. can be broken down into three segments: global enterprises, large companies, and small to medium size merchants.

Global enterprises are generally very large multinational corporations that are listed in the Global 1000, with annual sales over $3 billion. The middle tier represents large enterprises, with annual revenues ranging from $10 million to $3 billion. Most of these companies are service, distribution, manufacturing, mining and agricultural firms that distribute or offer their goods or services through established wholesale or retail sales channels. Although many of these companies participate in EDI and older forms of electronic commerce, very few traditionally have been active in e-Commerce.

The market segment of Small to Medium Merchants, includes businesses having annual revenues from $100,000 to $10 million, contains the largest number of companies with the fastest growth rates. In terms of new business formation, this market segment is also forecasted to have the highest rate of growth. This is the market segment TECH.com addresses.

Using information from the U.S. Census and Dunn & Bradstreet, Keenan Vision estimates that, as of January 1999, there are approximately 5 million businesses in the U.S. that fall into the Small and Medium Merchant segment. Based on a survey of major Internet merchant service providers and data from the Company, it is estimated that between 20,000 and 30,000 Internet merchants were able to collect payments via the Internet. This population is defined as "companies who have merchant accounts linked to a web site." By 2003, this number is expected to grow to 400,000 Internet merchants representing a 75% CAGR.

The E-merchant customer, particularly in the Small to Medium size business segment, has specialized requirements for transaction processing solutions and services. Technology that facilitates e-Commerce, employed by both the merchants and its customers, must to be easy to use, easy to modify, flexible and scalable. Customers will require solutions that provide:

1. Easy setup and credit card accounts
2. Low cost
3. Ready access to merchant numbers
4. Superior customer service and support

Through its "high-touch" (i.e., consultative selling approach) integrated product and service offerings, TECH.com provides the best solutions to address these customer requirements that exist on the market today.

Credit Card Market Size and Trends

Credit card transactions employed as part of the traditional "brick and mortar" retail market will also be an important part of the growth of e-Commerce. As a greater percentage of the population utilizes electronic payment methods, the growth of on-line electronic payment processing will expand. These growth trends and drivers can be expected to favorably impact TECH.com's business in the future.

Because of its obvious advantages, electronic means of payment are growing at ever-higher levels. During the past 10 years, the growth rate of global charge volume within the credit card industry has grown at a 26% annual growth rate over the most recent ten-year period. Credit card purchase volume has been expanding at a rate of about 15% a year for the last five years, about three times faster than the increase in overall U.S. purchases. Debit card purchases are accelerating even faster at over 50% per year. Despite these high rates of growth, the two payment methods together only make up about 20% of overall personal consumption expenditures in the U.S., leaving significant growth potential still remaining. According to a recent Nilson Report, credit and debit cards are expected to account for 33% of all purchases by 2000, and 43% by the year 2005.

These trends have been reinforced by changing attitudes about credit purchases. Due to aggressive marketing, incentive award, co-branding, and affinity programs over recent years, the average U.S. cardholder now holds roughly four bankcards. These programs have helped to change the way consumers think about paying with credit. Many consumers now view their credit cards as much more than a payment method and see them as lifestyle enhancers that can contribute to other areas of interest in their life.

Acceptance, and even promotion of electronic payment is occurring many places where credit card acceptance would have been low just a few years ago. A recent survey has found that 600,000 more merchants are now accepting credit cards compared to five years ago. (American Banker's Association Survey)

Additional factors driving the high growth and utilization rate of credit cards by customers and retailers include:

- *Increased Sales Revenues:* TECH.com's experience has been that credit card customers buy 2.5 times more merchandise than customers who pay cash. For Internet sales, credit card payment facilities can increase sales by 1500%.

- *Impulse Buying:* Credit cards give customers freedom to spend for previously unplanned merchandise.

- *Move Expensive Merchandise:* Credit card customers are often less conscious of slight price differences, and will seek out the business that offers credit rather than the discount or wholesale vendor who does not extend credit.

- *Enhanced Advertising:* Since customers are more likely to shop at businesses where they have credit acceptance, they tend to look for and read these store ads first.

- *Larger Volume:* Offering credit cards helps merchants achieve higher unit sales and extra orders.

- *Consistent Sales:* Credit smoothes out business peaks. Cash shoppers buy heavier only on paydays and just before holidays; credit customers buy whenever the need arises.
- *Customer Loyalty:* Research shows customers who spend on credit tend to return to the same business where they spent before.

e-Commerce: Market Size and Growth Rates

Global e-Commerce revenues are forecasted to reach $3.2 trillion in 2003 while U.S. based business trade on the Internet is projected to explode from $51 billion in 1998 to $1.4 trillion in 2003, an annual growth rate of 93% (Forrester Research, 1998). Of the $1.439 trillion of e-Commerce revenues projected in 2003, $1.331 trillion will be business-to-business and $108 billion will be business-to-consumer related commerce. In 1998 the number of on-line global users was estimated at 112 million (Hong Kong Standard, 1998), with 65% of all current on-line users making Net purchases (Greenfield On-line, 1998).

e-Commerce is now reaching a critical mass threshold where early adopters are being replaced with widespread industry acceptance and utilization. This has been made possible by the maturation of enabling infrastructure required to conduct e-Commerce. Mainstream commercial providers of systems and software like IBM, HP, SUN and Microsoft have entered the market with technology that supports advanced on-line market models such as auctions, exchanges and web malls.

Competition and Differentiation

Although there are no other companies that have the exact business model or compete in the exact space as TECH.com, the following list summarizes, in order of most relevant, those companies, which TECH.com considers its closest direct competition.

Total Merchant Services (**www.totalmerchantservices.com**)—Establishes payment solutions for virtual storefronts with secure payment processing services that include credit card and check processing on the web. Averages approximately 500 new accounts per month.

Electronic Clearing House, Inc (ECHO) (**www.echo-inc.com**)—provides credit card processing, check guarantee, inventory tracking services and various other services to over 19,000 retail merchants across the nation.

Cardservice International (CSI) (**www.cardservice.com**)—A division of First Data Corporation providing a complete range of traditional and Internet consumer payment options to small to middle sized business merchants. Services include credit and ATM/debit processing, check guarantee services, purchasing card programs and Internet capabilities. CSI has a cus-

Global Versus U.S. e-Commerce

(in billions)	1998	1999	2000	2001	2002	2003
Global	$80	$170	$390	$970	$2,000	$3,200
U.S. Business to Business	43	109	251	499	843	1,331
U.S. Business to Consumer	8	18	33	52	76	108
U.S. Total	$51	$127	$284	$551	$919	$1,439

Source: Forrester Research.

tomer base of over 150,000 merchants, processing an annual bankcard volume in excess of $6 billion.

CyberCash (**www.cybercash.com**)—Offers secure payment transaction services that encrypt credit card information. Other offerings include electronic cash payment software (CyberCoin) and electronic billing and payment software (PayNow). The company's ICVerify subsidiary provides retailers with point-of-sale credit card authorization software. CyberCash currently averages 700 new accounts per month.

CyberSource (**www.cybersource.com**)—A global provider of Internet Commerce Services that enable the secure sale, distribution and fulfillment of products and services via the Internet, including digital products, hard and soft goods, pay-per-use and subscription services. Services include enabling secure, reliable, real time multi-currency payment processing in local currencies worldwide.

iMall.com and stuff.com (**www.imall.com**)—Provider of fully integrated, "one-stop" e-commerce solutions. iMall's e-commerce tools and services allow businesses to create Web sites or use existing ones, establish accounts

The e-Commerce Threshold

Source: Forrester Research.

on-line, deliver shopping services to customers, drive traffic to their businesses and process customer orders. Unlike TECH.com, iMall.com outsources its payment gateway. Web sites receive more than 40 million hits and millions of shoppers each month. Recent strategic partnership with First Data Merchant Services Corporation a wholly owned subsidiary of First Data Corporation.

iBill (**www.iBill.com**)—Provides payment processing technology services worldwide. Provider of transaction processing and services that enable Web merchants to accept and process real-time payment for goods and services purchased over the Internet, and manage back-office functions associated with the transactions through iBill Commerce Management Interfaces. iBill has delivered commerce capabilities to more than 16,000 Web sites worldwide.

PaymentNet (**www.paymentnet.com**)—Provides e-Commerce transaction processing services on an outsourced basis to an estimated 300 businesses. Company does not issue a merchant number to its customers. Focuses on large customers such as Virtual Vineyards and Value America.

Billpoint (**www.billpoint.com**)—Facilitates person-to-person credit card payment over the Internet by addressing the payment needs of on-line trading communities such as auctions, classifieds and community sites. Billpoint's services include payment processing, shipment tracking, fraud protection, and business reporting.

Differentiation

TECH.com differentiates itself in the marketplace in several ways. First, it offers its customers a user-friendly application and easy set-up process backed by responsive customer service. A new merchant processing account can be setup within 5 days, compared to 15 to 45 days for most banks. Most banks are focused on servicing large traditional brick-and-mortar-based merchants and are not structured to efficiently process and service the smaller, Internet-based business accounts.

In contrast, TECH.com account representatives are on call 24 hours a day, 7 days a week to handle customer inquiries regarding their merchant accounts. One of the key factors to the Company's success has been its emphasis on educating potential merchants on all aspects of accepting non-cash payments. The Company has always maintained a "high-touch" approach to the sales process, where it figuratively takes the prospective new merchant by the hand and leads him or her through all the steps necessary to begin accepting non-cash transactions. The Company's current tagline, "Make E-Commerce Easy!" is an extension of its ongoing attention and commitment to its customers of delivering a professional and seamless merchant processing service. TECH.com's "high-touch" customer approach has enabled it to build a customer centric reputation, to differentiate its services and products, and to avoid price erosion, even as the marketplace has become more competitive. This "high-touch" approach to sales and service will continue to be a cornerstone of the Company's core culture and business strategy.

Second, TECH.com offers a complete bundled solution by providing merchants with all three of the critical elements of an e-Commerce solution a) merchant account number, b) payment processing software for Internet or retail store front, and c) a secure gateway for web transactions, compared to most of its competitors who do not provide a merchant account number. Traditional banks and institutions impose onerous credit restrictions on new merchants, will issue merchant accounts only to businesses with lengthy credit histories, and will require large security deposits for new merchants.

Finally, and consistent with acceptable credit risk parameters, TECH.com affords a 95 percent application to approval rate, compared to 60 to 70 percent by most banks. This high approval rate is the result of the Company's select banking and underwriting relationships, and capital commitments from companies that have reliable access to securitization markets.

III. THE COMPANY

Customer Segmentation

TECH.com targets primarily small and medium size Internet businesses, (as well as home-based businesses, new merchants, business owners with credit problems, and high risk or non-conventional businesses that banks or other credit card processors won't service) with annual revenues between $100,000 and $10,000,000. Approximately 60% of TECH.com's customers' businesses have A, B, or C credit ratings with the remaining 40% having D or E ratings. The Company believes that this small business segment has been under-serviced by traditional financial services companies, thereby affording a significant growth opportunity. This conclusion has also been reached by various independent sources such as Forrester Research, IDC and Cyber Dialogue.

For example, according to IDC, there are 38 million small-office, home-offices (SOHO) in the U.S., 70 percent of which have PC's. By 2002, there will be 50 million home offices, 38 million of which will have PC's. Another study by IDC indicates that SOHO's now account for 68 percent of U.S. households currently on the Internet. Over 19 million SOHO's have computers on the Internet: by 2002, this will grow to 30.2 million users, and spending on ISP services will increase from $6.5 billion to $10.5 billion a year.

Core Competencies and Strengths

- A single source supplier for all non-cash transactions Visa, MasterCard, American Express, Discover, ATM, Checks By Phone and Diners Club International with a 95% approval rate.

- A demonstrated ability to efficiently prospect and convert leads in the new and small business market niche, into profitable sales for the Company and its partners who comprise the entire value chain.

- A low cost and exceptional fulfillment operation that accurately tracks, processes, and compensates its Affiliate's referrals. TECH.com's infrastructure is also one of the largest in-house merchant account processing centers in the industry, rapidly scalable with increased volume.

- Considered to be one of the most effective sales and marketing organizations in the industry. With its CD-ROM inserts, telesales, seminar, display advertisements, television advertisements, TECH.com is a trendsetter in this industry.

- Key marketing and partner relationships that drive sales, reduce costs, and provide operational efficiencies.

- Strong brand name equity.

Products and Services

The major features and benefits that TECH.com provides are summarized below:

- ✓ A single source for equipment, service and support;
- ✓ Access to funds within 24 to 48 hours;
- ✓ SSL security protocol;
- ✓ Toll free 24 x 7 hour customer service, including holidays;
- ✓ Free temporary replacement of equipment within 24 hours;
- ✓ Reporting capabilities accessible via the Internet;
- ✓ Monthly merchant statements, and
- ✓ Purchase or lease plans at competitive rates.

Key components include:

1. Credit card processing merchant accounts
2. Internet-based credit card and check processing software (*QuickComm*)
3. Internet-based shopping cart programs (*Cartmanager*)
4. Computer-based credit card processing software (*PC or Mac*)
5. Credit card processing hardware (*terminals, printers, PIN pads*)

Credit Card Processing Merchant Accounts

A merchant account is a commercial bank account established by contractual agreement between a business and a sponsoring bank. A merchant account enables a business to accept credit card payments from its customers. Nearly all of TECH.com's customers receive a merchant account, the only exception being if the merchant wants to process electronic checks only, and not credit cards, or if the merchant already has a merchant account which is compatible with TECH.com's hardware or software.

TECH.com is a registered Independent Service Organization (ISO) and Merchant Service Provider (MSP) of both ABC Bank, Eureka, California and Third Bank of Beverly Hills, Calabasas, California. ISO and MSP are Visa's and Mastercard's terminology respectively, for a non-bank provider of credit card processing services. In order for an independent, non-bank company such as TECH.com, to offer merchant credit card services it must first register with a Visa/Mastercard Member Bank and submit an application for ISO/MSP status through that bank to the Visa/Mastercard card associations. There is an initial $10,000 and yearly $5,000 fee required in order to obtain and maintain an ISO/MSP status.

Internet-Based Credit Card and Check Processing Software

QuickComm is a versatile and easy-to-implement Internet-based secure payment gateway which enables merchants to either manually enter credit card and check transactions via the Virtual Terminal feature or link to their website order page through the WebLink so customers can submit their own orders automatically for processing. Approximately 70% of the Company's customers elect to use Internet-based payment gateways.

QuickComm is used by many phone order/mail order merchants to submit transactions, whether or not they presently sell on the Internet, since it performs the same functions as *Merchant Master* software, but offers the advantages of always being current (all updates are done on the server side and are thus available immediately to all merchants), and of having the potential of linking to their website should they decide to sell products on-line in the future.

The *QuickComm* WebLink feature requires only 5 lines of HTML code and can be added to a website order form or shopping cart interface in order to integrate with the secure payment gateway. The *QuickComm* servers are connected to the credit card processing network via a leased line, which results in extremely fast transaction times of two to eight seconds (depending on Internet traffic) and unsurpassed reliability.

Shopping Carts

A shopping cart is a type of software that keeps track of a customer's on-line order, including item numbers, descriptions, prices, size, weight and other details, and produces an order total including tax and freight when the customer is ready to check out.

The shopping cart then passes the total dollar amount of the order to the secure payment gateway for payment processing.

At present, Internet shopping carts account for a small portion of the Company's sales, since many of the Internet-based merchants are referred by web designers or hosting companies which offer shopping carts. For those merchants in need of only a shopping cart, the Company's *Cartmanager,* which is a cost-effective and simple to implement software that easily integrates with the *QuickComm* product, is the best solution.

Credit Card Processing Software

Non-storefront merchants that have a personal computer but do not have access to the Internet are offered either *Merchant Master* (for IBM-compatible) or *MacAuthorize* (for Macintosh) software. These products are designed for mail and phone order businesses that need credit card processing. They feature a simplified and automated method of credit card processing. Approximately 15% of the Company's customers elect to use credit card processing software.

Both of these software packages enable merchants to process all credit card transactions either singly or in batches of multiple transactions.

While *MacAuthorize* is an off-the-shelf product available to any of the Company's competitors, *Merchant Master* is a private-labeled product developed for TECH.com by a local software company called Domain Entertainment.

TECH.com chose *Merchant Master* as its primary software product because it is extremely easy to install and very user-friendly, which makes it perfect for the Company's small business/home-based business clients.

Credit Card Processing Hardware

TECH.com terminals and printers provide a cost-effective solution for traditional retail businesses that need a fast, easy way to authorize and manage credit card transactions. Merchants that utilize credit card processing hardware fall into two categories: 1) retail storefront, or other face-to-face merchants, and 2) home-based or mail order merchants who do not have a personal computer or access to the Internet. Approximately 15% of the Company's customers elect to use credit card processing hardware.

For retail storefront merchants, the Company provides a terminal/printer combination unit *(Nurit 2085)* or separate terminal and printer *(Nurit 2080 terminal* and *Nurit 505* printer) plus a PIN (Personal Identification Number) pad *(Verifone PIN Pad 1000)*. The terminal enables the merchant to swipe-read the credit card and enter the transaction amount. It then dials out to the credit card network for authorization and prints out the transaction receipt. The PIN pad is required for ATM/debit card transactions.

For home-based or mail order merchants that do not have a personal computer or access to the Internet, TECH.com provides the *(Nurit 2085)* terminal/printer combo or *(Nurit 2080)* terminal only. Both products enable the merchant to manually enter the credit card number, expiration date and sale amount, as well as address information for Address Verification Service (AVS), which checks the billing address provided by the customer against the issuing bank's records. AVS provides an important security feature and means of preventing losses due to fraudulent transactions. PIN pads cannot be used in non-face-to-face transactions, such as mail order and most home-based businesses.

Customer Support and Technical Services

Proactive, responsive and user-friendly customer support and technical services are important strengths of TECH.com. In addition to the 24 x 7 merchant bank support through Cards.com, the Company offers the following levels of technical support to its customers.

Level 1 (**support@TECH.com**) is designed to support basic questions and technical training aspects of the *QuickComm* product.

Level 2 (**premiumsupport@TECH.com**) is designed to support the linking of web site and shopping cart integration for the TECH.com merchants that require technical support beyond basic questions. TECH.com charges $75 per hour for premium service. This level of support requires HTML knowledge as well as CGI and Java experience.

Securitization of Leases

TECH.com provides the option to its customers of either purchasing or leasing its merchant processing software and/or hardware. Given the cash constraints of many new start-ups and an average lease payment of only $50 per month, over 95% of all TECH.com customers select the lease payment plan over purchasing. The average face value of each lease contract is $2,400 with a term of 48 months.

The following illustrates the parties involved in acquiring a new customer, processing the merchant application, securitization of the leases provision of a secure payment gateway, and issuance of a merchant account.

e-Commerce Exchange Value Chain

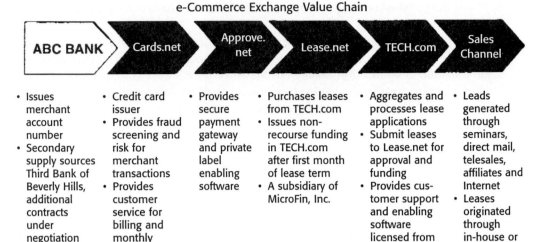

ABC BANK	Cards.net	Approve.net	Lease.net	TECH.com	Sales Channel
• Issues merchant account number • Secondary supply sources Third Bank of Beverly Hills, additional contracts under negotiation	• Credit card issuer • Provides fraud screening and risk for merchant transactions • Provides customer service for billing and monthly statement	• Provides secure payment gateway and private label enabling software	• Purchases leases from TECH.com • Issues non-recourse funding in TECH.com after first month of lease term • A subsidiary of MicroFin, Inc.	• Aggregates and processes lease applications • Submit leases to Lease.net for approval and funding • Provides customer support and enabling software licensed from Approve.net	• Leads generated through seminars, direct mail, telesales, affiliates and Internet • Leases originated through in-house or sub-agent channel

Lease.net—purchases the leases from TECH.com at a pre-negotiated price based upon the credit rating of each applicant's business. There are two credit categories—A,B,C, and D,E. Upon receipt of the merchant's first monthly payment, Lease.net accepts all credit risk for the lease and then securitizes them in the public markets. TECH.com has a seven-year relationship with Lease.net and is considered their number one vendor.

Lease.net is a subsidiary of MicroFin, Inc., headquartered in Waltham, Massachusetts, and with additional locations in Woburn, Massachusetts and Newark, California is a financial intermediary specializing in financing for products in the $500 to $10,000 range. The company has been in operation since 1986 and has been profitable since the second quarter of 1987. Through its operating subsidiary, Lease.net, MFI has provided funding for about 300,000, mostly commercial, accounts nationwide.

Cards.net—("C.net") located in Los Angeles, California provides TECH.com customers with the merchant number and is responsible for the backend loss prevention by monitoring merchant accounts for fraudulent transactions. In addition, inquiries from merchants concerning billing and monthly statements are handled by C.net on behalf of TECH.com.

Approve.net—provides the secure Internet payment gateway that enables TECH.com merchants to authorize, process and manage credit card and electronic check transactions in a real-time, on-line environment from any computer with an Internet connection and a Web browser. The Company currently enables commerce for more than 34,000 on-line merchants and was recently purchased by Go2Net.

ABC Bank—TECH.com is a registered ISO with ABC Bank, Eureka, California. ABC's only function is to provide the merchant numbers to C.net. Third Bank of Beverly Hills fulfills a similar function for TECH.com.

IV. FINANCIAL OVERVIEW

Historical Financial Statements

TECH.com Balance Sheet as of December 31, 1998	
Assets:	
Cash	$271,801
Due from Affiliates	1,314,523
Inventory	108,613
Current Assets	1,694,937
Fixed Assets, Net	457,657
Loans Receivable	196,152
Note Receivable	249,566
Financing Leases	933,396
Other Assets	793,783
Total Assets	**$4,325,491**
Liabilities & Stockholders' Equity	
Liabilities:	
Accrued Liabilities	303,837
Deferred Income	968,349
Shareholders' Equity:	
Beginning Retained Earnings	1,133,067
Current Income	4,559,295
Withdrawals/Income Tax	(2,639,057)
Ending Retained Earnings	3,053,305
Total Liabilities & Stockholders' Equity	**$4,325,491**

TECH.com Balance Sheet as of May 31, 1999	
Assets:	
Cash	$1,644,837
Due from Affiliates	383,133
Inventory	86,400
Current Assets	2,114,370
Fixed Assets, Net	507,983
Loans Receivable	127,562
Note Receivable	212,956
Financing Leases	1,150,641
Other Assets	812,738
Total Assets	**$4,926,250**
Liabilities & Stockholders' Equity	
Liabilities:	
Accrued Liabilities	103,694
Deferred Income	926,008
Shareholders' Equity:	
Beginning Retained Earnings	3,053,305
Current Income	2,515,022
Withdrawals/Income Tax	(1,671,779)
Ending Retained Earnings	3,896,548
Total Liabilities & Stockholders' Equity	**$4,926,250**

Balance Sheet at December 31, 1998 and May 31, 1999

1. **Cash and Cash Equivalents**—Represents cash and money market funds.

2. **Due from Affiliates**—Amounts due from companies wholly owned by [the Founder's Family] sic. and will be repaid before December 31,1999. $145,000 was repaid in June 1999.

3. **Inventory**—Stated at cost, inventory turns averaged 22 times per year in 1998 and is projected at 15 times per year in 1999 through 2003.

4. **Fixed Assets**—Includes $418,000 in capitalized equipment net of depreciation related financing leases held for investment at December 31, 1998 and May 31, 1999, respectively. This classification is subject to finalization of the accounting treatment for leases, and adjustments thereto, by the Company's independent auditors. The balance of $39,657 and $89,983 at December 31, 1998 and May 31, 1999 represents the net book value of office furniture and computer equipment.

5. **Loan Receivable**—Amounts due from employees and others. These loans are considered fully collectible and projected to be repaid during 1999.

6. **Note Receivable**—12% per annum, interest and principal paid monthly plus 50% profits interest in monthly receipts, after expenses, secured $903,000 in financing leases of which approximately 80% are current.

7. **Financing Leases**—Leases held for investment valued at market rates, net of an allowance of $101,202 at May 31, 1999 with an approximate interest rate to the company of 15% and an initial average lease term of 48 months.

8. **Other Assets**—Includes deposits of $75,000 and $133,793 at December 31, 1998 and May 31, 1999, respectively; deferred assets of $510,972 and deferred servicing expense of $165,470 at December 31, 1998 and May 31, 1999 related to the financing leases held for investment and projected future servicing costs. The classification of deferred assets and expense is subject to determination of the proper accounting treatment for accounting for leases and adjustment by our independent auditors.

9. **Accrued Liabilities**—Normal accruals accounting for differences in accounting periods.

10. **Deferred Income**—Represents the future principle payments on the Note receivable and future interest payments on financing leases that are recognized as income when received.

TECH.com Income Statement for the Year Ending December 31, 1998	
Revenues:	
Sales of Leases and Products	$19,977,231
Residual Income	409,709
Other Income	196,682
Net Revenues	20,583,622
Cost of Goods Sold	8,158,051
Gross Margin	12,425,571
Expenses:	
Advertising	267,612
Bad Debt Expense	296,100
Car and Truck	68,832
Data Base Programming	18,175
Depreciation	58,000
Entertainment	27,343
Insurance	113,138
Legal & Professional	65,145
New York Office	203,853
Office General	675,504
Postage	37,308
Promotion	31,091
Printing	271,175
Rent	133,375
Service Fee Expense	19,293
Super G Computer Expense	121,719
Taxes	21,205
Temporary Help	26,681
Telephone	294,455
Travel	379,440
Web Page Development	12,300
Wages	4,725,531
Total Expenses	7,867,275
Net Income Before Taxes	$4,558,296
EBITDA	**$4,419,614**

Projected Statement of Income

TECH.com Statement of Income for the Period Ending December 31					
	1999	**2000**	**2001**	**2002**	**2003**
Revenues:					
Lease Sales	$28,940,737	$42,156,381	$49,778,151	$62,222,688	$74,667,226
Cost of Goods Sold	17,924,028	24,478,539	28,613,625	35,492,600	42,365,063
Gross Profit	11,016,709	17,677,842	21,164,526	26,730,088	32,302,164
Residual Income	2,846,346	6,387,256	9,826,080	13,419,139	17,700,014
Net Revenues	13,863,056	24,065,098	30,990,605	40,149,227	50,002,178
Operating Expenses	6,430,413	8,645,415	10,854,688	13,482,148	16,101,985
Operating Income (Excluding Depreciation)	7,432,643	15,419,683	20,135,917	26,667,079	33,900,193
Depreciation Expense	(170,039)	(296,904)	(340,178)	(397,634)	(465,725)
Other Income/Expense	404,286	594,242	1,179,845	1,625,007	2,303,011
Net Income Before Taxes	**$7,666,890**	**$15,717,021**	**$20,975,584**	**$27,894,452**	**$35,737,479**
EBITDA	**$7,602,682**	**$15,716,587**	**$20,476,095**	**$27,064,713**	**$34,365,918**
EBITDA % of Sales	26.3%	37.3%	41.1%	43.5%	46.0%

Assumptions to Financial Projections

1. **Leases Funded**

   Growth in the number of leases funded in the Company's forecast is based on the expected increase in the overall market size as forecasted by industry research organizations; the existing and expected expansion of various joint venture marketing programs, and advertising campaigns; and on the Company's actual historical growth rates. Total year over year growth in leases funded is projected at 1999–43%, 2000–45%, 2001–18%, 2002–25%, and 2003–20%. As of July 1, 1999, the Company had approximately 14,000 active merchant accounts.

2. **Unit Revenue Model**

   The following table illustrates the revenue streams for a single ABC and DE credit rated lease contract assuming a 55% and 45% weighted average respectively, and the associated cost of goods sold and cost of sales. All leases have a face value of $2,400 and a term of 48 months.

Revenues:	ABC	DE	Wtd. Ave.
Gross lease value	$2,400	$2,400	$2,400
Discount to Lease.net	720	1350	1004
Gross lease proceeds (47 months)	1680	1050	1397
First month payment	50	50	50
Total cash proceeds	1730	1100	1447
Cost of Goods Sold:			
Wtd. Ave. software and hardware	85	85	85
Merchant application fee to C.net	25	25	25
Other (shipping and handling)	57	57	57
Total Cost of Goods Sold	167	167	167
Cost of Sales:			
Ave Internal Commissions/Overrides	509	363	443
Net Income (before G&A)	1054	571	836
G&A (1999)	328	328	328
Net Income Per Lease (before residual)	**$726**	**$242**	**$508**

Residual Income:	Monthly	Annual	
Approve.net Corporation	$5.0	$60	
C.net	18.0	216	
Gross residual income	23.0	276	
Payments to agents	4.0	48	
Net residual income per lease	$19	$228	**$228**
Total Proceeds Per Average Lease Contract Plus Residual Income for Year 1			**$736**

3. **Lease Revenues**

Proceeds from lease sales to Lease.net are calculated using an average 3.2% and 5.0% lease factor (the factor used to determine the present value of a lease contract), plus a 10.70% and 10.10% head office spread factor minus the first months lease payment of $50.00 for ABC and DE leases respectively. For example, the calculation for an ABC rated lease is $((50/.032)*(1.1070)-50.00)) = \$1,680.00$. All leases are sold to Lease.net without recourse to TECH.com after the second payment is received from the merchant. TECH.com estimates that 3% of total sales are paid in cash in the amount of $1,500 per sale.

4. **Residual Income**

Residual income is calculated based upon current contract rates and profit splits from Approve.net and Cards.net (C.net). The Company receives $5.00 of the $10.00 monthly payment gateway fee from Approve.net. Payment of the gateway fee by a merchant provides access to the Approve.net transaction server. The Company shares computed earnings with C.net based on a formula that includes a split of bank statement fees, minimum account fees for non-processing merchants, and a percentage of total dollars processed by merchants. An amount equal of residual income to $18.00 per month per lease (an amount consistent with historical experience) is assumed in the 5-year projections. Total gross residual income is therefore $23.00 per lease per month. The Company pays, on average, $4.00 of the gross residual income to its sales agents as a trailing commission. The net residual income is therefore $19.00 per active merchant per month.

5. **Merchant Lease Base and Attrition Rates**
   The following table contains the assumptions for the forecasted Merchant Base and the related percentage of the merchants that will terminate their leases each year. Early termination of the lease contract (after the second payment is made) does not impact the Company's revenue from lease sales. However, residual income from C.net will not be received and is therefore reflected in the net residual income amounts in the financial projections utilizing the following annual attrition rates.

	Q1/99	Q2/99	Q3/99	Q4/99	1999	2000	2001	2002	2003
Current Active									
Merchant Base	*	8,688	11,996	15,858	8,688	19,305	36,047	50,147	67, 565
Leases Funded	*	4,486	5,440	5,525	15,451	28,900	34,000	42,500	51,000
Less: Lease Termination	*	(1,178)	(1,578)	2,078)	(4,834)	(12,158)	(19,900)	(25,082)	(30,866)
Ending Balance									
Merchant Base	**8,688**	**11,996**	**15,858**	**19,305**	**19,305**	**36,047**	**50,147**	**67,565**	**87,699**
Attrition Rates	12%	12%	12%	12%	48%	46%	43%	39%	36%

* Historical numbers are currently being reconciled. Merchant balances as of Q2/99 are actual amounts.

The Company estimates that attrition rates will decline over the next 4 years due to the introduction of its *click-sold.com* and *sellitonline.com* (Internet mall and resource center services and support) that it believes will contribute significantly to the success of its merchants.

6. **Other Income (Expense)**
   This includes depreciation expense not included in operating expenses, interest computed on cash balances using a 4% money market rate, interest at 15% on financing leases held as an investment, note receivable at 12% from Axim Financial—a third party loan servicing company, profit participation on specific leases collected by Axim, and interest at 10% on employee loans.

   The financial projections include only revenues from the Company's core business and do not reflect the potential ancillary revenue streams described in the Business and Growth Strategy sections of this Offering Memorandum. The Company can generate ancillary revenues or increase its margins by 1) Bringing its credit card processing in-house, 2) Internally funding its own leases or bypassing the third party financing company, and 3) Reduce its cost of goods sold by becoming a software reseller.

7. **Cost of Goods Sold**

The cost of goods sold for all products (printers, terminals, and software) during the five year projection period are assumed to remain constant at the current prices: terminal and printer—$315.00, software with manual—$50, QuickComm software—$42.50, shipping and handling—$52.00, and C.net application fee—$25.00.

The Company's product mix is projected to shift for software sales from 82% in Q2 1999 to 90% in 2001, based on the following quarterly schedule:

Product Type	Q2/99	Q3/99	Q4/99	Q1/00	Q2/00	Q3/00	Q4/00	2001–2003
Terminal and Printer	17.30%	15.00%	15.00%	14.00%	13.00%	12.00%	11.00%	10.00%
PC Software	12.00%	11.00%	10.00%	9.00%	9.00%	8.00%	7.00%	5.00%
QuickCommSoftware	70.70%	74.00%	75.00%	77.00%	78.00%	80.00%	82.00%	85.00%
Total	100.00%	100.00%	100.00%	100.00%	100.00%	100.00%	100.00%	100.00%

8. **Cost of Sales**

The Company uses multiple sales channels to generate both referrals and direct sales, and compensates each channel based on the credit rating (i.e., ABC or DE) of each lease contract. Referrals are leads that are provided to TECH.com by third parties other than agent offices. These referrals are then converted to closed sales by the TECH.com internal sales team. Accordingly, for referral leads, total cost of sales is calculated by including the referral fee for a funded lease, plus the commission payable to the internal sales agent.

Referrals originate from either seminars or through affiliates on the Internet. For the seminar channel, average referral fees for ABC and DE credit rated leases are $600 and $200, respectively, per lease. For the Internet channel, average referral fees are, respectively, $200 and $100 for ABC and DE credit rated leases.

Direct sales are generated and commissions paid through the following three channels; VIP—$350–ABC and $225–DE credit; Internet—$600–ABC and $300—DE credit; Agent offices—an average of $795 for all credit.

Referrals and sales from the Internet channel, as a percentage of total revenues are projected to increase from 8.5% in May 1999 to 45% in 2003, although they are projected to decrease from 22% in May 1999 to 5% in 2003, for the seminar channel. The following Table summarizes the projected changes in sales mix, over the five year projected period.

Sales Channel	1999	2000	2001	2002	2003

Seminar (in-house)	16.00%	13.00%	9.00%	8.00%	5.00%
Internet (in-house)	20.00%	28.00%	36.00%	39.00%	45.00%
Chicago Agent	30.00%	25.00%	20.00%	19.00%	15.00%
New York Agent	7.00%	7.00%	7.00%	7.00%	7.00%
Utah Agent	14.00%	15.00%	14.00%	14.00%	15.00%
All Other Agents	13.00%	12.00%	14.00%	13.00%	13.00%
Total	100.0%	100.0%	100.0%	100.0%	100.0%

9. **Operating Expenses**

Operating expenses as a percentage of sales are projected as follows: 1999–22.19%, 2000–20.46%, 2001–21.76%, 2002–21.62%, and 2003–21.52%.

Advertising expense—Projected to increase from 2.16% to 3.34% of sales in 1999 and 2003 respectively. Increases are consistent with the Company's branding and lead generation strategies.

Bad Debt expense—One time reserve of $60,000 in 1999 related to accounts purchased from C.net.

Database and Systems—Anticipated expenditures to replace TECH.com database, future upgrades, and new accounting and processing systems.

Entertainment—Includes a budget for the annual Christmas party.

Legal and Professional—Budget for legal and consulting for systems analysis or acquisitions.

New York Office—Agent office that is anticipated to be acquired by year-end 1999. In 1999 the company incorporated the income and expenses of this office as if it were a branch office.

Rent—Actual expenses incurred and future rents that reflect lease terms of the new facility.

Telecom System Lease—Anticipated annual costs of a system for the new facility.

Web Page—New department reflecting additional wages.

Wages—Based on budgeted costs and planned expansion of various departments.

Depreciation and Amortization expense—Computed based on an average useful life of 4 years using the straight-line method as illustrated in the table below.

	Q1/99	Q2/99	Q3/99	Q4/99	2000	2001	2002	2003
Beginning Balance	$457,657	$507,657	$557,657	$777,657	$877,657	$1,197,657	$1,617,657	$2,137,657
Tenant Improvements	0	0	50,000	0	20,000	20,000	20,000	20,000
Computers & Furniture	50,000	50,000	120,000	50,000	300,000	400,000	500,000	600,000
Other Purchases	0	0	50,000	50,000	0	0	0	0
Ending Balance	507,657	557,657	777,657	877,657	1,197,657	1,617,657	2,137,657	2,757,657
Depreciation Expense	31,729	34,854	48,604	54,854	296,904	340,178	397,634	465,725
Accumulated Depreciation	(31,729)	(66,582)	(115,186)	(170,039)	(466,944)	(807,122)	(1,204,756)	(1,670,481)
Fixed Assets Net	475,928	491,075	662,471	707,618	730,713	810,535	932,901	1,087,176

Case 16

From Hattiesburg to Wall Street:
The Story of WorldCom

The WorldCom story begins in August 1983 with the court ordered break-up of AT&T. The break-up opened the long distance market to meaningful competition for the first time. Four investors—Bernard J. Ebbers, Bill Fields, David Singleton and Murray Waldron—while talking in a coffee shop in Hattiesburg, Mississippi, decided to take advantage of this new market opportunity. In September 1983, they bought LDDS (Long Distance Discount Service).

In November 1983, LDDS received permission from the Mississippi Public Utilities Commission to operate as a long distance carrier. Murray Waldron was named president of LDDS and Bill Fields became chairman of the board. The board began having monthly meetings at a local restaurant. Its first line of business was reselling AT&T long distance services to small- and mid-size businesses. A reseller is a carrier that does not own a network. It leases bulk capacity from the owner of the network and then resells portions of that capacity at a higher rate.

In early 1984, LDDS sold its first minute of long distance to the University of Southern Mississippi. A year later, Bernard J. Ebbers became president of the company. Under Ebbers, LDDS would embark on a massive acquisition campaign. In August 1988, LDDS acquired Telephone Management Corp. The acquisition expanded LDDS' service throughout Mississippi and into Tennessee. In March 1989, LDDS

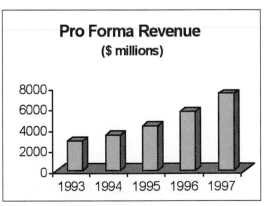

Pro Forma Revenue
(\$ millions)

Source: 1997 Annual Report.

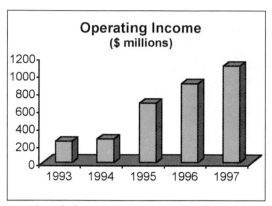

Operating Income
($ millions)

1996 figure before non-recurring one-time charges.

Source: 1997 Annual Report.

acquired ClayDesta Communications of Texas, followed by the acquisition of Micro-tel, Inc. in June and Galesi Telecommunications in November. The last acquisition expanded LDDS' service into Florida.

In 1991, LDDS acquired National Telecommunications of Austin, thereby expanding its service throughout the Southwest. LDDS also acquired Mid-America Communications Corp., expanding LDDS services throughout the Great Plains and from California to the Great Lakes. LDDS finished 1991 with an acquisition of BIZ-TEL Long Distance of Florida, which increased its presence throughout Florida.

LDDS began 1992 with the acquisition of AmeriCall and First Phone, expanding LDDS service to Kentucky and Massachusetts. Later in the year, LDDS acquired Prime Telecommunications, adding additional West and Southwest presence. In August, LDDS acquired TFN Group Communications. This acquisition added operations in California, Florida, Washington, New York and Virginia. LDDS increased its Midwest presence with the acquisition of TeleMarketing Investments in September.

LDDS' largest acquisition of the year was that of Advanced Telecommunications Corp. (ATC). The deal was announced on June 3, 1992, and closed in December. Under the terms of the deal, each ATC share would be exchanged for 0.83 shares of LDDS. LDDS' stock price on June 2, the last full trading day before the announcement, was $31.625 with 14.2 million shares outstanding. ATC's stock price was $20.00, with 20.9 million shares outstanding. The deal was valued at $549 million (0.83 x $31.625 x 20.9 million).

News of the deal sent LDDS' stock down $2.375 to close at $29.625 on June 3. ATC's stock rose $2.50 to close at $22.50. LDDS' market value fell by $33.7 million ($2.375 x 14.2 million), while ATC's market value rose by $52.3 million ($2.50 x 20.9 million). Overall, the market reacted favorably to the transaction, with a total increase of $18.6 million.

The $549 million merger, which was a pooling of interests, created the fourth-largest long distance provider in the country.

In early 1993, LDDS acquired Touch 1 Long Distance Inc., with operations in Alabama, Arizona, Colorado, Texas and Tennessee, and Dial-Net Inc., with operations spread throughout half the United States. In September 1993, LDDS acquired Resurgens Communications Group and billionaire John Kluge's Metromedia Communications Corp. in a three-way transaction. The three-way merger, which was valued at $1.2 billion, gave LDDS major long distance capacity in the Northeast and

California. Following the merger, the company was renamed LDDS Communications, Inc. Kluge became WorldCom's largest stockholder.

With only one major transaction, 1994 was a relatively quiet year for LDDS. On August 2, LDDS announced plans to acquired IDB WorldCom in a stock-for-stock transaction. Under the terms of the deal, each share of IDB would be exchanged for 0.476879 shares of LDDS. LDDS' stock price on August 1, 1994, the last full trading day before the announcement, was $19.50 with 121 million shares outstanding. IDB's stock price was $9.50, with 74 million shares outstanding. The deal was valued at $688 million (0.476879 x $19.50 x 74 million).

News of the deal sent LDDS' stock down $0.062 to close at $19.438 on August 2. IDB's stock fell $0.625 to close at $8.875. LDDS' market value fell by $7.5 million ($0.062 x 121 million), while IDB's market value fell by $46.25 million ($0.625 x 74 million). Overall, the market reacted unfavorably to the transaction, with a total decrease of $53.75 million.

The merger gave LDDS undersea cable capacity and networks in Germany and Britain. The deal closed in January 1995.

LDDS more than compensated for its single major transaction in 1994 with a slew of deals in 1995. Starting in January, LDDS formally acquired WilTel Network Services from The Williams Companies for $2.5 billion in cash. The acquisition was first announced on July 28, 1994. News of the deal sent LDDS' stock price up $0.25 to close at $19.00. This represented an increase in market value of $30.25 million ($0.25 x 121 million shares). The merger gave LDDS an 11,000-mile network of fiber-optic and wireless facilities and a big business supplying capacity to other long-distance carriers.

In May, LDDS was ranked in the *Fortune* 500 for the first time with a rank of 498. In the same month, it changed its name to WorldCom, Inc. In June 1995, WorldCom signed a $480 million carrier reseller agreement with UniDial of Kentucky. The deal was the largest such agreement in reseller history.

In August, WorldCom formed GridNet International, to provide enhanced data services for transaction processors, on-line service providers, and Internet Service Providers. In the same month, John Kluge, chairman of MetroMedia, announced the intention to sell its entire position of nearly 31 million common shares of WorldCom. Kluge continued to serve as chairman of the board of WorldCom.

In September, WorldCom signed a $600 million carrier reseller agreement with National Telephone and Communications, Inc. of Irvine, California. The deal became the largest in reseller history.

In December 1995, basketball superstar Michael Jordan became a corporate sponsor for WorldCom. He appeared in national television commercials and on prepaid phone cards.

WorldCom followed 1995 with an even more active 1996. In January it acquired a 30% stake in TCL Telecom, an Irish telecommunications company. In February, WorldCom signed an agreement with EDS, a global information services company, to become a major provider of data telecommunications services. It also signed a signed a five-year, $15 million agreement with AGIS, a leading global Internet service provider, to provide an array of data products and services.

WorldCom signed agreements to become the primary provider of long distance service for GTE, Ameritech, and SBC Mobile Systems. In March, Standard & Poor's announced that it would list WorldCom on the S&P 500. The *Wall Street Journal* also ranks WorldCom as the top performer for delivering shareholder value over a 10-year period.

In April 1996, WorldCom signed an operating agreement with Telecom Japan to provide bi-directional telephone services between Japan and the United States. In May, WorldCom's board of directors declared a two-for-one stock split.

WorldCom signed two major reseller agreements and continued its acquisitions in June. WorldCom signed $900 million and $1 billion reseller agreements with Excel Communications and National Telephone and Communications, respectively. The multi-year agreements were the largest in reseller history. WorldCom also acquired Choice Cellular, a Phoenix, Arizona cellular resale company. In July, WorldCom entered into an agreement with Telecommunications de Mexico for a network-to-network interface.

In August, it acquired BLT Technologies, the top U.S. supplier of prepaid phone cards through retail channels.

The landmark Telecommunications Act of 1996 altered the long distance market and WorldCom's acquisition strategy. Deregulation made the long distance market more competitive. It brought companies such as Qwest Communications International and the Baby Bells into the market. Instead of focusing on long distance, Ebbers decided to go after "one-stop shopping" in telecommunications. To accomplish this, on August 26, 1996, WorldCom announced that it had agreed to acquire MFS Communications. MFS Communications was a leading provider of local telephone service, particularly in large urban areas. The merger gave WorldCom first-class local networks in 41 cities and the largest Internet service provider, UUNET Technologies, which had just been bought by MFS.

The terms of the deal amount to a premium of 60% over MFS's previous stock price. WorldCom agreed to pay 2.1 shares of its stock for each share of MFS. With WorldCom's closing price, the total deal value amounted to (2.1 x $22.75 x 260 million shares) or $12.4 billion.

On the announcement date, WorldCom's stock fell 14%, or $3.625, to close at $22.75. Meanwhile, MFS rose $9.94 to close at $44.81, much closer to the proposed purchase price of $47.77 (2.1 x $22.75) per share at the closing price for WorldCom.

The combination of the two companies will be able to offer full telecommunications services, including local, long distance, and internet access, all brought under the supervision of one company. The company will continue to cater to the corporate world because of the high margins and profitability. Estimates of the combined savings the companies could experience by dealing with each other rather than outside providers reach as high as $240 to $440 million a year. Experts also noted WorldCom's good track record of integrating its acquisitions.

At the time of the merger, some doubts were expressed. Many felt the premium paid (60%) by WorldCom was much too high. Others argued that the newly formed company would not be a significant rival for the larger companies, ironically including MCI. There was also talk that many of the current allies of the companies may be turned off to doing business with the new combined company. Local phone companies such as GTE and SBC would be less likely to give business to WorldCom because of their rivalry with MFS. Similarly, long-distance companies would be more hesitant to deal with the former MFS.

The merger was approved by shareholders and completed on December 31, 1996. Bernard J. Ebbers is named president and chief executive officer, James Q. Crowe is named chairman and John Sidgmore is named chief operations officer.

In early-1997, WorldCom announced several plans to construct or expand fiber-optic networks in Europe. The plans, over time, will interconnect WorldCom's city networks in Europe and provide a platform for future national networks. The first phase will connect London, Amsterdam, Brussels, and Paris. In May 1997, Gemini, a joint venture between WorldCom and Cable & Wireless, announced the successful installation of the U.K. landing stage of its dual cable transatlantic cable. The undersea portion will begin when the U.S. landing stage is complete. Also in May, WorldCom announced that its German subsidiary had signed an agreed with Deutsche Telecom to interconnect their public networks.

Similarly, WorldCom's French subsidiary signed and agreement with France Telecom in June. The agreement will allow any WorldCom customer to communicate with any subscriber on France Telecom's network.

On September 7, 1997, WorldCom announced its intention to acquire CompuServe from H&R Block in a stock for stock transaction. Under the terms of the deal, each CompuServe share will be exchanged for 0.40625 shares of WorldCom. WorldCom's stock price on September 5, 1997, the last full day of trading before the announcement, was $31.50 with 910 million shares outstanding. CompuServe's stock price was $13.50, with 94 million shares outstanding. The deal was valued at $1.2 billion (0.40625 x $31.50 x 94 million).

News of the deal sent WorldCom's stock up $2.25 to close at $33.75 on September 8. CompuServe's stock fell $1.88 to close at $13.312. WorldCom's market value rose by $2.05 billion ($2.25 x 910 million), while CompuServe's market value fell by $176 million (-$1.88 x 94 million). Overall, the market reacted favorably to the transaction, with a total increase of $1.87 billion.

As a part of the deal WorldCom agreed to acquire America Online's network services company, ANS Communications. AOL will sign a five-year contract under which WorldCom will become AOL's largest network service provider in exchange for AOL receiving CompuServe's Online Services division and $175 million in cash. WorldCom will retain the CompuServe Network Services division. The merger was completed in January 1998.

On October 1, 1997, WorldCom announced its intention to acquire Brooks Fiber Properties (BFP) for $2.3 billion. The deal was complicated and virtually overlooked because it was announced on the same day as WorldCom's unsolicited bid to acquire MCI. BFP is a leading facilities-based provider of local telecommunications. It has constructed a series of fiber optic networks.

According to the terms of the deal, BFP shares were to be exchanged for between 1.65 and 1.85 shares of WorldCom, depending on the trading price of WorldCom. At WorldCom's price on the close of trading on the announcement date, this made the deal worth (1.7 x $34.48 x 39 million shares) or $2.3 billion.

The market reaction was largely dominated by the announcement of WorldCom and MCI. However, WorldCom fell $1, closing at $34.48 per share.

The logic provided for the merger included the fact that it would increase WorldCom's speed of entry to many secondary U.S. markets. The merger expanded the number of fiber optic networks operated by WorldCom from 52 to 86. The merger would contribute to WorldCom's expanding presence in local markets, and would help it serve more of the business customers it tries to cater to.

Possible problems with the merger hinged around the fact that WorldCom's stock was particularly volatile at that time, due to its interaction with MCI. BFP shareholders had to watch the events surrounding the MCI merger hoping that no bad news would break and hurt the price of WorldCom stock and therefore reduce the merger consideration. The merger was completed in January 1998.

On the same day, WorldCom announced its intention of making an unsolicited bid to acquire MCI. MCI, was the second largest provider of long distance service in the United States, behind only AT&T, and also had considerable assets within the developing world of the internet.

The deal was complicated by the fact that it came at a time when MCI had been preparing for a merger with British Telecom. It was prompted by BT's decision to cut its original offer from $21 billion to $17 billion. WorldCom followed with an initial offer valued at approximately $30 billion, but before the offer was accepted, GTE entered the fray with an all cash offer of about $28 billion. In response, on November 10, 1997, WorldCom increased it's bid to about $36 billion, and instead of sticking to its plan of an all stock transaction, agreed to buy some shares (particularly the 20% share of BT) for cash.

The initial deal of October 1 had World Com buying MCI for $41.50 per share with WorldCom stock. With 708 million shares of MCI stock outstanding, the deal was valued at (708 million x $41.50) or $29.4 billion.

After the challenge from GTE, WorldCom entered into negotiations with BT, and reached an agreement to buy that company's 20% stake for $7 billion in cash. For the remaining MCI shares, WorldCom offered $50 of stock per share. This led to a total deal value of (708 million x $50) or $35.4 billion.

Following the first offer, WorldCom fell $1 on the day of the announcement, closing at $34.48. Meanwhile, MCI rose $5.94, closing at $35.31. In addition, BT, whose shareholders found the proposed merger between that company and MCI undesirable rose $5.38 to $72, following news of the new deal.

Following the announcement of the second deal, WorldCom dropped another $2.13, closing at $31, which was a 13% decrease from what it had been before it began bidding for MCI. MCI rose $4.63, closing at $41.50 following the announcement.

Perhaps the most compelling logic provided for the merger is WorldCom's estimate of the massive savings that are possible within the combined company. The estimates include savings of $1.2 billion in operational costs, thanks to an elimination of MCI's need to pay for access to local phone companies. The estimates also note the possibility of up to $5 billion of other synergies by the year 2002.

The merger also creates a telecom giant, with considerable assets in long distance, local, and Internet provision. It helps the possibility for consumers to have all these services provided though one giant company, rather than many services provided by many smaller companies. MCI provides marketing power and name recognition, while WorldCom brings a wide variety of services to augment MCI's services. The new company would be second only to AT&T in the telecommunications realm.

Many problems have been noted about the merger. Antitrust regulation will force MCI to sell off some of its assets, particularly in the Internet areas that it overlaps with WorldCom. Also, the bidding war to arrive at the deal could create a situation in which WorldCom paid too much for what it gets. The structure of the deal itself was somewhat risky because it hinged on the continuing value of WorldCom. Fluctuations in the stock would make MCI shareholders uneasy. Another weakness of the merged company would be its absence from the rapidly growing area of wireless communications. The closing price of MCI WorldCom stock on January 13, 1999 was $73.938. With 1.83 billion shares outstanding, it had a market capitalization of $135.6 billion. (For further discussion of WorldCom, see the WorldCom/Sprint case).

In a 30 page report on August 20, 1999, Salomon Smith Barney research analyst Jack B. Grubman, group leader of the Global Telecom Team and highly regarded for his knowledge of the industry, analyzed in depth the outlook for MCI WorldCom, Inc. Financial analysts at other investment banking houses wrote detailed reports at about the same time. Some projections and their relationships are produced in Table 1. Figures 1 through 4 present graphically revenues and NOPAT on both arithmetic and semi-logarithmic scales.

QUESTIONS

1. Discuss WorldCom's history of growth by acquisition.
2. Present your valuation of WorldCom based on the background and data provided. Use Model 9.4 from the text.

TABLE 1 WorldCom Projections

	1999	2000	2001	2002	2003	2004	2005	2006	2007
Revenues	37,739	44,809	52,763	61,891	71,969	83,397	96,766	112,593	131,343
Depreciation	4,083	4,375	4,935	5,252	5,823	6,453	7,117	7,860	8,577
Capital Spending	7,000	7,500	7,750	8,000	8,365	9,125	9,995	11,000	13,000
Net Income	3,673	5,674	7,826	10,182	12,211	14,510	17,254	20,555	24,451
Interest Expense After Taxes	790	581	493	444	343	240	241	241	241
NOPAT	4,463	6,255	8,319	10,626	12,554	14,750	17,495	20,796	24,692
Change Revenue	7,070	7,954	9,128	10,078	11,428	13,369	15,827	18,750	
Cap Spending/Change Rev	99.0%	94.3%	84.9%	79.4%	73.2%	68.3%	63.2%	58.7%	
Depr/Change Rev	57.8%	55.0%	54.1%	52.1%	51.0%	48.3%	45.0%	41.9%	
Net Capital Spending	2,917	3,125	2,815	2,748	2,542	2,672	2,878	3,140	4,423
Net Cap /Change Rev	41.3%	39.3%	30.8%	27.3%	22.2%	20.0%	18.2%	16.7%	
Net Cap / Rev	7.7%	7.0%	5.3%	4.4%	3.5%	3.2%	3.0%	2.8%	3.4%
NOPAT / Rev	11.8%	14.0%	15.8%	17.2%	17.4%	17.7%	18.1%	18.5%	18.8%
NOPAT/Rev - Net Cap/Rev	4.1%	7.0%	10.4%	12.7%	13.9%	14.5%	15.1%	15.7%	15.4%
FCF	1,546	3,130	5,504	7,878	10,011	12,077	14,617	17,656	20,269
FCF/Rev	4.1%	7.0%	10.4%	12.7%	13.9%	14.5%	15.1%	15.7%	15.4%
Growth rate revenues	15.44%								
Growth rate NOPAT	20.44%								

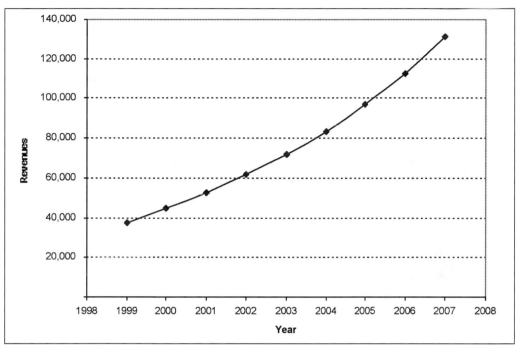

FIGURE 1 Revenues

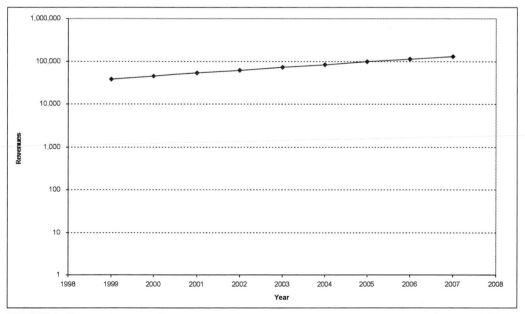

FIGURE 2 Revenues

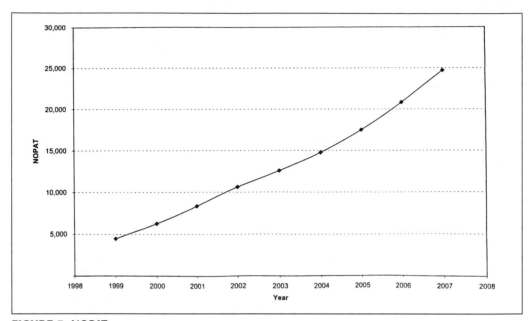

FIGURE 3 NOPAT

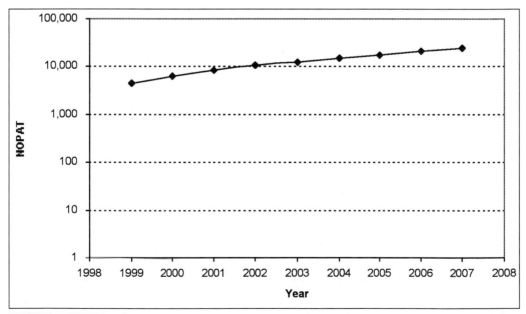

FIGURE 4 NOPAT

Case 17

The Viacom/CBS Merger

On September 7, 1999, it was announced that Viacom and CBS had agreed to merge. The deal terms are summarized in Table 1. The total market value of the Viacom shares, using a pre-announcement date price of $46.08, was $27.9 billion. For CBS, using a pre-announcement date price of $50 for both the common and preferred stock B, gives a total market value of $35.8 billion. So premerger Viacom shares represented 43.8% of the combined market values. The merger agreement called for CBS shareholders to receive 1.085 shares of Viacom for each share of CBS common and preferred stock B. The postmerger percentage of ownership remains at 43.8% for Viacom and 56.2% for CBS because there was virtually no premium reflected in the stock exchange terms. The background, rationale, and comparative valuation materials are presented below.

Background to the Merger

On August 5, 1999, the FCC announced that it had adopted new regulations that, for the first time, would permit a single person to own two television stations in a single market, subject to limitations. Since that date, it has been widely reported that numerous owners

TABLE 1 Viacom/CBS Deal Terms

	Viacom		CBS		
	Amount	Percentage	Amount	Percentage	**Total**
Number of common shares (million)	605.1	45.8%	705.2		
			10.1 (Pref. B)		
			715.3	54.2%	1,320.4
Share Price	$46.08		$50.00		
Total Market Value (billion)	$27.9	43.8%	$35.8	56.2%	$63.6
Post-Merger					
Number of Shares (million)	605.1	43.8%	776.1	56.2%	1,381.2

of television stations have been seeking opportunities to acquire or sell stations in reliance on the new rules.

On August 11, at the request of Mr. Karmazin, Mr. Karmazin and Mr. Redstone met at the offices of Viacom. Mr. Karmazin reviewed with Mr. Redstone the businesses of CBS and discussed with Mr. Redstone various possible transactions between the two companies, including an exchange of assets in the television and cable television businesses and ways in which various businesses of the two companies could be combined.

On August 12, Mr. Redstone called Mr. Karmazin and suggested that they meet again, together with Philippe Dauman and Thomas Dooley, Viacom's Deputy Chairmen and Executive Vice Presidents, to discuss further the possible transactions discussed at their August 11 meeting.

On August 16, Messrs. Redstone, Dauman and Dooley met with Mr. Karmazin. Mr. Karmazin proposed various alternative transactions involving the two companies, including swapping Viacom's television stations for the cable television networks of CBS and combining the entire businesses of Viacom and CBS. Mr. Karmazin emphasized the complementary nature of the assets of the two companies. Mr. Redstone indicated interest in the swap transaction, but did not express a conclusion regarding a possible merger. Mr. Karmazin said that he would like to make a more detailed presentation regarding the businesses of CBS to Messrs. Redstone, Dauman and Dooley. The parties agreed to meet again on August 24.

On August 24, Mr. Karmazin again met with Messrs. Redstone, Dauman and Dooley. Mr. Karmazin presented information regarding CBS, describing the performance of its assets, strategies for growth and the benefits of selling advertising across different advertising media. At the conclusion of the presentation, Mr. Karmazin again suggested a merger involving the two companies, proposing that CBS acquire Viacom at a premium to market value. Mr. Redstone indicated that he would not be interested in selling his stake in Viacom, but indicated that, in light of the strong strategic fit between the two companies, he would consider a merger of equals priced at market value, in which Mr. Redstone's controlling interest in Viacom was preserved in the combined company through the issuance of Viacom's non-voting Class B common stock to the shareholders of CBS. Mr. Redstone indicated that, if such a transaction was pursued, he would recommend a role for Mr. Karmazin in which he would serve as President and Chief Operating Officer of the combined company. Mr. Karmazin indicated his willingness to consider these terms and said that he would like to discuss such a transaction with members of the CBS board of directors.

On August 26, the CBS board held a special meeting at which Mr. Karmazin reviewed for the board the conversations and contacts he had had with Mr. Redstone to date and the current status of discussions regarding the structure and terms of a possible transaction with Viacom. Mr. Karmazin and Fredric G. Reynolds, CBS' Executive Vice President and Chief Financial Officer, also reviewed for the board the capital structure and share ownership of Viacom. The CBS board authorized Mr. Karmazin to continue his discussions with Mr. Redstone. Following the August 26 meeting, detailed publicly available information and analyst reports relating to the share ownership of Viacom were distributed to the CBS board.

On August 25 and 26, representatives of Shearman & Sterling, counsel to Viacom, held various discussions with representatives of Cravath, Swaine & Moore, legal counsel to CBS, and representatives of Evercore, financial advisors to CBS, concerning the structure of a possible transaction, exchange ratio mechanisms and related matters.

On August 26, Mr. Redstone and Mr. Karmazin met to continue their discussions regarding management of the combined company and ways to assure the CBS board of directors as to the management of the combined company in light of the controlling share-holdings of Mr. Redstone.

On August 27, representatives of Viacom, Morgan Stanley & Co. Incorporated, financial advisors to Viacom, and Shearman & Sterling met with representatives of CBS, Evercore and Cravath, Swaine & Moore to discuss the structure and exchange ratio for a possible transaction, board composition and management issues, the due diligence review process and related matters. The parties also finalized and executed a confidentiality agreement at this meeting.

On August 29, senior executives and professional advisors of each of Viacom and CBS met to exchange financial, legal and business due diligence information. The due diligence process, which included review of documents and interviews with executives and professional advisors of each company, continued through the signing of the merger agreement.

On August 30, Mr. Redstone and Mr. Karmazin discussed further the proposed governance of the combined company. The discussions related to Mr. Karmazin's proposed responsibilities and powers as Chief Operating Officer and Mr. Redstone's responsibilities and powers as Chief Executive Officer as well as whether the proposed responsibilities of the Chief Operating Officer were inconsistent with the continued involvement of Messrs. Dauman and Dooley as senior managers of Viacom following the merger. Mr. Redstone advised Mr. Karmazin that Messrs. Dauman and Dooley had indicated to Mr. Redstone that, in view of the strategic benefits to Viacom of the proposed transaction, they would be willing to resign from their respective management positions at Viacom at the closing of the transaction if that would facilitate the resolution of the governance arrangements for the combined company. Messrs. Redstone and Karmazin also confirmed their understanding that the combined board of directors would consist of a majority of Viacom representatives. These points were discussed further on August 31 between Mr. Redstone and Mr. Karmazin.

On August 30, Shearman & Sterling delivered a draft merger agreement to Cravath, Swaine & Moore.

On August 31, the CBS board held a special meeting to continue the board's previous discussions regarding a possible transaction between CBS and Viacom. Mr. Karmazin described in detail the discussions with Mr. Redstone leading up to the current proposal for a merger of CBS with Viacom. Mr. Karmazin and other members of CBS' senior management discussed with the CBS board their views of various aspects of the proposed transaction. Louis Briskman, CBS' Executive Vice President and General Counsel, and representatives of Cravath, Swaine & Moore discussed with the CBS board its fiduciary duties with regard to its consideration of the proposed transaction under applicable law. Representatives of Evercore discussed with the CBS board their views and preliminary analyses of the financial aspects of the proposed transaction. The CBS board reviewed and considered, among other things, the initial results of the due diligence investigation conducted to date, the proposed terms of the transaction, the impact of the proposed transaction on CBS' other pending transactions and the proposed terms relating to the management, board representation and governance of the combined company. Following extensive discussion of these matters, the CBS board directed Mr. Karmazin to negotiate further with Viacom on the basis of the CBS board's recommendations with respect to the matters discussed during the meeting. In particular, the CBS board directed Mr. Karmazin to negotiate arrangements substantially consistent with the management, board representation and governance arrangements, which are described later in this case.

Following the CBS board meeting on August 31, Cravath, Swaine & Moore and Shearman & Sterling reviewed and discussed those areas identified by the CBS board of directors as important for Mr. Karmazin to have delegated authority to manage, those areas which a majority of the board of directors of the combined company should have authority over and those areas requiring a supermajority board vote, and the conceptual framework for implementing this arrangement, Representatives of Cravath, Swaine & Moore and Shearman & Sterling negotiated the terns of these arrangements, including related changes to the Restated Certificate of Incorporation and by-laws of Viacom, together with the terns and conditions of the merger agreement and Mr. Karmazin's employment agreement, throughout the period from August 31 through the signing of definitive documentation on September 6. In addition, Morgan Stanley, on behalf of Viacom, and Evercore, on behalf of CBS, continued to negotiate the exchange ratio through September 2. The parties mutually agreed to an at market exchange ratio. The negotiation of the exchange ratio involved discussions concerning the appropriate measurement period for determining the market value of Viacom and CBS without any premium. No financial analysis was performed in determining the exchange ratio. A fixed exchange ratio at market was agreed to on or about September 3, subject to board approvals.

On September 2, the board of directors of Viacom, at a special meeting, received a presentation regarding the proposed terms of the transaction from Viacom's outside counsel, and a presentation from Morgan Stanley regarding the financial terms of the transaction and discussed the proposed terms and the risks and merits of the proposed transaction.

On September 2, the special meeting of the CBS Board reconvened and Mr. Karmazin recounted for the CBS board the events that had transpired since the meeting recessed on August 31. Mr. Karmazin described in detail the proposed terms that had been negotiated with Viacom with respect to the corporate governance of Viacom following consummation of the proposed transaction, and explained to the CBS board that such governance arrangements would be reflected in the proposed new Restated Certificate of Incorporation and by-laws of Viacom as well as in a voting agreement between National Amusements, the holder of a majority of Viacom's voting stock, and CBS. Following extensive discussion among the members of the CBS board, Mr. Karmazin, other members of CBS' senior management, representatives of Cravath, Swaine & Moore and representatives of Evercore, the CBS board directed Mr. Karmazin to negotiate definitive agreements and related documentation based on the terms outlined by Mr. Karmazin during the meeting.

On September 5, the CBS board held a special meeting to continue the board's discussions with respect to the proposed merger and to consider the merger agreement and the transactions contemplated thereby, including the proposed consideration to be issued to CBS shareholders and the proposed terms regarding the powers of the board of directors, the chief executive officer and the chief operating officer of Viacom following the merger. Mr. Karrnazin and other members of CBS' senior management, representatives of Cravath. Swaine & Moore and representatives of Evercore made presentations to the CBS board and discussed with the CBS board their views and analyses of various aspects of the proposed transaction. Evercore delivered its oral opinion, which was subsequently confirmed in writing, that, based upon the matters presented to the CBS board and as set forth in its opinion, as of such date, the exchange ratio was fair, from a financial point of view, to the shareholders of CBS.

After further deliberation, the CBS board unanimously approved the merger and the merger agreement and authorized, among other things, the execution of the merger agreement, the voting agreement and the stockholder agreement, and unanimously recommended that CBS shareholders vote to adopt the merger agreement.

On September 5, the Compensation Committee of the Viacom board met to review and, subject to approval of the merger by the Viacom board, approved the proposed terms of Mr. Redstone's and Mr. Karmazin's employment agreements, the resignation agreements for Messrs. Dauman and Dooley and the Viacom executive severance plans. For a more complete description of these terms, see the section entitled "Interests of Persons in the Merger-Senior Management Arrangements."

Also on September 5, at a special meeting of the Viacom board, the board heard presentations on the results of the due diligence investigation and the status of the negotiation of the merger agreement and related agreements and received an updated presentation from Morgan Stanley. Morgan Stanley also delivered to the Viacom board its oral opinion that the exchange ratio was fair from a financial point of view to Viacom.

Further, on September 5, the board also was briefed on and ratified the actions of the Compensation Committee, in the case of the resignation agreements of Messrs. Dauman and Dooley and the employment agreement of Mr. Redstone, without the participation of such individuals. The board then discussed the proposed terms and conditions of the transaction extensively, following which the board adjourned the meeting in order to consider the results of further negotiations.

During the evening of September 5, management of CBS and Viacom and their respective legal advisors continued their negotiations regarding the terms of the merger agreement and, in particular, the proposed terms regarding the respective powers of the board of directors, chief executive officer and chief operating officer.

On the morning of September 6, the board of directors of Viacom met and reviewed the finalized terms of the proposed transactions. Following a discussion, the Viacom board unanimously approved the merger agreement and the transactions contemplated thereby. In the afternoon of September 6, CBS and Viacom executed the merger agreement, National Amusements executed the voting agreement and the stockholder agreement, Viacom and Messrs. Redstone and Karmazin executed their respective employment agreements, and Viacom executed resignation agreements with Messrs. Dauman and Dooley.

On October 8, 1999, the merger agreement was amended and restated to provide for the issuance of Viacom Series C preferred stock in exchange for the CBS Series B preferred stock issued to Gaylord in connection with CBS' acquisition of KTVT-TV Dallas-Fort Worth from Gaylord. On November 23, 1999, the merger agreement was amended and restated again to provide for the alternative structure of the merger as a merger of CBS with and into Viacom/CBS LLC and to provide each company with additional flexibility to compensate its employees.

Reasons for the Merger and Board Recommendations

Viacom

The Viacom board carefully considered the terms of the merger and believes that the merger serves the best interests of Viacom and its shareholders. As a result, the Viacom board declared that the merger agreement was advisable, unanimously approved the merger agreement and unanimously recommends that the Viacom shareholders approve the adoption of the merger agreement and the other proposals described in this joint proxy statement/prospectus.

The Viacom board considered a number of factors, including those listed below. The Viacom board did not consider it practical, and did not try, to rank or weigh the importance of each factor, and different members of the Viacom board may have given different weight to different factors. The Viacom board also considered presentations by, and consulted with, members of Viacom's management as well as its financial advisors and outside and inside legal counsel. The list of factors set forth below is not exhaustive but is believed to include all material factors considered by Viacom's board.

CBS Assets and Relationship with the Existing Businesses of Viacom. The Viacom board considered the quality and breadth of the assets of CBS, including the radio and outdoor advertising assets of Infinity, and its financial condition, competitive position and prospects for growth. In particular, the board considered the complementary nature of the businesses of CBS and Viacom in that Viacom is a leader in the cable television programming, motion picture and television production businesses and CBS is a leader in the television network distribution, television and radio broadcasting and outdoor advertising businesses. The board recognized the tremendous opportunities for the combined company to reach large audiences and cross-promote and cross-market its assets among various distribution outlets. Similarly, the board recognized that the combined company would have greater opportunities to increase its advertising, licensing and other revenue than either company would on its own. The board also considered potential economies of scale by combining these businesses. The board took into account that the combined company would have an increased dependence on the advertising market, but concluded that the risk of such dependence was outweighed by the strategic benefits of the transaction.

Financial Terms. The Viacom board considered that the merger of equals structure, in which no premium would be paid to the shareholders of either company, would create a company with considerable financial resources. The Viacom board considered the historical trading ranges of Viacom Class B common stock and CBS common stock as compared with the proposed exchange ratio. The Viacom board also considered the fact that the merger would be tax-free to Viacom's shareholders. In addition, the Viacom board considered the pro forma effect of the proposed transaction on the financial condition and results of the combined company and the price of CBS as compared with other comparable companies using various methods of valuation.

Management and Governance Provisions. The Viacom Board considered the experience and accomplishments of Mr. Karmazin and other members of CBS management and the benefits of Mr. Karmazin's service as President and Chief Operating Officer and Mr. Redstone's continuing service as Chairman and Chief Executive Officer to the Viacom shareholders. The Viacom board weighed these benefits against the limitations the proposed governance structure would impose on its power to manage the combined company by majority vote of the board of the combined company and concluded that these limitations represented an acceptable balance of management responsibilities.

Support of Sumner Redstone. The Viacom board considered the fact that Viacom's controlling shareholder, National Amusements, which in turn is controlled by Mr. Redstone, supported the proposed transaction and was prepared to sign a voting agreement, in which National Amusements would agree to vote its shares in favor of the proposed transaction.

Presentation and Opinion of Morgan Stanley. At its meeting on September 6, the Viacom board considered the financial presentation made to the Viacom board on September 5 and the oral opinion rendered by Morgan Stanley on September 5, subsequently confirmed in writing, that, as of that date, the proposed exchange ratio was fair to Viacom from a financial point of view. Morgan Stanley's opinion as to the fairness of the exchange ratio to Viacom contributed to the Viacom board's determination that the merger is in the best interests of Viacom's shareholders. The Viacom board did not request an opinion as to the fairness of the exchange ratio specifically to the shareholders of Viacom because Viacom is the surviving corporation in the merger and its shareholders are not exchanging their shares in the merger. In contrast, the CBS shareholders will be exchanging their shares of CBS stock for shares of Viacom stock.

Regulatory Matters. The Viacom board considered the fact that Viacom might be required to divest or reduce its interest in United Paramount Network and Viacom and/or CBS would be required to divest a number of television and radio stations in the event that current law and regulations were not amended or waived. The Viacom board also considered the ability to obtain other necessary regulatory approvals.

Terms, Conditions, Termination Provisions and Termination Fee. The Viacom board reviewed the representations, warranties, covenants and conditions to consummation of the proposed transaction and the circumstances under which CBS would have the right to terminate the merger agreement. The Viacom board considered the fact that the vote of the Viacom shareholders was assured by reason of the voting agreement to be entered into by National Amusements and that CBS would have the right to terminate the merger agreement under specified circumstances if there was a superior proposal. The Viacom board considered the circumstances in which a termination fee would be payable in the event that the merger agreement was terminated. The Viacom board considered that there could be no assurance that the acquisition of Outdoor Systems by Infinity or King

World by CBS would be consummated. The Viacom board also considered the fact that the merger would not be conditioned on the completion of the pending CBS transactions with King World and Outdoor Systems.

The Viacom board unanimously recommends that the holders or Viacom Class A common stock approve the adoption or the merger agreement and the other proposals described in this joint proxy statement/prospectus.

CBS

Reasons for the Merger. At its meeting on September 5, 1999, the CBS board of directors determined that the merger is in the best interests of CBS and its shareholders, has unanimously approved the merger and the merger agreement and unanimously recommended that CBS shareholders vote to adopt the merger agreement.

In reaching its decision to approve the merger and the merger agreement and to recommend that CBS shareholders vote to adopt the merger agreement, the CBS board of directors consulted with senior management and its financial and legal advisors and considered a number of factors, including the following positive factors:

- recent trends in the entertainment and media industries and that a combination of Viacom, a leading "content provider" in the entertainment and media industries, with CBS, a leading distributor and marketer of programming, would create an even stronger global competitor in the entertainment and media industries;

- the opportunity to create the premier seller of advertising in the media industry, which could result in increased advertising revenue for the combined company;

- the opportunity for synergies and revenue generation through cross-promoting and cross-marketing the combined company's film, television, radio, theme park, home video, publishing, outdoor advertising and Internet businesses;

- that the merger would benefit the shareholders of CBS because they would participate in the value generated by increases in the opportunities for revenue generation through their equity participation in Viacom;

- the management and corporate governance arrangements agreed to between CBS and Viacom would provide for a strong management team drawn from both companies that would work together to integrate the two companies, to realize growth opportunities, to achieve synergistic benefits, and to successfully implement strategies of the combined company, including that:

  - the board of directors of the combined company would be expanded from ten to eighteen directors. The eight additional directors will initially be selected from and designated by the board of directors of CBS and vacancies in this group will be filled during the initial three-year term by independent directors designated by these eight CBS directors;

- Mr. Redstone, the current Chairman and Chief Executive Officer of Viacom, would continue to serve as Chairman and Chief Executive Officer of the combined company and would be responsible, in consultation with the President and Chief Operating Officer, for corporate policy and strategy;

- Mr. Karmazin, the current President and Chief Executive Officer of CBS, would serve as President and Chief Operating Officer of the combined company, would directly report to the CEO and consult with the CEO on all major decisions and would have responsibility for the supervision, coordination and management of the combined company's business;

- Mr. Karmazin, as President and Chief Operating Officer, would be entitled to manage the combined company's business, subject to the ability of the combined company's board of directors to take action with the approval of at least 14 directors. However, in a number of areas, the President and Chief Operating Officer would not be entitled to act without the approval of, and the combined company's board would be entitled to act by, a majority of the directors; and

- the governance arrangements described above would be in effect for a period of three years from the closing of the merger.

- the expected qualification of the merger as a tax-free reorganization;

- the oral opinion of Evercore, delivered on September 5, 1999, which was subsequently confirmed in a written opinion, a copy of which is attached as Annex I to this joint proxy statement/prospectus, that, subject to the assumptions and limitations contained in that opinion, as of that date, the exchange ratio was fair, from a financial point of view, to the shareholders of CBS, and the financial presentation made by Evercore to the CBS board of directors in connection with delivering that opinion;

- the terms and conditions of the merger agreement, including the right of CBS to consider and negotiate superior proposals;

- the financial condition, cash flows and results of operations of CBS and Viacom, on both a historical and prospective basis, which indicated that the combined company would enjoy financial strength immediately upon consummation of the merger;

- the historical market prices and trading information with respect to CBS common stock and Viacom non-voting Class B common stock, including that the Viacom non-voting Class B common stock and the Viacom Class A common stock have historically traded at comparable levels;

- that the complementary nature of the businesses of CBS and Viacom would enable the combined company to maintain important relationships with customers, suppliers and employees;

- the fact that CBS as an independent company has not fully participated in aspects of the media and entertainment industry where Viacom had particular strengths, such as MTV Networks and Paramount Pictures;
- the belief that the terms of the merger agreement, including the parties' representations, warranties and covenants, and the conditions to their respective obligations are reasonable;
- the fact that Viacom might be required to divest or reduce its interest in United Paramount Network and that Viacom and/or CBS would be required to divest a number of television and radio stations in the event that current law and regulations were not amended or waived;
- the regulatory approvals required to complete the merger and the favorable prospects for receiving those approvals; and
- satisfactory reports from CBS management and its advisors as to their due diligence investigations of Viacom.

The CBS board of directors also identified and considered a number of potentially negative factors in deliberations concerning the merger, including:

- the status, timing and tax considerations relating to the potential split-off of Blockbuster to the shareholders of Viacom;
- the existence of a controlling shareholder of the combined company following the merger and the non-voting security to be received by CBS shareholders in the merger;
- the possible effects of the provisions regarding termination fees on the ability of a third party to make an unsolicited superior proposal;
- the risk that the operations of CBS and Viacom might not be successfully integrated;
- the risk that, despite the efforts of CBS and Viacom, key management and other personnel might not remain employed by the combined company after the merger; and
- the risk that potential benefits of the merger might not be fully realized.

The CBS board of directors believed that some of these risks were unlikely to occur, while others could be avoided or mitigated by CBS, and that, overall these risks were outweighed by the potential benefits of the merger.

The discussion of the information and factors considered by the CBS board of directors in making its decision is not intended to be exhaustive but is believed to include all material factors considered by the CBS board of directors. In view of the variety of material factors considered in connection with its evaluation of the merger, the CBS board of directors did not find it practicable to, and did not, quantify or otherwise assign relative weights to the specific factors considered in reaching its determination. In addition, individual members of the CBS board of directors may have given different weight to different factors.

Recommendation of the CBS Board of Directors. After careful consideration, the CBS board of directors has determined that the merger is in the best interests of CBS and its shareholders, has unanimously approved the merger and the merger agreement and unanimously recommends that CBS shareholders vote "for" the adoption of the merger agreement.

Opinions of Financial Advisors

Viacom

Under a letter agreement dated as of September 2, 1999, Viacom engaged Morgan Stanley to act as its financial advisor in connection with a possible combination with CBS. The Viacom board of directors selected Morgan Stanley to act as its financial advisor based on Morgan Stanley's qualifications, expertise and reputation, as well as its knowledge of the business and affairs of Viacom. On September 5, 1999, Morgan Stanley delivered an oral opinion to the Viacom board of directors, which was subsequently confirmed in writing, that, as of that date, and based upon and subject to the considerations set forth in the written opinion, the exchange ratio was fair from a financial point of view to Viacom.

The full text of the opinion, which sets forth, among other things, the assumptions made, procedures followed, matters considered and limitations on the scope or the review undertaken by Morgan Stanley in rendering its opinion, is attached as Annex H to this joint proxy statement/prospectus. Morgan Stanley's written opinion is directed to the Viacom board of directors and only addresses the fairness of the exchange ratio to Viacom as of the date of the opinion. Morgan Stanley's written opinion does not address any other aspect or the merger and does not constitute a recommendation to any Viacom shareholder as to how to vote at the Viacom special meeting. The summary of the opinion set forth in this joint proxy statement/prospectus is qualified in its entirety by reference to the full text or the opinion attached as Annex H hereto. The following is only a summary of the Morgan Stanley opinion. Viacom shareholders are urged to, and should, read the opinion carefully and in its entirety.

In arriving at Morgan Stanley's opinion, Morgan Stanley, among other things:

- reviewed certain publicly available financial statements and other information of Viacom and CBS;

- reviewed and analyzed certain internal financial statements and other financial and operating data concerning Viacom and CBS prepared by the respective managements of Viacom and CBS;

- discussed the past and current operations and financial condition and the prospects of Viacom and CBS with senior executives of Viacom and CBS including their estimates of the strategic operating benefits of the merger and analyzed the pro forma impact of the merger on Viacom's financial ratios;

- reviewed the reported prices and trading activity for the Class B common stock of Viacom and the common stock of CBS;

- compared the financial performance of Viacom and CBS and the prices and trading activity of Viacom and CBS with that of certain other comparable publicly traded companies and their securities;

- participated in discussions and negotiations among representatives of Viacom, CBS and their respective financial and legal advisors;

- reviewed the merger agreement and certain related documents; and

- performed such other analyses and considered such other factors that Morgan Stanley deemed appropriate.

Morgan Stanley assumed and relied upon without independent verification the accuracy and completeness of the information it reviewed for the purposes of its opinion. With respect to the financial projections, Morgan Stanley assumed that they had been reasonably prepared on bases reflecting the best currently available estimates and judgments of the future financial performance of Viacom and CBS. Morgan Stanley has not made any independent valuation or appraisal of the assets or liabilities of Viacom and CBS, nor has Morgan Stanley been furnished with any such appraisals. Morgan Stanley has assumed that the merger will be consummated in accordance with the terms set forth in the merger agreement. Morgan Stanley's opinion is necessarily based on economic, market and other conditions as in effect on, and the information made available to it as of, the date of its opinion.

The following is a brief description of all material analyses performed by Morgan Stanley in connection with its oral opinion and the preparation of its written opinion letter. These summaries of financial analyses include information presented in tabular format. In order to understand the financial analysis used by Morgan Stanley, the tables must be read together with the text of each summary. The tables alone do not constitute a complete description of the financial analyses.

Historical Public Market Trading Value. Morgan Stanley reviewed the stock price performance of CBS based on an analysis of the historical closing prices and trading volumes for the one-year period beginning September 3, 1998 and ending September 3, 1999. The year-long time period chosen for the analysis of historical public market trading values is a traditional measurement period for stock prices chosen to reflect the impact of corporate events which might be deemed to have an impact on the current share price performance of two companies which are considering a stock-for-stock merger. The use of incremental measurement periods within the year-long review is designed to better capture the progression of each company's share price throughout the year and can better isolate the impact of specific corporate events on share price performance.

The following table lists the low, average and high daily closing prices of shares of CBS common stock for the periods indicated. These prices compare to $48.89, the price for CBS common stock implied by multiplying the exchange ratio by the price of Viacom Class B common stock on September 3, 1999.

| | **Historical CBS Common Stock Prices** | | |
	Low	**Average**	**High**
Last One Year	$18.00	$36.90	$50.44
Last Nine Months	26.75	40.93	50.44
Last Six Months	35.38	43.98	50.44
Last Three Months	40.56	45.07	50.44
Last One Month	44.13	46.71	50.44
Last Two Weeks	45.88	47.81	50.44

Comparative Stock Price Performance. As part of its analysis, Morgan Stanley reviewed the stock price performance of Viacom Class B common stock and CBS common stock and compared this performance with the following peer groups:

Viacom Peer Group	**CBS Peer Group**
The Walt Disney Company	A.H. Belo Corporation
Fox Entertainment Group, Inc.	Clear Channel Communications, Inc.
The Seagram Company Ltd.	Hearst-Argyle Television, Inc.
Time Warner Inc.	Sinclair Broadcast Group, Inc.
	Young Broadcasting Inc.

Morgan Stanley observed that over the one-year period from September 3, 1998 to September 3, 1999, the closing market prices appreciated as set forth below:

	% Total Appreciation
Viacom	56%
CBS	80
Viacom Peer Group	23
(equity market capitalization-weighted index)	
CBS Peer Group	42
(equity market capitalization-weighted index)	

Securities Research Analysts' Future Price Targets. Morgan Stanley reviewed and analyzed future public market trading price targets for Viacom Class B common stock and CBS common stock prepared and published by securities research analysts during the period from May 5, 1999 to August 18, 1999 for Viacom and May 26, 1999 to August 20, 1999 for CBS. Based upon discussions with senior executives of Viacom and CBS, these analysts' projections were viewed by Morgan Stanley as being representative of the future prospects of Viacom and CBS. These targets reflected each analyst's estimate of the future public market trading price of Viacom Class B common stock and CBS common stock at the end of the particular period considered for each estimate. Applying equity discount rates of 13.4% for Viacom and 12.8% for CBS, which reflect each company's cost of equity, Morgan

Stanley arrived at a range of present values as of September 3, 1999 of these targets as set forth below:

	Present Value Range	
	Low	High
Viacom Public Market Trading Price Target	$42	$50
CBS Market Trading Price Target	46	53

The present value range of the Viacom Public Market Trading Price Targets compares to a $45.06 price for the Viacom Class B common stock as of September 3, 1999. The present value range of the CBS Public Market Trading Price Targets compares to a $48.89 price for the CBS common stock implied by multiplying the exchange ratio by the price of Viacom Class B common stock on September 3, 1999. Morgan Stanley noted that the public market trading price targets published by the securities research analysts do not reflect current market trading prices and that these estimates are subject to uncertainties, including the future financial performance of Viacom and CBS and future financial market conditions.

Peer Group Comparison. Morgan Stanley compared financial information of Viacom and CBS with corresponding financial information for their respective peer groups.

Morgan Stanley analyzed, among other things, for each company the current aggregate value, i.e., equity value adjusted for capital structure, expressed as a multiple of earnings before interest, taxes, depreciation and amortization expense, or EBITDA.

As of June 30, 1999 and based on estimates of EBITDA taken from selected securities research analysts, the statistics derived from this analysis are set forth below:

		Viacom Peer Group				CBS Peer Group		
	Viacom	Median	High	Low	CBS	Median	High	Low
1999 EBITDA Multiple	17.1x	15.7x	19.0x	14.4x	22.7x	11.7x	25.7x	8.8x
2000 EBITDA Multiple	14.5	13.3	16.6	12.7	19.6	10.0	22.6	8.1

The trading multiples for Viacom, CBS and their respective peer groups compare to the transaction multiples implied by the exchange ratio of 22.7x 1999E CBS EBITDA and 19.6x 2000E CBS EBITDA.

Discounted Cash Flow Analysis. Morgan Stanley performed a discounted cash flow analysis of CBS' business. A discounted cash flow analysis involves an analysis of the present value of projected cash flows and a terminal value using discount rates and terminal year free cash flow perpetual growth rates as indicated below. Morgan Stanley analyzed CBS' business using a forecast for the period beginning January 1, 1999 and ending December 31, 2003, based on estimates published by securities research analysts. Based upon discussions with senior executives of CBS, these analysts' projections were viewed by Morgan Stanley as being representative of the future prospects of CBS. Morgan Stanley estimated the CBS common stock discounted cash flow value by using a discount rate of

10% and a perpetual growth rate applied to 2003 free cash flow ranging from 4.5% to 5.5%. This analysis yielded a range of per share values for CBS common stock of approximately $45 to $54. This range of per share values for CBS common stock compares to $48.89, the price for CBS common stock implied by multiplying the exchange ratio by the price of Viacom Class B common stock on September 3, 1999.

The discount rates used in the discounted cash flow analysis of Viacom and CBS reflect each company's weighted average cost of capital. The weighted average cost of capital represents the cost of capital for CBS and Viacom based on the relative proportion of debt, preferred equity and common equity employed by each company. The range of perpetual growth rates employed in the CBS discounted cash now analysis reflects certain assumption of CBS' cash flow growth in perpetuity. The terminal EBITDA multiple range used in the Viacom discounted cash flow analysis was based on a review of the trading multiples for Viacom and the companies in the Viacom peer group and a comparison of Viacom's business position relative to its peers.

Morgan Stanley also performed a discounted cash flow analysis of Viacom's business. Morgan Stanley analyzed Viacom's business using a forecast for the period beginning January 1, 1999 and ending December 31, 2003 based on estimates published by securities research analysts. Based upon discussions with senior executives of Viacom, these analysts' projections were viewed by Morgan Stanley as being representative of the future prospects of Viacom. Morgan Stanley estimated the Viacom Class B common stock discounted cash flow value by using a discount rate of 10% and terminal multiples of estimated 2003 EBITDA ranging from 13.0x to 15.0x. This analysis yielded a range of per share values for Viacom Class B common stock of approximately $39 to $45. This range of per share values for Viacom Class B common stock compares to a $45.06 price for the Viacom Class B common stock as of September 3, 1999.

Sum-of-the-Parts Analysis. Morgan Stanley performed a sum-of-the-parts analysis of CBS' business. A sum-of-the-parts analysis involves a separate valuation of each of CBS' core businesses. The valuation methodology applied to each component is set forth below:

Component	Valuation Methodology
Infinity Broadcasting Corporation	Market Value of CBS' 700 million shares
Television Assets[a]	13x–15x 2000E EBITDA
Cable Programming (CMT/TNN)	17x–19x 2000E EBITDA
King World Productions, Inc.	CBS net purchase price
Internet Holdings	Morgan Stanley equity research estimate

[a] Includes an analysis of CBS' Television Station group and Television Network which were each analyzed as separate components.

This analysis yielded a range of per share values for CBS common stock of approximately $42–$47. This range of per share values for CBS common stock compares to $48.89, the price for CBS common stock implied by multiplying the exchange ratio by the price of Viacom Class B common stock on September 3, 1999. The multiples for the Television Assets and Cable programming used in the sum-of-the-parts analysis were arrived at after a review of publicly traded companies with a similar operating profile to the CBS assets.

Market position, growth prospects and profitability were a few of the many factors used in comparing the CBS assets to the publicly traded comparables.

Relative Contribution Analysis. Morgan Stanley compared pro forma contribution of each of Viacom and CBS, based on securities research analyst estimates, to the resultant combined company assuming completion of the merger. Morgan Stanley adjusted these statistics to reflect each company's respective capital structure and then compared them to the pro forma ownership by Viacom shareholders of the common stock of the combined company, implied by the exchange ratio, of approximately 46%. Morgan Stanley performed this analysis with and without Blockbuster as part of Viacom to reflect Viacom's previously announced intention to split-off Blockbuster to the Viacom shareholders and, as a consequence, deconsolidate Blockbuster for accounting purposes. The results in terms of both EBITDA and after tax cash flow are set forth below:

| | Viacom Equity Contribution | |
	With Blockbuster	Without Blockbuster
2000E EBITDA	55.3%	46.9%
2001E EBITDA	54.5	45.9
2002E EBITDA	53.1	44.9
2000E After Tax Cash Flow	55.5	44.5
2001E After Tax Cash Flow	56.2	45.4
2002E After Tax Cash Flow	55.2	45.1

Historical Exchange Ratio Analysis. Morgan Stanley compared the exchange ratio of 1.085 to the ratio of the closing market prices of Viacom Class B common stock and CBS common stock on September 3. 1999. Morgan Stanley also compared this ratio to selected average historical ratios of the closing market prices of CBS common stock to Viacom Class B common stock over various periods ending September 3, 1999. Morgan Stanley then calculated the premiums represented by the exchange ratio over these ratios. The results of this analysis are set forth below:

	Market Price Ratio	% Premium/ (Discount) to Market Price Ratio
Current (9/3/99)	1.086x	(0.1)%
Prior 5 Days	1.109	(2.2)
Prior 10 Days	1.123	(3.4)
Prior 20 Days	1.116	(2.8)
Prior 30 Days	1.097	(1.1)
Prior 45 Days	1.071	1.3
Prior 60 Days	1.064	2.0
Last 6 months	1.043	4.0

As of September 3, 1999, the exchange ratio multiplied by the closing price for the Viacom Class B common stock implied a $48.89 share price for the CBS common stock or approximately a 5 cent discount to the closing price for CBS common stock.

The preparation of a fairness opinion is a complex process and is not necessarily susceptible to a partial analysis or summary description. In arriving at its opinion, Morgan Stanley considered the results of all of its analyses as a whole and did not attribute any particular weight to any particular analysis or factor considered by it. Furthermore, selecting any portion of Morgan Stanley's analyses, without considering all analyses, would create an incomplete view of the process underlying the Morgan Stanley opinion. In addition, Morgan Stanley may have deemed various assumptions more or less probable than other assumptions, so that the ranges of valuations resulting from any particular analysis described above should not be taken to be Morgan Stanley's view of the actual value of Viacom or CBS.

In performing its analysis, Morgan Stanley made numerous assumptions with respect to industry performance, general business and economic conditions and other matters, many of which are beyond the control of Viacom or CBS. Any estimates contained in the analyses performed by Morgan Stanley are not necessarily indicative of actual values, which may be significantly more or less favorable than suggested by such estimates. The analyses performed were prepared solely as a part of Morgan Stanley's analysis of the fairness of the exchange ratio to Viacom in connection with the delivery of Morgan Stanley's opinion to Viacom's board of directors. The analyses do not purport to be appraisals or to reflect the prices at which Viacom Class B common stock or CBS common stock might actually trade.

The exchange ratio was determined through arm's-length negotiations between Viacom and CBS and was approved by the Viacom board of directors. Morgan Stanley's opinion to the Viacom board of directors was one of many factors taken into consideration by the Viacom board of directors in making its determination to approve the merger. Consequently, the Morgan Stanley analyses described above should not be viewed as determinative of the opinion of the Viacom board of directors with respect to the value of CBS or of whether the Viacom board of directors would have been willing to agree to different consideration.

Morgan Stanley is an internationally recognized investment banking and advisory firm. Morgan Stanley, as part of its investment banking business, is continuously engaged in the valuation of businesses and securities in connection with mergers and acquisitions, negotiated underwritings, competitive biddings, secondary distributions of listed and unlisted securities, private placements and valuations for corporate and other purposes. In the ordinary course of Morgan Stanley's trading, brokerage and financing activities, Morgan Stanley or its affiliates may at anytime hold long or short positions, may trade, make a market or otherwise effect transactions, for its own account or for the accounts of customers, in the securities of Viacom or CBS.

In accordance with an engagement letter dated September 2, 1999, Viacom has agreed to pay Morgan Stanley a $10 million fee for advisory services rendered and to reimburse Morgan Stanley for reasonable expenses incurred. Of this $10 million fee, $7.5 million is contingent upon the closing of the merger. Viacom has also agreed to indemnify Morgan Stanley and its affiliates, their respective directors, officers, agents and employees and each person, if any, controlling Morgan Stanley or any of its affiliates, against liabilities and expenses, including certain liabilities under the federal securities laws, arising out of

Morgan Stanley's engagement. In the past, Morgan Stanley and its affiliates have provided financial advisory and financing services for Viacom and CBS and have received fees for the rendering of these services.

CBS

CBS retained Evercore to act as financial advisor to CBS and to render a fairness opinion, from a financial point of view, in connection with the merger. On September 5, 1999, Evercore delivered its oral opinion to the CBS board of directors, which was subsequently confirmed in a written opinion, that, as of that date, the exchange ratio was fair, from a financial point of view, to the shareholders of CBS.

The full text of the written opinion of Evercore is set forth as Annex I to this joint proxy statement/prospectus and describes the assumptions made, general procedures followed, matters considered and limits on the review undertaken. Evercore's opinion is directed only to whether the exchange ratio is fair, from a financial point of view, to the holders of CBS common stock and does not constitute a recommendation of the merger over other courses of action that may be available to CBS or constitute a recommendation to any CBS shareholder as to how that shareholder should vote with respect to the merger. The summary of the opinion of Evercore set forth in this joint proxy statement/prospectus is qualified in its entirety by reference to the full text of such opinion, attached as Annex I. **Shareholders of CBS are urged to read the opinion carefully and in its entirety.**

In connection with rendering its opinion, Evercore has, among other things:

- analyzed various publicly available financial statements and other information relating to CBS and Viacom;
- analyzed various internal financial statements and other non-public financial and operating data concerning CBS, which were prepared by and furnished to Evercore or reviewed for Evercore by the management of CBS, and concerning Viacom, which were prepared by and furnished to Evercore or reviewed for Evercore by the management of Viacom;
- analyzed various financial projections for 1999 concerning CBS, which were prepared by the management of CBS, and concerning Viacom, which were prepared by the management of Viacom;
- discussed the past and current operations and financial condition and the prospects of CBS with the management of CBS;
- discussed the past and current operations and financial condition and the prospects of Viacom with the management of Viacom;
- reviewed the reported prices and trading activity of the CBS common stock and Viacom Class B common stock;
- compared the market valuation and financial performance of CBS and Viacom with that of several other comparable publicly traded companies;

- reviewed the financial terms to the extent available of certain comparable acquisition transactions;

- participated in discussions and negotiations among representatives of CBS, Viacom, and their respective financial and legal advisers;

- reviewed the merger agreement and the related exhibits and schedules;

- reviewed various information concerning cost savings and combination benefits expected to result from the merger that was furnished to Evercore or reviewed for Evercore by the managements of CBS and Viacom; and

- performed other analyses and examinations and considered other factors as Evercore in its sole judgment deemed appropriate.

For purposes of its analysis and opinion, Evercore assumed and relied, without independent verification, upon the accuracy and completeness of the information reviewed by Evercore or reviewed for Evercore. With respect to the financial projections of CBS and Viacom for 1999 which were furnished to Evercore by the managements of CBS and Viacom, and certain analyses concerning the potential cost savings and combination benefits expected to result from the merger which were reviewed for Evercore by the management of CBS, Evercore assumed that they were reasonably prepared on bases reflecting the best currently available estimates and good faith judgments of the future competitive, operating and regulatory environments and related financial performance of CBS and Viacom, respectively. Evercore did not make nor assume any responsibility for making any independent valuation or appraisal of the assets or liabilities of CBS or Viacom, nor was Evercore furnished with any such appraisals: Evercore's opinion was necessarily based on economic, market and other conditions as in effect on, and the information and agreements made available to Evercore as of the date of its opinion. Evercore assumed, with the approval of CBS, that the merger would qualify as a tax-free reorganization within the meaning of Section 368 of the Internal Revenue Code of 1986. Evercore's opinion did not address CBS' underlying business decision to effect the merger nor constitute a recommendation to any CBS shareholder as to how that shareholder should vote with respect to the merger. Furthermore, Evercore expressed no opinion as to the price or range of prices at which the shares of Viacom Class B common stock would trade at any future time.

For purposes of its analyses, Evercore primarily relied upon publicly available Wall Street research estimates for each company, and subsequently compared those estimates to internal budgets for 1999 for each company to confirm the reasonableness of the analysts' expectations.

For purposes of rendering its opinion, Evercore assumed, in all respects material to its analysis, that the representations and warranties of each party contained in the merger agreement were true and correct, that each party would perform all the covenants and agreements required under the merger agreement, and that all conditions to the consummation of the merger would be satisfied without being waived.

In connection with a presentation to the CBS Board on September 5, 1999, Evercore advised CBS' board that, in evaluating the exchange ratio, Evercore had performed a variety of financial analyses with respect to CBS and Viacom, each of which material analysis is summarized below:

Historical Exchange Ratio Analysis. Evercore reviewed the daily closing prices of CBS common stock and Viacom Class B common stock to determine the implied exchange ratio based upon the relative prices of CBS common stock and Viacom Class B common stock for each considered time period. Evercore did so in order to analyze whether the agreed upon exchange ratio was consistent with the implied exchange ratio during these periods. Evercore analyzed the implied exchange ratio between CBS common stock and Viacom Class B common stock for various time periods between January 2, 1998 and September 3, 1999. Evercore noted that the agreed to exchange ratio of 1.085 was within the range of historical implied exchange ratios in the periods examined. The historical implied exchange ratios for the periods are shown below:

	CBS Share Price	Viacom Class B Share Price	Implied Exchange Ratio
September 3, 1999	$48.94	$45.06	1.0860
10-Day Average	47.81	42.59	1.1225
20-Day Average	46.71	41.86	1.1159
30-Day Average	46.15	42.10	1.0964
45-Day Average	45.86	42.91	1.0688
60-Day Average	45.07	42.43	1.0621
90-Day Average	44.63	41.73	1.0695
1999 Year-to-Date Avg. (through 9/3/99)	41.57	42.11	0.9871
1998 Full-Year Average	30.33	28.64	1.0591
Merger Exchange Ratio			1.0850

Contribution Analysis. Evercore analyzed the relative contributions of CBS and Viacom to the pro forma combined company with respect to revenues, consolidated EBITDA, EBITDA less minority interest, adjusted to exclude minority interests in the EBITDA of Infinity for CBS and in Blockbuster for Viacom, equity market value, and enterprise value for the projected fiscal years ending in 1999 and 2000. Evercore did so in order to compare CBS' relative contribution to the combined company on these measurements to CBS' pro forma ownership of the combined company based on the exchange ratio. Evercore also reviewed the pro forma ownership of the combined company, taking into account each company's outstanding options and warrants on common stock treated under the treasury stock method. Evercore noted that the pro forma ownership percentage based on the exchange ratio was consistent with CBS' contribution of the measurements set forth on the next page.

	FY 1999E		FY 2000E	
	CBS	**Viacom**	**CBS**	**Viacom**
Contribution Percentage:				
Revenue	39.9%	60.1%	39.5%	60.5%
Consolidated EBITDA	52.0%	48.0%	52.2%	47.8%
EBITDA Less Min. Int.[a]	47.2%	52.8%	47.6%	52.4%
Equity Market Value	54.7%	45.3%		
Enterprise Value	53.0%	47.0%		
Pro Forma Economic Ownership Based on Exchange Ratio:				
CBS	54.6%			
Viacom	45.4%			

[a] Excludes 35.8% minority interest in Infinity for CBS and 17.7% minority interest in Blockbuster for Viacom.

Pro Forma Merger Analysis. Primarily relying on Wall Street research estimates, Evercore analyzed the potential pro forma effects of the merger on CBS' projected free cash flow per share based on various assumptions regarding the merger. Evercore performed such analysis due to the fact that several Wall Street research analysts use projected free cash flow per share as one, among other, valuation measurements. For the purposes of this analysis, free cash flow was defined as EBITDA less interest expense less cash taxes less capital expenditures. This analysis indicated that the merger would initially be dilutive to CBS' free cash flow per share. The actual results achieved by the combined company may vary from projected results and the variations may be material.

Review of Selected Merger-of-Equals Transactions. Evercore reviewed the financial terms, to the extent publicly available, of nine selected merger-of-equals transactions, in order to compare the premiums implied in these transactions to the implied premium in the merger. Evercore reviewed the premiums implied in the selected merger-of-equals transactions relative to market value contributions, assuming a constant market capitalization based on closing stock prices prior to the announcement of such transactions.

Evercore noted that, if the merger had closed on September 3, 1999, utilizing the Viacom closing stock price on September 3, 1999, and assuming the exchange ratio of 1.085, CBS shareholders would have received Viacom Class B common stock having a market value representing a discount of 0.1% to the CBS common stock September 3, 1999 closing price. Evercore compared this implied discount to the implied premiums/discounts for similar periods prior to public announcement in the following comparable merger-of-equals transactions:

- Honeywell Inc./AlliedSignal Inc.;
- GTE Corporation/Bell Atlantic Corporation;
- Wells Fargo & Company/Norwest Corporation;
- Monsanto Company/American Home Products Corporation;
- BankAmerica Corporation/NationsBank Corp.;

- First Chicago NBD Corporation/Banc One Corporation;
- Citicorp/Travelers Group, Inc.;
- HFS Incorporated/CUC International Inc.; and
- NYNEX Corporation/Bell Atlantic Corporation

In each of the above transactions, the shareholders of the first-named company were to receive shares of the second-named company. Evercore considered these merger-of-equals transactions to be reasonably similar to the merger, but none of these precedents is identical to the merger.

The following table presents the premiums or discounts contemplated in the merger and implied in these other transactions, from the perspective of the shareholders of the first-named company, compared with the previous trading day closing price per share:

	Premium to Prior Day Closing Price
CBS/Viacom	−0.1%
Precedent "Merger-of-Equals Transactions:	
Average	3.5%
Median	5.5%
Low	−5.8%
High	9.3%

Evercore noted that the discount of 0.1% for the CBS/Viacom merger was within the range of 5.8%–9.3% discount/premium for the other transactions analyzed.

Selected Comparable Company Analysis. Evercore compared selected financial, market and operating information of CBS with corresponding data of other selected publicly traded companies with similar operations to those of CBS, in order to compare CBS' public market valuation to public companies with similar operations. Evercore compared the adjusted enterprise value to adjusted EBITDA multiples of the consolidated CBS Corporation to a selected group of publicly traded radio broadcasting and outdoor advertising companies. Adjusted enterprise value for a given company was defined as total enterprise value, which is equity market value plus total debt and preferred stock, less cash and cash equivalents, less the value of unconsolidated stakes in other companies, less the value of segments within the company that trade at multiples that are significantly different from the rest of the company, and plus the value of any minority stakes in consolidated businesses.

Adjusted EBITDA for a given company was defined as EBITDA less the EBITDA contributed by segments within the company that trade at multiples that are significantly different from the rest of the company. This selected group of publicly traded radio broadcasting and outdoor advertising companies was comprised of:

- AM/FM Inc.;
- Citadel Communications Corporation;
- Clear Channel Communications. Inc.;

- Cox Radio, Inc.;
- Cumulus Media, Inc.;
- Emmis Communications Corporation;
- Entercom Communications Corp.;
- Hispanic Broadcasting Corporation;
- Infinity Broadcasting Corporation;
- Radio One. Inc.; and
- Saga Communications, Inc.

Evercore selected these radio broadcasting and outdoor advertising companies because Evercore considered them to have operations similar to the operations of CBS in this business segment. All multiples were calculated based on closing prices as of September 3, 1999. For the comparable companies, EBITDA projections were based on publicly available Wall Street research estimates. Evercore noted that the closing price of CBS common stock on September 3, 1999 of $48.94 represented a multiple of EBITDA that was within the range found for the CBS-comparable companies set forth above. To illustrate, Evercore highlighted the following multiples of adjusted enterprise value to adjusted 1999E and 2000E EBITDA:

| | Adj. Enterprise Value to Adj. EBITDA | |
	FY 1999E	FY 2000E
CBS Consolidated	20.8x	18.2x
Radio & Outdoor Advertising[a]:		
Average	22.5x	19.5x
Low	13.4x	12.0x
High	28.7x	24.2x

[a] The analysis of Radio & Outdoor comparables excludes Hispanic Broadcasting because its multiples were not in line with other comparables.

Evercore compared the adjusted enterprise value to adjusted EBITDA multiples of CBS, excluding its majority-owned stake in Infinity, to a selected group of publicly traded television broadcasting companies. Evercore looked at CBS excluding Infinity due to the fact that many Wall Street research analysts also analyze CBS in this manner in order to isolate the implied valuation of the non-radio/outdoor advertising assets. In doing so, Evercore excluded the financial impact of Infinity on the EBITDA of CBS. Evercore also reduced the enterprise value of CBS used in the calculation by an amount equal to the market value of Infinity common stock held by CBS plus Infinity's net debt balance.

The group of publicly traded television broadcast companies selected for this comparative analysis was comprised of:

- A.H. Belo Corporation;
- Granite Broadcasting Corporation;

- Hearst-Argyle Television, Inc.;
- Paxson Communications Corporation;
- Sinclair Broadcasting Group. Inc.;
- United Television, Inc.; and
- Young Broadcasting, Inc.

Evercore selected these television broadcasting companies because Evercore considered them to have operations similar to the operations of CBS, excluding Infinity, in this business segment. All multiples were calculated based on closing prices as of September 3, 1999. For the comparable companies, EBITDA projections were based on publicly available Wall Street research estimates. Evercore noted that the closing price of CBS common stock on September 3, 1999 of $48.94 represented a multiple of EBITDA that was within the range found for the CBS-comparable companies set forth above. Evercore highlighted the following multiples of adjusted enterprise value to adjusted 1999E and 2000E EBITDA:

	Adj. Enterprise Value to Adj. EBITDA	
	FY 1999E	**FY 2000E**
CBS Excluding Infinity[a]	19.2x	16.8x
Television Broadcasting[b]		
Average	12.0x	10.9x
Low	9.0x	7.9x
High	14.2x	12.9x

[a] Also excludes TV network and Internet assets.

[b] The analysis of Television Broadcasting comparables excludes Paxson Communications because its multiples were not in line with other comparables.

Evercore also compared financial, market and operating information of Viacom with corresponding data of other selected publicly traded companies with similar operations. Evercore compared the adjusted enterprise value to adjusted EBITDA multiples of Viacom to a selected group of publicly traded entertainment companies. The selected group of publicly traded entertainment companies was comprised of:

- The Walt Disney Company;
- The News Corporation Limited;
- Time Warner Inc.;
- The Seagram Company Ltd.;
- Fox Entertainment Group, Inc.; and
- USA Networks, Inc.

Evercore selected these entertainment companies because Evercore considered them to have operations similar to the operations of Viacom. All multiples were calculated based on closing prices as of September 3, 1999. For the comparable companies, EBITDA projections were based on publicly available Wall Street research estimates. Evercore noted that the

closing price of Viacom Class B common stock on September 3, 1999 of $45.06 represent-
ed a multiple of Adjusted EBITDA that was within the range found for the Viacom-com-
parable companies set forth above. To illustrate, Evercore highlighted the following multiples of adjusted enterprise value to adjusted 1999E and 2000E EBITDA:

	Adj. Enterprise Value to Adj. EBITDA	
	FY 1999E	**FY 2000E**
Viacom[a]	20.2x	17.5x
Entertainment Comparable Firms[b]		
Average	16.3x	13.8x
Low	12.2x	9.8x
High	20.8x	17.8x

[a] Excludes Blockbuster.

[b] The analysis of Entertainment comparables excludes News Corp. due to its relatively high concentration
on publishing operations.

No company used in the comparable company analyses summarized above is identical to CBS or Viacom. Accordingly, any analysis of the fairness of the consideration to be
received by the holders of CBS common stock in the merger involves complex considerations and judgments concerning differences in the potential financial and operating characteristics of the comparable companies and other factors in relation to the trading values
of the comparable companies.

Selected Comparable Transaction Analysis. Evercore reviewed the implied transaction
multiples paid in selected comparable merger and acquisition transactions and compared
these multiples to the multiples implied by the consideration paid to CBS shareholders in
the merger. Evercore did so in order to compare the multiples paid in those transactions to
the multiple implied in the merger. Evercore noted that, if the merger had closed on
September 3, 1999, utilizing the closing price of Viacom Class B common stock on
September 3, 1999 of $45.06, and assuming the exchange ratio of 1.085, CBS shareholders
would have received Viacom Class B common stock having a market value equal to $48.89
per each share of CBS common stock owned. Evercore analyzed the adjusted enterprise
value of CBS, derived from this implied price per share, as a multiple or adjusted EBITDA
and compared this multiple to multiples of EBITDA paid in selected mergers and acquisitions of radio broadcasting and outdoor advertising companies. The following selection of
mergers and acquisitions or radio broadcasting and outdoor advertising companies was
used for purposes or this analysis:

- Chancellor Media Outdoor Corporation/Lamar Advertising Co.
- Outdoor Systems, Inc./Infinity Broadcasting Corporation
- Jacor Communications, Inc./Clear Channel Communications, Inc.
- Capstar Broadcasting Corporation/Chancellor Media Corp.
- Universal Outdoor Holdings, Inc./Clear Channel Communications, Inc.

- American Radio Systems Corporation/CBS Corporation
- SFX Broadcasting, Inc./Capstar Broadcasting Corporation
- Viacom Radio/Evergreen Media Corp.
- Chancellor Media Corp./Evergreen Media Corp.
- Infinity Broadcasting Corporation/Westinghouse Electric Corporation

Evercore also performed this analysis for the following selection of mergers and acquisitions involving television broadcasting companies:

- Gaylord Entertainment/CBS Corporation
- Kelly Broadcasting/Hearst-Argyle Television, Inc.
- Pulitzer Publishing Company (TV & Radio)/Hearst-Argyle Television, Inc.
- Sullivan Broadcasting/Sinclair Broadcast Group, Inc.
- LIN Television Corporation/Hicks Muse Tate & Furst
- Heritage Media Corporation/The News Corporation Limited
- Heritage Media Corporation/Sinclair Broadcast Group, Inc.
- A.H. Belo Corporation/Scripps Howard
- Argyle TV/Hearst-Argyle Television, Inc.
- Providence Journal Company/A.H. Belo Corporation
- First Media Television, L.P./Meredith Corporation
- New World Communications Group, Inc./The News Corporation Limited
- Renaissance Communications Corporation/Tribune Company
- Multimedia, Inc./Gannett Co., Inc.

Evercore selected these transactions because they involved companies in business segments in which CBS has operations. Evercore noted that the multiple implied by the merger as of September 3, 1999 is within the range of multiples paid in comparable transactions, and, therefore, that these analyses of multiples supported a fairness determination concerning the merger.

	Transaction Value to EBITDA
Merger Offer for CBS	
CBS Consolidated	20.8x
CBS Excluding Infinity	19.2x
Radio & Outdoor Transactions:	
Average	17.7x
Low	14.2x
High	21.0x
Television Broadcasting Transactions:	
Average	14.4x
Low	9.8x
High	23.3x

Additionally, Evercore analyzed the adjusted enterprise value of Viacom as a multiple of adjusted EBITDA and compared this multiple to multiples of EBITDA paid in a selection of mergers and acquisitions of entertainment companies. The following selection of mergers and acquisitions of entertainment companies was used for purposes of this analysis:

- PolyGram N.V./The Seagram Company Ltd.
- Metro-Goldwyn-Mayer Inc./Management
- Turner Broadcasting System, Inc./Time Warner Inc.
- CBS, Inc./Westinghouse Electric Corp.
- Capital Cities/ABC, Inc./The Walt Disney Company
- MCA, Inc./The Seagram Company Ltd.
- Blockbuster Entertainment Corporation/Viacom Inc.
- Paramount Communications Inc./Viacom Inc.

Evercore selected these transactions because they involved companies in business segments in which Viacom has operations. Evercore noted that the multiple implied by Viacom's closing price on September 3, 1999 is within the range of multiples paid in comparable transactions.

	Transaction Value to EBITDA
Viacom[a]	20.2x
Entertainment Transactions[b]:	
Average	15.9x
Low	12.3x
High	21.0x

[a] Excludes Blockbuster.

[b] The analysis of Entertainment transactions excludes Blockbuster Entertainment Corporation/Viacom Inc. transaction due to the retail nature of Blockbuster's business.

No transaction used in the comparable transaction analyses summarized above is identical to the merger. Accordingly, any analysis of the fairness of the consideration to be received by the holders of CBS common stock in the merger involves complex considerations and judgments concerning differences in the potential financial and operating characteristics of the comparable transactions and other factors in relation to the acquisition values of the comparable companies.

Discounted Cash Flow Analysis. Evercore estimated the present value of the future stand-alone, unlevered free cash flows that could be produced by CBS. Such analysis is performed to determine the value that a current share might be worth based on various assumptions as set forth below. The net present value ranges were estimated by applying one-year forward terminal value multiples ranging from 16.0x to 18.0x 2004E EBITDA and discount rates ranging from 11.0% to 14.0%. Terminal value multiples were determined based on both current public and private market-based valuations, as well as Wall Street research analyst estimates. The discount rates were determined based on the weighted average cost of capital formulation, which utilizes the cost of both debt and equity for a company/investment. This analysis indicated a value per share of CBS common stock ranging from approximately $42.03 to $52.60, as compared to the per share price of $48.89 for CBS common stock that was implied by the exchange ratio as of September 3, 1999.

Evercore also performed a discounted cash flow analysis for Viacom. Evercore estimated the present value of the future stand-alone, unlevered free cash flows that could be produced by Viacom. The net present value ranges were estimated by applying one-year forward terminal value multiples ranging from 16.0x to 18.0x 2004E EBITDA and discount rates ranging from 11.0% to 14.0%. Terminal value multiples were determined based on both current public and private market-based valuations, as well as Wall Street research analyst estimates. The discount rates were determined based on the weighted average cost of capital formulation, which utilizes the cost of both debt and equity for a company. This analysis indicated a value per share of Viacom Class B common stock ranging from approximately $42.80 to $53.18, as compared to the per share price for Viacom Class B common stock of $45.06 on September 3, 1999.

Sum-of-the-Parts Analysis. Evercore estimated the value of CBS by calculating the implied value of its different components at different multiples and then adding these values to arrive at a value for the consolidated entity. Evercore performed such analysis as it allows for the different business segments of a company to be valued consistently with its respective comparable peer group. This methodology is also commonly employed by Wall Street research analysts as one, among other, valuation measurements. For this sum-of-the-parts valuation, Evercore valued CBS' syndication business at a range of 10.0x to 12.0x 2000E EBITDA, CBS' television segment at a fixed amount for the network and at a range of 13.0x to l5.0x 2000E EBITDA for its television stations, and CBS' cable network division at a range of 16.0x to 18.0x 2000E EBITDA. The remaining businesses of CBS, consisting of corporate overhead, Internet assets, and CBS' stake in Infinity, were valued at fixed amounts. Evercore based its valuation ranges of these segments on both current public and private market-based valuations, as well as Wall Street analyst estimates. The sum-of-the parts valuation yielded a CBS common stock valuation range of $45.26 to $48.39 per share, as compared to the per share price of $48.89 for CBS common stock that was implied by the exchange ratio as of September 3, 1999.

Evercore also estimated the value of Viacom with a similar sum-of-the-parts analysis. Evercore used a range of values for each of Viacom's business segments and assets. These values were based on multiples of EBITDA, subscribers or revenues, or on other metrics such as market value or historical cost. The sum-of-the parts valuation yielded a Viacom Class B common stock valuation range of $44.60 to $51.83 per share, as compared to the per share price for Viacom Class B common stock of $45.06 on September 3, 1999.

The foregoing summary does not purport to be a complete description of the analyses performed by Evercore or of its presentation to CBS' board. The preparation of financial analyses and a fairness opinion is not susceptible to partial analysis or summary description. Evercore believes that its analyses and the summary set forth above must be considered as a whole and that selecting portions of its analyses and the factors considered by it, without considering all analyses and factors, could create an incomplete view of the processes underlying the analysis conducted by Evercore and its opinion. Evercore has not indicated that any of the analyses which it performed had a greater significance than any other.

In determining the appropriate analyses to conduct and when performing those analyses, Evercore made numerous assumptions with respect to industry performance, general business, financial, market and economic conditions and other matters, many of which are beyond the control of CBS or Viacom. The analyses which Evercore performed are not necessarily indicative of actual values or actual future results, which may be significantly more or less favorable than suggested by the analyses. The analyses were prepared solely as part of Evercore's analysis as to whether the exchange ratio is fair, from a financial point of view, to the holders of CBS common stock. The analyses are not appraisals and the estimates of values of companies do not reflect the prices at which a company might actually be sold or the prices at which any securities may trade at the present time or at any time in the future.

Evercore is a nationally recognized investment banking firm that is regularly engaged in the valuation of businesses and their securities in connection with mergers and acquisitions. CBS retained Evercore based on these qualifications as well as its familiarity with CBS and Viacom. Evercore has previously provided various investment banking and financial advisory services to CBS, for which Evercore received customary fees for the rendering of these services.

Pursuant to the terms of an engagement letter with Evercore, CBS agreed to pay Evercore a fee equal to $2.5 million following delivery of Evercore's fairness opinion and $7.5 million upon the completion of the merger. Whether or not the merger is completed, CBS has agreed under the engagement letter to reimburse Evercore for all its reasonable out-of-pocket expenses, including the reasonable fees and disbursements of its counsel, incurred in connection with its engagement by CBS, and to indemnify Evercore against liabilities and expenses in connection with its engagement.

Directors, Management and Corporate Governance or the Combined Company

Pursuant to the merger agreement, the proposed new Restated Certificate of Incorporation and By-laws. and the stockholder agreement between National Amusements and CBS, Viacom, CBS and National Amusements have agreed to corporate governance arrangements which generally cannot be changed for three years following the merger without approval of at least 14 directors and, in some cases, approval of the combined company's shareholders. These corporate governance arrangements are described below.

Chairman and Chief Executive Office: Mr. Redstone, the current Chairman and CEO of Viacom, will remain the Chairman and CEO of the combined company following the merger. Mr. Redstone, as CEO, will be responsible, in consultation with the President and COO, for the combined company's corporate policy and strategy and will chair all board and shareholder meetings at which he is present. If Mr. Redstone ceases to be the CEO at any time during the first three years following the merger, or if Mr. Redstone is no longer the CEO at the effective time of the merger, Mr. Karmazin will be the CEO and will retain the COO functions described below.

President and Chief Operating Office. Mr. Karmazin, the current President and CEO of CBS, will be the President and COO of the combined company following the merger. The COO will report directly to the CEO and must consult with the CEO on all major decisions affecting the combined company. Mr. Karmazin, as COO, will be responsible for supervising, coordinating and managing the combined company's business, operations, activities, operating expenses, capital allocation, officers other than the CEO, and employees, including hiring, terminating, changing positions and allocating responsibilities of those officers and employees, other than hiring of the Chief Financial Officer, Controller and General Counsel, which can only be done by majority vote of the combined company's board. All officers, other than the CEO, and employees will report directly or indirectly to the COO. During the three year period following the merger, Mr. Karmazin cannot be terminated or demoted, whether he is COO or CEO, and none of the COO functions may be changed, unless approved by a vote of at least 14 directors.

In a number of areas, Mr. Karmazin may not act without the approval of, and the combined company's board may act by, a majority of the directors. As described below, ten of the 18 directors of the combined company are expected to be designees of Viacom or their successors and could therefore control actions which may be taken by a majority of the combined company's directors. In all other areas, Mr. Karmazin's authority to manage the combined company may be limited only by a supermajority of the board of at least 14 directors. As a result, Mr. Karmazin will have an unusual degree of autonomy for a President and COO of a large corporation. For example, Mr. Karmazin may approve the acquisition or divestiture of an Internet or Internet related business meeting the criteria discussed below for under $100 million, subject to an aggregate $550 million limit, or the acquisition or divestiture of a radio or outdoor advertising business, subject to an aggregate $300 million limit, and can only be overruled in these decisions by a supermajority of 14 directors. Mr. Karmazin's ability to hire and terminate officers of the combined company without board approval is also unusual.

Board of Directors. At the effective time of the merger, the board of directors of Viacom will be expanded to 18 directors. The board size may not be changed during the three year period following the merger without the approval of at least 14 directors. Eight of the 18 directors initially will be individuals who were directors of CBS on September 6, 1999, or any independent directors of CBS subsequently appointed to the CBS board of directors, as selected by the CBS board of directors prior to the effective time of the merger. The Viacom board, subject to the fiduciary duties of its members, and National Amusements, pursuant to its voting agreement with CBS, are required to take all action necessary to fill any vacancy in any of the eight CBS directorships with an independent director designated by a majority of the remaining CBS directors. No CBS director serving on the Viacom board may be removed from office during the three year period following the merger unless the removal is for cause and is approved by at least 14 directors. The remaining ten directors will be the Viacom directors immediately prior to the effective time of the merger. Of these ten directors, two must either be the current independent directors of Viacom or other disinterested, independent persons that are chief executive officers, chief operating officers, chief financial officers or former chief executive officers of a Fortune 500 company or a non-U.S. public company of comparable size. Subject to the preceding sentence, National Amusements, which is controlled by Mr. Redstone through its majority ownership of Viacom Class A common stock, has the ability to cause the Viacom nominees to be elected to serve as the ten remaining directors.

Actions of the Board of Directors. All actions to be taken by the board of directors of Viacom following the merger will require the approval of at least 14 directors, except for the actions specified below, which will require approval only by a majority of the board:

Acquisitions, Divestitures, Joint Ventures, Guarantees

- Any acquisition, equity investment, or joint venture by Viacom or any of its subsidiaries for more than $25 million.
- Any divestiture or other sale of assets not in the ordinary course by Viacom or any of its subsidiaries for more than $25 million.
- Any real estate purchase, sale or lease by Viacom or any of its subsidiaries for more than $25 million.
- Any guarantee by Viacom or any of its subsidiaries of an obligation of a third party where the obligation guaranteed is more than $25 million.
- Notwithstanding any of the above, any acquisition or divestiture by Viacom or any of its subsidiaries of:

  —Internet or Internet related businesses for more that $25 million but less than $100 million, with the value thereof represented by multi-year commitments for advertising, promotion and content licensing is excluded, so long as the aggregate of these acquisitions or divestitures, in each case, does not exceed $550 million and

  —radio or outdoor advertising businesses for more than $25 million but less than $100 million is excluded, so long as the aggregate of these acquisitions or divestitures, in each case, does not exceed $300 million;

  provided that:

  —any divestiture of shares of a publicly traded Internet or Internet related business with a value of up to $75 million is excluded and will not be included in the calculation of any of the threshold amounts set forth above,

  —board approval may be secured, but is not required, for any transaction of more than $25 million but less than $100 million where the regular meeting schedule of the board so permits and is not otherwise required,

  —the board will be provided with information about and a status report on the transactions completed without board approval, and

—this limit of authority will be reviewed 12 months following the merger and may be amended only with the approval of 14 directors

- Any contract of Viacom or any of its subsidiaries not in the ordinary course with a value in excess of $25 million.

- Notwithstanding any of the above, any of the acquisitions, divestitures or other transactions described above that are approved by a majority of the board will not be included in the calculation of any of the threshold amounts for these transactions. For example, if a majority of the board elects to approve the acquisition of an Internet business for $100 million, the $100 million would not count against the $550 million aggregate threshold above which this type of transaction would require majority board approval.

Employee Matters

- Employee benefit plans of Viacom or any of its subsidiaries: (1) creating a new plan, (2) suspending or terminating an existing plan, or (3) adopting any amendment that materially increases costs to Viacom or any subsidiary.

- Entering into any modifications or amendments to the employment agreements with the CEO or the COO.

Viacom's proposed new Restated Certificate of Incorporation specifically provides for two committees—the Officers Nominating Committee and the Compensation Committee:

Officers Nominating Committee. The Officers Nominating Committee will be composed of the COO or, in the event Mr. Karmazin is CEO, the CEO. During the three year period following the merger, the Officers Nominating Committee has the power, subject to the powers of the Compensation Committee, to hire, elect, terminate, change positions, allocate responsibilities, and determine non-equity compensation of officers and employees, other than the Chairman, CEO and COO. The Officers Nominating Committee will not, however, have the power to fill the position of Chief Financial Officer, Controller or General Counsel without approval by a majority of the board of directors, although the Officers Nominating Committee will have the power to terminate the employment of the persons holding those positions. Any action taken by the Officers Nominating Committee may be overturned by a vote of at least 14 directors.

Compensation Committee. The Compensation Committee will be composed of three CBS directors who are independent directors and three non-CBS directors, all of whom are independent. Except as set forth in the following sentence, all compensation must be approved by the Compensation Committee. The Compensation Committee does not have the power to approve the annual compensation of any talent, as that term is commonly used in the media or entertainment industries, or of any employee whose annual cash compensation, measured as salary plus target bonus is less than $1 million. These powers are delegated to the Officers Nominating Committee.

Subsidiaries. The CEO and COO will be elected or appointed to the boards of directors of all public subsidiaries of Viacom following the merger. In addition, the board of directors of Viacom will have the right, in consultation with the COO, or, if Mr. Karmazin is the CEO, the CEO, to implement corporate governance arrangements for any public subsidiary of Viacom consistent with the corporate governance arrangements contained in Viacom's proposed new Restated Certificate of Incorporation.

Miscellaneous. The combined company may not issue any stock or other securities, including authorized shares of Viacom Class A common stock and Viacom preferred stock, giving the holder the right to vote on any matter on which shareholders are entitled to vote, if National Amusements would, as a result of the issuance, no longer own a majority of the outstanding voting stock of the combined company. Any amendment, alteration, repeal or waiver of the provisions of the new proposed Restated Certificate of Incorporation summarized above requires the approval of at least 14 directors of the combined company.

Accounting Treatment

The merger will be accounted for as a purchase for financial accounting purposes in accordance with generally accepted accounting principles. For purposes of preparing Viacom's consolidated financial statements, Viacom will establish a new accounting basis for CBS' assets and liabilities based upon their fair values, the merger consideration and the costs of the merger. Viacom believes that any excess of cost over the fair value of the net assets of CBS will be recorded as goodwill and other intangible assets. A final determination of the intangible asset lives and required purchase accounting adjustments, including the allocation of the purchase price to the assets acquired and liabilities assumed based on their respective fair values, has not yet been made. Accordingly, the purchase accounting adjustments made in connection with the development of the unaudited pro forma combined financial information appearing elsewhere in or incorporated by reference into this joint proxy statement/prospectus are preliminary and have been made solely for purposes of developing that pro forma information. Viacom will determine the fair value of CBS' assets and liabilities and will make appropriate purchase accounting adjustments, including adjustments to the amortization period of the intangible assets, upon completion of that determination.

Federal Income Tax Consequences

The following discussion summarizes the material United States federal income tax consequences of the merger assuming that it is consummated as contemplated by this joint proxy statement/prospectus. This discussion is based on the Internal Revenue Code, U.S. Treasury regulations, judicial decisions and administrative rulings as of the date hereof, all of which are subject to change, including changes with retroactive effect. The discussion below does not address any state, local or foreign tax consequences of the merger. This discussion assumes that shareholders hold such shares as capital assets. The tax treatment of a shareholder may vary depending upon the shareholder's particular situation, and some shareholders, including individuals who hold options in respect of CBS common stock, insurance companies, tax-exempt organizations, financial institutions or broker-dealers, and persons who are neither citizens nor residents of the United States or that are foreign corporations, foreign partnerships or foreign estates or trusts as to the United States, may be subject to special rules not discussed below.

Each CBS shareholder is urged to consult his, her or its own tax advisor as to the particular tax consequences to him, her, or it of the merger, including the applicability and effect of any state, local or foreign laws, and of changes in applicable tax laws.

Federal Income Tax Consequences of the Merger. The material federal income tax consequences of the merger of CBS directly into Viacom will be as follows and Cravath, Swaine & Moore, counsel to CBS, and Paul, Weiss, Rifkind, Wharton & Garrison, counsel to Viacom, have each rendered an opinion to such effect:

(1)   The merger will qualify as a reorganization under Section 368(a) of the Internal Revenue Code and each of CBS and Viacom will be a party to that reorganization within the meaning of Section 368(b) of the Internal Revenue Code.

(2)   CBS shareholders will not recognize any income, gain or loss as a result of the receipt of Viacom Class B common stock or Viacom Series C preferred stock, except for any payment received in lieu of fractional shares and to the extent that any payment by Viacom of transfer taxes is treated as taxable consideration received by the CBS shareholders.

(3)   A CBS shareholder's tax basis for the shares of Viacom Class B common stock or Viacom Series C preferred stock received in the merger, including any fractional share interest for which payment is received, will equal such shareholder's tax basis in the shares of CBS common stock or CBS Series B preferred stock exchanged therefore.

(4)   A CBS shareholder's holding period for the Viacom Class B common stock or Viacom Series C preferred stock received in the merger will include the period during which the shares of CBS common stock or CBS Series B preferred stock exchanged therefore were held.

Viacom's obligation to complete the merger is conditioned upon, among other things, its receipt of an opinion from Paul, Weiss, Rifkind, Wharton & Garrison that the merger will be treated as a reorganization under Section 368(a) of the Internal Revenue Code and that Viacom and CBS will each be a party to the reorganization within the meaning of Section 368(b) of the Internal Revenue Code. The obligation of CBS to complete the merger is conditioned upon, among other things, CBS's receipt of an opinion from Cravath, Swaine & Moore that the merger will be treated as a reorganization under Section 368(a) of the Internal Revenue Code and that Viacom and CBS will each be a party to the reorganization within the meaning of Section 368(b) of the Internal Revenue Code. These opinions of counsel will be based in part upon representations, made as of the effective time of the merger, by Viacom and CBS, which each counsel will assume to be true, correct and complete. If the representations are inaccurate, the opinions of counsel could be adversely affected.

Backup Withholding. Under the backup withholding rules, a holder of CBS common stock or CBS Series B preferred stock may be subject to backup withholding at the rate of 31% with respect to payment received in exchange for the fractional share interest unless the shareholder:

- is a corporation or comes within other exempt categories and, when required, demonstrates this fact, or
- provides a taxpayer identification number and certifies that the taxpayer identification number is correct and the taxpayer is not subject to backup withholding for specified reasons, and otherwise complies with applicable requirements of the backup withholding rules.

Any amount withheld under these rules will be credited against the shareholder's federal income tax liability.

Reporting Requirements. CBS shareholders will be required to attach a statement to their tax returns for the taxable year in which the merger is completed that contains the information set forth in Treasury Regulation 1.368-3(b) of the Department of Treasury regulations. The statement must include the tax basis in the CBS common stock or CBS Series B preferred stock surrendered and a description of the Viacom Class B common stock or Viacom Series C preferred stock received in the merger.

On the basis of the above materials, a plausible base scenario for the postmerger intrinsic value per share of the Viacom class B common stock is summarized from analyst reports. The year 2000 revenues for the combined companies are estimated to be $25 billion, which would represent the zero year revenues (R_0) for the valuation model to be applied. Other value drivers for the analysis are summarized on the next page.

n = Number of supernormal growth years	10
m = Net operating income margin	22.0%
T = Tax rate	35.0%
g_s = Supernormal growth period growth rate	20.0%
d_s = Supernormal growth period depreciation	7.0%
I_{ws} = Supernormal growth period working capital expenditures	4.0%
I_{fgs} = Supernormal growth period capital expenditures (gross)	1.0%
k_s = Supernormal growth period cost of capital	10.0%
g_c = Terminal period growth rate	4.0%
d_c = Terminal period depreciation	1.0%
I_{wc} = Terminal period working capital expenditures	0.0%
I_{fgc} = Terminal period capital expenditures	1.0%
k_c = Terminal period cost of capital	15.0%

QUESTIONS

1. For the levels of value drivers given for the base case, what is your estimate of the intrinsic value per share of the Viacom class B common stock? Additional-al inputs include no marketable securities, total interest bearing debt plus minority interest of $10 billion, and 1,541 million shares of class B Viacom stock outstanding. (Hint: Use Model 09-04A from the Models disk.)

2. For the following alternative assumptions, calculate alternative values per share of Viacom. 1) Net operating income margin of 20% of revenues. 2) Net operating income margin of 18% of revenues. 3) Supernormal growth period cost of capital of 10.5%. 4) Supernormal growth period capital expenditures of 5% of revenues. 5) Supernormal period growth rate of revenues of 15%.

3. Based on the background material in the case, what would be your best judgment of the intrinsic value of Viacom?

Case 18

The AOL/Time Warner Merger

The deal terms of the AOL/Time Warner (TWX) merger were formally announced on January 10, 2000. The basic financial relationships of the deal are summarized in Table 1. The respective closing market prices on Friday January 7 were $74 for AOL and $65 for TWX. Multiplying the price per share by the number of shares shown in Table 1 gives a market cap of $182 billion for AOL and $83.7 billion for TWX. Thus, premerger, the market cap of AOL represented 68.5% of the total market cap. The merger terms specified that TWX shareholders would receive 1.5 AOL shares per TWX share. Thus, the number of AOL shares received by TWX shareholders was 1.93 billion. Multiplying by the AOL price of $74 gives $142.8 billion as the price paid for TWX. This represented a premium over the premerger market cap of TWX of 70.7%. Other relationships are developed in the following pages.

TABLE 1 AOL Time Warner Merger Terms			
	AOL	**TWX**	**Combined**
Premerger			
Market price 1/7/00	$74	$65	
Number of shares (billion)	2.460	1.287	
Market cap ($ billion)	$182.0	$83.7	$265.7
Shares of market cap	68.5%	31.5%	100.0%
Postmerger			
Number of shares (billion)	2.460	1.930	4.390
Percent ownership	56.0%	44.0%	100.0%
Total paid by AOL ($ billion)		$142.8	
Premium paid		70.7%	

Background of the Merger

In September 1999, Stephen M. Case, Chairman and Chief Executive Officer of America Online, and Gerald M. Levin, Chairman and Chief Executive Officer of Time Warner, participated in a meeting of media and technology executives at the Global Business Dialogue on E-Commerce in Paris. Later in September, Messrs. Case and Levin participated in a number of meetings at the Fortune Global Forum and related events, which took place in Shanghai and Beijing. During the time they spent together at these conferences, Messrs. Case and Levin discussed a variety of topics related to their businesses. They did not, however, discuss the possibility of combining their businesses.

In mid-October, Mr. Case spoke with Mr. Levin to suggest that they consider a business combination involving America Online and Time Warner. Mr. Case proposed that the combination be accomplished through a stock-for-stock merger of equals. In addition, Mr. Case proposed that he would serve as chairman of the combined company and that Mr. Levin would serve as chief executive officer of the combined company. On October 25, 1999, Messrs. Case and Levin had another conversation to discuss further these matters.

On November 1, 1999, Messrs. Case and Levin met for dinner and continued their discussion about a possible business combination, elaborating on the mutual strategic benefits of a merger of equals and discussing the structure and implementation of a business combination. That discussion included a reaffirmation of the fundamental principles of the business combination first outlined in the mid-October conversation, and ended with a mutual intention to pursue discussions further.

In conjunction with the initial discussions, the companies began consulting with various financial and legal advisors about issues raised in the discussions among their executives. America Online retained Salomon Smith Barney as its financial advisor and Simpson Thacher & Bartlett and Mintz, Levin, Cohn, Ferris, Glovsky and Popeo, P.C., as its legal counsel. Time Warner retained Morgan Stanley as its financial advisor and Cravath, Swaine & Moore as its legal counsel. Working with these advisors, America Online and Time Warner began conducting their due diligence investigations using publicly available materials and began analyses of a possible combination. These consultations continued throughout the remaining merger discussions.

Following the November 1, 1999 dinner meeting between Messrs. Case and Levin, Kenneth J. Novack, Vice Chairman of America Online, and Miles Gilburne, then the Senior Vice President, Corporate Development of America Online, had several telephone conversations with Richard J. Bressler, Chairman and Chief Executive Officer of Time Warner Digital Media, to discuss the structure and implementation of a stock-for-stock merger of America Online and Time Warner. Over the next two months, Messrs. Novack and Bressler had periodic telephone conversations to discuss the proposed combination.

On November 9, 1999, Messrs. Novack, Gilburne and Bressler met to continue to discuss the strategic rationale for a merger, the appropriate exchange ratio and the governance and management structure of the resulting entity. The discussions remained at a general level, and no agreement regarding the specific terms of a possible stock-for-stock merger was reached.

Following the November 9, 1999 meeting, Messrs. Novack and Bressler engaged in numerous telephone discussions concerning a potential merger, culminating in another meeting among Messrs. Novack, Gilburne and Bressler in New York on November 16, 1999. During that meeting, there were again discussions, but no agreement, about an appropriate exchange ratio and a governance and management structure for the merged entity.

On November 17, 1999, Mr. Case met with R. E. Turner, the Vice Chairman of Time Warner, to discuss the potential merger and its strategic rationale. Later in the day, Messrs. Case and Levin met and discussed possible exchange ratios, but they concluded the meeting at an impasse. The parties determined at this point to discontinue discussions about a possible combination.

Mr. Novack and Mr. Bressler spoke by telephone on or about December 8, 1999, concerning the companies' relative market performance and the possibility of holding a meeting the following week to renew discussions. On December 10, 1999, America Online and Time Warner entered into a confidentiality agreement, which contained customary standstill provisions. On December 13, 1999, Mr. Novack and a representative of Salomon Smith Barney met with Mr. Bressler and a representative of Morgan Stanley in New York to discuss possible structures for a transaction and pricing terms, including exchange ratios and whether a collar would be used. The meeting concluded without agreement.

On the morning of December 23, 1999, Mr. Novack, and J. Michael Kelly, Chief Financial Officer of America Online, and a representative or Salomon Smith Barney met in Boston with Richard D. Parsons, President of Time Warner, Mr. Bressler and a representative of Morgan Stanley to continue discussions regarding a possible transaction. The exchange ratio for a possible merger was again discussed, but the parties' positions were not materially different than before, although alternative structures were discussed. The meeting concluded with no agreement on terms of a possible combination and no additional meetings or discussions were scheduled.

On January 5, 2000, Mr. Bressler and Mr. Novack renewed contact in a telephone conversation. On January 6, 2000, Mr. Novack telephoned Mr. Bressler to invite Mr. Levin and him to meet at Mr. Case's home in Virginia that evening. The four met that evening for approximately five hours to discuss the principal terms of a transaction. Messrs. Case and Levin agreed to fix the ratio for exchanging shares of common stock of Time Warner for shares of common stock of the combined company at 1.5 to 1, and they agreed in principle on other principal terms of the merger, subject to the approval of each company's board of directors and negotiation of definitive agreements.

Beginning on January 7, 2000, America Online, Time Warner and their respective advisors intensified due diligence activities, communications coordination and preparation of definitive documentation. On January 8 and 9, 2000, representatives of America Online, Time Warner and their respective advisors met to conduct due diligence, negotiate the merger agreement and related agreements, and plan and prepare for the announcement of the merger. These activities continued throughout the weekend, with negotiations on the merger agreement continuing through the evening of January 9, 2000.

On January 9, 2000, the board of directors of Time Warner met beginning at 2:00 P.M. at the offices of Cravath, Swaine & Moore to consider the proposed transaction. At this meeting, Mr. Levin and other members of management reviewed the transaction with the board, including the strategic reasons for the proposed transaction, the principal terms of the proposed transaction, a financial review of the proposed transaction, a review of America Online's financial condition and business operations and the results of Time Warner's due diligence review.

Time Warner's internal legal counsel and representatives of Cravath, Swaine & Moore discussed the board's fiduciary duties in considering a strategic business combination and further discussed the terms of the merger agreement and related documents. Representatives of Morgan Stanley presented to Time Warner's board of directors a summary of its analyses on the strategic rationale for and financial analyses related to the proposed transaction. In addition, Morgan Stanley delivered its opinion that the ratio for exchanging shares of Time Warner common stock and series common stock for shares of common stock and series common stock of AOL Time Warner pursuant to the merger agreement was fair, from a financial point of view, to holders of Time Warner's common stock and series common stock. Upon completing its deliberations, the board of directors of Time Warner unanimously approved the merger agreement and the related agreements and the transactions contemplated by those agreements, declared them advisable and resolved to recommend that Time Warner's stockholders adopt the merger agreement.

Also on January 9, 2000, the board of directors of America Online met beginning at 5:00 P.M. at the offices of Simpson Thacher & Bartlett to consider the proposed transaction. Dr. Thomas Middelhoff, Chairman and Chief Executive Officer of Bertelsmann, AG, chose not to participate in the meeting due to the potential conflict between the interests of America Online and Bertelsmann AG on whether to approve the proposed transaction. At this meeting, Mr. Case and other members of management reviewed the transaction with the board, including the strategic reasons for the proposed transaction, the principal terms of the proposed transaction, a financial review of the proposed transaction, a review of Time Warner's financial condition and business operations and the results of America Online's due diligence review.

America Online's internal legal counsel and representatives of Simpson Thacher & Bartlett discussed the board's fiduciary duties in considering a strategic business combination and further discussed the terms of the merger agreement and related documents. Representatives of Salomon Smith Barney presented to America Online's board of directors a summary of its analyses on the strategic rationale for and financial analyses related to the proposed transaction. In addition, Salomon Smith Barney delivered its opinion that the ratio for exchanging shares of Time Warner common stock for shares of common stock of AOL Time Warner contemplated by the merger agreement was fair, from a financial point of view, to America Online. Upon completing its deliberations, the board of directors of America Online, by action of those present at the meeting, unanimously approved the merger agreement and related agreements and the transactions contemplated by those agreements, declared them advisable and resolved to recommend that America Online's stockholders adopt the merger agreement.

At the conclusion of the respective board meetings, the boards of directors of America Online and Time Warner had a brief telephone conference call.

After negotiation of the final terms of the merger agreement and related agreements, representatives of America Online and representatives of Time Warner executed the agreements. In addition, Mr. Turner and certain of his affiliates entered into a voting agreement with America Online pursuant to which they agreed to vote substantially all of their shares of common stock of Time Warner in favor of adoption of the merger agreement.

On the morning of January 10, 2000, America Online and Time Warner issued a joint press release announcing the proposed merger of America Online and Time Warner.

America Online's Reasons for the Merger

America Online's merger with Time Warner will create the world's first fully integrated Internet-powered media and communications company. America Online's board of directors believes that AOL Time Warner will be uniquely positioned to expand the interactive medium's penetration into consumers' everyday lives—creating major new opportunities to deliver value to stockholders. By combining the leading interactive services and media companies, AOL Time Warner will advance the strategic goals of America Online and Time Warner and will provide the potential for stronger operating and financial results than either company could achieve on its own.

America Online's Internet resources will drive the digital transformation of Time Warner's divisions, and Time Warner's resources will advance the development of next-generation broadband and AOL Anywhere services, as well as build subscription and advertising and e-commerce growth throughout America Online's brands and products. With leading global brands, cost-efficient infrastructure, technological expertise and a shared vision for the Internet age, the two companies' complementary assets will act as catalysts to accelerate the growth of both subscription and advertising/e-commerce revenues, while also creating new business opportunities.

America Online's success has been guided by the principle that mass-market consumers seek convenience, ease-of-use and trusted brands in their Internet experience. AOL Time Warner will have an unmatched ability to provide these through a full range of interactive services delivered across current and emerging platforms. The combined company will be able to lead the next wave of Internet growth as interactivity extends beyond the personal computer to the television, wireless telephone and personal organizers, as well as other Internet-enabled devices—allowing consumers to access the Internet from anywhere and at anytime, and making the interactive experience even more convenient and valuable to them.

America Online's board of directors believes the following are key specific reasons that the merger will be beneficial to America Online and in the best interest of its stockholders:

Create a Portfolio of World-Class Consumer Brands and Advance Multiple-Brand Strategy. The board of directors of America Online believes that combining with Time Warner will dramatically advance America Online's multiple-brand strategy. Time Warner's leading global consumer brands cover the full spectrum of media entertainment and information—reaching from broadcast and cable television to film, music, publishing and the Internet. Together with America Online's family of premier interactive brands, the combined company will have a valuable portfolio of brands to deliver to consumers over multiple platforms.

Grow E-Commerce and Advertising Opportunities and Accelerate Multiple Revenue Stream Strategy. The board of directors of America Online believes the merger will advance America Online's strategy of multiple revenue streams by combining with Time Warner, which has grown its revenues across three major areas that reinforce America Online's: subscriptions, advertising and e-commerce and content. Putting together Time Warner's content properties with America Online's Internet and e-commerce infrastructure, AOL Time Warner will be able to create and distribute e-commerce products and services based on film, cable, broadcast, music, publishing and media properties. Recent successful collaborations to promote ""Austin Powers: The Spy Who Shagged Me" with AOL MovieFone and on "You've Got Mail" with Warner Bros. are small examples of what can be achieved in cross-promotion. The merger also will expand the opportunities for advertising across platforms and brands, including interactive properties, publishing, cable and broadcast television.

Advance AOL Anywhere Strategy to Extend and Enhance Communications and Convenience through Next-Generation Technology. The board of directors of America Online believes that combining with Time Warner will advance America Online's utilization of technology to extend and enhance its AOL Anywhere strategy to expand Internet communication, interactivity and convenience to devices beyond the personal computer. Time Warner's cable systems will expand the broadband delivery systems for America Online's interactive services and act as a catalyst for the development of AOL Plus— America Online's next generation multi-media/interactive services to personal computers. The combination also will further America Online's AOL Anywhere strategy of extending its interactive brands with their hallmark convenience and ease-of-use to new devices through television, wireless telephone and personal organizers as well as other companion devices. The merger also will provide a communications platform that gives AOL Time Warner the capability to offer instant messaging products and local telephony over cable systems.

Create Substantial Operating Synergies and New Business Opportunities. The board of directors of America Online believes that the combined company will benefit from substantial operating synergies as well as major new business opportunities. The following are representative potential cost synergies and revenue growth opportunities from the combination with Time Warner:

- revenue opportunities and synergies in areas such as advertising by providing companies "one-stop" shopping for their online as well as print and broadcast media advertising campaigns;

- increased subscriber growth through cross-promotion and marketing opportunities between Time Warner's brands and content and America Online's brands and interactive services;

- efficiency in marketing across different platforms and distribution systems, including cable, publishing and interactive services;

- cost synergies in areas such as technology and network infrastructure, direct mail and interactive marketing, use of "evergreen" billing systems, sales forces and other corporate services; and

- cost efficiencies in launching and operating interactive extensions of Time Warner brands.

In all, management estimated for the board of directors of America Online that total EBITDA synergies would be approximately $1 billion in the first full year of operations, producing an EBITDA growth rate of approximately 30% in that first year. It is anticipated that the combined company will have a revenue base in excess of $40 billion and EBITDA of approximately $11 billion, including synergies, in the first full year.

The board of directors also took note of the fact that the merger is with a long-time business partner of America Online with a proven history of successful collaborations, including cross-promotion and marketing activities between the two companies. Both companies also have management teams with demonstrated ability to manage the integration process of major business combinations.

Time Warner's Reasons for the Merger

The board of directors of Time Warner believes that the combination of Time Warner and America Online will create a preeminent global company that, for the first time, will fully integrate traditional and new media and communications businesses and technologies. The combined company, AOL Time Warner, will be uniquely positioned to deliver branded information, entertainment and communications services across rapidly converging media platforms and to take full advantage of the emergence of the Internet and the ongoing digital revolution.

In reaching the conclusion that the combination of Time Warner and America Online is in the best interests of Time Warner and its stockholders, the board of directors of Time Warner consulted with senior members of Time Warner's management team regarding the strategic and operational aspects of the merger and the results of the due diligence efforts undertaken by management. In addition, the board of directors of Time Warner consulted with representatives of Morgan Stanley, financial advisor to Time Warner, regarding selected financial aspects of America Online's business and future prospects and challenges facing Internet businesses in general and America Online in particular, as well as the fairness, from a financial point of view, to Time Warner's holders of common stock and series common stock of the proposed ratio for exchanging shares of Time Warner common stock or series common stock for shares of AOL Time Warner common stock or series common stock. The board of directors of Time Warner also consulted with Time Warner's internal counsel and with representatives of Cravath, Swaine & Moore, outside counsel to Time Warner, regarding the duties of the members of the board of directors, legal due diligence matters and the terms of the merger agreement and related agreements. In considering the information provided by senior members of Time Warner's management team, representatives of Morgan Stanley and representatives of Cravath, Swaine & Moore, in analyzing the terms of the merger agreement, and in coming to its endorsement of the merger, the board of directors of Time Warner considered a variety of factors, a number of which are summarized below.

Strategic Advantages. The board of directors of Time Warner reviewed presentations from senior members of Time Warner's management team regarding the strategic advantages of the combination of Time Warner and America Online. The Time Warner board of directors considered management's view that the combination of Time Warner's world-class media brands, subscriber bases and technologically advanced broadband delivery systems with America Online's renowned consumer online brands, subscriber base and extensive Internet infrastructure and expertise will provide AOL Time Warner with strengths and synergies in all its businesses. The Time Warner board considered management's view that AOL Time Warner's multiple brands, vast array of content, extensive infrastructure and strong distribution capabilities will provide it with a greater capacity to capitalize on and propel the convergence of media, entertainment and communications than Time Warner, or America Online, alone. The Time Warner board of directors also considered the strategic benefits of combining Time Warner's broadband infrastructure with America Online's established success in managing consumer migration online. The Time Warner board of directors also noted that this strategic combination would accelerate the digital transformation of Time Warner by infusing all of Time Warner's businesses with a heightened digital focus.

Potential for Growth. The board of directors of Time Warner considered the view of senior members of Time Warner's management team that the combination of Time Warner and America Online is expected to strengthen the ability of these companies to generate growth in revenue, earnings before interest, taxes and amortization, or "EBITA," earnings before interest, taxes, depreciation and amortization, or "EBITDA," and cash flow. In particular, the Time Warner board of directors considered management's view that:

- America Online's extensive Internet infrastructure is expected to provide a new and expanding distribution medium for Time Warner's popular brands, thereby giving its content businesses increased access to the consumer; and

- Time Warner's advanced broadband delivery systems are expected to provide an important distribution platform for America Online's interactive services, which is expected to result in incremental subscriber growth.

In addition, the Time Warner board noted management's view that:

- in the music business, AOL Time Warner will bring together Time Warner's prestigious labels and roster of established and new artists with America Online's established e-commerce capabilities, and

- in the publishing business, cross-marketing opportunities between Time Warner's prominent brands and America Online's interactive services are expected to provide new opportunities for subscriber growth.

Finally, the Time Warner board considered management's view that AOL Time Warner will have enhanced advertising and revenue potential due to its ability to offer promotional packages that include both traditional and online components.

Strengthened International Position. The board of directors of Time Warner considered the view of senior members of Time Warner's management team that the combination of Time Warner's strong international presence with America Online's global interactive services, will further strengthen the combined company's position in the international marketplace.

Increased Benefits for Consumers. The board of directors of Time Warner reviewed the potential for the combination of Time Warner and America Online to provide increased benefits for consumers. The Time Warner board of directors considered the view of senior members of Time Warner's management team that, through the combination of Time Warner's programming capabilities with America Online's Internet capabilities, AOL Time Warner is expected to be able to provide consumers with enhanced access to a broad selection of high quality content and interactive services. The Time Warner board of directors also considered management's view that, through the cooperative efforts of employees with creative and journalistic talents and employees with technological expertise, AOL Time Warner is expected to offer new and innovative products and services that are particularly suited to interactive media.

America Online's Business and Technology Infrastructure. In evaluating the combination of Time Warner and America Online, the board of directors of Time Warner considered information and analyses regarding the financial condition and results of operations of America Online. The Time Warner board of directors also considered information regarding America Online's Internet capacity and capabilities. Finally, the Time Warner board of directors considered information regarding prospects of and challenges facing Internet businesses in general and America Online in particular, including the view that the future of the Internet will be determined by companies that are able to take advantage of the distribution channels created by the Internet through providing compelling entertainment and informational content.

Expected Impact of the Combination. The board of directors of Time Warner noted that the combination of Time Warner and America Online is expected to strengthen the financial condition of both Time Warner and America Online. The Time Warner board of directors also noted that the combination of Time Warner and America Online would be accounted for as a purchase transaction.

Opinion of Morgan Stanley. The board of directors of Time Warner reviewed a detailed presentation by representatives of Morgan Stanley regarding the financial aspects of the proposed combination of Time Warner and America Online, including the ratio of exchanging shares of Time Warner common stock and series common stock for shares of AOL Time Warner common stock and series common stock. The board of directors of Time Warner considered the opinion of Morgan Stanley that the ratio for exchanging shares of Time Warner common stock or series common stock for shares of AOL Time Warner common stock or series common stock pursuant to the merger agreement was fair, from a financial point of view, to the holders of common stock and series common stock of Time Warner.

Ratio of Exchanging Shares of Time Warner Common Stock for Shares of AOL Time Warner Common Stock. The board of directors of Time Warner considered the fact that the proposed ratio of exchanging shares of common stock of Time Warner for shares of common stock of AOL Time Warner would provide Time Warner's stockholders with a substantial premium as compared to Time Warner's and America Online's stock market prices at the time of execution of the merger agreement.

The board of directors of Time Warner considered the fact that the value of the consideration to be received by holders of Time Warner's common stock could change depending upon the performance of America Online's common stock between the time of the execution of the merger agreement and the time of the completion of the merger, together with the fact that the multiple of underlying measures of financial performance reflected in the market price of America Online common stock differed from the multiple reflected in the market price of Time Warner common stock. The Time Warner board of directors also considered the fact that the merger agreement does not contain any provisions that limit the effect of declines in the market price of common stock of America Online prior to the completion of the merger on the value of the consideration to be received by holders of common stock of Time Warner in the merger. The Time Warner board of directors considered the absence of these provisions to be acceptable in the context of a "merger of equals" in which each of America Online and Time Warner will have the right to designate half of the directors of AOL Time Warner to serve for the first year after the merger is completed and the senior management of AOL Time Warner will be comprised of executive officers of both Time Warner and America Online and noted that, while the absence of these provisions exposes Time Warner stockholders to some market risk, the risk is mitigated by several factors. Holders of Time Warner's common stock will participate in any appreciation in the value of America Online's common stock between the time of the execution of the merger agreement and the time of the completion of the merger. In addition, any protection against declines in the market price of America Online's common stock would likely be coupled with a cap on the benefit Time Warner's stockholders would enjoy as a result of increases in the market price of America Online's common stock.

Continuing Equity Interest of Time Warner Stockholders in AOL Time Warner. The board of directors of Time Warner considered the fact that, by providing for the exchange of shares of common stock of Time Warner for shares of common stock of AOL Time Warner, the merger agreement provides for holders of Time Warner's common stock to participate in the value that may be generated by the combination of Time Warner and America Online through their continued equity participation in AOL Time Warner, while realizing through the exchange of shares a premium for their Time Warner shares, based on stock market prices at the time of execution of the merger agreement, and while obtaining tax-free treatment. The Time Warner board of directors also noted that the proposed ratio of exchanging shares of Time Warner common stock for shares of AOL Time Warner common stock would result in holders of Time Warner's common stock receiving a significant equity stake in AOL Time Warner, equal to approximately 45% of the common stock of AOL Time Warner after completion of the merger on a fully diluted basis.

Corporate Governance Arrangements. The board of directors of Time Warner noted that the merger agreement is structured as a "merger of equals" and provides that the board of directors of AOL Time Warner will initially consist of sixteen individuals, eight of whom will be designated by America Online and eight of whom will be designated by Time Warner. In addition, the Time Warner board of directors noted that the merger agreement provides that Stephen M. Case, the Chairman of the Board and Chief Executive Officer of America Online, will initially serve as Chairman of the Board of AOL Time Warner, and Gerald M. Levin, the Chairman and Chief Executive Officer of Time Warner will initially serve as Chief Executive Officer of AOL Time Warner. The Time Warner board of directors also noted that the affirmative vote of 75% of the members of the board of directors of AOL Time Warner will be required to change the size of the board of directors and that, until December 31, 2003, the affirmative vote of 75% of the members of the board of directors of AOL Time Warner will be required to remove the chairman or chief executive officer. The Time Warner board of directors concluded that these arrangements would reasonably assure the continuity of the management of AOL Time Warner following completion of the merger and allow a strong management team drawn from both Time Warner and America Online to work together to integrate the two companies.

Alternatives to the Merger. The board of directors of Time Warner considered information presented by senior members of Time Warner's management team that, in seeking a digital transformation of Time Warner, they had explored alternatives to the proposed combination of Time Warner and America Online, including the internal development of an Internet distribution infrastructure and growth through acquisitions. The Time Warner board of directors also considered the view of senior members of Time Warner's management team that the combination of Time Warner with America Online provides Time Warner with an extensive Internet distribution infrastructure in a relatively brief period of time and cost-effective manner. In addition, the Time Warner board of directors considered management's view that the combination of Time Warner and America Online accelerates Time Warner's Internet distribution plan by several years and provides significant cost savings with greater distribution capabilities, opportunities for cross-marketing products and potential to offer consumers new and innovative products than would other potential avenues for exploiting the potential of the Internet.

Integration of Time Warner and America Online. The board of directors of Time Warner considered the fact that the combination of the businesses of Time Warner and America Online would be challenging, and the success of the combination is not certain. The Time Warner board of directors noted, however, that the management teams of Time Warner and America Online have a shared vision of the potential created by the combination of traditional and new media. The Time Warner board of directors further noted that the businesses of both Time Warner and America Online are based, in part, on the acquisition and retention of subscribers. In addition, the Time Warner board of directors noted that both management teams share a consumer and marketing focus, a new media interactive service orientation and a sense of social commitment and responsibility. The Time Warner board of directors then noted that these similarities in experiences and views are likely to facilitate the efforts of the management teams of Time Warner and America Online to integrate their businesses effectively and efficiently.

Potential Adverse Consequences of the Combination. The board of directors of Time Warner considered several risks associated with the combination of Time Warner and

America Online that have the potential to create adverse consequences for Time Warner. In particular, the Time Warner board of directors considered the risk that the attention and efforts of senior members of Time Warner's management team may be diverted from Time Warner's businesses while they are working to implement the merger and that valuable strategic opportunities may be lost. The Time Warner board of directors also considered the risk that receipt of the various regulatory approvals necessary to complete the merger may require the acceptance of certain regulatory conditions that may have the effect of imposing additional costs on the combined company or limiting the combined company's revenues and the risk that the combination of Time Warner and America Online may not be completed.

This summary of the factors considered by the board of directors of Time Warner in evaluating the merits of the combination of Time Warner and America Online is not intended to be exhaustive but is believed to include all material factors considered by the Time Warner board of directors. Due to the wide variety of the factors that the Time Warner board of directors considered in evaluating the merits of the combination of Time Warner and America Online, the Time Warner board of directors did not find it practicable to, and did not attempt to, quantify or otherwise assign relative weights to the specific factors considered in its evaluation. In addition, the Time Warner board of directors did not undertake to make any specific determination as to whether any particular factor, or any aspect of any particular factor, should be regarded as favorable or unfavorable; instead the Time Warner board of directors analyzed all of the factors as a whole and determined that, overall, the factors support its conclusion that the combination of Time Warner and America Online is in the best interests of Time Warner and its stockholders. Individual members of the Time Warner board of directors may have considered some factors to be more important than other factors and may have considered some factors, or aspects of some factors, to be favorable while other members considered them to be unfavorable.

Recommendation of America Online's Board Of Directors

The America Online board of directors believes that the merger is fair to and in the best interest of America Online's stockholders, and recommends the adoption of the merger agreement.

In considering the recommendation of the America Online board of directors with respect to the merger agreement, you should be aware that certain directors and executive officers of America Online have interests in the merger that are different from, or are in addition to, the interests of America Online stockholders. Please see the section entitled "Interests of Certain America Online Directors and Executive Officers in the Merger."

Opinion or America Online's Financial Advisor

America Online retained Salomon Smith Barney to act as its financial advisor in connection with a possible business combination transaction with Time Warner. In connection with its engagement, America Online instructed Salomon Smith Barney to evaluate the fairness, from a financial point of view, of the Time Warner common stock exchange ratio to America Online. At the January 9, 2000 meeting of the board of directors of America Online, Salomon Smith Barney delivered its written opinion to the board of directors of America Online to the effect that, as of the date of such opinion and based upon the various qualifications and assumptions set forth therein, the exchange ratio of 1.5 shares of AOL Time Warner common stock for each share of Time Warner common stock is fair, from a financial point of view, to America Online.

Salomon Smith Barney's opinion is directed only to the fairness, from a financial point of view, of the Time Warner common stock exchange ratio to America Online and is not intended and does not constitute a recommendation to any stockholder of America Online as to how such stockholder should vote at the America Online special meeting. No limitations were imposed by America Online upon Salomon Smith Barney with respect to the investigations made or procedures followed by it in rendering its opinion. Although Salomon Smith Barney evaluated the financial terms of the merger and participated in discussions concerning the determination of the Time Warner common stock exchange ratio. Salomon Smith Barney was not asked to and did not recommend this exchange ratio, which was the result of arm's length negotiations between America Online and Time Warner.

In connection with rendering its opinion, Salomon Smith Barney, among other things:

- reviewed a draft of the merger agreement;
- held discussions separately with certain senior officers and other representatives and advisors of America Online and Time Warner concerning the business, operations and prospects of America Online and Time Warner, respectively;
- examined publicly available business and financial information relating to America Online and Time Warner as well as certain estimates and other data for America Online and Time Warner prepared by Salomon Smith Barney's and Morgan Stanley's research analysts;
- examined information relating to some of the strategic implications and operational benefits anticipated from the merger; and
- evaluated the potential pro forma financial impact of the merger on America Online.

In addition, Salomon Smith Barney conducted other analyses and examinations and considered other financial, economic and market criteria as it deemed appropriate.

In rendering its opinion, Salomon Smith Barney assumed and relied, without independent verification, upon the accuracy and completeness of all financial and other information publicly available or furnished to or otherwise reviewed by or discussed with it. Salomon Smith Barney relied on estimates prepared by Salomon Smith Barney's research analysts, based on Salomon Smith Barney's own independent evaluation of this information and indications by the management of America Online that the estimates regarding America Online were reasonably consistent with their own and indications by the management of Time Warner that estimates regarding Time Warner prepared by Morgan

Stanley's research analysts were reasonably consistent with their own. Salomon Smith Barney determined that its research analysts' estimates regarding Time Warner were generally consistent with Morgan Stanley's research analysts' estimates regarding Time Warner, which was acknowledged by the managements of America Online and Time Warner. With respect to the anticipated strategic, financial and operational benefits of the merger, Salomon Smith Barney assumed that the information provided was reasonably prepared on bases reflecting the best currently available estimates and judgments as to the strategic implications and operational benefits anticipated to result from the merger. Salomon Smith Barney assumed that the merger agreement would be substantially the same as the draft that Salomon Smith Barney reviewed. Salomon Smith Barney further assumed, with the consent of America Online, that the merger will be treated as a tax-free "reorganization" for federal income tax purposes.

Salomon Smith Barney did not express any opinion as to what the value of AOL Time Warner common stock actually will be when issued pursuant to the merger or the price at which the AOL Time Warner common stock will trade subsequent to the merger. Salomon Smith Barney did not make and was not provided with an independent evaluation or appraisal of the assets or liabilities, contingent or otherwise, of America Online or Time Warner nor did Salomon Smith Barney make any physical inspection of the properties or assets of America Online or Time Warner. Salomon Smith Barney was not requested to consider, and Salomon Smith Barney's opinion does not address, the relative merits of the merger as compared to any alternative business strategies that might exist for America Online or the effect of any other transaction in which America Online might engage.

Salomon Smith Barney's opinion was necessarily based on the information made available to it, and financial, stock market and other conditions and circumstances existing and disclosed to Salomon Smith Barney as of the date of its opinion.

In preparing its opinion, Salomon Smith Barney performed a variety of financial and comparative analyses. The following is a summary of the material financial analyses performed by Salomon Smith Barney in connection with the preparation of its opinion. These analyses were presented to the board of directors of America Online at its meeting on January 9, 2000. The following summary of the material financial analyses contains information in tabular format. In order fully to understand the financial analyses used by Salomon Smith Barney, the tables must be read in conjunction with the text of each summary. The tables alone do not constitute a complete description of the financial analyses.

Historical Stock Price Performance. Salomon Smith Barney reviewed the relationship between movements of the America Online common stock, the Time Warner common stock and the Standard & Poor's 400 Composite Index for the period from and including January 7, 1999 through January 7, 2000, the average closing prices for the Time Warner common stock and the America Online common stock over various periods during the 3-year period ended January 7, 2000 as set forth in the table below, and the trading volume and price history of the America Outline common stock and the Time Warner common stock for the period from and including January 7, 1999 through January 7, 2000.

Period (prior to January 7, 2000)	Average Share Price of America Online	Average Share Price of Time Warner
January 7, 2000	$73.75	$64.75
1 Week	$75.34	$67.50
1 Month	$81.88	$67.45
3 Months	$74.03	$65.35
6 Months	$62.02	$65.99
1 Year	$58.78	$66.95
3 Years	$22.56	$43.46

Implied Historical Exchange Ratio Analysis. Salomon Smith Barney reviewed the implied historical exchange ratio between the America Online common stock and the Time Warner common stock determined by dividing the average and the volume weighted average, respectively, prices per share of Time Warner common stock by the average and the volume weighted average, respectively, prices per share or America Online Common Stock over various periods during the three-year period ended January 7, 2000. This review indicated the following implied historical exchange ratios:

Period ending January 7, 2000	Implied Exchange Ratios	
	Average Share Price	Volume Weighted Average Share Price
1 Week	0.896x	0.888x
1 Month	0.824	0.806
3 Months	0.883	0.887
6 Months	1.064	1.083
1 Year	1.139	1.159
3 Years	1.926	1.595

Implied Exchange Ratio Analysis. Salomon Smith Barney derived a range of values for Time Warner and America Online by utilizing a sum-of-the-parts valuation analysis, which separately values distinct assets and businesses of a company by applying various valuation methodologies to those assets and businesses and uses the derived valuations to arrive at a range of values for the consolidated entity. Salomon Smith Barney then used the derived valuation ranges to determine the implied exchange ratios. The following are the three principal valuation methodologies used by Salomon Smith Barney in this analysis:

- *Public Market Valuation Analysis.* A public market analysis reviews a business' operating performance and outlook relative to a group of publicly traded peer companies to determine an implied unaffected market trading valuation range.

- *Private Market Valuation Analysis.* A private market analysis provides a valuation range based upon financial information of companies involved in selected recent business combination transactions or in business combination transactions that have been publicly announced and which are in the same or similar industries as the business being valued.

- *Discounted Cash Flow Analysis.* A discounted cash flow analysis derives the intrinsic value of a business based on the net present value of the future free cash flow anticipated to be generated by the assets of the business.

Salomon Smith Barney considered the values derived for various Time Warner businesses from the public and private market valuations and the discounted cash flow analyses under two scenarios. In the "100% Synergies" scenario, Salomon Smith Barney included merger-related revenue enhancements and cost savings, commonly referred to as "synergies," provided by the management of America Online as well as tax savings estimated to be achieved through the application by the combined company of existing and expected net operating losses of America Online over five years. The synergies were discussed with America Online and Time Warner managements, although Time Warner did not participate in the quantification of the synergies. In the "No Synergies" scenario, Salomon Smith Barney did not give effect to any synergies or to any tax savings that may be achieved from the application of the net operating losses. Salomon Smith Barney considered the values derived for various America Online businesses from public market valuations and discounted cash flow analyses. Salomon Smith Barney used the valuation ranges per share listed in the table below in order to derive a range of implied exchange ratios for each valuation methodology. Salomon Smith Barney calculated these valuation ranges per share by dividing the aggregate equity values of Time Warner and America Online derived as described under "Time Warner Valuation" and "America Online Valuation" below by the respective number of each company's diluted shares outstanding as of September 30, 1999.

	Low	High
Time Warner ("No Synergies" scenario)	(per share)	(per share)
Public market value	$69.58	$ 81.46
Private market value	83.47	92.37
Discounted cash flow	71.45	78.16
Time Warner ("100% Synergies" scenario)		
Public market value	$90.85	$102.03
Private market value (does not reflect any synergy or tax savings)	83.47	92.37
Discounted cash flow	92.72	99.44
America Online		
Public market value	$45.47	$136.28
Discounted cash flow	50.93	107.24
Synergies	$20.22	$ 20.22
Net operating losses	$ 1.05	$ 1.05

The implied exchange ratios which were derived from the above valuation ranges per share are set forth in the table below.

| | Implied Exchange Ratio | | | |
| | "No Synergies" Scenario | | "100% Synergies" Scenario | |
Valuation Methodology	**Low**	**High**	**Low**	**High**
Time Warner public market valuation to				
America Online public market valuation	0.511x	1.792x	0.667x	2.260x
Time Warner discounted cash flow to				
America Online discounted cash flow	0.666x	1.535x	0.865x	1.952x
Time Warner discounted cash flow to				
America Online public market valuation	0.524x	1.719x	0.680x	2.187x
Time Warner private market valuation to				
America Online public market valuation	0.612x	2.032x	0.612x	2.032x

The low implied exchange ratios in these ranges were determined by dividing the low Time Warner share value that had been calculated using the indicated valuation methodology by the high America Online share value that had been calculated using the indicated valuation methodology. Similarly, the high implied exchange ratios in these ranges were determined by dividing the high Time Warner share value that had been calculated using the indicated valuation methodology range by the low America Online share value that had been calculated using the indicated valuation methodology.

Time Warner Valuation

Salomon Smith Barney derived a valuation for Time Warner by performing financial analysis with respect to the following consolidated and non-consolidated assets and businesses of Time Warner:

- cable systems business;
- cable networks business;
- filmed entertainment business;
- publishing business;
- music business;
- WB network business; and
- non-consolidated investments of Time Warner, including:
  - equity interest in the Road Runner joint venture;
  - equity interest in cable joint ventures;
  - equity interest in Time Warner Telecom Inc.;
  - Comedy Central and Court TV business;
  - Internet assets; and
  - equity interests in other businesses.

Minority Interest. Part of Time Warner's cable, cable networks and filmed entertainment businesses is held by TWE. In connection with deriving the public and private market and discounted cash flow valuations of Time Warner's interest in TWE, Salomon Smith Barney excluded the equity values in TWE of the other partners of TWE. Salomon Smith Barney derived an implied value for TWE using the same sum-of-the parts valuation methodology as for Time Warner but applied a 20% minority discount to reflect the other partners' minority interests.

Public Market Analysis of Time Warner. Salomon Smith Barney reviewed and compared various actual and forecasted financial, operating and stock market information of the individual Time Warner businesses listed below, collectively referred to as the "Time Warner businesses" and, together with the WB network business, the "Time Warner consolidated businesses," with that of various publicly traded companies in corresponding industries, which companies Salomon Smith Barney believed are comparable in relevant respects to the applicable Time Warner business:

- cable systems;
- cable networks;
- filmed entertainment;
- publishing; and
- music.

Salomon Smith Barney calculated various financial multiples for each of the Time Warner businesses and for each of the applicable groups of comparable companies including, in certain cases, firm value to historical EBITDA and to estimated 2001 EBITDA. Salomon Smith Barney then calculated, among other things, a range of estimated 2001 EBITDA multiples, as summarized in the table below. Salomon Smith Barney utilized the multiples of the applicable comparable companies for purposes of calculating the implied value of the Time Warner businesses. The multiple ranges for the comparable companies that Salomon Smith Barney deemed relevant to this analysis are summarized below.

Businesses	Public Market 2001E EBITDA Multiples	
	Low	High
Cable systems	16.0x	19.0x
Cable networks	19.0	21.0
Filmed entertainment	16.0	19.0
Publishing	14.0	16.0
Music	12.0	14.0

None of the comparable companies used in the public market valuation analyses summarized above is identical to the applicable Time Warner business. Accordingly, an examination of the results of the comparable companies used in this analysis necessarily involved complex considerations of the businesses and judgments concerning differences in financial and operating characteristics and other factors that could affect the public trading values or the acquisition values of these companies. In addition, Salomon Smith Barney performed its analyses using published analyst reports for forecasted financial and operating information, including EBITDA estimates for the comparable companies. Actual results may vary from such estimates and the variations may be material. Salomon Smith Barney takes no responsibility for any of the published analyst reports.

Private Market Valuation Analysis of Time Warner. Salomon Smith Barney reviewed and analyzed certain financial, operating and stock market information relating to comparable selected transactions in the cable systems, cable networks, diversified media, filmed entertainment, publishing and music industries. To the extent that the relevant information was publicly available, Salomon Smith Barney calculated the multiples of firm value to estimated 2001 EBITDA represented by the transaction prices of the subject companies in the cable systems industry and the multiples of firm value to last twelve month revenue and firm value to last twelve month EBITDA represented by the transaction prices of the subject companies in the other industries described below. Using this information and other factors relevant in the valuation of the Time Warner businesses, Salomon Smith Barney determined an estimated 2001 EBITDA multiple range for each of the Time Warner businesses and calculated an implied value of the Time Warner businesses utilizing those multiples. The multiple ranges for the selected transactions that Salomon Smith Barney deemed relevant to this analysis are summarized below.

Businesses	Public Market 2001E EBITDA Multiples	
	Low	**High**
Cable systems	20.0x	22.0x
Cable networks	22.0	24.0
Filmed entertainment	16.0	18.0
Publishing	14.0	16.0
Music	14.0	16.0

No transaction used in the private market valuation analysis described above is identical to the merger and none of the constituent companies are identical to the respective Time Warner business being analyzed. Accordingly, any analysis of the selected comparison transactions necessarily involved complex considerations and judgments concerning differences in financial and operating characteristics and other factors that would necessarily affect the value of the given Time Warner business versus the values of the transactions to which that business was being compared.

WB Network. Salomon Smith Barney calculated the implied firm value of approximately $1.0 billion for the WB Network using published analyst reports. This implied firm value was included by Salomon Smith Barney in its public and private market valuations which derived the aggregate implied firm value of Time Warner.

Discounted Cash Flow Analysis. Salomon Smith Barney performed a discounted cash flow analysis of the various Time Warner consolidated businesses to estimate ranges of intrinsic values for each of the Time Warner consolidated businesses. Salomon Smith

Barney applied a terminal value multiple ranges to the forecasted EBITDA in calendar 2004 for each of the Time Warner consolidated businesses. The ranges of terminal value multiples used for each of the Time Warner consolidated businesses are set forth in the table below. The unlevered free cash flows of each of the Time Warner consolidated businesses were then discounted to present value using various discount rates. The ranges of discount rates and multiples used for each of the Time Warner consolidated businesses are set forth in the table below.

Consolidated Businesses	Discount Rates	Terminal Values
Cable systems	10.0%–12.0%	16.0x–18.0x
Cable networks	10.00 –12.0	19.0 –21.0
Filmed entertainment	11.0 –13.0	16.5 –18.5
Publishing	10.0 –12.0	14.0 –16.0
Music	11.0 –13.0	13.0 –15.0
WB television network	10.0 –12.0	19.0 –21.0

Time Warner Non-Consolidated Assets. Salomon Smith Barney reviewed and compared various actual and forecasted financial, operating and stock market information, as applicable, with respect to Time Warner's non-consolidated investments identified below. For Time Warner's investments in publicly traded companies, such as Time Warner Telecom, Salomon Smith Barney derived the implied firm value using the current market trading prices of those companies' securities. With respect to other non-consolidated investments, including the unconsolidated cable and Road Runner joint ventures, Salomon Smith Barney performed applicable analyses using subscriber multiples and other subscriber information to derive an implied firm value. For the remaining non-consolidated investments, Salomon Smith Barney calculated the implied firm value using forecasted EBITDA and published analyst reports.

The aggregate implied firm value for Time Warner's non-consolidated investments was included by Salomon Smith Barney in its public and private market valuations and its discounted cash flow analyses in order to derive the aggregate implied firm value ranges for Time Warner.

Net Operating Losses. Based on management estimates of aggregate existing and expected net operating losses of the combined company, assuming that these net operating losses could be used without limitation through fiscal 2005, and based upon a 35% federal tax rate and an 11% discount rate, Salomon Smith Barney derived an implied present value of approximately $1.5 billion for the tax savings estimated to be achieved from these net operating losses.

Synergies. Salomon Smith Barney considered the value of the net synergies related to the merger provided by the management of America Online. The synergies were discussed with America Online and Time Warner managements, although Time Warner did not participate in the quantification or the synergies. The net synergies are estimated to increase EBITDA by $1 billion in fiscal 2001. The estimates of synergies are based on numerous estimates, assumptions and judgments, and are subject to significant uncertainties. In addition, the actual synergies realized in the merger may vary materially from the estimates used in Salomon Smith Barney's analysis.

America Online Valuation

Public Market Analysis of America Online. Salomon Smith Barney reviewed and compared various actual and forecasted financial, operating and stock market information of the individual America Online businesses listed below, collectively referred to as the "America Online businesses," with that of various publicly traded companies in corresponding industries, which companies Salomon Smith Barney believed are comparable in relevant respects to the applicable America Online business:

- internet access;
- online portals (advertising/e-commerce); and
- enterprise solutions.

Salomon Smith Barney calculated various financial multiples for the America Online businesses and for each of the applicable groups of comparable companies including firm value to historical revenues and to estimated forward revenues. Salomon Smith Barney then calculated, among other things, a range of estimated Year 2000 revenue multiples, as summarized in the table below. For purposes of calculating the implied value of the America Online businesses, Salomon Smith Barney utilized these multiples. The multiple ranges for the comparable companies that Salomon Smith Barney deemed relevant to this analysis are summarized below.

	Public Market 2001E Revenue Multiples	
Business	**Low**	**High**
Internet access	6.0x	8.0x
Online portals (advertising/e-commerce)	44.0x	171.0x
Enterprise solutions	13.0x	15.0x

None of the comparable companies used in the public market valuation analyses summarized above is identical to the applicable America Online business. Accordingly, an examination of the results of the comparable companies used in this analysis necessarily involved complex considerations of the businesses and judgments concerning differences in financial and operating characteristics and other factors that could affect the public trading values or the acquisition values of these companies. In addition, Salomon Smith Barney performed its analyses using published analyst reports for forecasted financial and operating information, including EBITDA estimates for the comparable companies. Actual results may vary from such estimates and the variations may be material. Salomon Smith Barney takes no responsibility for any of the published analyst reports.

Discounted Cash Flow Analysis. Salomon Smith Barney performed a discounted cash flow analysis of America Online to estimate a range of intrinsic values of America Online. Salomon Smith Barney applied a terminal value multiple range of 40.0x to 80.0x to America Online's forecasted EBITDA for calendar 2004. The unlevered free cash flows were then discounted to present value using various discount rates ranging from of 14.0% to 16.0%.

Contribution Analysis. Salomon Smith Barney performed an exchange ratio analysis comparing the relative contributions of Time Warner and America Online to the combined company. The following table displays each company's relative contribution to the combined company's actual 1998 and estimated 1999, 2000 and 2001 revenues, EBITDA and net income, as well as the combined company's market fully-diluted equity value as of January 7, 2000 and derived implied exchange ratios from such relative contributions.

	Period	% Contribution America Online	Time Warner	Implied Exchange Ratio
Revenues	1998A	11.2%	88.8%	12.6x
	1999E	17.1	82.9	7.7
	2000E	20.4	79.6	6.2
	2001E	24.0	76.0	5.0
EBITDA	1998A	9.0%	91.0%	16.0x
	1999E	15.3	84.7	8.9
	2000E	21.7	78.3	5.7
	2001E	29.0	71.0	3.9
Net Income	1998A	NM	NM	NM
	1999E	45.4%	54.6%	2.2x
	2000E	55.3	44.7	1.5
	2001E	57.5	42.5	1.4
At Market	Equity Value	67.6%	32.4%	0.9x

Pro Forma Earnings Per Share Impact to America Online. Salomon Smith Barney reviewed certain pro forma financial effects of the merger on the estimated earnings per share of America Online common stock. Using First Call estimates, Salomon Smith Barney compared the earnings per share of America Online common stock, on a stand-alone basis assuming the merger was not consummated to the estimated earnings per share of America Online common stock following consummation of the merger on a pro forma basis. Salomon Smith Barney's analysis gave effect to the issuance of shares of AOL Time Warner common stock to America Online and Time Warner stockholders pursuant to the merger agreement and gave effect to the net estimated synergies. Based on such analysis, Salomon Smith Barney determined that the merger would be: (a) dilutive to, or result in a decrease in, the earnings per share of America Online common stock on a pro forma basis by approximately 404.7% in calendar 2000 and approximately 267.0% in calendar 2001 using First Call GAAP earnings per share estimates, and (b) accretive to, or result in an increase in, the earnings per share of America Online common stock on a pro forma basis by approximately 63.6% in calendar 2000 and approximately 48.5% in calendar 2001 using cash earnings per share estimates which are based on the First Call GAAP earnings per share estimates and adding goodwill amortization per share.

Other Analyses. Salomon Smith Barney conducted such other analyses as it deemed necessary, including reviewing selected investment research reports on, and earnings estimates for, America Online and Time Warner.

Salomon Smith Barney is an internationally recognized investment banking firm and was engaged as financial advisor to America Online in connection with the merger because of its experience and expertise and its familiarity with America Online. As part of its investment banking business, Salomon Smith Barney is regularly engaged in the valuation of businesses and their securities in connection with mergers and acquisitions, negotiated underwritings, competitive biddings, secondary distributions of listed and unlisted securities, private placements and valuations for estate, corporate and other purposes.

Pursuant to the terms of an engagement letter dated January 9, 2000, America Online agreed to pay Salomon Smith Barney a financial advisory fee of: $5 million upon the execution of the merger agreement; $7.5 million upon receipt of requisite shareholder approvals to complete the merger; and $47.5 million upon completion of the merger. Additionally, America Online has agreed to reimburse Salomon Smith Barney for reasonable out-of-pocket expenses incurred by Salomon Smith Barney in performing its services, including the fees and expenses of its legal counsel, and to indemnify Salomon Smith Barney and related persons against certain liabilities, including liabilities under the federal securities laws, arising out of Salomon Smith Barney's engagement. In the ordinary course of business, Salomon Smith Barney and its affiliates may actively trade or hold the securities of America Online and Time Warner for their own account or for the account of customers and, accordingly, may at any time hold a long or short position in such securities.

Salomon Smith Barney has in the past provided investment banking services to America Online unrelated to the merger. From January 1, 1998 through January 6, 2000, Salomon Smith Barney received approximately $14.5 million for these services. In addition, Salomon Smith Barney and its affiliates including Citigroup Inc. and its affiliates, may maintain relationships with America Online or Time Warner.

Opinion of Time Warner's Financial Advisor

Time Warner retained Morgan Stanley to provide it with financial advisory services and a financial fairness opinion in connection with the merger. The Time Warner board of directors selected Morgan Stanley to act as Time Warner's financial advisor based on Morgan Stanley's qualifications, expertise and reputation and its knowledge of the business and affairs of Time Warner. At the meeting of the Time Warner board on January 9, 2000, Morgan Stanley rendered its oral opinion, subsequently confirmed in writing, that as of January 9, 2000, and subject to and based on the considerations in its opinion, the exchange ratio pursuant to the merger agreement is fair from a financial point of view to the holders of Time Warner common stock and series common stock.

The full text of Morgan Stanley's opinion, dated as of January 9, 2000, which sets forth, among other things, the assumptions made, procedures followed, matters considered and limitations on the review undertaken by Morgan Stanley is attached as Annex F

to this joint proxy statement-prospectus. We urge you to read this opinion carefully and in its entirety. Morgan Stanley's opinion is directed to the board of directors of Time Warner, addresses only the fairness from a financial point of view of the exchange ratio pursuant to the merger agreement to the holders of Time Warner common stock and series common stock, and does not address any other aspect of the merger or constitute a recommendation to any Time Warner stockholder as to how to vote at the special meeting. This summary is qualified in its entirety by reference to the full text of the opinion.

In connection with rendering its opinion, Morgan Stanley, among other things:

- reviewed certain publicly available financial statements and other information of America Online and Time Warner;

- discussed the past and current operations and financial condition and the prospects of America Online and Time Warner with senior executives of America Online and Time Warner, respectively;

- discussed with senior executives of America Online and Time Warner certain strategic, financial and operational benefits they anticipate from the merger;

- reviewed the reported prices and trading activity for America Online's common stock and Time Warner's common stock;

- compared the financial performance of America Online and Time Warner and the prices and trading activity of America Online's common stock and Time Warner's common stock with those of other comparable publicly traded companies and their securities;

- reviewed the financial terms, to the extent publicly available, of precedent transactions that Morgan Stanley deemed relevant;

- participated in discussions and negotiations among representatives of America Online and Time Warner and their financial and legal advisors;

- reviewed the draft of the merger agreement, the draft of the voting agreement to be entered into between America Online and Mr. Turner and his affiliates and the draft of the stock option agreements to be entered into between America Online and Time Warner, each substantially in the form of the draft dated January 9, 2000, and related documents; and

- performed other analyses and considered other factors as Morgan Stanley deemed appropriate.

Morgan Stanley assumed and relied upon, without independent verification, the accuracy and completeness of the information reviewed by it for the purposes of its opinion. Morgan Stanley did not receive financial forecasts for America Online or Time Warner and instead relied on the publicly available estimates of selected analysts, including those at Morgan Stanley, who report on America Online and Time Warner. With respect to the anticipated strategic, financial and operational benefits of the merger, including assumptions regarding America Online's and Time Warner's existing and future products and technologies, Morgan Stanley assumed that the information provided has been reasonably prepared on the bases reflecting the best currently available estimates and judgments of the future financial and operational performance of America Online and Time Warner. Morgan Stanley did not make and did not assume responsibility for making any independent valuation or appraisal of the assets or liabilities of Time Warner or America Online, nor was Morgan Stanley furnished with any appraisals of those assets and liabilities. Morgan Stanley assumed that the executed versions of the merger agreement, the voting agreement and the stock option agreements would not differ in any material respect from the last drafts of these agreements reviewed by Morgan Stanley. Morgan Stanley assumed that the merger will be completed in accordance with the terms provided in the merger agreement without material modification or waiver and that the merger will be a tax-free reorganization or exchange under the Internal Revenue Code of 1986. The opinion of Morgan Stanley is necessarily based on financial, economic, market and other conditions as in effect on, the information made available to Morgan Stanley as of, and the financial condition of Time Warner and America Online on, January 9, 2000.

The following is a summary of the material financial analyses performed by Morgan Stanley in connection with its oral opinion and the preparation of its written opinion. These summaries of financial analyses include information presented in tabular format. In order to fully understand the financial analyses used by Morgan Stanley, the tables must be read together with the text of each summary. The tables alone do not constitute a complete description of the financial analyses.

Historical Share Price Performance. Morgan Stanley reviewed the price performance and trading volumes of the common stock of each of Time Warner and America Online from January 7, 1999 through January 7, 2000. The table below shows the twelve-month high and low closing prices during that period, compared with a closing price on January 7, 2000 of $64.75 per share for the Time Warner common stock and $73.75 per share for the America Online common stock:

	January 7, 1999 through January 7, 2000 High	January 7, 1999 through January 7, 2000 Low
Time Warner	$78.25	$58.50
America Online	$93.81	$35.11

Morgan Stanley then compared the price performance of the Time Warner common stock from January 7, 1999 through January 7, 2000 with that of the S&P 500 Index and of a group of selected media and entertainment companies and the price performance of the America Online common stock over the same period with that of the Nasdaq Composite Index and of a group of selected Internet companies.

The group of selected media and entertainment companies included CBS Corporation, Comcast Corporation, Viacom, Inc., News Corp. Ltd., Cablevision Systems Corporation, Cox Communications, Inc., The Seagram Company Ltd., The Walt Disney Company and Fox Corporation. The group of selected Internet companies included CNET,

Inc., Yahoo! Inc., Lycos, Inc., eBay Inc., Excite, Inc. and Amazon.com, Inc. Morgan Stanley selected CNET, Excite, Lycos and Yahoo! because they are publicly traded companies with Internet portal operations that, for purposes of this analysis, may be considered similar to those of America Online. Morgan Stanley also selected Amazon.com and eBay because they are publicly traded companies that are leaders in e-commerce retail and because their leading positions in this market may be considered, for purposes of this analysis, similar to America Online. None of the companies utilized in this analysis as a comparison is identical to Time Warner or America Online.

This analysis showed that the closing market prices during the period from January 7, 1999 through January 7, 2000 appreciated as follows:

	Appreciation
Time Warner	6.3%
S&S 500 Index	13.5%
Group of selected media and entertainment companies:	
Mean	43.1%

	Appreciation
America Online	97.5%
Nasdaq Composite Index	66.9%
Group of selected Internet companies:	
Mean	104.2%

Comparable Companies Analysis. Morgan Stanley calculated aggregate value, i.e., equity value adjusted for capital structure, to EBITDA multiples for Time Warner for fiscal years 1999 through 2001 based on publicly available Morgan Stanley research estimates. Morgan Stanley then compared the EBITDA multiples obtained for Time Warner with multiples obtained for a group of selected media and entertainment companies. Morgan Stanley calculated aggregate value to revenue multiples for America Online for fiscal years 1999 through 2001 based on publicly available Morgan Stanley research estimates, Morgan Stanley then compared the revenue multiples obtained for America Online with multiples obtained for a group of selected Internet companies.

The group of selected media and entertainment companies included Cablevision Systems Corporation, The Walt Disney Company, Fox Corporation, News Corp. Ltd., The Seagram Company Ltd. and the combined Viacom/CBS Corporation entity. Morgan Stanley selected these companies because they are publicly traded companies with media and entertainment operations that for purposes of this analysis may be considered similar to those or Time Warner.

The group of selected Internet companies included Excite, Inc., Lycos, Inc., Yahoo! Inc., Amazon.com. Inc. and eBay Inc. Morgan Stanley selected Excite, Lycos and Yahoo! because they are publicly traded companies with Internet portal operations that, for purposes of this analysis, may be considered similar to those of America Online. Morgan Stanley also selected Amazon.com and eBay because they are publicly traded leaders in e-commerce retail which, because or their trading positions in this market, may be considered for purposes or this analysis similar to America Online.

| | **Estimated Aggregate Value/EBITDA** | | |
	1999	**2000**	**2001**
Time Warner	19.4x	17.5x	15.4x
Group of selected media and entertainment companies:			
Mean	18.7x	15.8x	13.8x
Median	16.2x	14.7x	12.8x

| | **Estimated Aggregate Value/Revenue** | | |
	1999	**2000**	**2001**
America Online	33.6x	25.8x	21.1x
Excite, Lycos, Yahoo:			
Mean	89.9x	57.6x	40.1x
Median	38.8x	24.0x	16.8x
Amazon.com, eBay:			
Mean	48.5x	29.5x	20.3x
Median	48.5x	29.5x	20.3x

Securities Research Analysts' Future Price Targets Analysis. Morgan Stanley reviewed the 12-month price targets for the shares of common stock of each of Time Warner and America Online as projected by analysts from various financial institutions in recent reports. These targets reflected each analyst's estimate of the future public market trading price or Time Warner common stock and America Online common stock at the end of the particular period considered for each estimate. Morgan Stanley then arrived at the present value for these targets using an estimated equity discount rate of 12.7% for the Time Warner common stock and 18.5% for the America Online common stock.

This analysis showed the following mean and median values for the Time Warner and America Online common stock:

| | **12-Month Analysts' Price Target** | |
Time Warner	**Nominal**	**Present Value**
Mean	$82	$74
Median	$81	$73

| | **12-Month Analysts' Price Target** | |
America Online	**Nominal**	**Present Value**
Mean	$97	$84
Median	$108	$94

Morgan Stanley noted that the exchange ratio pursuant to the merger agreement implied a value of $110.625 for the common stock of Time Warner resulting from the merger, based on the trading price of the America Online common stock on January 7, 2000.

Historical Exchange Ratio Analysis. Morgan Stanley reviewed the implied historical exchange ratios for the shares of common stock of each of Time Warner and America Online determined by dividing the price per share of Time Warner common stock by the price per share of America Online common stock over the three-year period from January 7, 1997 through January 7, 2000, and over the twelve-month period from January 7, 1999 through January 7, 2000. Morgan Stanley performed this analysis to compare the premium represented by the exchange ratio in the merger with the premium/(discount) represented by historical exchange ratios prevailing in the open market.

This analysis indicated the following premiums/(discounts) represented by the average historical exchange ratios prevailing in the open market:

Period Ending January 7, 2000	Premium/(Discount) Over Average Historical Exchange Ratio
Last one month	81%
Last three months	66%
Last six months	34%
Last one year	25%
Last 18 months	(16)%
Last two years	(37)%
Last three years	(61)%

Morgan Stanley noted that the 1.5x exchange ratio in the merger agreement implied a 71% premium to the market ratio implied by the trading prices of the America Online and Time Warner common stock on January 7, 2000.

Relative Contribution Analysis. Morgan Stanley compared pro forma contribution of each of Time Warner and America Online, based on publicly available Morgan Stanley research estimates, to the resultant combined company assuming completion of the merger. Morgan Stanley adjusted these statistics to reflect each company's respective capital structures and then compared them to the pro forma ownership by Time Warner stockholders of the common stock of the combined company of approximately 45%, implied by the exchange ratio.

This analysis indicated the following equity contribution for Time Warner to the combined company on a pro forma basis:

	Time Warner Equity Contribution
Estimated Net Revenues:	
2000	79%
2001	77%
Estimated EBITDA:	
2000	79%
2001	74%
Estimated Net Income (after preferred dividends):	
2000	46%
2001	48%
Market equity value (based on 1/7/00 closing prices and	
fully diluted shares using treasury method)	32%

Pro Forma Merger Analysis. Morgan Stanley analyzed the pro forma effect of the merger on each of Time Warner's and America Online's actual and projected revenue and EBITDA for fiscal 1998 to fiscal 2001, based on publicly available Morgan Stanley research estimates, compared to the revenue and EBITDA growth rates of Time Warner and America Online on a standalone basis in each of the selected years.

The analysis indicated that the merger would increase the revenue and EBITDA growth rates of Time Warner compared to the revenue and EBITDA growth rates of Time Warner on a standalone basis for the period selected as follows:

	Estimated 1999–2001 Compound Annual Growth Rate
Revenue:	
Time Warner	10.1%
America Online	26.2%
Pro forma	13.0%

	Estimated 1999–2001 Compound Annual Growth Rate
EBITDA:	
Time Warner	12.5%
America Online	61.0%
Pro forma	20.1%

Premiums Paid in Selected Precedent Transactions Analysis. Morgan Stanley reviewed nine recent selected business combinations structured as mergers of equals and analyzed the premiums/discounts paid in these transactions over prevailing market prices before the announcement of these transactions. Morgan Stanley selected these transactions because they were structured as mergers of equals of large publicly-traded corporations and not because they involved companies engaged in industries that would be similar or related to those in which Time Warner or America Online operate.

These transactions are: the Viacom, Inc./CBS Corporation transaction, the Vodafone PLC/AirTouch Communications, Inc. transaction, the British Petroleum Company/Amoco Corporation transaction, the Bell Atlantic Corporation/GTE Corporation transaction, the Norwest Corporation/Wells Fargo & Company transaction, the SBC Communications Inc./Ameritech Corporation transaction, the Daimler-Benz Aktiengesellschaft/Chrysler Corporation transaction, the NationsBank Corporation/Bank of America Corporation transaction and the Travelers Group Inc./Citicorp transaction.

The table below provides the high and low premiums/discounts at 30 days and at one day before the announcement of these transactions, compared with the 71% premium to be received by the shareholders of Time Warner in the merger, based on the trading price for the America Online and Time Warner common stock as of January 7, 2000:

	Premium/(Discount) to Stock Price at 30 Days	Premium/(Discount) to Stock Price at One Day
Selected transactions:		
High	72.1%	70.4%
Low	(4.5)%	(1.5)%

No company or transaction utilized in the peer group comparison analysis is identical to Time Warner or America Online or the merger. In evaluating the peer groups, Morgan Stanley made judgments and assumptions with regard to industry performance, general business, economic, market and financial conditions and other matters, many of which are beyond the control of Time Warner or America Online, such as the impact of competition on the business of Time Warner, America Online, or the industry generally, industry growth and the absence of any adverse material change in the financial condition and prospects of Time Warner, America Online or the industry or in the financial markets in general, which could affect the public trading value of the companies and the aggregate value of the transactions to which they are being compared. Mathematical analysis, such as determining the mean or median, or the high or the low, is not in itself a meaningful method of using peer group data.

In connection with the review of the merger by Time Warner's board of directors, Morgan Stanley performed a variety of financial and comparative analyses for purposes of rendering its opinion. The preparation of a fairness opinion is a complex process and is not necessarily susceptible to a partial analysis or summary description. In arriving at its opinion, Morgan Stanley considered the results of all of its analyses as a whole and did not attribute any particular weight to any analysis or factor considered by it. Morgan Stanley believes that the summary provided and the analyses described above must be considered as a whole and that selecting portions of these analyses, without considering all of them, would create an incomplete view of the process underlying its analyses and opinion. In addition, Morgan Stanley may have given various analyses and factors more or less weight than other analyses and factors and may have deemed various assumptions more or less probable than other assumptions, so that the range of valuations resulting from any particular analysis described above should therefore not be taken to be Morgan Stanley's view of the actual value of Time Warner or America Online.

In performing its analyses, Morgan Stanley made numerous assumptions with respect to industry performance, general business and economic conditions and other matters, many of which are beyond the control of Time Warner or America Online. Any estimates contained in Morgan Stanley's analysis are not necessarily indicative of future results or actual values, which may be significantly more or less favorable than those suggested by these estimates. The analyses performed were prepared solely as a part of Morgan Stanley's analysis of the fairness from a financial point of view to the holders of common stock and series common stock of Time Warner of the exchange ratio pursuant to the merger agreement and were conducted in connection with the delivery by Morgan Stanley of its opinion dated January 9, 2000 to the board of directors of Time Warner. Morgan Stanley's analyses do not purport to be appraisals or to reflect the prices at which shares of common stock or series common stock of Time Warner or America Online might actually trade. The exchange ratio in the merger was determined through arm's length negotiations between Time Warner and America Online and was approved by Time Warner's board of directors. Morgan Stanley did not recommend any specific exchange ratio to Time Warner or that any given exchange ratio constituted the only appropriate exchange ratio for the merger.

Morgan Stanley is an internationally recognized investment banking and advisory firm. Morgan Stanley, as part of its investment banking and financial advisory business, is continuously engaged in the valuation of businesses and their securities in connection with mergers and acquisitions, negotiated underwritings, competitive biddings, secondary distributions of listed and unlisted securities, private placements and valuations for corporate and other purposes. In the past, Morgan Stanley and its affiliates have provided financial advisory and financing services for Time Warner and America Online and have received customary fees for the rendering of these services. During 1998 and 1999, Morgan Stanley received approximately $23.8 million for services provided to Time Warner and its affiliated entities. In the ordinary course of business, Morgan Stanley may from time to time trade in the securities or indebtedness of Time Warner and America Online for its own account, the accounts of investment funds and other clients under the management of Morgan Stanley and for the accounts of its customers and, accordingly, may at any time hold a long or short position in these securities or indebtedness.

Time Warner has agreed to pay Morgan Stanley a financial advisory fee of $12.5 million upon execution of the merger agreement and, upon completion of the merger, $47.5 million plus a contingent amount, not to exceed $15 million, based on the enterprise value of Time Warner implied by the average trading price of AOL Time Warner common stock for five days after completion of the merger. Time Warner has also agreed to reimburse Morgan Stanley for its expenses incurred in performing its services and to indemnify Morgan Stanley and its affiliates, their respective directors, officers, agents and employees and each person, if any, controlling Morgan Stanley or any of its affiliates against certain liabilities and expenses, including certain liabilities under federal securities laws, related to or arising out of Morgan Stanley's engagement and any related transactions.

Risk Factors

Fluctuations in market prices may cause the value of the shares of AOL Time Warner stock that you receive to be less than the value of your shares of America Online stock or Time Warner stock.

Upon completion of the merger, all shares of America Online stock and Time Warner stock will be converted into shares of AOL Time Warner stock. The ratios at which the shares will be converted are fixed, and there will be no adjustment for changes in the market price of either America Online common stock or Time Warner common stock. Any change in the price of either America Online common stock or Time Warner common stock will affect the value Time Warner stockholders and America Online stockholders will receive in the merger. America Online common stock has historically experienced significant volatility, and the value of the shares of AOL Time Warner stock received in the merger may go up or down as the market price of America Online common stock, or Time

Warner common stock, goes up or down. Stock price changes may result from a variety of factors that are beyond the control of America Online and Time Warner, including changes in their businesses, operations and prospects, regulatory considerations and general market and economic conditions. Neither party is permitted to "walk away" from the merger or resolicit the vote of its stockholders solely because of changes in the market price of either party's common stock.

The prices of America Online common stock and Time Warner common stock at the closing of the merger may vary from their respective prices on the date of this joint proxy statement-prospectus and on the dates of the special meetings. Because the date the merger is completed will be later than the dates of the special meetings, the prices of America Online common stock and Time Warner common stock on the dates of the special meetings may not be indicative of their respective prices on the date the merger is completed.

The combination of America Online and Time Warner to form an integrated media and communications company creates a new business model that the marketplace may have difficulty valuing.

The market value of shares of common stock generally reflects a "multiple" of selected measures of financial performance, such as operating profits or earnings per share. The market price of shares of common stock of Internet companies, such as America Online, typically reflects a higher multiple of the underlying measures of financial performance than does the market price of shares of common stock of media companies, such as Time Warner. The multiple for shares of AOL Time Warner common stock may be similar to the multiple for shares of America Online common stock, or it may be similar to the multiple for shares of Time Warner common stock, or it may reflect a "blending" of the two. AOL Time Warner will be the first global, fully integrated media and communications company, and financial analysts and investors may have difficulty identifying and applying measures of financial performance that reflect the value of the combined company. As a result, shares of AOL Time Warner common stock may not achieve a valuation in the public trading market that fully reflects the true value of the combined company, including its synergies and benefits.

AOL Time Warner may fail to realize the anticipated benefits of the merger.

The success of the merger will depend, in part, on the ability of AOL Time Warner to realize the anticipated growth opportunities and synergies from combining the businesses of America Online with the businesses of Time Warner. To realize the anticipated benefits of this combination, members of the management team of AOL Time Warner must develop strategies and implement a business plan that will:

- effectively combine Time Warner's media, entertainment and news brands and its broadband delivery systems with America Online's interactive services, technology and infrastructure;

- successfully use the anticipated opportunities for cross-promotion and sales of the products and services of Time Warner and America Online and for increasing revenues from advertising and e-commerce;
- effectively and efficiently integrate the policies, procedures and operations of America Online and Time Warner;
- successfully retain and attract key employees of the combined company, including operating management and key technical personnel, during a period of transition and in light of the competitive employment market; and
- while integrating the combined company's operations, maintain adequate focus on the core businesses of AOL Time Warner in order to take advantage of competitive opportunities and to respond to competitive challenges

If members of the management team of AOL Time Warner are not able to develop strategies and implement a business plan that achieves these objectives, the anticipated benefits of the merger may not be realized. In particular, anticipated growth in revenue, earnings before interest, taxes and amortization, or "EBITA," earnings before interest, taxes, depreciation and amortization, or "EBITDA," and cash flow may not be realized, which would have an adverse impact on AOL Time Warner and the market price of shares of AOL Time Warner common stock.

Directors of America Online and Time Warner have potential conflicts of interest in recommending that you vote in favor of adoption of the merger agreement.

A number of directors of America Online and a number of directors of Time Warner who recommend that you vote in favor of the adoption of the merger agreement have employment or severance agreements or benefit arrangements that provide them with interests in the merger that differ from yours. Following completion of the merger, Stephen M. Case, Chairman and Chief Executive Officer of America Online, will serve as Chairman of the Board of AOL Time Warner, and Robert W. Pittman, President and Chief Operating Officer of America Online, will serve as Co-Chief Operating Officer of AOL Time Warner. In addition, Gerald M. Levin, Chairman and Chief Executive Officer of Time Warner, will serve as Chief Executive Officer of AOL Time Warner, Richard D. Parsons, President of Time Warner, will serve as Co-Chief Operating Officer of AOL Time Warner and R.E. Turner, Vice Chairman of Time Warner will serve as Vice Chairman of AOL Time Warner.

The receipt of compensation or other benefits in the merger, including the vesting of stock options and restricted stock, or the continuation of indemnification arrangements for current directors of America Online and Time Warner following completion of the merger, may influence these directors in making their recommendation that you vote in favor of the adoption of the merger agreement.

AOL Time Warner may be subject to adverse regulatory conditions.

Before the merger may be completed, various approvals must be obtained from, or notifications submitted to, among others, competition authorities in the United States and abroad, the Federal Communications Commission and numerous state and local authorities. Many of these governmental entities from whom approvals are required may attempt to condition their approval of the merger, or of the transfer to the combined company of licenses and other entitlements, on the imposition of certain regulatory conditions that may have the effect of imposing additional costs on AOL Time Warner or of limiting AOL Time Warner's revenues. In addition, the regulatory environment in which AOL Time Warner's businesses will operate is complex and subject to change, and adverse changes in that environment could have either of these adverse effects.

QUESTIONS

1. Summarize the reasons for the merger from AOL's standpoint.

2. Summarize the reasons for the merger from Time Warner's standpoint.

3. A number of analyst reports from various sources made ten-year projections of the combined AOL Time Warner company. Using a DCF spreadsheet analysis, the target price placed on the combined company was mostly in the range of $105 to $115 per share. The year 2000 revenues for the combined companies were estimated to be $33 billion, representing the zero year revenues (R_0). From the analysis related to these DCF valuations, we arrived at the following value drivers as a basis for calculating the intrinsic value per share of the AOL Time Warner stock.

n	=	Number of supernormal growth years	10
m	=	Net operating income margin	28.0%
T	=	Tax rate	39.0%
g_s	=	Supernormal growth period growth rate	25.0%
d_s	=	Supernormal growth period depreciation	6.0%
I_{ws}	=	Supernormal growth period working capital expenditures	2.0%
I_{fgs}	=	Supernormal growth period capital expenditures (gross)	3.0%
k_s	=	Supernormal growth period cost of capital	10.0%
g_c	=	Terminal period growth rate	5.0%
d_c	=	Terminal period depreciation	1.0%
I_{wc}	=	Terminal period working capital expenditures	0.0%
I_{fgc}	=	Terminal period capital expenditures	1.0%
k_c	=	Terminal period cost of capital	12.0%

Using the basic revenue growth formula, M 09-04 from the models disk, calculate the base case estimate of the intrinsic value per share of the AOL Time Warner stock. Additional inputs include no marketable securities, total interest bearing debt of $21 billion, and 4.39 billion shares of common stock outstanding.

4. During the months of May through July 2000, when most analyst reports were calculating a target price of $105 to $115 for AOL, the market price of AOL continued to drift down from a price of $56 to around $52. It appears that the market was not agreeing with the glowing analyst valuations of a much higher intrinsic value for AOL. What might be the reasons for this divergence?

Case 19

Scott Paper and Sunbeam: A Contrast*

The narratives of Scott Paper and Sunbeam provide sharp contrasts that illuminate the nature of corporate restructuring and the turnaround process. Albert J. Dunlap was the central figure in both stories. This case will describe what appeared to happen in each of these case histories. We draw on information from a wide range of sources in the attempt to present as fair and as balanced accounts as possible. Our focus is not on the people involved, but rather on the goal of improving our understanding of what is required for successful corporate restructuring. Other cases on these two companies were written earlier; this one tells the "rest of the story" as it looked in July 2000.

THE SCOTT PAPER STORY

When Albert Dunlap was hired by Scott Paper in April, 1994 the market value of shareholders equity was $1.4 billion. Scott Paper was sold to Kimberly-Clark in December, 1995 for $6.9 billion. Its value had increased by 393 percent. The cost of goods sold as a percentage of sales for Scott Paper had been reduced from 65.5 percent in 1993 to 61.2 percent for 1995. These results were widely heralded as an example of a turnaround of outstanding success.

Characteristics of the Paper and Allied Products Industry

The paper manufacturing industry is capital intensive. Large investments are required for the machinery to produce paper products. The acceleration principle from economic theory operates in capital expenditure patterns in the paper industry. When demand-supply relationships are strong, individual companies place orders for plant

---

*This case was stimulated by Sanford C. Sigoloff and was improved by the opportunity of presenting it to his classes on Crisis Management and Corporate Renewal.

and equipment to increase capacity. By the time the machinery is delivered, the cumulative decisions of the individual producers result in industry excess capacity. Downward pressure on paper prices results. Historically, paper companies added much capacity during the 1980's, but the quantity of paper products demanded did not match supply capacity until early 1995. Thus, there was a downward pressure on prices during the early 1990's. An upward price cycle began to accelerate in late 1994 and was very strong through 1995.

Six major types of paper industry products are manufactured, each with somewhat distinctive characteristics. (1) Paper pulp is the basic raw material for paper production. Some paper manufacturers are integrated backward to pulp production. (2) Newsprint quality paper is used for newspaper production. (3) Printing papers are of two types. Uncoated papers used for office supplies, envelopes, and forms. Coated papers use clay to produce a smooth surface. This paper is used in glossy magazines, corporate annual reports, textbooks, and catalogs. (4) Tissue paper includes bathroom and facial tissues, paper towels and napkins. Consumption of tissue products is sensitive to changes in per capita income after taxes. (5) Packaging paper includes heavy brown paper used for grocery bags and the linerboard for corrugated boxes. Linerboard prices are highly sensitive to rates of change in gross domestic product. (6) Bleached paperboard is used for folding cartons, milk cartons, and disposable cups and plates. Some product differentiation is achieved by branding and differences in paper textures. But most paper products are commodities with a relatively high degree of price sensitivity.

The U.S. paper and allied products industry is the world's leading producer and exporter of a variety of consumer-directed commodities, trading many of them with more than 125 countries. A large modern manufacturing base, combined with an adequate transportation and distribution network and a highly skilled labor force, makes the U.S. industry the most competitive and highest-volume supplier in the world. Although the domestic market consumes more than 90 percent of its output, this industry has become a major player in the world paper and allied products market. After 1993 exports as a proportion of total U.S. paper and allied products shipments increased from 7.3% in that year to nearly 9% in 1998 as exports on a value basis grew from over $9 billion to nearly $15 billion. As much as 65% of the industry's growth in shipments over the past decade is directly attributable to increases in foreign shipments of paper and allied products.

After a poor performance in 1996, the U.S. paper and allied products industry has experienced consecutive years of increased domestic and foreign demand, slowly improving prices, higher capacity utilization rates, and inventory drawdowns. As a result, total shipments of paper and allied products increased 1.5% in real terms and 4.1% in current dollar terms in 1998. A general upward movement in prices for a number of primary commodity grades of paper and paperboard and certain converted paper products and packaging materials resulted in the increase in the current value of shipments. Real GDP increased about 3.7 percent in 1998 (first quarter to first quarter), leading to noticeable increases in real disposable income, total U.S. industrial production, and purchases of nondurable goods; all these factors combined to increase domestic paper and paperboard demand and improve the industry's level of shipments.

The earnings of domestic paper and paperboard companies were estimated to improve slowly in 1998 as a result of increasing demand, slightly higher prices, increased operating rates, and the end of a major inventory drawdown cycle. Virtually every major U.S. pulp and paper company saw overall sales, net profits, and average earnings per share improve slightly in 1998 from the same period in 1997. Labor, chemicals, and wood raw materials costs generally were kept in check, but energy prices fell for the industry in 1998 as the mild winter resulted in an excess supply of heating fuel oil and natural gas.

With U.S. GDP forecast to continue to expand in 1999, product shipments by the U.S. paper and allied products industries should follow suit with a 2.2% increase. Over the 1999-2003 forecast period, product shipments should expand 2% annually in real terms. The move by this industry to improve its fundamentals over the past several years should allow it to reap positive benefits, especially if demand remains high and the industry is better able to control capacity additions.

The Background on Scott Paper before Dunlap

Scott Paper was the second largest tissue producer in the U.S. after Procter & Gamble. It held the number one position in Europe in the tissue market. It had operations in 22 countries and its own products in 80 countries. It had an excellent distribution network with a good reputation. It owned more than two-dozen manufacturing facilities in the Americas as well as an additional two-dozen facilities in Europe and in the Pacific region. In the late 1920's the company became vertically integrated by acquiring timberlands and pulp mills. Later, it began to operate its own energy facilities to power its mills.

In 1967, Scott Paper acquired S.D. Warren, a manufacturer of coated printing papers. As S.D. Warren grew, Scott Paper's sales were three-quarters in the tissue segment and one-quarter in coated printing paper.

In 1990, the earnings per share of Scott Paper declined to $2.01 from $5.11 in 1989. The earnings decline reflected cyclical over capacity in paper products generally and particularly in the coated paper business. Scott Paper attempted several restructuring efforts. Between 1990 and 1993, employment was reduced from 30,800 to 25,900. Special restructuring charges of $167 million and $249 million were taken in 1990 and 1991, respectively, to cover cost of workforce reductions and sale of a number of asset that were nonstrategic such as a foodservice container business and a bulk "nonwovens" business. On 1/26/94, Scott Paper announced an additional restructuring charge of $490 million to cover an additional 3,000 job cuts and plant shut downs.

Despite the restructuring efforts, inefficiencies remained. Employment remained excessive and the shop floor culture was unfavorable. Salaried administrative support was substantially higher than competitors. The corporate staff spent more than $30 million per year on consultants. The decision making process was cumbersome. The product family was fragmented without a focused strategy.

Dunlap at Scott Paper

On 4/19/94, Scott Paper announced that Albert J. Dunlap would become Chairman and Chief Executive Officer. Albert Dunlap had begun his business career at Kimberly-Clark. He occupied managerial positions at numerous companies, most of them in the paper industry. He had past turnaround experience in Lily-Tulip (paper-cup maker), Diamond International, Crown-Zellerbach (timber company), and Consolidated Press Holdings (Australian conglomerate).

Dunlap began a swift restructuring program. During the first year, he discharged 70% of upper management. By June 1994, eight of the companies eleven senior executives had been terminated or resigned. He added three new senior executives who were part of the team that had worked with him in prior restructuring assignments. He hired fourteen experienced marketing executives from Kimberly-Clark, Procter & Gamble, Colgate-Palmolive, and Coca-Cola. He reduced payroll by 35% by cutting 11,200 jobs with annual savings estimated at $425 million.

A divestiture program generated gross proceeds of $2.2 billion within the first year. The S.D. Warren operation was closed in mid-December of 1994 for $1.57 billion. The Mobile, Alabama energy complex sold to Southern Company for $350 million. Energy complex at Chester, Pennsylvania was sold to CRSS Inc. for $170 million. Three smaller businesses, Scott Healthcare and food service units in the U.S. and UK were sold for a total of $110 million.

Dunlap developed a new business plan with a strategy which "focuses like a laser, not a shotgun." Dunlap pared down the product line, eliminating 31% of consumer product items offered. The number of products was reduced by more than 500 and domestic warehouses were reduced from 70 to 10. Marketing efforts were refocused around this unified product line, saving millions in advertising and promotional expenses. A new marketing plan included revitalized packaging for existing products, new advertising campaigns, and new consumer products.

Dunlap invested his personal wealth plus substantial borrowings. The top ten executives owned $10 million of company stock. Dunlap felt that executive pay should be tied to shareholder value.

Sale of Scott Paper to Kimberly-Clark

On July 17, 1995, the sale of Scott Paper to Kimberly-Clark was announced. Just short of fifteen months had elapsed since Dunlap had taken the helm at Scott Paper. The deal terms are summarized in Table 1. The respective share prices 30 days before the announcement were $59.13 for Kimberly-Clark and $43.38 for Scott Paper. Based on the

TABLE 1 Kimberly Clark/Scott Deal Terms

Pre-Merger	Dollar Amounts		Total	Percentage	
	K-Clark	Scott		K-Clark	Scott
Share Price [1]	$59.13	$43.38			
Shares Outstanding (million)	160	152			
Total Market Value (billion)	$9.5	$6.6	$16.1	59.0%	41.0%
Exchange Terms	0.765 for	1			
Post-Merger					
Number of Shares (million)	160	116	276	58.0%	42.0%

(1) Share Prices as of 30 days before announcement

Total Paid (billion)	$6.9
Premium Over Market	
Amount (bilion	$0.3
Percent	4.3%

total market values of the two companies, Kimberly-Clark represented 59% ownership and Scott Paper 41% ownership. The exchange terms were 0.765 shares of Kimberly-Clark for each share of Scott Paper. The total amount paid by Kimberly-Clark in the market value of shares exchanged was $6.9 billion. This represented a $0.3 billion premium or 4.3%. These amounts were smaller than ordinary stock price fluctuations so that virtually no premium was paid by Kimberly-Clark.

Some comparisons of Kimberly-Clark versus Scott Paper relationships are summarized in Table 2. The sales of Scott Paper were about one-half the sales of Kimberly-Clark. But net income was about two-thirds of Kimberly-Clark. The market value to sales ratio was much higher for Scott than for Kimberly-Clark. However, the ratio of market value to net income was only slightly higher for Scott.

TABLE 2 Comparison of Multiples, Kimberly-Clark vs. Scott

	Kim-Clark	Scott	Total	Scott %
Total market value	$9.5B	$6.6B	$16.1B	41.0%
Sales	$8.1B	$4.0B	$12.1B	33.1%
Operating profit	$1,015M	$635M	$1,650M	38.5%
Operating margin	12.6%	16.0%		
Pretax income	$895M	$575M	$1,470M	39.1%
Net income	$582M	$392M	$974M	40.2%
Market to Sales	1.17	1.65		
Market to Operating Profit	9.36	10.39		
Market to Pretax Income	10.61	11.48		
Market to Net Income	16.32	16.84		

The merger appeared to have much strategic logic from the standpoint of Kimberly-Clark. Clearly it broadened its product line to cover every segment from premium brands to low price competitive brands. Contemporaneous financial analyst reports commented on the complementary brand patterns. Operating synergies and potential cost savings were estimated to be in the $400-$600 million range. Duplicate facilities and excess capacity would be eliminated. While Kimberly-Clark had a strong position in the United Kingdom, its entry into Europe was late and it lacked a strong distributions system on the continent. Kimberly-Clark had superior technology with an excellent history of developing new products which created whole new markets like Pull-Ups training pants. Analysts regarded Kimberly-Clark's marketing organization as superior to Scott's. Scott's strong brands could be further exploited in the Kimberly-Clark marketing organization.

After the merger Kimberly-Clark learned that Dunlap's cost cutting program had impaired its long run viability. Deferment of equipment maintenance had impaired factory efficiency. Cost cutting of the R&D functions had dried up the new product pipeline. Scott's inventory channel was stuffed with products that had been sold at discounted prices. Analysts noted that it took Kimberly-Clark almost three years and two restructuring charges to recover from the impaired condition of Scott Paper. However, over the ten year period 9/30/89 to 9/30/99 Kimberly-Clark achieved about sixteen percent annualized return to shareholders only slightly below the S&P 500 of 16.83 percent for the same period.

Several financial analysts noted that Dunlap had a record of cutting muscle along with fat in his turnaround operations. Some expressed admiration for his ability to sell off the companies he had "turned around" at top prices. It was widely reported that Dunlap had increased his wealth by over $100 million in his Scott Paper experience. To some he became a folk hero. His record in reducing employment and cutting costs earned him the sobriquet, "Chainsaw Al." With Bob Andelman he wrote a book entitled *Mean Business: How I Save Bad Companies and Make Good Companies Great* published in 1996. In it he summarized his philosophy for turning around companies. He set forth a list of ten rules:

1. Get the right management team
2. Cut costs
3. Focus on the core business
4. Get a "real strategy"
5. Use consultants sparingly, if at all
6. Reduce debt
7. Get rid of "self-aggrandizing corporate royalty"
8. Use stock options generously to motivate executives

9. Board members should be paid in stock and top executives should put their personal fortunes at risk

10. Don't worry about being liked. "If you want a friend, get a dog."

Dunlap said that business is remarkably simple. It only required that his ten rules be followed. He observed that the knowledge and application of his ten rules would put business schools and most consulting firms out of business. With regard to his tenth rule that the cheap executive should not worry about being liked and that to have a friend get a dog, he said that to play it safe he had two dogs. Thus at the pinnacle of his reputation he was hired to rescue Sunbeam.

DUNLAP AT SUNBEAM

Sunbeam had a long and turbulent history. It was founded in Dundee, Illinois in 1897. Its early products included agricultural tools such as sheep shearing machines and hand-clippers. In 1910 it began manufacturing electrical appliances, creating the lightweight Princess iron. At about the same time it adopted the Sunbeam brand name in advertising. In the 1930s it achieved a number of product triumphs including the Sunbeam Mixmaster, Shaver, the first automatic coffee maker, and the first pop-up electric toaster. In 1946 the company changed its name to Sunbeam. By 1960 it had introduced a hair dryer, humidifiers, knife sharpeners, massage pillows, egg cookers, controlled-heat frying pans, electric blankets, a cordless hand mixer, a snow blower, and a rotisserie.

In 1960 Sunbeam acquired its arch-rival, Oster, made famous by its Osterizer food processor. In 1981 Sunbeam was acquired by Allegheny International, a conglomerate firm. A sharp decline in sales in its other divisions pushed Allegheny into bankruptcy in 1988. In 1990 the company was bought from Allegheny's creditors by three financial investors: Michael Price, Michael Steinhardt, and Paul Kazarian. They renamed the company, The Sunbeam-Oster Company. Two years later the company had made sufficient progress to make it possible to take it public. However, in 1993 some problems caused chairman Kazarian to be forced out. The new head of the company was an experienced General Electric executive named Roger Schipke. In 1994 Sunbeam-Oster bought Rubbermaid's outdoor furniture business. In 1995 the company changed its name back to Sunbeam.

However, the company's problems continued and after some deliberations among the major owners the decision was made to hire Albert J. Dunlap to perform a Scott Paper-type miracle at Sunbeam. On July 19, 1996 Dunlap became the head of the company. The day before the announcement that Dunlap would take the helm, Sunbeam stock closed at $12.50. On the announcement day the Sunbeam stock rose sixty percent to close at $20.00. Truly the market expected much from the new chief executive.

Dunlap seemed to follow his historical pattern. Executives were discharged. He had demanded as a condition of taking the job that he select his board of directors;

some outside directors resigned so that Dunlap directors could be appointed. Plants were closed and employment sharply reduced. Staffing was shrunk at human resources and R&D departments. New sales programs were formulated and launched.

By early 1998 the price of Sunbeam stock had reached $53, up 324 percent from the $12.50 pre-Dunlap level. Dunlap hired an investment banker and later a second to try to sell the company. But buyers could not be found.

An alternative strategy was formulated by Dunlap. If he couldn't sell Sunbeam he would acquire other companies. Negotiations were made with Ronald Perelman, the major owner of Coleman Company, a camping-gear maker. The asking price seemed high to Dunlap so no progress was made for some months. In the meantime it appeared that Sunbeam was having problems meeting the projections it had made to analysts on its sales and its earnings. In his book, *Chainsaw, Business Week* senior editor John A. Byrne writes that Dunlap became "what every seller so badly wants: a desperate buyer." (p.202) In early 1998 in quick succession acquisitions of three companies were announced by Sunbeam. Coleman was bought for $1.6 billion plus an assumption of $440 million debt. This represented about $30 a share for the stock of a troubled company that had traded at $14 a share a month earlier. Sunbeam also bought First Alert (smoke alarms) for $133 million in cash and $45 million of assumed debt. Signature Brands, best known for its Mr. Coffee product, was bought for $84 million in cash and $169 million in assumed debt. These deals were completed by March 2, 1998.

But rumors persisted that the sales and earnings reports of Sunbeam had been manipulated. On March 19, 1998 the company announced that first quarter sales and earnings might not meet Wall Street analysts' estimates. But the company said that it was still "highly confident" about the full year outlook. On April 3, 1998 at 9:09 a.m. the PaineWebber downgrade of Sunbeam hit the First Call website. Skepticism about Sunbeam's future grew. The major owners and board of directors of Sunbeam became concerned. On June 13, 1998 Albert J. Dunlap was discharged as the chief executive of Sunbeam. Sunbeam's price quickly dropped to a low of $4.625. This represented a decline of 91.3% from its peak value. In relation to the $12.50 value on 7-18-96, the day before the Dunlap announcement was made, Sunbeam stock price had declined 63%.

What Happened at Sunbeam?

In fifteen months at Scott Paper Dunlap achieved a great triumph. In twenty-three months at Sunbeam controversy and doubt led to Dunlap's departure. Why did the Sunbeam experience turn out so differently for Albert Dunlap? One difference that readily emerges is that Dunlap grew up in the paper business, but had no prior experience with the household appliance business. In addition he caught a rising price wave for paper products in 1994 and 1995. At Sunbeam the Dunlap years of the second half of 1996 through 1998 were difficult years for the U.S. household appliances industry.

The patterns are shown in Table 3. The value of shipments produced in the United States consistently declined from the peak value of $22.8 billion in 1994 to $22.3 in 1999. Shipments were flat in units sold but prices were falling. The value of imports rose from $4.3 billion in 1992 to $7.1 billion in 1998. The Asian crisis caused producers

TABLE 3 Household Applicances (SIC 363) Trends and Forecasts (billions of dollars)

		1992	1993	1994	1995	1996	1997	1998	1999
Industry data									
Value of shipments		18.6	20.4	22.8	21.8	22.2	22.1	22.1	22.3
3631	Household cooking equipment	3.0	3.0	3.8	3.9	3.6	3.6	3.6	3.7
3632	Household refrigerators	4.2	4.5	5.1	5.2	5.6	5.4	5.4	5.5
3633	Household laundry equipment	3.3	3.9	4.6	4.1	4.2	4.3	4.3	4.4
3634	Electric housewares and fans	2.9	3.1	3.1	3.3	3.0	2.9	2.8	2.7
3635	Household vacuums	1.9	2.1	1.9	2.0	2.4	2.3	2.3	2.3
3639	Home appliances nec	3.3	3.9	4.2	3.2	3.3	3.6	3.7	3.8
Value of shipments (1992$)		18.6	20.2	22.5	21.5	21.7	22.0	22.4	22.6
3631	Household cooking equipment	3.0	2.9	3.8	3.9	3.5	3.6	3.7	3.7
3632	Household refrigerators	4.2	4.4	5.1	5.2	5.5	5.5	5.7	5.8
3633	Household laundry equipment	3.3	3.9	4.7	4.2	4.3	4.4	4.6	4.7
3634	Electric housewares and fans	2.9	3.1	3.1	3.3	3.1	3.0	2.9	2.8
3635	Household vacuums	1.9	2.0	1.8	1.9	2.3	2.2	2.3	2.3
3639	Home appliances nec	3.3	3.8	4.1	3.0	3.1	3.2	3.3	3.4
Total employment (thousands)		103	105	111	110	108	104		
Production workers (thousands)		83.2	85.0	90.6	87.7	87.0	82.2		
Average hourly earnings$		11.34	11.72	11.74	12.23	12.81	13.02		
Capital expenditues		556	481	517	630	721			
Product data									
Value of shipments		16.8	18.0	19.8	20.1	20.6	20.5	20.5	20.7
3631	Household cooking equipment	3.0	3.2	3.8	3.9	3.8	3.8	3.8	3.9
3632	Household refrigerators	4.0	4.3	5.0	5.1	5.4	5.2	5.1	5.2
3633	Household laundry equipment	3.0	3.3	3.7	3.5	3.7	3.7	3.7	3.8
3634	Electric housewares and fans	2.7	2.7	2.7	2.9	2.5	2.4	2.3	2.2
3635	Household vacuums	1.8	2.0	1.8	1.9	2.3	2.2	2.2	2.2
3639	Home appliance nec	2.3	2.5	2.9	2.7	2.9	3.2	3.3	3.3
Value of shipments (1992$)		16.8	17.8	19.6	19.8	20.2	20.4	20.8	21.0
3631	Household cooking equipment	3.0	3.1	3.7	3.8	3.7	3.8	3.9	3.9
3632	Household refrigerators	4.0	4.3	4.9	5.1	5.3	5.3	5.5	5.6
3633	Household laundry equipment	3.0	3.3	3.7	3.6	3.7	3.9	4.0	4.1
3634	Electric housewares and fans	2.7	2.7	2.7	2.9	2.5	2.5	2.4	2.3
3635	Household vacuums	1.8	2.0	1.7	1.8	2.2	2.2	2.2	2.2
3639	Home appliance nec	2.3	2.5	2.8	2.6	2.7	2.9	2.9	3.0
Trade data									
Value of imports		4.3	4.5	4.9	5.1	5.4	5.8	7.1	
Value of exports		2.3	2.5	2.6	2.6	2.8	3.0	3.2	

there to cut prices in the desperate attempt to increase exports to the U.S. for dollars badly needed to meet short-term debt repayment requirements. The economic environment of the household appliance industry while Dunlap was at the helm of Sunbeam was highly unfavorable. It was difficult to cut costs enough to meet the conditions of a depressed sales environment and sharp price-cutting by the competition. It was difficult to achieve sales increases; it was even more difficult to maintain profitability. Other firms were experiencing similar difficulties and were attempting to make adjustments.

Household Appliances Industry

In addition to increased foreign trade, there has been a substantial increase in investments by appliance companies in foreign countries through acquisitions and joint ventures. The investing companies are seeking low-cost sources of appliances and/or a share in rapidly growing markets. Much of this investment has taken place in the former communist countries as well as in rapidly industrializing countries in Asia and Latin America.

In the U.S. appliance market in 1998, pressure on prices was keen and persistent. Much of the pressure resulted from sharply increased imports led by soaring imports from the two largest foreign suppliers, China and Mexico. In addition, imports from several other Asian countries, such as South Korea and Japan, were also up sharply because of the weakness of their currencies in foreign exchange markets stemming from the Asian economic crisis. Pressure on prices from increased imports was a major factor in causing U.S. appliance producer prices to decline during 1998.

Severe competition has induced several companies to restructure, often resulting in major layoffs and plant closings. For Example, Black & Decker, a leading small appliance producer exited the household appliance industry, selling its household products division to Windmere-Durable Holdings, Inc., in early 1998. Restructuring was not restricted just to the small appliance producers. In mid-1997, Raytheon began exiting from the industry when it sold its Amana home appliance business to Goodman Holding company. This was followed in early 1998 by the sale of its Speed Queen laundry equipment business to Bain Capital Inc. Meanwhile, A.B. Electrolux of Sweden was closing its Frigidaire headquarters in Dublin, Ohio, after that division was combined with the lawn products divisions. This was part of a long-term global restructuring by Electrolux to eliminate 12,000 jobs. Whirlpool, going through a restructuring to cut 7,900 positions worldwide, terminated two of its four joint ventures in China. However, Whirlpool was moving forward in Brazil as it completed the purchase of a majority voting interest in Brasmotor S.A., a holding company that controlled Multibras S.A., the largest appliance company in Latin America. Whirlpool has had an interest in these two Brazilian companies for several years.

In the unfavorable environment of the household appliance industry critics argue that Dunlap broke his own rules for how to successfully turnaround a company. For example, at Scott Paper employment reductions in the factory were based on review of production flow processes. At Sunbeam outside consultants calculated a volume to employee relationships based on samples of similar companies.

In addition it is alleged that to show higher sales some questionable accounting practices were employed. Big buyers agreed to accept the practice of a massive sell-and-hold program. Sales were billed but the product was shipped to rented warehouses and the "customer" had the right to reverse the order.

Without detailing each one, a list of criticisms were made of Dunlap's practices at Sunbeam:

1. No product or marketing strategies related to Sunbeam's industry, competitors, strengths and weaknesses

2. Early change of computer systems without backup; blackout in orders and invoicing for weeks

3. Reduced employment by shutting plants; sought to increase sales, but lacked product

4. Layoffs based on target reductions without analysis of production planning systems

5. Closed plants making precision products requiring worker experience and commitment; moved to plants in Mexico using unskilled labor

6. Cost cutting methods impaired Sunbeam's ability to compete

    a. In manufacturing, deferred maintenance

    b. In marketing, cut advertising

    c. In product development, cut R&D

    d. In human resources, cut training budget

7. Sharp cuts in prices in an effort to increase sales

8. Window dressing – prepaid expenses in 1996 to make 1997 look better

9. To boost sales, adopted a massive sell-and-hold practice; sales were billed, but product shipped to rented warehouses, and "buyer" had the right to reverse the order

10. Tried to sell company before the debacle, but could find no buyers

11. Made three quick acquisitions, overpaid, took on $2 billion debt to be able to "restructure" the books

12. Managed acquisitions poorly

The histories of Scott Paper and Sunbeam provide the basis for discussion questions. The aim of these questions is to stimulate a better understanding of the restructuring and turnaround process.

QUESTIONS

1. Discuss the characteristics of the paper industry and how they affected the performance of Scott after Dunlap became CEO.

2. Describe the turnaround concepts that Dunlap used at Scott. Are they "simple" to apply?

3. Describe the small appliance industry and how it affected Dunlap's performance at Sunbeam.

4. What did Dunlap do wrong at Sunbeam?

5. What are the pros and cons of doing a turnaround within twelve months?

6. Present your own list of prescriptions of how restructuring can make a firm more efficient.

Case 20

The GM-Toyota Vows:
A Reply to the Critics

In the January Across the Board, *two antitrust specialists weighed the competitive benefits and antitrust risks of joint ventures by American firms. Among the ventures examined was the disputed General Motors-Toyota plan to jointly produce a subcompact car in Fremont, California.*

Delayed for more than a year, the plan—as detailed in a consent order—was tentatively approved by a 3-to-2 majority of the Federal Trade Commission last December.

The following commentary was written as a reply to the articles by Sanford M. Litvack ("The Urge to Rewrite the Antitrust Laws") and Joseph F. Brodley ("Joint-Venture Marriages").

by J. Fred Weston

Critics of the Federal Trade Commission's approval of the GM-Toyota venture argue that antitrust laws are being rewritten and relaxed. On the contrary, the decision reflects new thinking on industrial economics during the past decade that has been recognized by the courts.

Under the old structural theory, the courts measured market concentration to determine whether businesses were violating the antitrust laws; they looked at the sales shares of the top firms in an industry as a predictor of how firms might behave. The new approach looks at how firms actually conduct themselves in real-world markets by measuring efficiency and how firms serve consumers.

This common-sense way of looking at markets began 10 years ago. It was first applied in merger cases (for example, U.S. Supreme Court approval in 1974 of General

Reprint from *Across the Board*, The Conference Board Magazine, Vol. XXI, No. 3, March 1984.

Dynamics' acquisition of the Material Service Company), then in monopoly cases (for instance, a U.S. Court of Appeals decision in 1975 in favor of IBM against the Telex complaint), and later in cases involving a manufacturer selling to distributors (for example, *Continental TV v. Sylvania*, 1977). With the tentative approval of the GM-Toyota joint venture, antitrust policy has extended what Conference Board economist Betty Bock has termed the "new realism" to a major joint-venture case. Applying an efficiency test does not represent an abrupt change in policy, but rather further recognition that the antitrust game should not be "played by the numbers."

The business reasons underlying the GM-Toyota joint venture are straightforward. GM hopes to obtain day-to-day, hands-on experience in the advanced management technology of building small cars, and to add this experience to other efforts underway to become more cost efficient in producing a family of small cars. Such learning is essential because U.S. production suffers a small-car landed cost disadvantage vis-à-vis production in Japan of up to $2,000 per unit.

For its part, Toyota aims to test its production methods in a new setting with different labor and supplier relationships. Each firm is seeking to become more efficient to meet the tough competition in the automobile industry. Because the cars will be produced at an unused plant in Fremont, California, the new investment costs are reduced. Hence, the risk/return prospects of the venture are improved compared with alternative methods of achieving their objectives.

In contrast to previous joint ventures that have been found illegal, this agreement expresses the intention of both parties to compete vigorously in all their markets for every product. This joint venture, as codified by the conditions of the FTC consent order, is quite circumscribed. It limits the annual volume of the one model the joint venture can produce for GM to 250,000. It limits the duration of the venture to a maximum of 12 years. It restricts the exchange of information that can pass between the parties. The order also requires that records be kept of certain contacts between the parties, and that both companies file annual compliance reports with the FTC.

Yet, despite all these safeguards, the critics have voiced skepticism. The many darts thrown at the joint venture do not pierce its fundamental efficiency motive. While some of the criticisms make good rhetoric, they do not stand up to careful analysis.

The first criticism is that the joint venture will increase the already excessive concentration of market positions in the auto industry. Only under the outdated structural theory would concentration measures command center stage. The new wisdom recognizes that the economic facts of life of an industry are more to the point.

For example, take the Government's prosecution of IBM for anticompetitive behavior, which was dropped in 1982. Carl Kaysen, who as an economic advisor to U.S. District Judge Charles Wyzanski in the early 1950s set the pattern for the structural theory in a shoe-industry case, has argued that the circumstances in the IBM case were different and that the Government's position was without merit. While IBM's share of the computer market was large, Kaysen has written, it had been declining. Superior new technologies were appearing with "breathtaking speed." IBM's main customers were large and sophisticated, with the ability to seek out and even create alternative sources of supply. These arguments were the thrust of the IBM defense and evidently helped persuade the Justice Department to drop the case.

But even under the older structuralist standards, the data on the venture are consistent with dynamic competition. One of the ways of measuring concentration (endorsed by the Department of Justice guidelines of June 1981) is called the HHI index, which sums the squares of the market percentage shares of each firm (the squaring has the impact of giving greater weight to the large-firm shares). An HHI index above 1800 in an industry is considered excessive concentration; below 1000 is considered unconcentrated. Between the two ranges, the guidelines suggest further study of such market factors as prices, product quality, and service to customers. The HHI for the world auto market in 1981 was 680—clearly in the acceptable range and even lower than the HHI of 896 ten years earlier.

To narrow the market definition to subcompact autos sold in the United States would be to carve up the market in an artificial way because of the competition between different models. But this is how the structuralists like to define the game, and we will therefore play it for the moment. For the subcompact segment, the HHI was, predictably, somewhat higher, at a level of 1316 for 1982 car deliveries. There was no dominant firm: Ford had slightly over 20 percent of the market, with GM and Toyota following close behind. In all there were 13 major international competitors with appreciable market shares.

A wide range of assumptions could be made about how the single joint-venture car model would impact this narrow subcompact segment. It is likely that there would be some increase in subcompact sales overall, and some substitution of the joint-venture car for other subcompacts. But a reasonable assumption is that the market share of the joint venture would be about 6 percent. And if the venture is treated as a separate entity, the HHI for this industry segment would drop to under 1200, near the acceptable area under the Government guidelines. All reasonable assumptions point to a negligible impact of the joint venture on concentration measures. Thus, even under the older structural approach, the GM-Toyota joint venture does not raise serious antitrust concerns.

But looking at concentration numbers is the outmoded way of judging the joint venture. The right way is to recognize that there are many substitutes for the products sold by GM and Toyota. Since consumers have good alternatives, and since other firms are ready to augment output if GM or Toyota individually or jointly attempt to control supply, one conclusion is inescapable: The two firms do not have monopoly power, nor do they have the potential to collude effectively. The original provisions for limiting the venture, now codified in the FTC consent order, further guarantee against anticompetitive effects.

A second criticism leveled at the joint venture is that it will help solidify "collusive price leadership" in autos (that is, all of the automakers will march in step with the industry leader's prices). Past studies of the U.S. auto industry found no evidence to support such claims, and the joint venture will not change the situation. The special conditions that must be present for collusive price leadership do not exist in the auto industry. Its products are highly differentiated. Costs vary greatly among rival firms. Fluctuations in demand and supply are large and continuous. Technology is subject to continuous change. Entry by foreign firms has taken place in markets throughout the world. The market shares of the auto firms have been fluctuating, and concentration has been decreasing in all major market segments. The cross-elasticity of demand among auto models is high, so that any attempt to elevate prices in some segments of the market would be met by a loss of sales to competing firms and models.

There is no basis in logic or fact to support allegations of collusive price leadership in the industry. While it is argued that some firms announce prices before others, what is more relevant is that prices continually change throughout a given model year. The forms of price change are numerous, including such things as extra bonuses to dealers for exceeding quotas, different strategies for pricing "extras," and so forth.

Thus, the idea that Toyota and GM can ignore market forces and raise prices at will is pure fantasy. To do so would mean huge losses in sales and profits and corresponding gains to competitors. Such behavior would clearly be irrational.

The FTC majority saw no basis for concern, even if concentration, by some measures, were to increase under the joint venture. A preponderance of theory and evidence support the FTC decision, which, rather than creating new rules, is consistent with both the older structural theory and the newer emphasis on efficiency in antitrust policy.

A third criticism is that the pricing formula, based on the prices of competing models, would lead to an upward spiral in auto prices. Such an argument is pure conjecture and fails to take into account market mechanisms that determine auto prices. What is fundamentally involved is supplier relationships. All kinds of purchasing activity is required in doing business and supplier-buyer prices must be "set." To call the GM-Toyota relationship "price fixing" in any sense is to regard all supplier-price relationships as suspect—which they clearly are not.

More important, after the car is transferred to General Motors, neither the joint venture nor Toyota plays any further part in pricing the vehicle. General Motors, within the boundaries set by the competition of the marketplace, arrives at a set of price relationships with dealers. Dealers, of course, then negotiate final prices with consumers, and at this point even GM is out of the picture.

The joint venture realizes a net amount which is equal to a competitive price less a relatively fixed distributor margin. If the joint venture is highly efficient and keeps its costs low, it has the potential for making high profits. If the joint venture is inefficient, it will suffer losses.

It is important to note that the pricing of the joint-venture car produces an inherent conflict of interest between GM and Toyota that is procompetitive. GM as a distributor would like to buy at as low a price as possible; it receives 100 percent of the benefits of a low purchase price, whereas it receives only half the profits from the joint venture. However, Toyota shares only in the profit from the joint venture's sales; it would thus be motivated to have as high a price as possible while keeping costs low.

GM also wants the joint venture to achieve low costs, so that it can learn to manufacture small cars more efficiently. The logic of the joint venture is to provide the correct efficiency incentives at each stage of the relationship.

Lastly, opponents of the venture argue that it will lead to the exchange of competitive-sensitive information. Obviously, they speculate, GM and Toyota will have to talk about such things as new models, outputs, and prices, and it will be to their advantage to exchange as much information as possible.

Of course, by jointly investing in this particular project, GM and Toyota will have to produce and share some information. GM will seek to learn about Toyota's superior approaches to stamping facilities, plant layout, quality control, inventory control, assembly and related production activities and management of the work force. For its part, Toyota will learn about operating in the United States, particularly in connection with supplier and labor relations.

But there will be self-limiting controls on the exchange of information. Consider, for example, GM's marketing of the joint-venture product. Advance information of GM's consumer-research and marketing strategy would be useful to its rivals, among them Toyota. Since such information could be used to inflict competitive harm on General Motors, GM is not likely to want to share it with anybody. Similarly, it would not be rational for Toyota to share with GM product design and research for other vehicles, since it is competing for the same customers.

This logic is reinforced by the absence of collateral restraints in the joint-venture agreement. By means of collateral restraints, parties to a venture impose limits on competition between themselves in certain areas. For example, collateral restraints were the reason that the joint-venture agreement in 1972 between Yamaha and Brunswick to produce outboard motors was declared illegal. These included division of markets in which each could sell and limits on each to produce competing products. But no such limits are found in the GM-Toyota agreement. The significance of the absence of these collateral restraints is that each firm intends to be a more vigorous competitor with the other as well as with all other rival companies.

Other critics say that it is not just sharing of information that poses a competitive threat but the fact that the venture will make GM more efficient in general. Indeed, some of GM's competitors have stated publicly that the venture will enable GM to produce cars at a lower cost. The following syllogism is then implicit: As a consequence of the joint venture, GM will become more efficient. If GM is more efficient, this will make life more difficult for its other domestic rivals. Therefore, the knowledge gained by GM and the joint venture will be anticompetitive.

But our antitrust laws were not intended to protect competitors. They were designed to stimulate competition. Greater efficiency forces greater competition. In addition, history tells us that when superior efficiency enters into the management experience of some companies in the United States, it becomes diffused to other companies. If the joint venture is successful, the new management technology learned by GM will be diffused to other firms in the auto industry as well as to other industries.

Another claim is that the GM-Toyota joint venture would stimulate similar arrangements by other companies. But this is evidence of the basic procompetitive nature of the joint venture. Other firms may indeed be forced to strive harder, by whatever means they can, to stay competitive. But this is the essence of the competitive process.

Furthermore, the GM-Toyota joint venture is of limited scope and duration. The histories of other joint ventures tell us that most were dissolved before their half-lives had been completed. This is so, in part, because the purposes of the joint ventures had been achieved, but perhaps also because the inherent difficulties and animosities that arise in operating under a long-term contractual arrangement will cause joint ventures to come asunder. A joint venture is not a marriage intended to bind the parties for eternity (as Mr. Brodley suggests). Rather, it is a temporary arrangement that the parties will terminate when short-term needs have been satisfied. Thus, very likely the GM-Toyota venture will be of shorter duration than the 12-year maximum life.

The FTC majority weighed efficiency benefits against anticompetitive costs: "To the extent the Fremont venture can demonstrate successfully that the Japanese system can work in America, the Commission finds that this will lead to the development of a more efficient, more competitive U.S. automobile industry."

The GM-Toyota joint venture will achieve an important management technology transfer to the U.S. It reinforces GM's strong commitment to the small-car market and provides incentives for other U.S. firms to do likewise.

In the shorter term, the venture will yield substantial benefits to consumers and workers. Consumers will benefit from lower prices and a greater range of choice in new cars. Workers will benefit from the reopening of the Fremont plant, which will create approximately 3,000 jobs (closer to 12,000 if jobs stemming from new orders to suppliers are taken into account). Without the joint venture's cars, more Japanese imports might be sold in the U.S., which means fewer jobs for Americans.

In the longer term, the improved efficiency will spur other U.S. rivals to improve efficiency, enhancing total U.S. competitiveness in the industry. The joint venture thus has the potential to produce thousands of new jobs that might well be lost to other countries unless the U.S. companies become more efficient. Ford's proposed new joint-venture plan in Mexico and rumors of similar moves by other U.S. firms are clear warnings of what could happen.

The dynamics of competition in the auto industry, despite various artificial barriers created by governments, guarantee against effective collusion. Attempts at collusion would, indeed, be ineffectual. High product substitutability and numerous rivals will continue to guarantee strong competition in the industry.

In an increasingly competitive, international economy, joint ventures are likely to continue to proliferate. To limit U.S. firms would place them at a further competitive disadvantage. The FTC decision joins the antitrust treatment of joint ventures to the mainstream of Government policy, reflecting a more enlightened view of competitive processes.

QUESTIONS

1. What did General Motors hope to gain from the joint venture?

2. Why would Toyota agree to help GM learn how to build competitive small cars?

3. List the criticisms of the joint venture and evaluate them.

Case 21

Daimler-Benz/Chrysler Corporation

In January 1998, Daimler-Benz CEO Jürgen Schrempp visited the Auburn Hills, Michigan headquarters of Chrysler for what was ostensibly a courtesy call. In a 17 minute meeting with Chrysler CEO Robert Eaton, the groundwork was laid for the merger of Daimler and Chrysler. According to Schrempp in an interview with Fortune (6/8/98), Daimler believed that the industry was beginning a period of consolidation. "The answer can't be joint venture here, joint venture there. We said to ourselves, 'We have to find a partner.' Once we did the studies of Japanese, European and American companies, it became obvious that Chrysler was the ideal partner." The combination of the two companies, announced on May 6, 1998, was the largest automobile merger in history. However, the entire industry was in the process of consolidating.

CHARACTERISTICS OF THE AUTO INDUSTRY

The automobile industry is one of the most global and competitive industries. Following the end of World War II, the large American companies thrived. However, a resurgence in the German and Japanese economies increased the number of companies in the international market. Even following recent consolidation, the industry is still spread throughout the world. GM and Ford remain the leaders in America (see Figure 1). German firms such as Daimler-Benz (now DaimlerChrysler), Volkswagen, and BMW are strong in Europe and play a role in the American market. Japanese firms are still important. Toyota and Honda are the leading independent firms, with Nissan (Renault) and Mitsubishi (DaimlerChrysler) recently selling significant shares to outside buyers. Many other auto firms play a role in the world market, such as Renault, Hyundai, and Fiat, to name a few. Such firms have distinct competitive advantages within their home nations. This plethora of large firms has made the auto industry very competitive on a global scale.

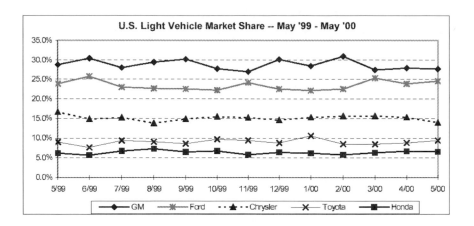

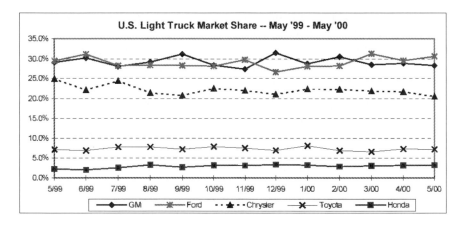

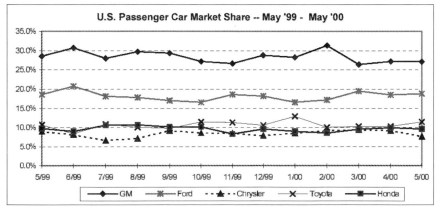

FIGURE 1

Furthermore, the existence of many large firms has led to global excess capacity. Analysts estimate that automobile firms sold about 54 million cars in 1999. However, auto plants had the capacity to produce about 77 million cars. Were plants to run to their full capacity, auto firms would find it nearly impossible to make a profit. This imbalance creates an impetus for mergers to eliminate some of the capacity of the industry. Complicating the capacity problem is the recent trend away from passenger cars. Consumers have shown an increasing preference for minivans and SUVs, as shown in Figure 2.

National pride is often wrapped up in automobile firms. They usually employ tens of thousands of workers in their home countries, making them an integral part of the local economy. This was a large source of the motivation behind the bailout of Chrysler by the United States government in the early 1980s. Chrysler was seen as a critical part of the U.S. economy. Politicians were not willing to risk the disenchantment of thousands of unhappy voters. In addition, many people felt threatened by the success of the Japanese auto firms. There was some surprise that there was little outcry over the Daimler-Chrysler merger. Rather than dismay over a key American firm selling out to Germans, there was rejoicing about the value created for Chrysler shareholders. As the global economy becomes more integrated, cross border mergers will likely face reduced nationalistic sentiment.

Technology plays a pivotal role in the auto industry. Auto firms must have sufficient technology to compete with new developments of other firms to produce a competitive product. With many large firms offering many similar products, new technology can be the key in producing a car that is significantly different and better than competitors. In addition, rising environmental concerns are making the quest for alter-

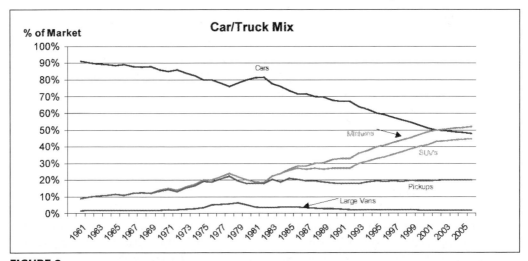

FIGURE 2

Source: DLJ.

native sources of power critical to the future success of firms. Most firms estimate that it costs about $500 million to develop a new conventional engine, but this price is only a fraction of the cost for development of environmentally friendly gas-electric hybrids or fuel-cell powered engines.

THE COMPANIES

Daimler-Benz

Daimler-Benz was the largest industrial group in Germany with 1997 revenues of DM 124 billion. Daimler-Benz operated in four business segments— Automotive (Passenger Cars and Commercial Vehicles), Aerospace, Services, and Directly Managed Businesses. Daimler-Benz was primarily active in Europe, North and South America, and Japan and was continuing to expand in markets such as Eastern Europe and East and Southeast Asia, which were assuming strategic importance as production locations.

Daimler was in the midst of a strategic shift. The company had become very diversified in the 1980s and had only begun to really try to focus the company in the mid 1990s. The aerospace division (which owned a significant stake in Airbus) and other divisions still made up a significant portion of Daimler's revenues (in the neighborhood of 25%). The automotive division made primarily luxury cars and commercial vehicles. Daimler was strong in Europe, but it had only about a 1% share of the lucrative United States market. In addition, Daimler-Benz automobiles had a reputation for superior engineering.

Chrysler

Chrysler Corporation, a Delaware corporation, operated in two principal industry segments: Automotive Operations and Financial Services. Automotive Operations included the research, design, manufacture, assembly and sale of cars, trucks, and related parts and accessories. Substantially all of Chrysler's automotive products were marketed through retail dealerships, most of which were privately owned and financed. Financial Services include the operations of Chrysler Financial Corporation and its consolidated subsidiaries, which are engaged principally in providing consumer and dealer automotive financing for Chrysler's products.

Chrysler was focused entirely on the automobile industry. Chrysler had a reputation for innovative designs, and an ability to bring new designs quickly to market. This earned it the reputation of being the most nimble of the "Big Three" United States auto firms. Chrysler was an industry leader in sport utility vehicles (SUVs) and minivans. It had been one of the first firms to benefit from the SUV's popularity, and it had a commanding lead in the minivan market throughout the 1990s. Although Chrysler was strong in the United States, it was weak abroad. Chrysler had very few dealerships in Asia, and only a 1% market share in Europe.

Background of the Transactions

In mid-January 1990, Jürgen E. Schrempp, Chairman or the Daimler-Benz Management Board, visited Robert J. Eaton, Chairman and Chief Executive Officer of Chrysler, while Mr. Schrempp was attending the Detroit International Auto Show. Mr. Schrempp discussed with Mr. Eaton some of his thoughts about the likelihood of consolidation in the worldwide automotive industry and suggested it might be mutually beneficial if Daimler-Benz and Chrysler were to consider the possibility of a business combination. Mr. Eaton indicated that Chrysler had been conducting its own studies of the industry and had similar views of the likely direction it would be taking. Mr. Eaton indicated that he would telephone Mr. Schrempp in response to his inquiry within the next couple of weeks. Toward the end or January, Mr. Eaton telephoned Mr. Schrempp to suggest a meeting early in February.

On February 5, 1998, the Chrysler Board was briefed on the discussion between Messrs. Schrempp and Eaton.

On February 12, 1998, Mr. Eaton and Gary C. Valade, Executive Vice President and Chief Financial Officer of Chrysler, met with Mr. Schrempp and Dr. Eckhard Cordes, Daimler-Benz Management Board member responsible for Corporate Development and Directly Managed Businesses, to discuss the possibility of combining Daimler-Benz and Chrysler. Following a discussion concerning, among other things, the consolidation likely to take place in the automotive industry and the complementary nature of their companies' respective product lines and markets, they decided to consult with their respective financial advisors and to meet again on February 18, 1998. Messrs. Schrempp and Eaton believed industry consolidation was timely because of industry overcapacity and the potential benefits of combining automotive companies arising from joint product design, development and manufacturing, combined purchasing, other economies of scale and brand expansion and diversification. In discussing the possibility of a business combination between Daimler-Benz and Chrysler, they considered it essential that their respective companies play a leading role in this process of expected industry consolidation and choose a partner with optimal strategic fit. In this respect, both the timing of the proposed business combination and the selection or the parties thereto were considered highly appropriate in order to secure and strengthen their respective market positions.

On February 17 and 18, 1998, Drs. Cordes and Rüdiger Grube, Director of Corporate Strategy and Planning for Daimler-Benz, and representatives of Goldman Sachs met with Messrs. Valade, Thomas P. Capo and WIlliam J. O'Brien, Vice President and Treasurer, and Vice President and General Counsel of Chrysler, respectively, and representatives of CSFB, financial advisor to Chrysler, to discuss the combination of the two companies generally and, specifically, various transaction structures. During the course of that week and the next week, representatives of Chrysler, CSFB and Debevoise & Plimpton, United States counsel to Chrysler ("Debevoise"), met with representatives of Goldman Sachs, Skadden, Arps, Slate, Meagher & Flom LLP, United States counsel to Daimler-Benz ("Skadden, Arps"), and Shearman & Sterling, German counsel to Daimler-Benz ("Shearman"). During the course of these discussions and thereafter, representatives of Chrysler stated that it was important to Chrysler that any potential transaction maximize value for its stockholders, that it be tax-free to Chrysler's U.S. stockholders and tax efficient for DaimlerChrysler AG, that it have the post-merger governance structure of a "merger-of-equals," that it have the optimal ability to be accounted for as a pooling-of-interests, that it result in the combination of the respective businesses of Daimler-Benz and Chrysler into one public company and that it limit any post-effective contingencies arising out of the Transactions, including limiting any rights that might result from a German valuation proceeding *(Spruchver-fahren)*. Representatives of Daimler-Benz indicated that it was important to Daimler-Benz that any potential transaction maximize value for its stockholders, that it be tax-free to Daimler-Benz' German stockholders and tax efficient for DaimlerChrysler AG and that the surviving entity of any combination be a German stock corporation, thereby enhancing the likelihood of acceptance of the Transactions by all important constituencies of Daimler-Benz. During these meetings, various tax, corporate and management issues were discussed with a view to developing a transaction structure that would accommodate the parties' objectives.

On March 2, 1998, Mr. Schrempp and Dr. Cordes met with Messrs. Eaton and Valade in Lausanne, Switzerland, to discuss governance and business organizational structures for a possible combined entity. The organizational issues discussed by the parties included, among other things, the impact of the jurisdiction of incorporation of the combined company on its corporate governance, the composition of the combined company's management and the most effective way to foster the integration of the two business organizations. Over the course of their discussions, the parties considered various alternative transaction structures for the combination of the two enterprises, including through (1) a newly-incorporated U.S. company, (2) a company incorporated in The Netherlands and (3) either a newly organized German *Aktiengesellschaft* or Daimler-Benz itself. The simplest structural solution, a direct merger of Daimler-Benz and Chrysler, was not possible under German law. The parties believed that the structure for the Transactions was the preferable alternative to a combination through a newly-incorporated U.S. company or a company incorporated in The Netherlands because this structure was believed to be the most tax efficient for the combined entity on an ongoing basis, could be tax-free to Chrysler's U.S. stockholders and to Daimler-Benz' German stockholders and was the only structure which would enable the elimination of all minority stockholders of Daimler-Benz and Chrysler thereby creating a parent corporation with one group of stockholders holding a single publicly traded equity security. The structure for the Transactions was therefore selected because it best achieved both parties' objectives.

On March 5, 1998, the Chrysler Board was updated concerning the status of the discussions with Daimler-Benz.

Mr. Valade and Dr. Cordes met on March 6, 1998, to discuss the progress of their respective working teams. They concluded that the working teams should continue to meet in an effort to refine the structural alternatives then under discussion. In addition, Mr. Valade requested that Daimler-Benz provide Chrysler with its preliminary thoughts on valuation.

On March 5 and 17 representatives from each party's legal and investment banking teams met in New York to continue their discussion with respect to alternative transaction structures. On March 19, representatives of Chrysler and CSFB met with representatives of Daimler-Benz and Goldman Sachs to discuss valuation matters.

On March 23, the Chrysler Board was updated concerning the status of discussions with Daimler-Benz. On March 26, representatives of Chrysler and Daimler-Benz met at the offices of CSFB to discuss the progress of the working teams, valuation analyses, governance and structural matters.

On April 7, the Chrysler board was updated concerning the status of discussions with Daimler-Benz. On April 9, at a meeting in London, Messrs. Schrempp and Eaton agreed that the valuations and preliminary views on the transaction structure being discussed were approaching a point where they could each recommend them to their respective Boards, and they discussed a governance structure for the combined company. During late March and the month of April, the legal and investment banking teams, including representatives of the law firm of Bruckhaus Westrick Heller Löber, German counsel to Chrysler, continued to discuss and refine their analysis with respect to the appropriate business combination structure.

Major points or discussion during that period and thereafter involved: (a) valuation, particularly in light of the fact that Daimler-Benz shares have had a higher price/earnings multiple than Chrysler's, although Chrysler has had higher earnings; (b) identifying a governance structure that would take into account the parties' goals of incorporating the best U.S. and German practices; (c) finding a structure that would (i) result in a tax-free transaction in the United States and Germany for both companies' stockholders and result in ongoing tax efficiency, (ii) involve one publicly traded class or equity security, (iii) minimize the risk of non-consummation, and (iv) create the possibility that the transactions would be accounted for as a pooling-of-interests under U.S. GAAP; (d) determining how best to meet the requirements of a cross-border transaction between a U.S. corporation and a German stock corporation; and (e) creating a management organization for the combined company that achieves a meaningful sharing of management roles consistent with the parties' conception of the Transactions as a "merger of equals."

The parties recognized that acceptance of the Transactions by important constituencies of Daimler-Benz (including German stockholders, employees and management) would be enhanced if the combined parent company were a German stock corporation *(Aktiengesellschaft)* because such constituencies were familiar and comfortable with that form of organization. Consequently, the parties decided that a new company organized under the laws of the Federal Republic of Germany should be the new public parent company and that the Transactions would be the best means to accomplish the parties' objectives for a business combination transaction, including implementing a merger of equals combining both companies' businesses, stockholder groups, managements and other constituencies, and further that the governance structure that had been discussed would be an appropriate management structure for the combined company in the future.

On April 7, 1998, Mr. Schrempp and Dr. Cordes presented the Daimler-Benz Management Board with an overview of the discussions with Chrysler regarding a potential transaction.

On April 16, 1998, Mr. Schrempp and Dr. Cordes discussed the status of the proposed Chrysler transaction with Mr. Hilmar Kopper, the Chairman of the Daimler-Benz

Supervisory Board *(Aufsichtsrat),* and on April 19, 1998, Mr. Schrempp and Dr. Cordes gave a detailed presentation of the transaction to the Daimler-Benz Management Board.

On April 21, 1998, Messrs. Eaton and Valade met with Mr. Schrempp and Drs. Cordes and Grube to refine their thinking with respect to, among other things, valuation and key governance and management positions. In addition, they agreed that the working teams should work with the objective of completing all elements necessary to announce a transaction on May 7, 1998.

Between April 23 and May 6, 1998, members or the working teams met at various times to negotiate the Combination Agreement and related documentation. On April 22 and 29, the Chrysler Board was updated concerning the status of discussions with Daimler-Benz. On May 3, 1998, the Daimler-Benz Management Board met to review the Transactions and unanimously approved the Combination Agreement and the Transactions.

At meetings on May 5 and May 6, the Chrysler Board reviewed the proposed Combination Agreement and the Transactions. At the May 6, 1998 meeting the Chrysler Board unanimously approved the Combination Agreement and the Transactions. On May 6, 1998, the Daimler-Benz Supervisory Board met in Stuttgart and received a full briefing and the recommendation of the Management Board with respect to the proposed Combination Agreement. Although no resolution was proposed at the meeting, there was substantial discussion and several members indicated their general satisfaction with the proposed transaction. The discussion at the meeting focused on the reasons for the business combination including, among other things, general consolidation in the automotive industry and the strong potential for synergies between the constituent companies, the company profile of Chrysler, the transaction structure, organizational issues relating to the structure and composition of the DaimlerChrysler Management Board and Supervisory Board and the prospects for enhancing the value of the combined entity in the future. The Daimler-Benz Supervisory Board scheduled a second meeting on May 14, 1998, to consider and vote on the proposed Combination Agreement.

On May 6, in response to newspaper stories about discussions between Chrysler and Daimler-Benz, the companies announced that they were in discussions.

Late in the evening of May 6, 1998, in London, all constituent parties signed the Combination Agreement. In the morning of May 7, the signing of the Combination Agreement was publicly announced.

On May 14, 1998, the Daimler-Benz Supervisory Board unanimously approved the Combination Agreement and the Transactions.

In July 1998, the parties discussed how best to maximize the likelihood that the Minimum Condition to the Daimler-Benz Exchange Offer would be satisfied in order to enable the Transactions to be accounted for as a pooling-of-interests. Both parties believe this accounting treatment is desirable because purchase accounting would cause reported earnings per share of DaimlerChrysler AG to be reduced as a result of the amortization of the excess of purchase consideration over the book value of the net assets acquired. The parties decided to increase the likelihood of satisfying the Minimum Condition to the Daimler-Benz Exchange Offer by amending the Combination Agreement to provide that the Daimler-Benz

Exchange Offer Ratio would be 1.005, rather than 1.000, if the Minimum Condition is satisfied so that the Transactions can be accounted for as a pooling-of-interests.

Opinion of Financial Advisor of Chrysler

Chrysler Discounted Cash Flow Analysis. CSFB performed a discounted cash flow analysis for fiscal years 1998 to 2002 to estimate the present value of the stand-alone unlevered free cash flows Chrysler is expected to generate if Chrysler performs in accordance with scenarios based on certain financial forecasts. For purposes of this analysis, unlevered free cash flows were defined as unlevered net income plus depreciation plus amortization less capital expenditures less investment in working capital.

CSFB performed its analyses based on financial forecasts provided to it by Chrysler for two separate business scenarios: a base case (the "Chrysler Base Case") and a sensitivity case (the "Chrysler Sensitivity Case"). The Chrysler Base Case reflects Chrysler's current business plan, including Chrysler management forecasts for fiscal years 1998 through 2002. The Chrysler Sensitivity Case includes management's adjustments to the Chrysler Base Case to provide for an industry downturn, lower market share and higher sales incentives.

The Chrysler Base Case projections included (i) projected revenues of $63.7 billion, $71.1 billion, $71.2 billion, $76.4 billion and $80.5 billion in 1998, 1999, 2000, 2001 and 2002 and (ii) projected net income of $3.1 billion, $3.3 billion, $3.3 billion, $4.1 billion and $4.9 billion in 1998, 1999, 2000, 2001 and 2002.

Chrysler informed CSFB that the Chrysler Base Case projection was based on several significant assumptions. The Chrysler Base Case projections are influenced significantly by North American vehicle sales, the level of retail incentives per unit and the success of new product models. The Chrysler Base Case projections assume North American vehicle sales of approximately 16.6 million in 1998 and remaining relatively constant through 2002. The assumed level of retail incentives in 1998 was approximately $1,250 per unit with slight increases in the incentive levels for 1999 and 2000 during the launch of new models and declines in incentive levels during 2001 and 2002 after the successful launch of the new models.

CSFB calculated terminal values for Chrysler by applying a range of multiples of earnings before interest, taxes, depreciation and amortization ("EBITDA") to the fiscal year 2002 EBITDA from 3.00x to 3.75x in each of the above two scenarios. These EBITDA multiples were based on Chrysler's and comparable U.S. automobile manufacturers' trading multiples of fiscal year 1997 EBITDA. The unlevered free cash flow streams and terminal values were then discounted using a range of discount rates from 12.5% to 13.5%. The discount rate range was selected based on an analysis of Chrysler's weighted average cost of capital. Based on this analysis, the implied equity values for Chrysler ranged from approximately $49 to approximately $58 per fully diluted share of Chrysler Common Stock for the Chrysler Base Case and approximately $30 to approximately $35 per fully diluted share of Chrysler Common Stock for the Chrysler Sensitivity Case.

Daimler-Benz Discounted Cash Flow Analysis. CSFB performed a discounted cash flow analysis for fiscal years 1998 to 2002 to estimate the present value of the stand-alone unlevered free cash flows that Daimler-Benz is expected to generate if Daimler-Benz performs in accordance with scenarios based on certain financial forecasts. For purposes of this analysis, unlevered free cash flows were defined as unlevered net income plus depreciation plus amortization less capitol expenditures less investment in working capital.

CSFB performed its analyses based on financial forecasts provided to it by Daimler-Benz for two separate business scenarios: a base case (the "Daimler-Benz Base Case") and a sensitivity case (the "Daimler-Benz Sensitivity Case"). The Daimler-Benz Base Case reflects Daimler-Benz' current strategic plan, including Daimler-Benz management forecasts for fiscal years 1998 through 2000 and forecasts developed by CSFB for fiscal years 2001 through 2002 based upon the first three years' projected performance. The Daimler-Benz Sensitivity Case was developed by CSFB after discussions with Daimler-Benz management to reflect adjustments to the Daimler-Benz Base Case to provide for slower sales growth and lower operating margin expansion.

CSFB was informed by Daimler-Benz that the Daimler-Benz Base Case included projections of each of its major operating segments. Passenger Cars projections included (i) projected revenues of DM59.4 billion, DM66.6 billion and DM69.2 billion in 1998, 1999 and 2000 and (ii) earnings before interest and taxes ("EBIT") of DM3.4 billion, DM5.4 billion and DM5.9 billion in 1998, 1999 and 2000. Commercial Vehicles included (i) projected revenues of DM40.2 billion, DM42.4 billion and DM44.2 billion in 1998, 1999 and 2000 and (ii) EBIT of DM1.3 billion, DM2.1 billion and DM2.3 billion in 1998, 1999 and 2000. DASA projections included (i) projected revenues of DM16.0 billion, and DM17.6 billion and DM17.8 billion in 1998, 1999 and 2000 and (ii) EBIT of DM0.5 billion, DM1.3 billion and DM1.5 billion in 1998, 1999 and 2000. Directly Managed Businesses projections included (i) projected revenues of DM8.4 billion, DM9.9 billion and DM10. 9 billion in 1998, 1999 and 2000, debis* projections included (i) projected revenues of DM17.3 billion, DM20.4 billion, and DM23.5 billion in 1998, 1999 and 2000 and (ii) EBIT of DM0.5 billion, DM0.7 billion and DM1.0 billion in 1998, 1999 and 2000. Corporate Eliminations projections included (i) projected revenues of DM(5.9) billion, DM(7.2) billion and DM(7.4) billion in 1998, 1999 and 2000 and (ii) EBIT of DM(0.5) billion, DM(0.4) billion and DM(0.4) billion in 1998, 1999 and 2000.

Daimler-Benz informed CSFB that the Daimler-Benz Base Case projections were based on several assumptions. The growth in Passenger Car revenues and EBITDA stem from the assumed successful launch of the new S-Class automobile and the continued growth of the recently introduced C-Class and M-Class lines. The continued growth in Commercial Vehicle revenues and the increases in the EBITDA arise from the assumed improvement in the European truck market and the successful launch of its new line of vehicles. The revenue increases for DASA are assumed to arise from the high demand in the commercial aircraft business and from increased European defense spending while the improvements in EBITDA in addition stem from the continued successful implementation of the restructuring program of this business segment. The improvement in the Directly Managed Businesses is assumed to continue after the successful rationalization of the businesses in this segment and the success of recently entered into joint ventures. The growth in debis' revenues and EBITDA are assumed to track the growth of the Passenger Car

---

*debis is the financial services unit of Daimler. It corresponds to GMAC of General Motors.

segment and the continued growth of its telecommunications and information technology services.

CSFB calculated terminal values for Daimler-Benz by applying a range of multiples of EBITDA to the fiscal year 2002 EBITDA from 5.5x to 6.5x for the passenger cars business segment; from 5.0x to 7.0x for the commercial vehicles business segment; from 8.0x to 10.0x for the aerospace (DASA) business segment; from 8.0x to 9.0x for the non-financial services businesses within the debis business segment; and from 7.0x to 9.0x for the Directly Managed Businesses (DMB) business segment in each or the above two scenarios. These EBITDA multiples were based on current comparable companies trading multiples of fiscal year 1997 EBITDA. CSFB calculated terminal multiples for Daimler Benz' financial services business within the debis business segment by applying a range of net income multiples for the fiscal year 2002 net income from 16.0x to 17.0x. These net income multiples were based on current comparable companies (including, in the case of the passenger cars segment, comparable European automobile companies) trading multiples of fiscal year 1997 net income. The unlevered free cash flow streams and terminal values were then discounted using a range of discount rates from 9.5% to 10.5% for the passenger cars business segment; from 9.5% to 10.5% for the commercial vehicles business segment; from 9.0% to 10.0% for the aerospace (DASA) business segment; from 11.0% to 13.0% for the financial services businesses within the debis business segment; from 9.0% to 10.0% for the non-financial services businesses within the debis business segment; and from 10.0% to 12.0% for the Directly Managed Businesses (DMB) business segment in each of the above two scenarios. The discount rate ranges for the business segments were selected based on an analysis of the comparable companies' weighted average cost of capital. Based on this analysis, the equity values for Daimler-Benz ranged from approximately DM183 to approximately DM221 ($102 to $123 assuming DM/US$ exchange rate of 1.80/1.00) per fully diluted Daimler-Benz Ordinary Share for the Daimler-Benz Base Case and approximately DM143 to approximately DM172 ($79 to $95 assuming DM/US$ exchange rate of 1.80/1.00) per fully diluted Daimler-Benz Ordinary Share for the Daimler-Benz Sensitivity Case.

CSFB reviewed the ratios of Chrysler's to Daimler-Benz' discounted cash flow equity valuation per fully diluted share based on the discounted cash flow analysis and computed the premium or discount of the U.S. Exchange Ratio in relation to the aforementioned ratios. The ratios of equity valuations per fully diluted share of Chrysler to Daimler-Benz for the Chrysler Base Case and the Daimler-Benz Base Case ranged from 0.472 to 0.480. CSFB observed that the U.S. Exchange Ratio represented a premium of approximately 14% to 16% over the ratios of Chrysler's to Daimler-Benz' discounted cash flow equity valuations per fully diluted share.

DEAL TERMS

The deal was announced on May 6, 1998. Chrysler shareholders would receive 0.6235 shares of the combined DaimlerChrysler for each Chrysler share. Daimler-Benz shareholders would receive 1.005 shares for each Daimler-Benz share. On May 5, the day before the merger, Daimler-Benz ADRs were trading at $102.06, and Chrysler stock was trading at $41.44. The 0.6235 exchange rate implied a purchase price of $63.63 per share of Chrysler stock, or $41 billion for the company as a whole. This translates into a 54% premium. Table 1 conveys the key details about the terms of the deal.

Figure 3 conveys the structure of the transaction. Chrysler became a wholly owned subsidiary of the newly formed DaimlerChrysler AG. Daimler-Benz shareholders exchanged their shares for shares of the new DaimlerChrysler. Chrysler renamed itself as DaimlerChrysler Corporation. The transactions had the final effect of giving the shareholders of the two companies control over DaimlerChrysler AG, a German company that included Daimler-Benz. This company in turn owned all the shares of the former Chrysler.

Table 2 shows the performance of Daimler-Benz and Chrysler stocks around the time of the announcement of the merger. The returns are adjusted by the returns on the S&P 500. There was virtually no runup prior to the merger. On the day of the announcement, both firms gained significantly — Chrysler, almost 19% (adjusted) and Daimler almost 8% (adjusted). For the window from 5 days before the announcement of the merger to 5 days after, the CAR for Chrysler was about 25%, and Daimler was about 10%. These significant positive returns indicate that the market approved of the merger.

Historical data for Daimler-Benz and Chrysler are presented in Tables 3-6. Tables 3 and 4 are the income statement and balance sheet information, respectively, for Daimler-Benz from 1990-1997. Tables 5 and 6 are the same financials for Chrysler for the same time period.

The combination had little difficulty with antitrust considerations. Perhaps the most critical regulatory hurdle to pass was that of convincing Americans that Daimler-Benz had done enough to compensate Jewish slave laborers who were used by the com-

TABLE 1 Daimler-Benz/Chrysler Deal Terms

Pre-Merger	Dollar Amounts			Percentage	
	Daimler	Chrysler	Total	Daimler	Chrysler
Share Price	$102.06	$41.44			
Shares Outstanding (million)	517	647			
Total Market Value (billion)	$52.8	$26.8	$79.6	66.3%	33.7%
Exchange Terms	0.6235 for	1.005			
Post-Merger					
Number of Shares (million)	520	403	923	56.3%	43.7%
Premium Calculation					
Total Paid (billion)	$41.2				
Premium Over Market					
Amount (billion)	$14.4				
Percent	53.6%				

The diagrams set forth below are intended to provide a graphic illustration of the corporate mechanics and the immediate corporate structuring results of (1) the Daimler-Benz Exchange Offer and the Chrysler Merger and (2) the Daimler-Benz Merger.

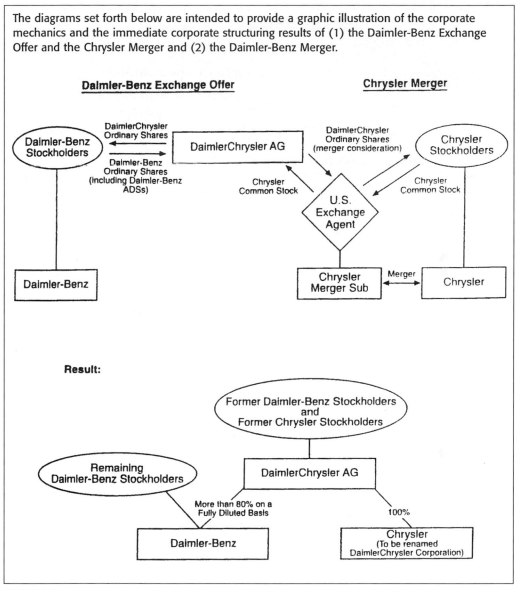

FIGURE 3

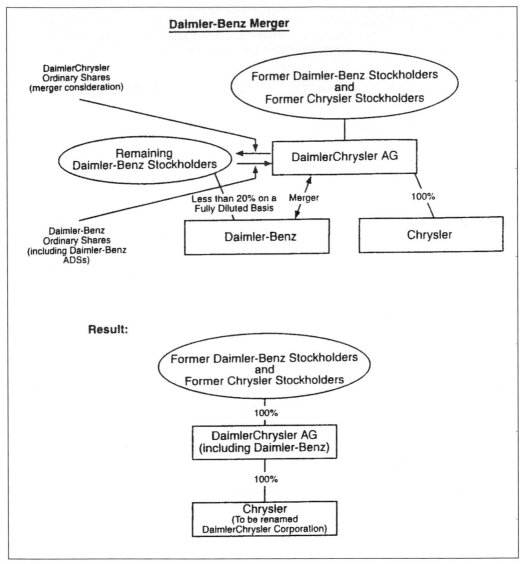

FIGURE 3 (Continued)

TABLE 2 Daimler-Benz & Chrysler Stock Returns

Date	S&P 500 index	Return on S&P 500 index	DAI	DAI Return	Cumulative Adjusted Return	C	C Return	Cumulative Adjusted Return
4/28/98	1085.11		98.50			39.50		
4/29/98	1094.63	0.877%	98.94	0.445%	-0.433%	40.56	2.691%	1.814%
4/30/98	1111.75	1.564%	101.00	2.084%	0.087%	40.25	-0.772%	-0.522%
5/1/98	1121.00	0.832%	101.88	0.866%	0.122%	40.38	0.311%	-1.043%
5/4/98	1122.07	0.095%	103.00	1.104%	1.131%	41.00	1.548%	0.409%
5/5/98	1115.50	-0.586%	102.06	-0.910%	0.806%	41.44	1.068%	2.063%
5/6/98	1104.92	-0.948%	108.56	6.369%	8.124%	48.81	17.798%	20.809%
5/7/98	1095.14	-0.885%	106.38	-2.015%	6.993%	53.50	9.602%	31.296%
5/8/98	1108.14	1.187%	111.38	4.700%	10.507%	53.81	0.585%	30.694%
5/11/98	1106.64	-0.135%	111.63	0.224%	10.866%	52.50	-2.440%	28.390%
5/12/98	1115.79	0.827%	108.00	-3.247%	6.792%	51.00	-2.857%	24.706%
5/13/98	1118.86	0.275%	108.13	0.116%	6.633%	51.44	0.859%	25.289%

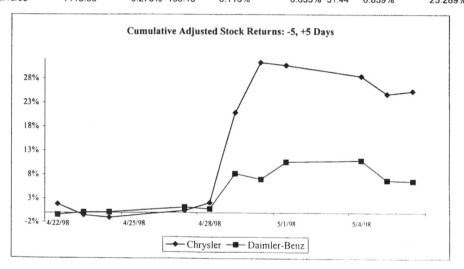

pany during World War II. Some analysts were surprised that American regulators did not closely investigate the increase in size and market share of one of the "Big Three." European analysts also were surprised that such a large combination did not face serious scrutiny from any European regulatory bodies. It is rare for such a large-scale horizontal merger to be largely overlooked by regulatory bodies.

ISSUES OF INTERNATIONAL CORPORATE GOVERNANCE

Corporate governance in Germany has traditionally emphasized giving weight to the position of all stakeholders. German firms focus on balancing the interests of shareholders, employees, communities, and creditors. There is a supervisory board, which consists of directors and representatives of labor groups. Half of the representatives are elected by shareholders, and half are elected by employees. In addition, there is the

TABLE 3 Summary Income Statement for DaimlerChrysler AG
(All Amounts Are in Millions of Dollars)

	1990	1991	1992	1993	1994	1995	1996	1997
Sales (Net)	59,011	65,832	62,283	57,197	67,170	72,185	62,132	68,951
Cost of Goods Sold	30,119	33,367	30,611	29,585	54,435	61,320	45,549	50,816
Selling, General, and Administrative Expense	25,989	28,851	29,176	26,428	9,276	9,978	12,499	12,838
Operating Income Before Depreciation	2,902	3,615	2,496	1,184	3,459	887	4,084	5,297
Depreciation and Amortization	3,453	3,992	4,374	4,633	4,642	4,864	4,047	4,180
Operating Income After Depreciation	(550)	(377)	(1,879)	(3,449)	(1,183)	(3,977)	37	1,117
Interest Expense	(822)	(1,151)	(1,423)	(1,166)	(1,389)	(842)	(538)	(578)
Nonoperating Income (Expense)	3,744	3,883	4,559	5,551	3,912	4,237	1,647	1,823
Special Income (Expense) Items	39	(363)	0	(1,782)	C	C	C	C
Pretax Income	2,411	1,991	1,258	(846)	1,340	(582)	1,146	2,362
Income Taxes - Total	1,212	694	362	296	763	708	(416)	(2,213)
Minority Interest	74	47	20	8	(103)	(42)	(52)	105
Income Before Extraordinary Items	1,125	1,250	875	(1,150)	680	(1,248)	1,614	4,470
Dividends - Preferred	0	0	0	0	0	0	0	0
Income Before Extraordinary Items	1,125	1,250	875	(1,150)	680	(1,248)	1,614	4,470
Common Stock Equivalents - Dollar Savings	0	0	0	0	0	0	0	0
Income Before Extraordinary Items	1,125	1,250	875	(1,150)	680	(1,248)	1,614	4,470
Extraordinary Items	0	0	0	1,496	0	(2,707)	0	0
Extraordinary Items and Discontinued Operations	0	0	0	1,496	0	(2,707)	0	0
Net Income Adjusted for Common Stock Equivalents	1,125	1,250	875	346	680	(3,955)	1,614	4,470
Net Income (Loss)	1,125	1,250	875	346	680	(3,955)	1,614	4,470

management board, which consists of the firm's top managers and is responsible for the day-to-day operation of the firm. Banks also tend to dominate under the German governance system. Banks tend to be very risk averse. Their main concern is to avoid risky growth and to reduce costs to increase the price of the shares they hold; they focus on the financial security of the company in order to be sure that bank debt will be repaid. Furthermore, German accounting standards make it relatively easy for firms to smooth their revenue, by making good years look a little worse and make bad years look fine.

Prior to 1995 when Schrempp took over the leadership of Daimler-Benz, the firm was very typical of the German governance system. Daimler-Benz was Germany's largest firm. Its largest shareholder was Deutsche Bank, and the chairman of Daimler's

TABLE 4 Summary Balance Sheet for DaimlerChrysler AG (All Amounts Are in Millions of Dollars)	1990	1991	1992	1993	1994	1995	1996	1997
Assets								
Cash and Short-Term Investments	5,972	5,166	5,592	5,659	8,638	7,369	8,379	11,406
Receivables - Total	7,562	8,262	12,927	16,220	18,508	20,554	19,060	23,344
Inventories - Total	8,770	9,955	10,859	9,741	9,666	10,989	7,947	7,998
Current Assets - Other	6,025	6,534	2,163	0	0	2,745	3,654	4,548
Current Assets - Total	28,329	29,917	31,540	31,620	36,812	41,657	39,040	47,296
Property, Plant, and Equipment - Total (Net)	14,412	16,474	17,924	17,706	18,030	18,433	17,625	19,780
Investments and Advances - Equity Method	150	178	783	629	1,370	1,174	419	143
Investments and Advances - Other	898	2,332	1,681	1,688	3,421	2,031	1,647	1,776
Intangibles	203	517	377	301	C	C	1,140	1,065
Assets - Other	991	1,151	904	327	736	518	5,838	6,144
Assets - Total	44,982	50,569	53,210	52,271	60,368	63,813	65,709	76,204
Liabilities and Net Worth								
Debt in Current Liabilities	2,989	4,085	6,085	5,416	6,659	8,631	8,938	12,277
Accounts Payable	4,246	4,602	4,011	3,878	4,950	4,993	4,898	6,037
Income Taxes Payable	606	595	559	650	622	687	680	492
Current Liabilities - Other	3,102	3,985	7,721	7,510	8,936	11,973	10,626	10,836
Current Liabilities - Total	10,943	13,266	18,376	17,454	21,167	26,284	25,142	29,642
Long-Term Debt - Total	2,859	4,463	4,462	6,496	6,633	5,406	6,944	9,569
Liabilities - Other	19,272	19,851	18,197	17,890	19,498	22,474	16,339	15,728
Deferred Taxes and Investment Tax Credit	0	0	0	0	0	0	1,316	1,113
Minority Interest	589	811	758	323	97	612	547	650
Liabilities - Total	33,663	38,391	41,794	42,163	47,396	54,776	50,288	56,702
Preferred Stock - Carrying Value	0	0	0	0	0	0	0	0
Common Equity - Total	11,320	12,178	11,416	10,108	12,973	9,037	15,421	19,502
Stockholders' Equity - Total	11,320	12,178	11,416	10,108	12,973	9,037	15,421	19,502
Liabilities and Stockholders' Equity - Total	44,982	50,569	53,210	52,271	60,368	63,813	65,709	76,204
Common Share Outstanding - millions	N/A	N/A	N/A	466	513	514	515	517

supervisory board was the chairman of Deutsche Bank's management board. Daimler had engaged in a series of unprofitable diversifying investments, which became a drag on the performance of the firm. Diversification is generally in the interests of the banks because it reduces the risks that the firm is exposed to. Reduced risk makes the bank loans more secure.

TABLE 5 Summary Income Statement for Chrysler Corp.
(All Amounts Are in Millions of Dollars)

	1990	1991	1992	1993	1994	1995	1996	1997
Sales (Net)	29,797	28,162	35,501	42,260	50,736	51,190	59,333	58,622
Cost of Goods Sold	23,933	24,533	29,467	33,906	39,580	42,089	47,068	47,470
Selling, General, and Administrative Expense	2,785	2,909	3,412	3,377	3,933	4,064	4,730	4,957
Operating Income Before Depreciation	3,079	720	2,622	4,977	7,223	5,037	7,535	6,195
Depreciation and Amortization	1,398	1,465	1,610	1,640	1,944	2,220	2,312	2,696
Operating Income After Depreciation	1,681	(745)	1,012	3,337	5,279	2,817	5,223	3,499
Interest Expense	(2,598)	(2,031)	(1,581)	(1,280)	(1,114)	(1,199)	(1,163)	(1,200)
Nonoperating Income (Expense)	963	1,370	1,572	1,516	1,665	2,209	2,220	2,719
Special Income (Expense) Items	101	596	(69)	265	0	(378)	(188)	(461)
Pretax Income	147	(810)	934	3,838	5,830	3,449	6,092	4,557
Income Taxes - Total	79	(272)	429	1,423	2,117	1,328	2,372	1,752
Minority Interest	C	C	C	C	C	C	C	C
Income Before Extraordinary Items	68	(538)	505	2,415	3,713	2,121	3,720	2,805
Dividends - Preferred	0	0	69	80	80	21	3	1
Income Before Extraordinary Items	68	(538)	436	2,335	3,633	2,100	3,717	2,804
Common Stock Equivalents - Dollar Savings	0	0	0	0	0	0	0	0
Income Before Extraordinary Items	68	(538)	436	2,335	3,633	2,100	3,717	2,804
Extraordinary Items	0	(257)	218	(4,966)	0	(96)	(191)	0
Extraordinary Items and Discontinued Operations	0	(257)	218	(4,966)	0	(96)	(191)	0
Net Income Adjusted for Common Stock Equivalents	68	(795)	654	(2,631)	3,633	2,004	3,526	2,804
Net Income (Loss)	68	(795)	723	(2,551)	3,713	2,025	3,529	2,805

Deutsche Bank began to reduce its stake in Daimler-Benz, helping to make the firm focus on shareholder value. Jürgen Schrempp began to divest some of the unrelated businesses of Daimler. In Germany, he was referred to derogatorily as "Mr. Shareholder Value." As Daimler became more focused, its stock price began to improve. Daimler also implemented new, stock based compensation for its managers. It became listed on the New York Stock Exchange in 1993, requiring the disclosure of its financial statements under U.S. GAAP. These and other factors pushed the firm to adopt a more American style of business.

Some scholars view the DaimlerChrysler merger within this larger trend of Daimler-Benz's move toward emphasizing shareholder value (Logue and Seward, 1999; Gordon, 2000). If Daimler-Benz were still fully under the influence of German banks, it would not be willing to take on the risks associated with such a large merger. The willingness of Daimler to merge is a sign that it is seeking American ways to increase shareholder value. Furthermore, the addition of a large block of American shareholders, who used to hold Chrysler stock, made it even more important that the combined company emphasize shareholder value, or risk losing American investors.

TABLE 6 Summary Balance Sheet for Chrysler Corp.
(All Amounts Are in Millions of Dollars)

	1990	1991	1992	1993	1994	1995	1996	1997
Assets								
Cash and Short-Term Investments	1,572	2,041	2,357	4,040	5,145	5,543	5,158	4,898
Receivables - Total	20,631	14,239	9,661	12,007	14,258	15,626	14,465	15,164
Inventories - Total	3,150	3,571	3,090	3,629	3,356	4,448	5,195	4,738
Current Assets - Other	565	618	747	833	1,330	985	1,929	2,193
Current Assets - Total	N/A	N/A	N/A	N/A	N/A	N/A	N/A	N/A
Property, Plant, and Equipment - Total (Net)	9,468	10,508	11,531	12,774	14,482	16,161	18,829	22,540
Investments and Advances - Equity Method	N/A	N/A	N/A	N/A	N/A	N/A	N/A	N/A
Investments and Advances - Other	1,783	994	1,292	1,055	3,226	2,582	2,594	2,950
Intangibles	5,299	5,191	4,619	4,328	2,162	2,082	1,995	1,573
Assets - Other	3,906	5,914	7,356	5,164	5,580	6,329	6,019	6,362
Assets - Total	46,374	43,076	40,653	43,830	49,539	53,756	56,184	60,418
Liabilities and Net Worth								
Debt in Current Liabilities	10,150	4,458	2,117	4,580	5,456	4,335	6,212	6,479
Accounts Payable	4,920	5,475	5,798	6,863	7,826	8,290	8,981	9,512
Income Taxes Payable	0	0	0	0	0	0	0	0
Current Liabilities - Other	3,423	3,921	4,090	4,650	5,582	7,032	8,864	9,717
Current Liabilities - Total	18,493	13,854	12,005	16,093	18,864	19,657	24,057	25,708
Long-Term Debt - Total	12,750	14,980	13,434	6,871	7,650	9,858	7,184	9,006
Liabilities - Other	6,787	7,310	7,416	14,030	12,331	13,282	13,372	14,342
Deferred Taxes and Investment Tax Credit	1,210	748	260	0	0	0	0	0
Minority Interest	285	75	C	C	C	C	C	C
Liabilities - Total	39,525	36,967	33,115	36,994	38,845	42,797	44,613	49,056
Preferred Stock - Carrying Value	0	0	2	2	2	0	0	0
Common Equity - Total	6,849	6,109	7,536	6,834	10,692	10,959	11,571	11,362
Stockholders' Equity - Total	6,849	6,109	7,538	6,836	10,694	10,959	11,571	11,362
Liabilities and Stockholders' Equity - Total	46,374	43,076	40,653	43,830	49,539	53,756	56,184	60,418
Common Share Outstanding - millions	225	292	296	354	355	378	703	648

DAIMLERCHRYSLER DIFFICULTIES AFTER THE MERGER

The performance of the combined company following the combination has been disappointing. The stock, which was about $100 following the combination of the firms in November 1998 has fallen below $60 at the beginning of May 2000. Estimates are that the number of American shareholders has fallen from about 40% of the combined company after the combination to about 25%. Analysts attribute this decline to two factors: (1) Americans are reluctant to invest in firms based in foreign countries. (2) Because the combined firm was primarily based in Germany, it was dropped from the S&P 500. This caused all the funds that tracked the S&P 500 or invested only in S&P 500 firms to have to sell their stakes in the firm.

Another issue that arose over the international nature of the deal was that of executive compensation. German and American systems of compensation were vastly different. German firms tend to give their managers higher salaries, and little equity consideration. Meanwhile, American firms usually grant generous option packages that are often worth much more than the salary of executives. The combination of DaimlerChrysler vividly illustrated the disparity. While Daimler's CEO, Schrempp, had compensation valued at about $2 million, Chrysler's Eaton had compensation valued at more than eight times that amount. Similar differences existed between most of the top managers of the two firms. Naturally, this led to dissatisfaction among the Daimler managers, who felt underappreciated. In order to try to solve the problem, Daimler has moved to increase the option packages of the German managers and reduce that of the Americans. However, the firm has drawn fire within Germany. Germans are skeptical of the benefits of giving managers large option bonuses. This kind of culture difference is one of the greatest difficulties faced by cross-border merging firms.

Labor unions posed another challenge to the combined firm. While German labor groups are allowed to elect members to the supervisory board under the German corporate system, there was some question about how Chrysler's United Auto Workers (UAW) union members would fit into this system. The combined company granted one seat on the supervisory board to the president of the UAW. Another issue arose over the fact that Daimler already operated non-union factories in the United States. The UAW wanted the right to organize these factories. In September 1999, the UAW's bargaining agreement expired, and the group underwent negotiations with DaimlerChrysler. UAW workers briefly went on strike before the deal was finalized. DaimlerChrysler agreed to remain neutral in UAW efforts to organize the non-union plants. However, as of early 2000, the UAW had found that they had at most 22% support among the workers for unionization.

DAIMLERCHRYSLER POSTMERGER STRATEGIC DEVELOPMENTS

Despite the complications of the international merger between Daimler and Chrysler, the company quickly decided to pursue more automobile industry combinations. In 1999, it became involved in discussions to take a major equity stake in Nissan. Although these talks did not result in a deal, DaimlerChrysler remained committed to expanding their presence in the Asian market, where the company was weak. This was accomplished through a deal with Mitsubishi that was announced on March 28, 2000. DaimlerChrysler took a significant equity stake in Mitsubishi, which was weak financially. In exchange for $2 billion, DaimlerChrysler gained about 34% of the firm, three seats on the Mitsubishi board, and the right to veto Mitsubishi decisions. In addition, DaimlerChrysler did not have to consolidate the $14 billion of debt on Mitsubishi's books.

The combination with Mitsubishi made sense for three main reasons: (1) Mitsubishi has a strong position in Asia. DaimlerChrysler has set a goal of having 25%

of its sales from Asia. The deal with Mitsubishi gains half of that figure, and gives the firm the opportunity to sell Chrysler cars through existing Mitsubishi dealerships. Currently, Chrysler has only 25 dealerships in the entire region. (2) Mitsubishi has considerable knowledge and experience with producing small cars. DaimlerChrysler has committed to voluntarily reducing European emissions to a low level by 2008, and will probably need to produce more small cars to achieve this goal. (3) Cooperation with Mitsubishi offers the opportunity to combine technologies. Mitsubishi is a leader in Gasoline Direct Injection engines, which may prove to be highly efficient. Combining R&D investment should provide long-term benefits for both firms.

While DaimlerChrysler is primarily an automobile firm, it does have significant interests in other industries. The DASA unit is one of Europe's leading aerospace and defense firms. On October 14, 1999, DaimlerChrysler and Aerospatiale Matra, a French company, agreed to merge their aerospace businesses into a new company. The combined firm would have about $22 billion in revenues. The combined firm would be known as European Aeronautic, Defense and Space Company (EADS), and would have control over Airbus Industrie, the second largest maker of commercial airliners. Analysts felt that combining DASA into a new company would help to focus DaimlerChrysler on its core automobile business. DaimlerChrysler would retain a significant stake in the new firm, but would not retain the responsibility over day-to-day operations that it had over DASA.

Another division that DaimlerChrysler has decided to divest is its IT services segment. In March 2000, DaimlerChrysler agreed to sell 50.1% of the unit to Deutsche Telekom. This decision was arrived at because only 25% of the unit's sales were to DaimlerChrysler. Since 75% was to outside firms, it was determined that IT was a non-core business.

One division that Daimler Chrysler is seeking to expand is its financial services branch, debis. In the May 15, 2000 issue of *Forbes*, Jürgen Schrempp remarked that he envisioned the future of DaimlerChrysler as being 50% services and 50% hardware. This would be a major change from the firm's 7% services. It is estimated that only 30 to 40% of the cost of car ownership is accounted for by the initial purchase. By expanding its services, DaimlerChrysler hopes to capture some of the remaining costs of car ownership. Schrempp also envisions it as a means of increasing the margins of the firm. However, competition with focused financial firms may make such a goal relatively difficult to achieve.

By July 2000, the suffering stock price of DaimlerChrysler had become a serious problem for the firm. The Germans felt that it was the Americans' fault. Chrysler's sales had slipped significantly in early 2000, largely because it had many old models. However, Chrysler expected to recover with the release of many redesigned models in late 2000 and early 2001. Despite this promise, the Chrysler division came under the focus of its German parent for cost cutting measures. Many analysts felt that, if anything, Chrysler needed a cash infusion to help bring some new models to market. These same analysts tended to point out that Germany was more in need of cost cutting, recalling how Daimler had been surprised by Chrysler's efficiency when the merger was consummated.

IMPACT ON COMPETITORS

Despite the predictions of many analysts that the combination of Daimler and Chrysler would be the first of many mergers, the auto industry has not undergone many other large-scale mergers. Firms are reluctant to undergo the massive restructuring that is implicit in a large combination between automobile firms. Even with such concerns, Ford has purchased the car producing division of Volvo. Ford also bought Land Rover from BMW. Although these are large transactions, they are not on the scale of the DaimlerChrysler combination.

While formal business combinations have been scarce, there have been numerous other forms of M&A activity in the auto industry. The financial crisis in Asia helped to shake out some of the weak auto firms. The poor performing Japanese manufacturers have been the subjects of equity investments by rivals. Renault took a significant equity stake in Nissan, gaining significant control over the firm. Renault managed to outbid the combined DaimlerChrysler for its stake. DaimlerChrysler went on to instead secure a deal with Mitsubishi. DaimlerChrysler later bought a stake in Hyundai with the added hope of making a successful bid for Daewoo, which was being auctioned in summer 2000. As of June 30, 2000, Ford had become the winner in the auction of Daewoo. In addition, General Motors has recently secured large equity stakes in Fiat and Subaru. While these equity stakes are not the massive consolidation that was envisioned by most analysts, they should aid in reducing the capacity in the industry and eventually lead to just a few completely global firms.

Other forms of consolidation include cooperation between the large auto companies. GM, Ford, and DaimlerChrysler have formed a joint venture to purchase parts over the Internet. GM and Toyota have formed a research alliance. DaimlerChrysler has allied with Ford and Ballard Power Systems (a fuel cell company) to pursue research in fuel cells. Such cooperation between three of the largest manufacturers could well prove to be a trend for the future.

QUESTIONS

1. What are the fundamental economic characteristics of the automobile industry that have created the pressures leading to widespread merger activity?

2. Discuss the relationship between the control struggle between Kirk Kerkorian's Tracinda investment vehicle (allied with Lee Iacocca) and Chrysler management and the subsequent takeover of Chrysler by Daimler-Benz.

3. Did this merger run into any major antitrust obstacles with the Federal Trade Commission, Department of Justice, or the European regulators, such as the European Commission? Why or why not?

4. What were the major advantages and disadvantages to the Daimler-Benz/Chrysler deal? Based on the subsequent history of the combined company, would you judge the deal to be a good one?

Case 22

Vodafone's International Acquisitions

Vodafone Group PLC started as a division of British defense and electronics company, Racal Electronics. Vodafone launched its cellular network on January 1, 1985 in England. It was the first cellular network in the United Kingdom. By the 1990s, Vodafone was a major cellular provider in the UK, but did not have a strong international presence. Vodafone's vision of the future of wireless communications was that customers would require geographic flexibility that could only be provided by a massive global corporation. Between January 1999 and February 2000, Vodafone arranged deals to acquire Airtouch and Mannesmann, and also set up a massive joint venture, Verizon Wireless, with Bell Atlantic and GTE.

THE CHARACTERISTICS OF THE WIRELESS COMMUNICATIONS INDUSTRY

The wireless telecommunications industry is in a period of rapid growth. Not only is the number of people using wireless devices increasing, but the number of wireless devices on the market is also booming. Wireless phones have become standard equipment for many individuals. There is a large and growing market for wireless Internet connection with the importance of laptop computers to many executives. In addition, the proliferation of other devices, such as Palm organizers, is increasing the potential uses for wireless communications.

Wireless technology has primarily impacted developed countries. Europe and Japan have emerged as the leading markets for wireless technology. These countries have established accepted standards that have allowed the technology to spread easily. They also include leading manufacturers of electronic devices that utilize wireless technology. These include some of the consumer electronics device companies in Japan, Nokia of Finland, Ericsson of Sweden, and others. Most wireless organizations in each nation are joint ventures between multiple telecom organizations. This is a typical means of structuring international wireless businesses, particularly in Europe. Thus, companies benefit when they can gain a controlling interest in wireless ventures.

The U.S. has also experienced rapid growth in wireless customers, as indicated in Table 1. However, this growth has lagged behind that of Europe and Japan. This is often blamed on the system of awarding licenses. For the most part, the licensing of wireless

TABLE 1 U.S. Cellular Telephone Subscribers

		Number of Systems	Subscribers
1984	December	32	91,600
1985	June	65	203,600
	December	102	340,213
1986	June	129	500,000
	December	166	681,825
1987	June	206	883,778
	December	312	1,230,855
1988	June	420	1,608,697
	December	517	2,069,441
1989	June	559	2,691,793
	December	584	3,508,944
1990	June	592	4,368,686
	December	751	5,283,055
1991	June	1,029	6,390,053
	December	1,252	7,557,148
1992	June	1,483	8,892,535
	December	1,506	11,032,753
1993	June	1,523	13,067,318
	December	1,529	16,009,461
1994	June	1,550	19,283,506
	December	1,581	24,134,421
1995	June	1,581	28,154,415
	December	1,627	33,785,661
1996	June	1,629	38,195,466
	December	1,740	44,042,992
1997	June	2,005	48,705,553
	December	2,228	55,312,293
1998	June	2,300	60,831,431
	December	3,073	69,209,321
1999	June	3,447	76,284,753

Source: Cellular Telecommunications Industry Association.

technology remained regional, causing many companies to haphazardly patch together networks. The standards for both digital and analog systems have been uneven through time and geography. Furthermore, they have generally been incompatible with the standards of Europe and other countries. This complicated the establishment of nationwide systems. Eventually, AT&T and Sprint were able to offer wireless national coverage. The Verizon joint venture followed suit soon after. AT&T also raised the stakes in the wireless industries by introducing a "one-rate" national calling plan, in which local and long distance wireless calling were all charged at the same rate. Such a plan increases the need for U.S. wireless firms to have a viable means of offering long distance and other telecom services. The emergence of nationwide networks has increased the potential for growth in the U.S.

Developing technology will likely increase the possibilities of wireless communications. Before 2003, it is forecast that 3G (third generation) wireless will become widely available. 3G has many potential advantages. It should allow U.S. wireless standards to achieve more consistency, as well as compatibility with Europe and other nations. It allows faster speeds of data transfer, which will be important for users who make use of Internet and other wireless data exchange devices. 3G will likely be useful for corporate intranets, where the cost of installing wire-based systems throughout many buildings or floors would be prohibitive. There is also the potential that 3G will allow residential customers in remote locations to gain fast Internet access where it was not previously available. As wireless services increasingly provide Internet access, there is the possibility that they may become major players in the Internet portal market. Customers would choose to use the portals of the wireless providers because they would be more supportive of various wireless devices than a conventional portal, such as Yahoo! The main potential drawback to 3G is the potentially prohibitive cost of obtaining licensing. Licensing costs are projected to run into the billions of dollars. Analysts have estimated that Vodafone will have to pay in the neighborhood of $40 billion to obtain 3G licenses in the countries in which it currently operates.

This highlights an increasing need for scale in the wireless industry. Because of the high costs of making available the newest technologies, small operators will not be able to compete. Larger firms have the advantage of greater resources to be able to offer new and innovative services. They also have the ability to spend more for research and development of new products and technologies. In addition, there has been a movement in which companies that offer wireless service purchase communications devices for customers. This is another development that favors large companies that have the resources and bargaining power to gain favorable terms with equipment manufacturers. Another factor favoring large firms is globalization. As executives are increasingly required to travel throughout the world, they require wireless service that can do the same. This kind of coverage is not yet readily available, but a few large firms will likely provide it in the near future.

THE AIRTOUCH ACQUISITION

On January 15, 1999, Vodafone announced the acquisition of Airtouch Communications for about $62 billion. The offer involved an exchange of Airtouch shares for one-half share of Vodafone ADRs and $9 cash. This was valued at about $97 per share. Vodafone managers arrived at this figure because under United Kingdom tax laws the original Vodafone shareholders had to maintain at least 50% of the combined company's shares to receive favorable accounting treatment. Meanwhile in the U.S., because the offer involved a cash element, the exchange could not qualify for pooling of interests accounting.

Following is an excerpt of the background on the merger from the prospectus issued to Airtouch shareholders in connection with the merger.

Description of Vodafone

Vodafone is a leading international provider of mobile telecommunications services. It owns interests in mobile operations in the United Kingdom and 12 other countries which, as of March 31, 1999, served over 10.4 million customers based on Vodafone's ownership share of its telecommunications ventures, of which over 9.5 million are connected to digital networks. Vodafone was formed in 1984 as a subsidiary of Racal Electronics Plc. Approximately twenty percent of Vodafone, then known as Racal Telecom Limited, was offered to the public in October 1988. Vodafone was spun off from Racal Electronics and became an independent company in September 1991.

Vodafone's principal business consists of the operation in the United Kingdom of digital and analog cellular radio telephone and paging networks. Vodafone was the first cellular operator in the United Kingdom to open its network for service. After commencing service on its analog network on January 1, 1985 it subsequently launched one of the world's first digital networks in July 1992. It has been the U.K. market leader since 1986 and is presently the largest of the four United Kingdom operators with more than 5.5 million customers at March 31, 1999, of which over 1.8 million are on its innovative "Pay As You Talk" prepaid service.

Outside of the United Kingdom, Vodafone currently has interests, including, in most cases, board representation and significant operating influence, in cellular operators in Australia, Egypt, Fiji, France, Germany, Greece, Malta, the Netherlands, New Zealand, South Africa, Sweden and Uganda. These cellular interests are licensed to serve over 360 million people. At March 31, 1999, Vodafone's customer base outside of the U.K. was almost 4.9 million, based on its ownership shares of its ventures. Vodafone also owns an approximate 3.0% interest in Globalstar, which is constructing and will operate a 48 low-earth orbit satellite communications system. Vodafone is licensed to be the exclusive service provider for Globalstar in Australia, Greece, Lesotho, Malta, South Africa, Swaziland and the United Kingdom.

Description of Airtouch

AirTouch is a leading international mobile telecommunications company, with a significant presence in the United States, Europe and Asia. As of March 31, 1999, AirTouch had over 18.8 million customers based on its ownership share of the cellular, paging and personal communications service ventures in which it has an interest. At that date, those ventures were licensed to serve an estimated 723 million people.

In the United States, AirTouch's cellular and PCS ventures had over 10.3 million customers at March 31, 1999, of which AirTouch's proportionate share was approximately 8.7 million customers. AirTouch's interests in its U.S. cellular and PCS ventures at March 31, 1999 represented over 95 million POPs, a number reflecting the population of a market multiplied by AirTouch's ownership interest in a licensee operating in that market. AirTouch controls or shares control over cellular systems in 15 of the 30 largest cellular markets in the United States, including Los Angeles, Detroit, San Francisco, Atlanta, San Diego, Minneapolis, Phoenix, Seattle, Denver, Cleveland, Portland, San Jose, Kansas City, Cincinnati and Sacramento. In addition, through PrimeCo Personal Communications, L.P., AirTouch shares control over PCS systems operations in over 30 major U.S. cities, including Chicago, Dallas, Tampa, Houston, Miami, New Orleans and Milwaukee.

Outside the U.S., as of March 31, 1999, AirTouch's cellular ventures were licensed to serve more than 570 million people and had over 26 million customers, of which AirTouch's proportionate share was approximately 6.6 million. AirTouch holds significant ownership interests, with board representation and significant operating influence, in cellular systems operating in Belgium, Egypt, Germany, India, Italy, Japan, Poland, Portugal, Romania, South Korea, Spain and Sweden.

Industry surveys indicate that AirTouch is also among the largest providers of paging services in the United States, with approximately 3.5 million units in service as of March 31, 1999. AirTouch also owns an approximate 5.2% interest in Globalstar and is licensed to be the exclusive service provider for Globalstar in the United States and the Caribbean region, Indonesia, Japan, Malaysia and owns interests in the exclusive service providers in Mexico and Canada.

The Merger

Background of the Merger

Both Vodafone and AirTouch are leading international providers of mobile telecommunications services. Vodafone provides cellular service in the United Kingdom and has interests in wireless companies operating in 12 other countries. AirTouch operates cellular and PCS networks that reach most of the major markets in the United States and has interests in wireless companies operating in 12 other countries. Vodafone and AirTouch have highly complementary operations and together have interests in companies that provide service in 13 European countries, including all major European markets. At the time of the execution of the merger agreement, the companies owned interests in competing ventures only in Germany.

As is common in the wireless telecommunications industry, AirTouch and, outside the U.K., Vodafone conduct much of their business through partnerships and other joint ventures. Internationally, AirTouch generally operates through joint ventures and other consortia, including in Sweden and Egypt, where Vodafone and AirTouch both have ownership interests in the same ventures. Vodafone and AirTouch are also both limited partners in Globalstar, L.P., a satellite communications venture. In the United States, AirTouch is a partner in a number of partnerships, including with Bell Atlantic in PrimeCo Personal Communications, L.P., a company providing PCS services in more than 30 major cities, and in TOMCOM, L.P., a partnership formed to provide technical, operating and marketing services for the partners' United States wireless properties.

In light of the complementary nature of AirTouch's and Vodafone's European properties, in late 1996 and on several occasions in 1997, executives of Vodafone and AirTouch explored possible operational synergies. Alternatives discussed included a joint venture, contractual roaming and purchasing arrangements and a merger of the companies. The discussions were conceptual only, and no subsequent steps were taken.

In September and early October of 1998, Chris Gent, chief executive of Vodafone, Sam Ginn, chairman and chief executive officer of AirTouch, and other executives of the companies met on several occasions. The parties discussed the possible benefits and principal objectives of a potential merger as well as issues regarding the then current valuation of AirTouch and how management of a combined company would be organized. Those discussions, however, were inconclusive on many important issues and did not result in the formation of a combination proposal.

On October 14, 1998, the AirTouch board held its annual meeting to discuss the company's strategic direction. The AirTouch board analyzed the United States and international wireless environments and AirTouch's position as an independent company as well as the strategic aspects of a potential merger with Vodafone. The AirTouch board also discussed the strategic aspects of the formation of a new wireless company with Bell Atlantic in response to an indication by Bell Atlantic in September 1998 that it might make a proposal of this kind to AirTouch in the near future. The AirTouch board reaffirmed AirTouch's strategy as an independent company but determined that management should be open to discussions with both interested companies to explore further the potential benefits of both transactions.

On October 21, 1998, Messrs. Gent and Ginn had a telephone conversation to discuss again several of the issues key to a potential merger but were unable to resolve them and agreed to terminate their negotiations. There were no further negotiations between executives or other employees of the two companies until the week of January 4, 1999, although in the interim the two companies' financial advisors had several discussions regarding the financial aspects of a potential merger.

On November 13, 1998, Bell Atlantic presented its proposal to AirTouch regarding the formation of a new wireless company. The proposal contemplated that both Bell Atlantic and GTE, which companies have entered into a merger agreement, would contribute their wireless assets to AirTouch and receive a controlling interest in the new company. During November and December, senior management of AirTouch and Bell Atlantic engaged in discussions regarding the Bell Atlantic proposal and, in late November, AirTouch and Bell

Atlantic also began to explore a possible merger of AirTouch with Bell Atlantic in exchange for Bell Atlantic stock.

On December 31, 1998, media reports circulated to the effect that Bell Atlantic and AirTouch were in merger discussions. Over the next two days, Mr. Gent and Ken Hydon, financial director of Vodafone, and representatives of Goldman Sachs International discussed the Bell Atlantic proposal described in the media reports and the propriety and timing of informing AirTouch of Vodafone's renewed interest in a transaction with AirTouch. On January 2, 1999, Vodafone sent AirTouch a letter indicating its desire to make a merger proposal but did not set forth the elements of its proposal. On January 3, 1999 the AirTouch board had a special meeting to discuss the status of merger negotiations and AirTouch's options. Although AirTouch has a long-standing policy not to comment on market speculation, in light of Bell Atlantic's stated intention to issue a press release and the extensive and detailed media coverage of the AirTouch and Bell Atlantic discussions, on January 3, 1999 AirTouch and Bell Atlantic issued a joint press release confirming that they were in merger discussions. At or about that time, AirTouch's financial advisors requested that, if Vodafone was interested in making a proposal, it make a specific proposal promptly.

By letter dated January 4, 1999, Vodafone invited AirTouch to enter into discussions for a merger in which AirTouch stockholders would receive five Vodafone shares, equivalent to 0.5 of an ADS, and $6.00 in cash for each share of AirTouch common stock. Vodafone structured the offer as a share exchange with a cash element in order both to make the offer attractive to AirTouch in light of competing proposals and, at the same time, fair to Vodafone as well as to ensure tax-free treatment (to the extent possible) for AirTouch's U.S. stockholders.

Vodafone's approach was rumored in the media, and on January 5, 1999, in response to a request from the London Stock Exchange in light of the media rumors, Vodafone issued a press release confirming that it had made a proposal to AirTouch. On that same day, AirTouch issued its own press release stating that it had received a merger proposal from Vodafone. Mr. Hydon, Mohan Gyani, executive vice president and chief financial officer of AirTouch, and the companies' financial advisors met on January 6 and January 7, 1999 to discuss the financial terms of Vodafone's proposal and the potential cost savings and revenue opportunities which might be achieved through a merger.

On January 7, 1999 and January 10, 1999, the AirTouch board held special meetings to discuss AirTouch's strategic alternatives, the status of negotiations with Bell Atlantic and Vodafone, the potential benefits and disadvantages of each of the proposed transactions and the status of due diligence and related legal and financial issues. At the meetings, the AirTouch board received advice from Morgan Stanley regarding the financial aspects of both proposals and from AirTouch's legal counsel regarding the relevant legal considerations in evaluating AirTouch's options. At the January 7 meeting, the AirTouch board was also briefed about a possible MCI WorldCom proposal as a result of an exploratory call from that company's chairman, Bernard Ebbers, to Mr. Ginn. However, later that week Mr. Ebbers informed Mr. Ginn that MCI WorldCom would not be making an acquisition proposal.

Following the January 10, 1999 meeting of the AirTouch board, Vodafone and AirTouch, advised by their respective financial advisors and lawyers, negotiated the terms and conditions of the merger agreement. At the same time, AirTouch continued its merger negotiations with Bell Atlantic. AirTouch informed both Bell Atlantic and Vodafone that it intended to present both companies' final proposals and the final forms of the respective merger agreements to the AirTouch board at a special meeting on January 15.

The financial terms of the merger being proposed by Bell Atlantic varied during the period of negotiations between Bell Atlantic and AirTouch, although each proposal after late November 1998 involved the exchange of Bell Atlantic common stock for AirTouch common stock. During the week of January 10, Bell Atlantic's proposal involved an exchange of each share of AirTouch common stock for 1.54 shares of Bell Atlantic common stock, subject to an upward adjustment in the exchange ratio commencing in nine months to reflect dividend payments on Bell Atlantic common stock, and was conditioned on the transaction being accounted for as a pooling of interests under U.S. GAAP. Bell Atlantic's proposal also involved a "collar" pursuant to which the exchange ratio would be adjusted to produce a price of $80.08 if the price of Bell Atlantic common stock ranged from $48 to $52. If the average closing price of Bell Atlantic common stock was below $48 during the specified period, the exchange ratio would be 1.6683; if the price was above $52, the exchange ratio would be 1.54. The closing price per share of Bell Atlantic's common stock on the NYSE ranged from $53 1/8 to $54 15/16 during the week of January 11.

On January 14, 1999, the Vodafone board met and considered, together with its financial advisors, the progress of the negotiations with AirTouch of the merger agreement and the results of Vodafone's due diligence with respect to AirTouch. The Vodafone board confirmed its view of the strategic importance to Vodafone's future of the proposed merger with AirTouch. The Vodafone board also discussed the possibility of increasing the cash component and therefore the value of its then current offer to AirTouch following indications received by the executive management of Vodafone from AirTouch that an increase in the cash consideration would substantially improve the competitiveness of Vodafone's offer as compared to Bell Atlantic's offer. The Vodafone board then considered an increase in the terms of Vodafone's offer from five Vodafone shares and $6.00 in cash for each share of common stock of AirTouch to five Vodafone shares and $9.00 in cash. At the meeting, Goldman Sachs International rendered its oral opinion to the Vodafone board, subsequently confirmed in writing, that the increased merger consideration contemplated was fair from a financial point of view to Vodafone. The Vodafone board then unanimously approved the merger agreement and the offer of five Vodafone shares and up to $9.00 in cash for each share of common stock of AirTouch in the hope of securing a successful transaction with AirTouch.

On January 15, 1999, immediately prior to the AirTouch board meeting, Vodafone increased its offer to five shares of Vodafone and $9.00 in cash for each share of AirTouch common stock. Senior management of Bell Atlantic indicated that it was prepared to raise its offer, but did not specify by what amount and further indicated both that the exchange ratio would not reach 1.60 Bell Atlantic shares for each AirTouch share and also that no "collar" would be provided to the stockholders of AirTouch.

At the AirTouch board meeting, AirTouch's executive management reviewed the principal terms of the two offers and the results of AirTouch's due diligence of the two companies. Morgan Stanley then presented its financial analysis of each proposed transaction and AirTouch's legal counsel reviewed the two proposed merger agreements as well as the standards of Delaware law applicable to the board's decision. The AirTouch board, executive management, legal counsel and Morgan Stanley engaged in a discussion of the two proposals. Morgan Stanley delivered its oral opinion, which was later confirmed in a written opinion dated as of January 15, 1999, that, as of that date and based upon and subject to the matters stated in its opinion, the merger consideration offered by Vodafone was fair from a financial point of view to the holders of AirTouch common stock. See "—Opinions of Financial Advisors—Opinion of AirTouch's Financial Advisor" for a description of the Morgan Stanley opinion. The AirTouch board concluded that the Vodafone proposal was superior to the Bell Atlantic proposal and in the best interests of AirTouch and its stockholders for the reasons set forth below under "—Recommendation of the AirTouch Board; Additional Considerations of the AirTouch Board." The AirTouch board voted unanimously to approve and declare advisable the merger, the merger agreement and each of the transactions contemplated thereby, and to recommend that the AirTouch stockholders approve and adopt the merger agreement and the agreement providing for the internal reorganization.

After the January 15 meeting of the AirTouch board, the parties executed the merger agreement. On January 15, 1999, Vodafone and AirTouch issued a joint press release announcing the execution of the merger agreement.

Reasons for the Merger

Vodafone and AirTouch believe that the merger of two of the world's leading mobile telecommunications companies will create a more competitive, global wireless telecommunications company than either Vodafone or AirTouch would be on its own and will generate significant opportunities to deliver greater value to shareholders.

- **Shared Strategic Vision.** The global market for mobile telecommunications is undergoing rapid growth as consumers have endorsed the benefits of mobile telephony, enhanced by increasingly lightweight, secure and attractive equipment. Both Vodafone and AirTouch believe that mobile telecommunications will continue to be one of the fastest growing segments of the telecommunications industry as, over time, mobile voice telephony will replace large amounts of telecommunications traffic currently carried by fixed line networks and will serve as a major platform for voice and data communications. The companies expect that the combined entity will be in a better position to take advantage of the opportunities presented by the rapidly growing mobile telecommunications industry and data services market. Vodafone and AirTouch believe that mobile penetration rates in most developed countries will reach 50% by the year 2003 and will reach 55% in the United States and 65% in most developed European countries by 2005.
- **Scale, Operational Strength and Complementary Assets.**

THE VERIZON WIRELESS JOINT VENTURE

The Vodafone/Airtouch deal closed on June 30, 1999. On September 21, 1999, Vodafone Airtouch reached an agreement with Bell Atlantic Corporation to create a new wireless business, which came to be known as Verizon Wireless. Verizon combined the U.S. wireless assets of Airtouch, Bell Atlantic, and GTE (which was awaiting approval to merge with Bell Atlantic).

The deal was said to have many advantages. The combination of the firms' wireless assets would give Verizon nearly complete national coverage in the United States. The combined firm would be able to compete with AT&T's national coverage and "one-rate" pricing plan. Verizon would become by far the largest wireless company in the U.S., with almost twice as many customers as AT&T. It would have a footprint covering 90% of the U.S. population, and 49 of the top 50 wireless markets. Vodafone contributed about 40% of the subscribers to the deal. However, Vodafone holds 45% of the joint venture because it agreed to cede managerial control to Bell Atlantic. Bell Atlantic also holds four of the seven members of Verizon's board, with Vodafone appointing the other three.

THE MANNESMANN ACQUISITION

The following materials were issued in connection with Vodafone's hostile bid for Mannesmann.

Description of Vodafone Airtouch

General

Vodafone AirTouch is one of the world's leading international telecommunications companies with a significant presence in the United Kingdom, the United States, Europe and the Asia Pacific region. The company provides a full range of wireless telecommunications services, including cellular, broadband personal communications (PCS), paging and data communications.

On June 30, 1999, Vodafone Group Plc and AirTouch Communications, Inc. merged to create the world's largest wireless telecommunications company in terms of the number of proportionate customers. As a result of the merger, Vodafone Group Plc changed its name to Vodafone AirTouch Plc and AirTouch Communications, Inc. became a majority owned subsidiary of Vodafone AirTouch. The merger facilitated a major step in Vodafone AirTouch's declared strategy to extend the reach, range and penetration of mobile services to as many customers as possible, in as many geographical territories throughout the world that can sustain viable and profitable operating environments. The merger enabled the creation of a more competitive, global telecommunications company than either Vodafone Group or AirTouch would have been alone.

Following the merger, Vodafone AirTouch now has interests in 24 countries across five continents. The major geographical markets in which it has interests in cellular network operations are Australia, Belgium, Egypt, France, Germany, Greece, Italy, Japan, The Netherlands, New Zealand, Poland, Portugal, South Africa, Spain, Sweden, the United Kingdom and the United States. Vodafone AirTouch also has interests in cellular network operations in Fiji, Hungary, India, Malta, Romania, South Korea and Uganda. As of September 30, 1999, the company had approximately 31.5 million proportionate customers (excluding paging customers). The company and its ventures serve approximately 417 million people worldwide, calculated on a proportionate basis in accordance with Vodafone AirTouch's percentage interest in its ventures.

Regional Operations

Vodafone AirTouch operations are divided into three geographical regions: the United Kingdom; Europe, Middle East and Africa; and the United States and Asia Pacific region.

In the United Kingdom, Vodafone AirTouch is the largest of the four cellular operators with more than 6.8 million customers at September 30, 1999 and has been the market leader in terms of number of customers since 1986. Vodafone AirTouch's networks cover 99% of the U.K. population. Vodafone U.K. currently has roaming agreements covering over 100 countries. It also successfully introduced the "Pay as You Talk" prepaid service, which represented 46% of its customer base as of September 30, 1999.

Vodafone AirTouch's operations cover most of the European continent and span into areas of future growth such as Eastern Europe, Africa and the Middle East. In total, the company had over 12 million proportionate customers in this region as of September 30, 1999. It has controlling stakes in key wireless telecommunications operators in Greece (Panafon), Portugal (Telecel), Sweden (Europolitan) and The Netherlands (Libertel), strategic stakes in operators in Spain (AirTel) and Belgium (Proximus) and longstanding relationships with Mannesmann in operators in Germany (02), Italy (Omnitel) and France (SFR). Vodafone AirTouch is currently considering increasing its stake in Airtel, the Spanish mobile telecommunications operator. Vodafone AirTouch is one of the pioneers in developing the rapidly growing Eastern European markets, having already established a presence in Poland, Romania and Hungary. In the Middle East and Africa, Vodafone AirTouch holds interests in Egyptian, South African and Ugandan mobile telecommunications operators.

In the United States, Vodafone AirTouch is one of the largest providers of wireless services, serving approximately 9.1 million proportionate cellular and PCS customers as of September 30, 1999 and representing over 96 million proportionate POPs. Vodafone AirTouch controls or shares control over cellular systems in 22 of the 30 largest U.S. markets, including Atlanta, Chicago, Dallas, Detroit, Houston, Los Angeles, Phoenix, San Diego, San Francisco and Seattle. Vodafone AirTouch's U.S. PCS operations are carried out jointly through its PrimeCo partnership with Bell Atlantic, its equal partner in the venture. PrimeCo's markets complement the existing U.S. cellular operations of Vodafone AirTouch and Bell Atlantic. As of September 30, 1999, PrimeCo had over 1.2 million customers.

In the Asia Pacific region, Vodafone AirTouch operates networks extensively in Australia, New Zealand, Fiji, India, Japan and South Korea, with over three million customers as of September 30, 1999. Vodafone AirTouch is considering an initial public offering of its Australasian business during the first half of 2000 but intends to maintain a controlling stake following the offering.

Other

Vodafone AirTouch holds an approximate 8% interest in Globalstar and has the exclusive rights to provide Globalstar service in the United Kingdom, the United States, Australia, Botswana, Canada, Greece, Malta, Mexico, Mozambique, Namibia, South Africa, Zimbabwe and the Caribbean.

Vodafone AirTouch was incorporated in England in July 1984 as a subsidiary of Racal Electronics Pic and became an independent company in September 1991.

Recent Developments

Joint Venture with Bell Atlantic. On September 21, 1999, Vodafone AirTouch and Bell Atlantic Corporation reached a definitive agreement to create a new wireless business with a nationwide U.S. footprint, a single brand and a common digital technology composed of Vodafone AirTouch's and Bell Atlantic's U.S. wireless assets (which will also include GTE's U.S. wireless assets if the Bell Atlantic/GTE merger is completed). Upon its formation, the new venture will serve approximately 20 million wireless customers and 3.5 million paging customers throughout the United States based on each party's customers as of September 21, 1999, making it the largest wireless telecommunications operator in the United States. It will have a footprint covering over 90% of the U.S. population and 49 of the top 50 U.S. wireless markets, with 254 million gross POPs.

Under the transaction agreements, the contribution of assets will take place in two stages. In Stage I, Vodafone AirTouch will contribute certain of its U.S. wireless interests to an existing partnership which holds Bell Atlantic's U.S. wireless interests and is currently doing business as Bell Atlantic Mobile. Following the Stage I closing, Vodafone AirTouch will hold 65.1% of the partnership and Bell Atlantic will retain the remaining 34.9%. Stage II of the closing will occur on the earlier of the first anniversary of Stage I shortly after Bell Atlantic completes its merger with GTE or Bell Atlantic's right to merge with GTE is terminated. It is possible that Stage I and Stage II could occur simultaneously. In Stage II, Vodafone AirTouch will contribute the rest of its U.S. wireless assets and Bell Atlantic will contribute the U.S. wireless assets of GTE if the Bell Atlantic/GTE merger has been completed. In this case, Vodafone AirTouch will own 45% of the partnership and Bell Atlantic 55%. If for any reason the U.S. wireless assets of GTE are not contributed to the venture, the partners' interests will be adjusted so that Vodafone AirTouch will have a 67% interest in the partnership and Bell Atlantic will have 33%. In such a case, however, Bell Atlantic will have the right to acquire up to a 50.5% interest in the partnership by acquiring a portion of Vodafone AirTouch's interest at fair market value.

Bell Atlantic will manage the joint venture and will designate four of the seven members to the joint venture board of directors. Vodafone AirTouch will designate the other three directors. The new business will initially assume or incur $10 billion in existing and new debt, approximately $5.5 from Bell Atlantic and GTE Corporation and $4.5 from Vodafone AirTouch, thus causing Vodafone AirTouch's net consolidated debt to decline by $4.5 billion. Vodafone AirTouch will account for its interest in the joint venture on an equity basis, recognizing a proportionate share of the joint venture's financial results. Vodafone AirTouch can elect to sell shares through an initial public offering of a company fonned to hold ownership interests in the wireless business at any time after three years from the closing of the transaction. Bell Atlantic may initiate an initial public offering at any time after the Stage II closing, in which instance Vodafone AirTouch will be entitled to a pro rata participation. Vodafone AirTouch can also put up to $20 billion worth of its interest in the joint venture to Bell Atlantic or the wireless venture between three and seven years from the closing of the transaction.

On December 6, 1999, the U.S. Department of Justice approved the joint venture transaction, subject to an anticipated consent decree that calls for the disposition of one or two competing wireless properties in each market where an overlap would be created by the venture. The overlapping operations are estimated to serve approximately 3 million customers in several major U.S. markets covering a total of approximately 49 million POPs. Under the terms of the consent decree, Vodafone AirTouch, Bell Atlantic and GTE plan to eliminate their wireless overlaps upon the closing of their respective transactions; however, the decree gives the companies until June 30, 2000 to resolve more than half of the overlapping wireless properties. Vodafone AirTouch believes that the decree gives the three companies sufficient time to dispose of the overlapping properties in an orderly manner and in a way that will maximize the value of the assets and minimize the impact on customers.

The transaction is still subject to approval by various other regulatory authorities, the approval of shareholders of Vodafone AirTouch and the receipt of an exemptive order from the SEC or other satisfactory resolution regarding the application of the Investment Company Act of 1940 to Vodafone AirTouch and AirTouch and is subject to third-party claims which may or may not affect the scope of the transaction. See "—Litigation" below. The transaction is expected to be completed within three to six months from the date of this prospectus.

Disposition of E-Plus. On October 4, 1999, Vodafone AirTouch reached agreement with France Telecom S.A. for the sale of Vodafone AirTouch's 17.24% equity interest in E-Plus Mobilfunk GmbH, the German cellular network operator, for a cash consideration net of debt of DM3.42 billion (approximately £1.14 billion). The sale is subject to various regulatory and other consents and will be carried out in accordance with the existing agreements among the shareholders of E-Plus Mobilfunk GmbH. On December 9, 1999, Bell South Corporation announced that it had exercised its right of first refusal to purchase Vodafone AirTouch's 17.24% interest. Vodafone AirTouch announced in May 1999 that it would divest this interest pursuant to the undertaking it gave to the European Commission at that time in connection with its merger with AirTouch Communications.

Acquisition of CommNet Cellular, Inc. In July 1999, Vodafone AirTouch reached an agreement to acquire 100% of the outstanding capital stock of CommNet Cellular, Inc., which provides wireless technology services in the midwest of the United States, for $764 million in cash plus debt of approximately $600 million. The transaction is expected to close in January 2000.

Increase in Ownership in Japan. On October 7, 1999, Vodafone AirTouch announced a series of transactions that will give it an equity interest of more than 20% in each of Japan's nine regional mobile telecommunications companies. These transactions included the acquisition of the entire equity stake owned by Cable and Wireless Plc (Cable and Wireless) in Tokyo Digital Phone Co., Ltd., Kansai Digital Phone Co., Ltd. and Tokai Digital Phone Co., Ltd., the acquisition from Japan Telecom of additional shares in the six Digital Tu-Ka Group companies, which have been consolidated under the "J-Phone" brand name, an agreement with Cable and Wireless to acquire its entire equity stake in each of the Digital Tu-Ka Group companies and the acquisition of Metrophone Service Co., Ltd. from Distacom Communications Ltd. of Hong Kong and Tiger Spirit Developments Limited. Total consideration relating to the increase of ownership in Japan was approximately $550 million. Upon completion of these transactions, Vodafone AirTouch will become the second largest shareholder behind Japan Telecom in the carriers that serve each of Japan's nine mobile telecommunications regions.

Agreement with British Broadcasting Company. On December 16, 1999, Vodafone AirTouch and the BBC announced an agreement under which they will jointly develop and deliver continuously updated news, sport, entertainment and business services via text, audio and video to mobile phone users. Through this agreement, Vodafone AirTouch is positioned to be one of the leaders in defining the standards for future mobile, Internet and multimedia services.

Description of Mannesmann

General

Mannesmann is an international, German-domiciled company with activities in four business segments: telecommunications, engineering, automotive and steel tubes and tubular products. Mannesmann has majority stakes in the leading German mobile operator (02), the second-largest Italian mobile operator, Omnitel, and the U.K. mobile operator, Orange, and provides fixed network services in Germany and Italy. It is one of Europe's largest telecommunications providers.

Principal Business Segments

Mannesmann's principal business segments are as follows:

Mannesmann Telecommunications. Mannesmann is one of Europe's largest telecommunications providers with interests in D2 Mannesmann and Mannesmann Arcor in Germany, Omnitel and Infostrada in Italy, Cegetel in France and tclc.ring in Austria. D2 Mannesmann (65.2% owned by Mannesmann and the remainder owned by Vodafone AirTouch) is the largest player in mobile communications in Germany, with more than 8 million D2 Mannesmann network customers.

Mannesmann Arcor (70.0% owned by Mannesmann) provides fixed network services in Germany. Arcor's network is also linked to that of the French telecommunications company, Cegetel, and the Austrian network telephone company, tele.ring. Together with o.tel.o, which is wholly owned by Arcor, Arcor follows a two-brand strategy in the German fixed-line market. Arcor offers Internet access and online services together with wholly owned germany.net. Omnitel (55.2% owned by Mannesmann) is the second-largest Italian mobile operator with more than 9 million subscribers. Infostrada provides fixed network services in Italy. With Italia Online, its wholly-owned Internet service provider, Infostrada offers Internet access and also offers online services in Italy.

Mannesmann Eurokom is a strategic telecommunications holding company which manages Mannesmann's international assets and extends Mannesmann's reach through acquisitions and applications for new licenses. Mannesmann's international assets include a 15% stake in the French telecommunications operator, Cegetel, which also provides mobile services through SFR, and tele.ring, the Austrian telecommunications provider (53.8% owned), which is currently preparing the launch of its mobile service. Other interests include Ipulsys, which develops Internet protocol-based international voice and data services throughout Europe by using its partners' existing network capacities, and Mannesmann Passo, which provides a traffic information service under the brand name, Passo, that can be accessed via mobile telephone.

Mannesmann Engineering. The Mannesmann engineering business is a leading global supplier in the fields of hydraulics, materials handling and plastics technology with three main divisions: Mannesmann Rexroth (drives and controls), Mannesmann Oematic (material flow and logistics) and Mannesmann Oemag Krauss-Maffei (plastics machinery, compressors, process and laser technology).

Mannesmann Automotive. The Mannesmann automotive business is a systems developer and partner to the global automobile industry, with two main divisions: Mannesmann VDO (information systems, cockpit systems and audio and navigation systems) and Mannesmann Sachs (components and systems primarily for chassis and powertrain).

Mannesmann Tubes. The Mannesmann tubes business is one of the world's largest producers of steel tubes.

Recent Developments

Disposition of Engineering and Automotive. In September 1999, Mannesmann announced that it intended to create two separate corporations with their own identities for Mannesmann Engineering and Automotive on the one hand and Mannesmann Telecommunications (including Mannesmann Tubes) on the other and to conduct an initial public offering of the engineering and automotive business by 2001. On November 23, 1999, Mannesmann announced that it would accelerate the timing of the initial public offering of its engineering and automotive division to as early as mid-2000.

Offer for Orange. On October 20, 1999, Mannesmann and Orange, a British public limited liability company that operates a digital mobile network in the United Kingdom, announced that they had agreed to terms pursuant to which Mannesmann would make an offer to purchase Orange. On November 23, 1999, Mannesmann announced that approximately 74.9% of the outstanding Orange ordinary shares had been tendered into the offer and declared the offer unconditional. In the offer, Mannesmann offered 0.0965 newly issued shares of Mannesmann and £6.40 in cash per each Orange unconditionally allotted or issued and fully paid ordinary share of 20p each, subject to certain elections on the part of Orange shareholders to adjust the payment received. On December 20, 1999, the European Commission approved the acquisition of Orange by Mannesmann. As a condition to such approval, Mannesmann agreed to dispose of Orange's 17.5% stake in Connect Austria.

Orange is a mobile telecommunications company that provides a range of communications services, particularly through its digital mobile network in the United Kingdom and sells Orange products and services both in the United Kingdom and internationally. In 1994 the company was formed when Hong Kong-based Hutchison Whampoa established a mobile phone service provider in the United Kingdom under the name Hutchison Telecommunications. In 1996, Hutchison Whampoa took that company public as Orange Plc and retained a 44.82% interest.

In the United Kingdom, Orange is one of four operators of mobile telephone networks providing wireless communications and paging services. Orange provides digital network coverage over more than 98% of that country's population. As of June 30, 1999, Orange had a total of 2.96 million mobile service customers and a 17.6% share of the United Kingdom mobile subscribers market. Orange's "Just Talk" pre-pay service accounted for 33% of the Orange customer base at June 30, 1999. As of July 31, 1990, subscribers to Orange mobile services were able to roam on 182 networks in 90 countries. Orange also provides paging services in the United Kingdom through Hutchison Paging Limited's two networks and re-sells BT Cellnet and Vodafone AirTouch services through Hutchison Cellular Services Limited.

Orange also provides mobile and data communications services in Europe. Orange also has a 17.45% interest in Connect Austria GmbH, which launched Austria's third mobile network service in October 1998; a 45.50% interest in Orange Communications S.A., which won the third Swiss mobile license in April 1998 and commenced operations on June 29, 1998; and a 50% interest in KPN Orange Belgium N.V., which was awarded the third Belgian mobile license in June 1998 and began a regional service through city by city launches, starting on June 3, 1999. Beyond Europe, Orange has licensed the Orange brand to Hutchison Whampoa affiliated companies Partner Communications for its operations in Israel and to Hutchison Telecom for its operations in Hong Kong.

As part of the offer for Orange, Mannesmann and Hutchison entered into a shareholding agreement pursuant to which the parties agreed that for a period of 18 months following the issuance of new Mannesmann shares to Hutchison, Hutchison will abstain from any disposal of any interest in 42,700,423 Mannesmann shares. Subject to certain conditions, Hutchison may make a disposal or any interest in the remainder of the new Mannesmann shares at any time. Moreover, Hutchison may, upon expiration of the lock-up period, make a disposal of any interest in new Mannesmann shares at any lime subject to certain limitations. The transfer restrictions do not prevent Hutchison from accepting a general offer for Mannesmann shares if the acceptance of such offer is recommended by the Mannesmann management board or following a change of control having occurred without the disposal of the lock-up shares. At present however, the Mannesmann management board has not made any such recommendation and such change of control has not occurred. Hutchison has announced in a press release that it will not tender its Mannesmann shares in the offer.

Background to the Offer

Vodafone AirTouch began offering mobile telecommunications services in the United Kingdom in 1985 as one of the first companies to be awarded a mobile telecommunications license in the U.K. Beginning in 1988, it started to expand its operations by making acquisitions and participating in consortia to apply for mobile network operating licenses in European countries. In 1993, Vodafone AirTouch had its first year of major international expansion by entering the German, Australian, Greek, South African and Fijian mobile markets. By the end of 1998, prior to the merger with AirTouch Communications, Inc., Vodafone AirTouch had interests in mobile operations in 12 countries other than the U.K., including a 70% interest in Libertel in the Netherlands and a 20% interest in Societé Française du Radiotelephone SA, the French mobile telecommunications operator. The merger with AirTouch in 1999 created a global telecommunications leader with a presence in 23 countries.

Mannesmann began offering mobile telecommunication services in Germany in 1992. In 1996, Mannesmann became an indirect partner of Vodafone AirTouch when it acquired a 10% interest (later increased to 15%) in Cegetel, the French telecommunications group, which is the owner of the remaining 80% in SFR.

As is common in the wireless telecommunications industry, Vodafone AirTouch conducts much of its business through partnerships and other joint ventures. In late December 1998, Dr. Klaus Esser, chairman of the Mannesmann management board, contacted Chris Gent, formerly chief executive of Vodafone Group and currently chief executive of Vodafone AirTouch, to arrange a meeting in order to discuss matters of mutual interest. On January 15, 1999, Mr. Gent and Julian Horn-Smith, an executive director of Vodafone AirTouch, met with Dr. Esser and Kurt Kinzius, managing director of Mannesmann Eurokom GmbH, a wholly owned subsidiary of Mannesmann, in London to explore possible opportunities to build upon their partnership relationship. The parties discussed the potential for combining or transferring assets or shareholdings in certain markets. The discussions were conceptual only, and no subsequent steps were taken.

On January 15, 1999, Vodafone AirTouch, then known as Vodafone Group Plc, entered into an agreement to merge with AirTouch Communications, Inc., a wireless company based in the United States with interests in mobile operators in Europe. Among AirTouch's interests were a 34.8% interest in the German mobile operator, Mannesmann Mobilfunk (D2), and a 17.8% interest in the Italian mobile telecommunications operator, Omnitel Pronto Italia. At that time, Mannesmann owned the other 65.2% of D2 and held a 37.5% interest in Omnitel Pronto Italia. In addition, AirTouch owned a 4.5% interest in a consortium led by Mannesmann to hold a 74.9% interest in Mannesmann Arcor, Germany's second largest wireline telecommunications company. Mannesmann owned 94% of the consortium.

In late January 1999, media speculation focused on Mannesmann as a possible takeover target. Dr. Esser telephoned Mr. Gent to inquire about Vodafone's intentions in this regard and Mr. Gent reassured Dr. Esser that Vodafone would discuss any such intentions with him first.

On February 21, 1999, Sam Ginn, then chairman and chief executive officer of AirTouch and currently Chairman of Vodafone AirTouch, and Arun Sarin, formerly director, president and chief operating officer of AirTouch and currently an executive director of Vodafone AirTouch, met with Professor Dr. Joachim Funk, chairman of the supervisory board of Mannesmann, in New York. In this meeting, Dr. Funk expressed a concern on the part of Mannesmann that Vodafone AirTouch might have hired an investment bank to review the possibility of making an unsolicited bid for Mannesmann. Mr. Ginn confirmed, however, that no such appointment had been made and that Vodafone and AirTouch were satisfied with the existing partnership arrangements with Mannesmann.

On April 27, 1999, Mr. Gent telephoned Dr. Esser to arrange a meeting. On May 6, 1999, Mr. Gent and Mr. Horn-Smith met with Dr. Esser in Düsseldorf to discuss areas of mutual cooperation and operational synergies. The parties discussed further areas of mutual cooperation, including the potential for cross shareholding arrangements in light of Mannesmann's desire to enter the U.K. market, and the growth opportunities in data. These discussions were conceptual only and no steps were taken. The parties agreed to engage in further discussions.

On May 25, 1999, Mr. Horn-Smith and other executives of Vodafone met with Lars Berg, a member of the management board of Mannesmann, and other executives of Mannesmann to discuss further possible operational synergies. After this meeting, Mr. Horn-Smith had discussions with Mr. Kinzius regarding various matters concerning their partnership interests and commercial operations, including possible cooperation on the development of mobile Internet access technology.

On June 30, 1999, the merger between Vodafone and AirTouch was completed and, as a result, the new entity, called Vodafone AirTouch, formally became a partner with Mannesmann in D2, Omnitel Pronto ltalia and Arcor.

On September 8, 1999, Mr. Gent, Mr. Horn-Smith and Peter Bamford, an executive director of Vodafone AirTouch, met with Dr. Esser, Mr. Kinzius and Mr. Berg in England. The parties discussed possibilities for cooperation in making further investments in Europe and the development of mobile Internet access technology.

On October 18, 1999, Mr. Horn-Smith and Mr. Kinzius had a further conversation regarding future investments in Europe. On the following day, the press reported Mannesmann's interest in Orange pic, a competitor of Vodafone AirTouch in the U.K. wireless telecommunications market. Mr. Gent telephoned Dr. Esser to suggest trying to determine a more constructive route for the two companies to follow.

On Wednesday, October 20, 1999, Mr. Gent contacted Dr. Esser again after further media coverage reporting that Mannesmann had made a bid for Orange. In that telephone call, the parties agreed to meet in Berlin as an adjunct to a previously arranged social occasion to celebrate the tenth anniversary of D2 and Mannesmann's relationship with AirTouch, to discuss a more cooperative way to go forward. However, later that evening Dr. Esser phoned Mr. Gent to suggest that the meeting be canceled because he had already signed an agreement with Orange and its principal shareholder for Mannesmann to make a part-cash, part-share offer for all of the outstanding shares of Orange.

On Friday, October 22, 1999, Mr. Gent separately contacted Goldman Sachs International and Warburg Dillon Read to act as Vodafone AirTouch's financial advisors in connection with a potential acquisition of Mannesmann. Vodafone AirTouch subsequently engaged both of these financial advisors to assist it with an unsolicited bid.

Beginning on Monday, October 25, 1999, Mr. Gent, senior management of Vodafone AirTouch and Vodafone AirTouch's financial and legal advisors met at various times to discuss the viability of, and to formulate a strategy for, an all share exchange offer for all of the outstanding Mannesmann shares and to commence preparations for a possible transaction.

On Tuesday, November 9, 1999, the Vodafone AirTouch board met with its advisors and authorized management to continue to pursue a strategic transaction. The board also discussed a potential price range. On Friday, November 12, 1999, Dr. Esser telephoned Mr. Gent. Dr. Esser inquired about press speculation suggesting that Vodafone AirTouch was pursuing an offer for Mannesmann and invited Mr. Gent to a meeting in Düsseldorf. Mr. Gent agreed to attend a meeting to discuss constructive proposals for putting their businesses together.

Also on Friday, November 12, 1999, in response to an inquiry from the London Stock Exchange and press speculation regarding a possible offer for Mannesmann, Vodafone AirTouch issued a statement to the effect that the further development of Vodafone AirTouch's partnership with Mannesmann remained an important strategic priority, that Vodafone AirTouch was continuing to evaluate a broad range of opportunities to participate in the further consolidation of the global wireless markets, including possible ways to develop its existing long standing relationship with Mannesmann, but that it would only consider such opportunities that would add value for its shareholders and that no decisions had yet been taken with regard to any specific options.

On Sunday, November 14, 1999, Mr. Gent wrote a letter to Dr. Esser setting forth the strategic case for combining the two companies and various terms of the proposed offer. On the same day, Mr. Gent and Mr. Horn-Smith traveled to Mannesmann headquarters in Düsseldorf to meet with Dr. Esser and Mr. Kinzius to discuss the strategy and terms of the proposed offer. At this meeting, Dr. Esser rejected Mr. Gent's proposal. He commented, however, that if Mannesmann was ever to lose its independence, Vodafone AirTouch would be its natural partner/"white knight." Dr. Esser also stated that he would refuse to present the proposed offer to Mannesmann's supervisory board because he considered it to be inadequate. Mr. Gent left his letter with Dr. Esser. Following that meeting, Mannesmann issued a statement which referred to the Vodafone AirTouch proposal as wholly inadequate and not in the best interests of Mannesmann and its shareholders and which stated that Mannesmann did not consider a combination with Vodafone AirTouch strategically attractive.

On Monday, November 15, 1999, the Vodafone AirTouch board issued a statement noting with regret the decision of the Mannesmann management board announced earlier that evening.

Also on Monday, November 15, 1999, Dr. Esser sent a letter to Mr. Gent rejecting the proposed offer and attaching a copy of the press statement issued by Mannesmann on the prior day. On the same day, Mannesmann filed an application with the U.K. High Court for an injunction seeking to restrain Goldman Sachs International from acting on behalf of Vodafone AirTouch. In the application, Mannesmann argued that Goldman Sachs International had given an undertaking to Mannesmann not to act for any third party which might be contemplating an acquisition of Mannesmann and that Goldman Sachs International had a conflict of interest because of its involvement in previous matters affecting Mannesmann in which, Mannesmann argued, Goldman Sachs International had acquired confidential information.

Also on November 15, 1999, the Vodafone AirTouch board met to discuss how to respond to Mannesmann's rejection of its proposed offer.

On Tuesday, November 16, 1999, Mr. Gent sent a letter to certain members of the supervisory board of Mannesmann reinforcing the strategic rationale for the proposed offer.

Also on Tuesday, November 16, 1999, Vodafone AirTouch, in conjunction with an announcement of its results for the six months ended September 30, 1999, issued a press release which discussed the strategic and commercial rationale for Vodafone AirTouch's approach to Mannesmann regarding a merger of the two companies. The release stated that the transaction would be an all share exchange offer of Vodafone AirTouch ordinary shares for Mannesmann shares and ADSs and set forth the reasons for, and anticipated benefits of, the proposal. In the release, Mr. Gent stated that Vodafone AirTouch was disappointed with Mannesmann's reaction to the Vodafone AirTouch proposal.

Also on November 16, 1999, following a regularly scheduled meeting with analysts to discuss Vodafone AirTouch's results for the six months ended September 30, 1999, Vodafone AirTouch made a presentation to analysts regarding the proposed transaction. In the presentation, Vodafone AirTouch highlighted the strategic rationale and set forth the synergies that Vodafone AirTouch expects to realize from the transaction.

On Thursday, November 18, 1999, Dr. Esser sent a letter to Mr. Gent and Mr. Ginn requesting that Vodafone AirTouch stop its unsolicited approach to Mannesmann. On the same day, the U.K. High Court dismissed Mannesmann's application for an injunction to restrain Goldman Sachs International from advising Vodafone AirTouch, which it found was based on an affidavit which contained "totally false evidence of great importance." The Court concluded that the application was "completely hopeless," that it "must be dismissed" and "should never have been made."

Later on November 18, 1999, the Vodafone AirTouch board met and considered, together with Vodafone AirTouch's financial advisers, the continued rejection by the Mannesmann management board of Vodafone AirTouch's proposed offer and the management board's refusal to negotiate. At the meeting, Goldman Sachs and Warburg Dillon Read made financial presentations to the Vodafone AirTouch board regarding the proposed offer. The Vodafone AirTouch board considered and then approved the terms of a proposed offer to be made directly to the Mannesmann shareholders at an exchange ratio of 53.7 Vodafone AirTouch ordinary shares for each Mannesmann share and ADS.

On Friday, November 19, 1999, Mr. Gent sent a letter to Dr. Esser reiterating Vodafone AirTouch's desire to negotiate with Mannesmann, but stating that because Mannesmann refused to do so, Vodafone AirTouch was compelled to put a new proposal directly to Mannesmann shareholders. The proposed offer, as stated in the letter, would be 53.7 Vodafone AirTouch ordinary shares for each Mannesmann share and ADS. The letter stated that this offer was a final offer. The letter also emphasized that no redundancies would result from the transaction and that senior management would be offered important roles in the combined group. On the same day Vodafone AirTouch issued a press release announcing the proposed terms of the all share offer at an exchange ratio of 53.7 Vodafone AirTouch shares for each Mannesmann share and ADS and stating that Vodafone AirTouch continued to believe that a combination of the two companies has compelling logic and is in the best interests of shareholders of both Vodafone AirTouch and Mannesmann.

The Mannesmann supervisory board met later that day and considered Vodafone AirTouch's proposal. In a statement issued in the evening of Friday, November 19, 1999, Mannesmann management advised shareholders to reject the offer, stating that the proposal did not reflect the potential offered to Mannesmann shareholders by the combination of Mannesmann and Orange. The Mannesmann supervisory board said that it supported the decision of Mannesmann management, but that it would meet on Sunday, November 28, 1999 to consider further Vodafone AirTouch's proposed offer.

On Monday, November 22, 1999, Mannesmann's offer for Orange became wholly unconditional. On Tuesday, November 23, 1999, Mannesmann announced that it would significantly accelerate the separation and initial public offering of its engineering and automotive businesses, stating that the initial public offering would occur as soon as mid-2000 and that it had decided upon a separation procedure that would ensure that the proceeds from the sale would not be significantly impaired by taxation.

Also on November, 22, 1999, Mr. Ginn spoke with Dr. Funk by telephone with a view to arranging a direct meeting between Mr. Ginn and members of the supervisory board. On Tuesday, November 23, 1999, Mr. Ginn sent a letter to Dr. Funk expressing the disappointment of the Vodafone AirTouch board that a direct discussion with the supervisory board could not take place. Mr. Ginn reiterated the benefits of creating a joint company and urged Dr. Funk to explore ways to allow the combination to come together.

On Wednesday, November 24, 1999, Mr. Gent sent a letter to Mannesmol1n employees confirming Vodafone AirTouch's commitment to the Mannesmann employees, businesses and community.

On Friday, November 26, 1999, Mannesmann issued a press release denying speculation in the press about friendly negotiations between Mannesmann and Vodafone AirTouch.

On Sunday, November 28, 1999, Mannesmann issued a press release stating that the Mannesmann supervisory board unanimously supported the decision of the management board to oppose the possible takeover attempt by Vodafone AirTouch.

On Monday, November 29, 1999, Vodafone AirTouch issued a press release noting

Mannesmann's rejection of its offer, but reiterating Vodafone AirTouch's belief that a combination of the two companies would be in the best interests of shareholders of both companies.

Also, on Monday, November 29, 1999, at a conference in London, Mannesmann made a presentation to investors describing the basis for its opposition to Vodafone AirTouch's offer in which it forecast growth levels for Mannesmann for the years 2000 through 2003.

On Tuesday, November 30, 1999, Vodafone AirTouch issued a press release in response to Mannesmann's presentation to investors on November 29, stating that Vodafone AirTouch shared Mannesmann's confidence that voice, data and Internet telecommunications services would be strong drivers of growth.

In a press conference in Düsseldorf on Wednesday, December 8, 1999, Mannesmann again rejected the Vodafone AirTouch proposed offer on the grounds of valuation and strategy. Later that day, Vodafone AirTouch issued a press release in response noting Mannesmann's comments and stating its disappointment in the renewed rejection particularly given the positive reaction to its proposals that Vodafone AirTouch had received from many Mannesmann shareholders both in Germany and elsewhere. Vodafone AirTouch also expressed its surprise at the lack of justification for the increasing valuations Mannesmann was placing on itself. As of December 8, 1999, Mannesmann was valuing itself at over £350 per share whereas just six weeks earlier, Mannesmann had offered shares at around £157.8 per share in connection with its offer for Orange, less than half its new valuation. Finally, Vodafone AirTouch reiterated its belief that, because Vodafone AirTouch and Mannesmann are leading participants in the same industry and pursue similar strategies, the growth of both businesses would be accelerated if the businesses were combined.

On December 17, 1999, the Vodafone AirTouch board met with its financial and legal advisors to review the documentation and to authorize various actions in connection with the commencement of the offer.

On December 23, 1999, Vodafone formally launched its hostile bid for Mannesmann. The deal valued Mannesmann at 260 euros per share or $132 billion. Vodafone also filed with the U.S. Securities Exchange Commission in order to be sure that the estimated 25% of Mannesmann held by American individuals and institutions would count in a possible proxy fight.

On January 10, 2000, Mannesmann CEO, Esser, confirmed that he had met with Vivendi's CEO, Messier. However, Esser denied that Mannesmann would seek any kind of white knight, asserting that the company was well positioned as an independent firm.

On January 19, 2000, with the Vodafone bid looming, Vodafone announced that it would be willing to increase its offer price if the deal were to become friendly.

On January 28, 2000, Mannesmann announced that it had begun talks with AOL Europe.

On January 30, 2000, Vodafone and Vivendi announced a broad Internet venture. Central to the deal was the establishment of an Internet portal between the two companies. This venture became known as Vizzavi. It is projected to combine some of Vivendi's content properties with Vodafone's potentially large subscriber base of Internet devices. In addition, Vodafone agreed to give Vivendi half of Mannesmann's 15% share (assuming Vodafone would win Mannesmann) of the French fixed-line firm, Cegetel. Also, Vodafone agreed to take no stake in Vivendi for three years without approval of Vivendi's management. Some critics of this deal said that Vodafone in essence gave "three gifts" to Vivendi.

On February 1 and 2, 2000, Vodafone and Mannesmann managers engaged in extensive negotiations regarding a possible friendly deal.

On February 3, 2000, Vodafone and Mannesmann announced that they had reached a friendly deal. Vodafone agreed to pay 353 euros per share for Mannesmann. This valued Mannesmann at about $180 billion. Vodafone's offer had increased by almost 75% from its initial offer on November 14 for 203 euros per share.

On the same day that the Mannesmann board approved the deal, they voted for a $16 million "appreciation award" for Esser, the CEO. This was seen as a sort of golden parachute to reward him for maximizing shareholder value. Golden parachutes were extremely rare in Europe, so the award gained considerable notice. However, many contrasted the award with the compensation of Airtouch's CEO, Sam Ginn, who received in the neighborhood of $150 million in options and other benefits.

Vodafone had faced some criticism for being overagressive in its pursuit of Mannesmann. Vodafone and observers were aware that the company would be forced to spin off Mannesmann's recently acquired Orange division. After regulators mandated it, an arrangement was reached to sell Orange to France Telecom. Vodafone also made what had seemed to be a foolish decision by launching the bid without the help of a German bank. Deutsche Bank was one of Mannesmann's large shareholders and was therefore unable to work for Vodafone. Vodafone was not able to find another suitable bank that was willing to launch the largest hostile bid in history.

Mannesmann's defensive strategy also came under criticism. Although the firm's shareholders gained significantly by the resistance, critics found many missteps. Shortly after Vodafone's initial bid, Mannesmann give a presentation for analysts. The analysts were very disappointed, saying that they were bored for four hours. Mannesmann elected to use a strategy of pointing out its strengths and stating that its true value was far above Vodafone's bid. This helped to increase Mannesmann's share price, but as a side effect, it also helped Vodafone by showing Vodafone's investors the value of the company that was being pursued. Such information helped to keep Vodafone's share price strong. And since it was offering all stock to Mannesmann, the offer price remained high.

Mannesmann also had to deal with added complications. It was somewhat vulnerable to a hostile bid because it was estimated to be only 30 to 35% held by German investors. About 25% was estimated to be held in the U.S., and a significant portion of the remainder was held by British shareholders following the Orange transaction.

Vodafone management essentially conceded that the German investors would vote for management. However, the company campaigned strongly for the rest of the votes.

QUESTIONS

1. How did the Airtouch deal lead Vodafone to both the Verizon and Mannesmann deals?
2. What were the advantages and disadvantages to Bell Atlantic and Vodafone of the Verizon deal?
3. What logic was there for the timing of Vodafone's bid for Mannesmann?
4. Why was Vodafone willing to give Vivendi "three gifts"?
5. How did international considerations complicate these deals?

Case 23

Tribune/Times Mirror

BACKGROUND ON TIMES MIRROR

The *Los Angeles Times* has been an institution in Southern California for over 100 years. The Chandler and Otis families have controlled the paper for virtually its entire existence. The *L. A. Times* was a booster for civic growth in Los Angeles in the late 19th and early 20th centuries, and the Chandler family made millions of dollars on the resulting real estate boom. However, by the mid 1900s, the Chandler interests in the newspaper had been tied up in trusts that controlled the Times Mirror Company, the parent of the *L. A. Times*. The influence of the Chandlers through the trusts would continue to shape the course of the company.

In 1962, Otis Chandler, the great-grandson of the founder of the *Times* took over as the publisher of the newspaper. He changed the paper from being a conservative paper that espoused the views of the Chandler family to a paper recognized for the quality and independence of its reporting. When Otis Chandler stepped down from the chairmanship of the company in the mid 1980s, it marked the end of direct control over the paper for any Chandler family member. However, the Chandlers would maintain control over Times Mirror through the stock ownership of their trusts.

Because it was difficult for the family to sell its shares of Times Mirror due to the structure of the trusts, the value of the shares was of limited interest to the Chandler family. Instead, the family put pressure on management to maintain a high level of dividend payment. Robert Erburu took over as CEO of the company following Otis Chandler's retirement. Erburu continued Chandler's strategy of expanding operations by acquiring other newspapers. Times Mirror also expanded into other businesses, including television, newsprint, forest products, and book and magazine publishing. Meanwhile, operating income and operating margins reached a peak around 1987 before a sharp decline. During the early 1990s, Times Mirror lagged considerably behind its newspaper industry peers in virtually all operating measures.

The decline of Times Mirror's operating income put pressure on Erburu and Times Mirror management to find a source of cash to continue funding dividends. The pressure of dividend-seeking shareholders forced the management to sell off certain units. The firm sold many properties it had acquired during its previous expansion, calling into question its strategic decisions. The *Denver Post* was sold at a loss in 1987 (for notes on which the buyer defaulted) seven years after being acquired. A group of magazines, including *Broadcasting*, was sold in 1991 for $32 million after being acquired for $75 million in 1986. In 1993, Times Mirror sold four television stations for $320 million. The buyer subsequently resold them a year later for $717 million. This deal in particular raised the ire of shareholders, particularly the Chandlers.

However, the deal that probably resulted in a change of management was the sale of Times Mirror's cable television division. In June 1994, Times Mirror agreed to sell its cable business to Cox Enterprises for $2.3 billion. Times Mirror would receive $1.36 billion cash. Times Mirror shareholders besides the Chandlers would receive stock in the new Cox Cable stock. Meanwhile, the Chandlers would get a new class of Times Mirror preferred stock that would pay immediate dividends. Times Mirror also announced plans to cut its common stock dividend.

The market had a negative reaction to the deal. The initial announcement of the deal caused an increase of 11.7% in Times Mirror stock. However, management announced later that it would use the money to invest in new technology and would not maintain the same level of dividends. This realization in the markets caused the stock to fall back to virtually the same levels as before the cable deal was announced.

Furthermore, within days a suit had been filed by Times Mirror's minority shareholders objecting to the favoritism shown to the Chandlers. The Chandlers did not suffer a reduction in dividends, and were allowed to participate in the negotiation of the deal. The minority shareholders had insufficient power to block the deal. Litigation was settled by Times Mirror's agreement to offer an exchange of common stock for dividend-paying preferred stock. However, the controversy was a black eye for the publicity-shy Chandler family, which was seen as protecting its own financial interests at the expense of the minority shareholders and the firm.

The CEO succession process became the board's means of expressing its displeasure with management. The search for a successor to Erburu was initially an internal process. It appeared that one of the executives within Times Mirror would take over the CEO position. However, in June 1994, about the same time as the cable divestiture, the board decided to consider outside candidates. This can be seen as a rejection of the strategy of the old management.

The new CEO, Mark Willes, was announced in May 1995. Willes was known as a disciplined cost cutter. He presided over further streamlining of the Times Mirror operations. Times Mirror closed the unprofitable *Baltimore Evening Sun* and *New York Newsday*. Even the *L. A. Times* underwent its largest layoff ever, removing over 300 people. Moves such as these helped bring operating margins more in line with other firms in the newspaper industry.

Times Mirror stock performed well under Willes. The stock increased 4.1% when Willes was announced to be the new CEO, and 11.9% when Willes made it clear he would close unprofitable papers. Similar positive returns resulted from the closure of the unprofitable papers. Willes also began a stock repurchase plan, which further aided Times Mirrors stock price. This plan was unpopular with the Chandlers, who preferred to see free cash flows distributed as dividends. Because they could not freely sell their stock, the family did not share in the benefits of the repurchase plan.

Willes drew criticism from many people for his push to bring the business and reporting portions of the paper closer together. Such a structure was questioned as a betrayal of journalism's need for clear independence. The incident that drew the most fire was the decision of Times Mirror to run a section in the *L. A. Times* in connection with the new Staples Center arena. Times Mirror and Staples Center shared in the profits from the section, but the arrangement was not disclosed. The incident alienated many reporters, and Otis Chandler made a rare public comment criticizing the decision.

Despite the improvements in Times Mirror that Willes achieved, he was essentially fired when Times Mirror agreed to merge with Tribune Company. The deal was largely negotiated directly between Tribune and the Chandlers, leaving Willes out of the negotiations. It had been widely believed that under the terms of the Chandler trust the family would not be able to sell the paper. In early 1999, Willes had refused to listen to any offers from Tribune, believing that a deal was impossible. However, upon closer inspection following Tribune's first expression of interest, it was revealed that the family needed to maintain only some control over the *Los Angeles Times*. In early 2000, when Tribune decided to pursue Times Mirror again, it decided to bypass the CEO, going directly to the Chandlers. The conditions of the trust were met by the structure of the deal, giving the Chandlers about 10% of Tribune stock, and the power to fill multiple board seats on a newly created sub-board for the *Los Angeles Times*.

THE DEAL WITH TRIBUNE

On March 13, 2000, Tribune Company and Times Mirror Company announced plans to merge. The deal would combine two of the leading newspaper companies. Tribune had its roots in the *Chicago Tribune*, which was founded in the mid 19th century. In more recent years, it had expanded to become a "media" company, owning the Chicago Cubs, numerous television broadcasting stations, and some radio stations.

CHARACTERISTICS OF THE NEWSPAPER INDUSTRY

The newspaper industry has been undergoing many significant changes. The technological impact of the Internet is perhaps the most important. Many believe it is the most ominous for the outlook of the industry. The Internet has the potential to replace print media. As fewer people read newspapers due to the attraction of the Internet, advertising revenues will be reduced. Some analysts believe that the advertising revenue of newspapers will be moved to the Internet, leaving papers in a relatively unprofitable position. Some newspaper people say that the market for classifieds has "softened" already due to the competition of the Internet. Many alliances among newspapers have sought to establish online help wanted and other classified Web sites, but these alternatives still offer lower margins than traditional classifieds.

However, some analysts feel that newspapers have the capabilities to keep up with the changes being wrought by the Internet. Tribune and Times Mirror have two of the most visited regional web sites. This illustrates that newspapers remain an important source of cutting edge local and regional information. Newspapers are one of the few media outlets with sufficient news gathering resources to provide a viable amount of coverage. Websites such as Yahoo may provide news, but they lack the resources to give readers fully localized coverage. Becoming leaders on the Internet also could potentially allow newspapers to cut out the costs of circulation. Roughly 40% of the cost of running a newspaper comes from the cost of materials (paper and ink) and the cost of delivery. By eliminating such costs, newspapers potentially can gain efficiency in the future as primarily Internet companies.

Despite the uncertain challenges of the Internet, the newspaper industry has been undergoing a wave of consolidation. The trend is for companies to own collections of either large metropolitan papers, or smaller community papers centered in specific regions. The *New York Times* has decided to sell seven of its smaller papers in order to concentrate on larger newspapers. Firms like Gannet Co. and Lee Enterprises Inc. have assembled collections of smaller papers. These firms hope to buy many papers in the same geographical area in order to benefit by combining certain aspects of operations. In addition, other firms like Thomson have decided to shift away from newspapers toward electronic information. Merger activity has increased as many firms seek to implement these varied strategies.

Background of the Merger

On April 25, 1999, John Madigan, Chairman, President and Chief Executive Officer of Tribune, met with Mark Willes, Chairman of the Board, President and Chief Executive Officer of Times Mirror. At this meeting, Mr. Madigan proposed to Mr. Willes the possibility of a business combination between Tribune and Times Mirror. At the end of the meeting, Mr. Willes requested more detailed information about the proposal.

On May 27, 1999, Mr. Madigan sent a letter to Mr. Willes describing Tribune's view of the strategic benefits of the proposed combination. On June 8, 1999, Mr. Willes called Mr. Madigan to request financial projections supporting the benefits of the combination. Mr. Madigan responded to Mr. Willes' request with a letter dated June 9, 1999, which contained pro forma projections for the combination. These projections were based on a merger between Tribune and Times Mirror in which 50% of the consideration would be paid in Tribune common stock and 50% of the consideration would be paid in cash, at a price of $82.50 per share.

Mr. Willes replied with a letter to Mr. Madigan dated June 17, 1999. Mr. Willes' letter requested that correspondence regarding a business combination between Tribune and Times Mirror cease, citing the perceived inability of the Chandler Trust to be able to agree to this type of transaction, but expressed interest in a possible joint venture between Tribune's Los Angeles television station and Times Mirror's Los Angeles newspaper. On June 21, 1999, Mr. Madigan and Mr. Willes discussed by telephone the possibility of a Los Angeles television/newspaper joint venture.

On July 1, 1999, Mr. Willes sent Mr. Madigan a letter stating that, after consulting with his associates, Times Mirror would decline Tribune's offer to explore the possible joint venture. On July 15, 1999, Mr. Madigan responded with a letter to Mr. Willes stating that he regretted Mr. Willes' decision to abandon the discussions. There were no further discussions between Tribune and Times Mirror on the subject of a business combination until November 1999.

On November 9, 1999, Jack Fuller, President of Tribune Publishing, und Thomas Untermun, then Chief Financial Officer of Times Mirror and the Manager of Rustic Canyon Partners, LLC, the general partner of TMCT Ventures, which is a venture capital fund in which the Chandler Trusts have an 80% interest, met at a regularly scheduled meeting of the board of another company on which they both serve. During a break in the meeting, the participants engaged in a general discussion of issues regarding Times Mirror. At the end of the break, Messrs. Fuller and Unterman had a brief discussion regarding whether a transaction between Times Mirror and Tribune could be feasible for the Chandler Trusts. Mr. Unterman said he would be in Chicago over Thanksgiving and might be available then to talk.

On November 11, 1999, Mr. Fuller spoke with Mr. Unterman by telephone to arrange a meeting with Mr. Unterman on November 27. On November 27, 1999, Messrs. Madigan and Fuller met with Mr. Unterman and told him that Tribune would be interested in exploring the possibility of a combination. Mr. Unterman explained his understanding of certain transaction parameters resulting from certain requirements of the Chandler Trusts that might affect the ability of the Chandler Trusts to engage in such a transaction, At the end of this meeting, a meeting between Messrs, Madigan and Fuller and representatives of the Chandler Trusts was suggested.

On January 5, 2000, Messrs. Madigan and Fuller met with representatives of the Chandler Trusts to discuss the possibility of a business combination between Tribune and Times Mirror. At the conclusion or this meeting, it was agreed that discussions should continue and that representatives of the Chandler Trusts would visit Tribune management in Chicago in February. On Fehruary 9, 2000, members or Tribune's senior management made a presentation to representatives of the Chandler Trusts regarding the strategic and financial rationale supporting a transaction between the companies.

On February 14, 2000, Tribune's board of directors met at a regularly scheduled meeting and discussed the possible combination. The Tribune board authorized continued discussions with the Chandler Trusts and discussions with Times Mirror. Thereafter, representatives of Tribune and representatives of the Chandler Trust continued their discussions. This included discussion of the structure of the proposed transaction because of the desire of the Chandler Trusts to engage in a tax-free transaction and discussion of possible participation in governance by some persons associated with the Chandler Trusts. The governance participation discussed was with respect to the Tribune board of directors and a separate board that would be created to oversee the *Los Angeles Times*.

On February 29, 2000, representatives of the Chandler Trusts met with Mr. Willes to inform him of their intention to pursue a transaction with Tribune and to propose that the Times Mirror board of directors approve such a transaction. Times Mirror contacted Goldman, Sachs & Co. and engaged Goldman, Sachs & Co. as its financial advisor in connection with the possible sale of all or a portion of Times Mirror.

On March 1, 2000, representatives of the Chandler Trusts met with members of the senior management of Times Mirror and representatives from Times Mirror's regular outside corporate counsel, Gibson, Dunn & Crutcher LLP, and Goldman, Sachs & Co., to describe the status of the discussions between the Chandler Trusts and Tribune, the requirements of the Chandler Trusts in order to proceed with a transaction and their interest in addressing the Times Mirror board of directors on the transaction and in moving forward with a transaction promptly. Representatives of the Chandler Trusts indicated that they expected that Times Mirror would receive a proposal from Tribune shortly, possibly as early as March 3, 2000, following a scheduled meeting of the Tribune board of directors.

On March 2, 2000, during an executive session of a regularly scheduled meeting of the Times Mirror board of directors, Mr. Willes advised the non-Chandler Trusts members of the Times Mirror board of the status of developments and Gibson, Dunn & Crutcher LLP and Times Mirror's financial advisors addressed various aspects of the proposed transaction. The directors approved the retention of Goldman, Sachs & Co. as Times Mirror's financial advisor with respect to the proposed transaction, and decided to retain Skadden, Arps, Slate, Meagher & Flom LLP as special counsel to the non-Chandler Trusts members of the Times Mirror board of directors, with Gibson, Dunn & Crutcher LLP continuing to represent Times Mirror. The Chandler Trusts directors and the legal advisors (Munger, Tolles & Olson LLP) and financial advisors (Morgan Stanley & Co., Incorporated) to the Chandler Trusts then joined the meeting and made a presentation regarding the background of their discussions with Tribune, the specific requirements of a transaction that were necessary for the Chandler Trusts to proceed, the strategic advantages of a combination with Tribune and the desire of the Chandler Trusts to move forward with a transaction. The representatives of the Chandler Trusts indicated that there had been no detailed discussions about price.

On March 3, 2000, the Tribune board or directors met and approved an offer to acquire Times Mirror through a merger at $90 per share of Times Mirror common stock, on the terms described below, subject to the offer not being disclosed to the public or any third party. Mr. Madigan then sent a letter to the Times Mirror board of directors and the Trustees of the Chandler Trusts setting forth Tribune's offer. The offer provided for a 50% cash/50% stock election merger, at a price of $90 in cash per share of Times Mirror common stock or its equivalent in Tribune common stock. The offer also contemplated participation in governance by some persons associated with the Chandler Trusts, both with respect to the Tribune board and a separate *Los Angeles Times* board. The offer was conditioned on the agreement of the Chandler Trusts to commit to vote all of their shares of Times Mirror common stock in favor of the proposed merger and against any competing transactions, and on the merger agreement not being terminable if a competing proposal was made to Times Mirror unless the stockholders of Times Mirror failed to approve the transaction at a meeting of such stockholders.

On March 6, 2000, counsel for Tribune provided Gibson, Dunn & Crutcher LLP, Skadden, Arps, Slate, Meagher & Flom LLP and counsel for the Chandler Trusts with a proposed form of merger agreement and voting agreement reflecting the terms or Tribune's offer. On March 8, 2000, the non-Chandler Trusts members of the Times Mirror board of directors convened with their financial and legal advisors to review the Tribune offer. Representatives of Skadden, Arps, Slate, Meagher & Flom LLP reviewed with the directors their duties in the context of the proposal as well as the impact of the provision of Times Mirror's restated certificate of incorporation that would permit the directors in their sole discretion in connection with their approval of a merger to convert shares of the high voting Times Mirror series C common stock (including those held by the Chandler Trusts) to shares of low voting Times Mirror series A common stock. Goldman, Sachs & Co reviewed Times Mirror's current and projected financial performance, Tribune's business, strategy, financial performance and reputation in the market, and various valuation models for Times Mirror and other newspaper acquisitions which had been recently completed. Goldman, Sachs & Co. also addressed the potential interest of other acquirors. After an extended discussion, these directors directed their advisors to indicate to Tribune and the Chandler Trusts that the price of $90 per share of Times Mirror common stock was too low and would need to be increased before Times Mirror was prepared to pursue a transaction with Tribune. These directors further indicated that they had significant reservations about the scope or the voting agreement required by Tribune, particularly in light of the Times Mirror restated certificate of incorporation provisions permitting the conversion of the shares of Times Mirror series C common stock into shares of Times Mirror series A common stock in certain circumstances.

On March 9, 2000, representatives of Times Mirror met with representatives of the Chandler Trusts and reviewed the Times Mirror board's reaction to the proposal, the need for an increased price and the board's resistance to the scope of the voting agreement. In the course or those discussions, the Times Mirror restated certificate of incorporation provision providing for conversion of the shares of Times Mirror series C common stock was discussed. The representatives of the Chandler Trusts forcefully objected to the non-Chandler Trusts directors' view of the availability of that provision, indicating their belief that any conversion pursuant to such provision was intended to be effective only upon consummation of a transaction and not in advance of such consummation, and stated that any attempt to utilize the provision would be litigated by the Chandler Trusts. The parties discussed possible alternative structures for the transaction that might ensure that the public stockholders were treated at least as favorably as the Chandler Trusts and would permit another potential acquiror to make a competing proposal.

On March 10, 2000, representatives of Tribune, Times Mirror and the Chandler Trusts met to discuss the terms of the proposed merger and to commence management interviews and due diligence. The representatives of Times Mirror told the representatives of Tribune that, while the Times Mirror board of directors had not yet authorized any transaction, they believed that any transaction would need to be at a higher price than $90 per share of Times Mirror common stock, and with a structure that would ensure that the public stockholders had the opportunity to receive all stock for their shares of Times Mirror common stock if they so desired. The Times Mirror representatives also suggested the possibility of a cash tender offer as a first step in a two-step acquisition, in order to allow Times Mirror stockholders the opportunity to receive cash for their shares of Times Mirror common stock significantly earlier than they would in a one-step merger. The representatives of the Chandler Trusts told the Tribune representatives that the Chandler Trusts agreed with the foregoing Times Mirror position and further required a structure that would guarantee that the Chandler Trusts could elect to receive all stock in the transaction. Finally, the Times Mirror representatives also objected to Tribune's requirement that the Chandler Trusts enter into a proposed voting agreement unconditionally obligating them to vote their shares of Times Mirror common stock, representing approximately 67% of the Times Mirror voting power, in favor of the merger.

On March 11, 2000, the Tribune board of directors met to approve increasing the price of the cash portion of its offer to $92.50 per share of Times Mirror common stock (leaving the stock portion at $90 per share or Times Mirror common stock), to provide for a tender offer preceding the merger for up to 28 million shares of Times Mirror common stock, and to provide for an unlimited stock election in the merger, subject to the Chandler Trusts entering into a voting agreement requiring the Chandler Trusts to vote their shares of Times Mirror series C common stock in favor of the merger at their full voting power. Following this meeting, representatives of Tribune informed representatives of Times Mirror and of the Chandler Trusts of these revisions to Tribune's proposal.

In the afternoon of March 11, the non-Chandler Trust members of the Times Mirror board met with their legal and financial advisors to consider the status of the discussions with representatives of Tribune and the Chandler Trusts as well as the terms of the revised proposal from Tribune. Representatives from Goldman, Sachs & Co. and Skadden, Arps, Slate, Meagher & Flom LLP advised these directors that, while the revised Tribune proposal now provided all Times Mirror stockholders who desired to receive all Tribune common stock for their shares of Times Mirror common stock with the opportunity to do so, the proposal still did not permit termination of the merger agreement by Times Mirror in the event of a proposal from a third party and continued to be conditioned upon the Chandler Trusts entering into a voting agreement at the time of execution of any merger agreement requiring the Chandler Trusts to vote their shares of Times Mirror series C common stock at their full voting power in favor of the merger, thus assuring stockholder approval of the transaction proposed by Tribune. The advisors also conveyed to these directors the views of the representatives of the Chandler Trusts that the Times Mirror board did not have the right to convert the shares of Times Mirror series C common stock into shares of Times Mirror series A common stock in a manner that would prevent the shares of Times Mirror series C common stock from voting on the proposed merger at their full voting power, and that any attempt to do so would be vigorously resisted by the Chandler Trusts. At the end of the meeting, these directors instructed their advisors to continue to seek to improve the economic terms of the proposed transaction and to seek to modify the terms of the voting agreement.

The directors who are associated with the Chandler Trusts then joined the meeting and the full Times Mirror board reviewed and approved various actions taken by the Executive Compensation Subcommittee of the Compensation Committee on March 2, 2000 with respect to severance and other employee benefits upon a change of control of Times Mirror. Following that portion of the meeting, Mr. Madigan and other Tribune executives made a presentation to the full Times Mirror board of directors, joined by certain trustees of the Chandler Trusts, regarding the financial performance and future prospects of Tribune and the perceived benefits of the Tribune-Times Mirror combination.

In the evening of March 11, representatives of Times Mirror and representatives of the Chandler Trusts informed the Tribune representatives that Times Mirror and the Chandler Trusts would be willing to agree to a transaction at $95 in cash per share of Times Mirror common stock for up to 28 million shares of Times Mirror common stock and an exchange ratio of 2.5 shares of Tribune common stock for each share of Times Mirror common stock that did not elect cash (representing a value of $93 in Tribune common stock for each share of Times Mirror common stock electing Tribune common stock based on the closing price of the Tribune common stock on March 10, 2000). The representatives of Times Mirror and of the Chandler Trusts also said that they would agree to the proposed voting agreement; provided, however, that, in the event a third party were to submit a competing bid prior to completion of the Tribune tender offer that caused the Times Mirror board to change its recommendation, the Chandler Trusts' commitment to vote in favor of the transactions with Tribune would apply only to 28% of the total voting power of Times Mirror, with the remaining shares of Times Mirror common stock held by the Chandler Trusts voted in proportion to the vote of the shares of Times Minor common stock not held by the Chandler Trusts. The representatives of Tribune informed the Times Mirror representatives and the Chandler Trusts' representatives that they would be willing to recommend that the Tribune board approve these economic terms, but only if the Chandler Trusts agreed unconditionally to vote all of their shares of Times Mirror common stock in favor of the transaction and the board did not take any action to convert the shares of Times Mirror series C common stock into shares of Times Mirror series A common stock. Tribune also indicated that its proposal, by its terms, would expire on March 13 if it was not accepted by that time.

On March 12, 2000, counsel for Tribune met with Skadden, Arps, Slate, Meagher & Flom LLP to discuss possible means of resolving the parties' disagreement with respect to the terms of the voting agreement with the Chandler Trusts. Following these meetings, the Tribune representatives informed the Times Mirror representatives and the Chandler Trusts' representatives that they would be willing to recommend to the Tribune board that it approve a voting agreement providing that the Chandler Trusts' vote in favor of the transaction with Tribune would be reduced to 40% of the total voting power of Times Minor (with the remaining shares of Times Mirror common stock held by the Chandler Trusts voted in proportion to the vote of the shares of Times Mirror common stock not held by the Chandler Trusts) in the event a competing offer were made that caused the Times Mirror board to change its recommendation of the Tribune offer within 20 days of the announcement of the execution of the merger agreement, but only in the event that the exchange ratio was 2.35 shares of Tribune common stock for each share or Times Mirror common stock that did not elect cash. The representatives of Times Mirror responded that, based upon the overall terms of the proposed transaction, they would be willing to support these terms in their presentation to the Times Mirror board if the exchange ratio remained at the previously proposed 2.5. The representatives of Times Mirror and of the Chandler Trusts also provided the Tribune representatives with their other comments on the proposed forms of merger agreement and voting agreement.

In the evening of March 12, 2000, the board of directors of Tribune met, approved the revisions to the Tribune proposal described above, but with an exchange ratio of 2.5, authorized Tribune to enter into the merger agreement and the voting agreement on these terms, and resolved to recommend approval of the transaction to Tribune stockholders. Following the meeting of the Tribune board of directors, the board of directors of Times Mirror met, and after reviewing all aspects of the proposed transaction, approved the transaction on these revised terms, authorized Times Mirror to enter into the merger agreement and resolved to recommend approval of the transaction to Times Mirror stockholders. On March 13, 2000, following finalization of the merger agreement and the voting agreement on these terms, Tribune and Times Mirror executed the merger agreement, and Tribune, the Chandler Trusts and the other parties to the voting agreement executed the voting agreement.

On March 21, 2000, Tribune commenced a tender offer for up to 28 million shares of Times Mirror common stock. Pursuant to the tender offer, Tribune purchased 23,148,044 shares of Times Mirror common stock, or approximately 40% of the outstanding shares of Times Mirror common stock, at the price of $95 net, in cash, per share of Times Mirror common stock. The tender offer was completed as of midnight on April 17, 2000.

Recommendation of the Tribune Board and Tribune's Reasons for the Merger

On March 3, March 11 and March 12, 2000, the Tribune board of directors met to review and evaluate the terms of a potential transaction with Times Mirror. On March 12, the Tribune board of directors unanimously determined that it is advisable, consistent with, in furtherance of, and otherwise in the best interests of Tribune and its stockholders for Tribune to acquire up to 50% of the outstanding shares of Times Mirror common stock in a tender offer for $95 per share in cash followed by a merger of Times Mirror with and into Tribune in which each of the remaining outstanding shares of Times Mirror common stock would be converted into the right to receive either 2.5 shares of Tribune common stock or, to the extent available, $95 in cash. In reaching its decision regarding the transaction with Times Mirror, the Tribune board of directors considered, among other things:

- financial and strategic factors in connection with such a transaction;
- the results of its due diligence analysis;

- the analysis of Tribune management and Merrill Lynch of the financial information of Times Mirror, Tribune and the combined company, which included financial forecasts provided by Tribune relating to the earnings, cash flow, assets, liabilities and prospects of Tribune and Times Mirror, as well as the amount and timing of the cost savings and related expenses and synergies expected to result from the transaction;

- legal considerations for the Tribune board of directors in applying its fiduciary responsibilities to the proposed transaction;

- the terms and conditions of the merger agreement and the voting agreement; and

- the support of the Chandler Trusts for the proposed transaction and their willingness to enter into the voting agreement.

Moreover, the board of directors considered its view of or belief in each of the following factors:

- Following completion of the merger, Tribune will have 11 daily newspapers, 22 television stations and four radio stations. The combined company will be one of the largest providers of interactive news and information services in the U.S. and the largest multi-media company in four of the nation's five most populous states—California, New York, Illinois and Florida.

- Led by top interactive sites in New York, Los Angeles and Chicago, the merger will create an Internet company with approximately $55 million in projected 2000 revenue and an estimated 3.4 million unique monthly visitors. This will place the combined company in the top 20 ranking for news/information/entertainment interactive services.

- The combined company's Internet assets will provide marketers with a powerful network that reaches a national audience and delivers deep local market impact. The scale will enable Tribune to bring powerful news and information services to its markets, as well as world-class technology. The combined multi-media newsgathering resources and technology assets will allow the combined company to deliver compelling broadband news, advertising and information choices to consumers in the future.

- The merger will enable Tribune to provide a compelling set of marketing solutions in top metro newspaper markets and increase revenue from the rapidly expanding national advertising category, including national retailers.

- The merger will bring together a worldwide newsgathering organization of extraordinary quality, scope and depth, providing the public in the communities served with news and opinion that is both diverse and comprehensive. The combined company will have an expanded presence in foreign bureaus and Washington, D.C., and increased national coverage from other bureaus around the U.S.

- The combined company will provide opportunities for advertisers to reach major market consumers in any media form—broadcast, newspapers or interactive services. In addition, the combined company will benefit consumers by giving them rich and diverse choices for obtaining news, information and entertainment.

- The combined company can achieve significant cost savings related to the consolidation of Internet operations, back office efficiencies and newsprint purchasing and Times Mirror's newspaper margins can move closer to Tribune's higher margins.

- Times Mirror is one of only a few very large, profitable, quality news and information companies in the country. Its reputation for quality and integrity complements that of Tribune. Consequently, Tribune management believes that there is a strong cultural fit between the two institutions. The combined company has won 82 Pulitzer Prizes.

In addition, the board received a report from Merrill Lynch, including its written opinion to the effect that, as of the date of the opinion and based upon and subject to the factors and assumptions set forth therein, the consideration into which each outstanding share of Times Mirror common stock would be converted in the tender offer and the merger, taken together and not separately, was fair from a financial point of view to Tribune. A copy of Merrill Lynch's written opinion, dated March 12, 2000, which sets forth the procedures followed, the matters reviewed and the assumptions made by Merrill Lynch, is attached as Annex D to this proxy statement/prospectus, and is incorporated herein by reference. Tribune's stockholders are urged to read Merrill Lynch's opinion in its entirety. See "The Merger—Opinion of Tribune's Financial Advisor."

The foregoing discussion of the information and factors considered and given weight by the Tribune board of directors is not intended to be exhaustive. In view of the variety of factors considered in connection with its evaluation and approval of the tender offer, the merger, the merger agreement and the transactions contemplated thereby, the Tribune board did not find it practicable to, and did not, quantify or otherwise assign relative weights to the specific factors considered in reaching its determination. In addition, individual members of the Tribune board may have assigned different weights to different factors.

Recommendation of the Times Mirror Board and Times Mirror's Reasons for the Merger

On March 12, 2000, the Times Mirror board of directors unanimously:

- determined that the merger agreement and the transactions contemplated thereby, including the tender offer and the merger, are advisable, fair to, and in the best interests of the stockholders of Times Mirror;

- approved and adopted the merger agreement, the tender offer, the merger and the other transactions contemplated thereby; and

- recommended that the holders of shares of Times Mirror common stock who desire cash consideration for their shares of Times Mirror common stock accept the tender offer and tender their shares of Times Mirror common stock pursuant to the tender offer, and approve and adopt the merger agreement and the transactions contemplated thereby.

In making its determination and recommendation with respect to the transaction with Tribune, the Times Mirror board of directors considered a number of factors, including, without limitation, the factors mentioned in the section entitled "Background of the Merger" above and the following:

- The financial and other terms of the tender offer, the merger, the merger agreement and the related transaction agreements.

- The historical and recent market prices for the shares of Times Mirror common stock, and that the $95 per share cash consideration to be paid in the tender offer and the 2.5 shares of Tribune common stock to be exchanged in the merger, on a blended basis, represented a significant premium of approximately 100% over the closing price on the New York Stock Exchange of the Times Mirror series A common stock ($47.94) on the last trading day prior to the announcement of the execution of the merger agreement.

- The oral opinion of Goldman, Sachs & Co. received by the Times Mirror board of directors on March 12, 2000, which was subsequently confirmed by its written opinion, that as of the date of the opinion, the stock consideration and cash consideration to be received by the holders of Times Mirror common stock in the aggregate is fair from a financial point of view to the holders of shares of Times Mirror common stock receiving such consideration. A copy of Goldman Sachs & Co.'s written opinion, dated March 13, 2000, which sets forth the procedures followed, the matters reviewed and the assumptions made by Goldman Sachs & Co., is attached as Annex E to this proxy statement/prospectus, and is incorporated herein by reference. Times Mirror's stockholders are urged to read Goldman, Sachs & Co.'s opinion in its entirety.

- The terms and conditions of the merger agreement and the tender offer and, in particular, the structure of the transaction providing Times Mirror stockholders with the option of receiving (i) cash for their shares of Times Mirror common stock pursuant to the tender offer, subject to certain conditions, (ii) shares of Tribune common stock on a tax-free basis or (iii) a combination of cash and shares of Tribune common stock.

- The fact that the Times Mirror stockholders will have the opportunity to hold equity in Tribune, a corporation with significant and diverse businesses and moreover, that stockholders electing to receive shares of Tribune common stock will continue to have the opportunity to obtain a control premium in a future transaction involving Tribune.

- The fact that Tribune's editorial independence and journalism quality is consistent with Times Mirror's traditions and integrity in the media field.

- The fact that the Chandler Trusts, who are parties to the voting agreement and hold approximately 32% of the outstanding shares of Times Mirror common stock (including their interests in TMCT, LLC and TMCT II, LLC) and control approximately 67% of the voting power of Times Mirror, were in favor of the merger, the tender offer and the transactions contemplated thereby.

- The high likelihood that the transactions contemplated by the merger agreement and the tender offer would be consummated, particularly in light of Tribune's reputation, ability to finance the transactions, lack of any financing condition in the merger agreement and ability to terminate the tender offer and the merger agreement only in limited circumstances.

- Times Mirror's future prospects, financial resources and condition, ability to access the capital markets, as well as the increased competition in all segments of Times Mirror's business from other companies and the significant challenges that Times Mirror would face if it did not proceed with the proposed transaction with Tribune.

- The belief by the Times Mirror board that, after review by independent members of the Times Mirror board, the transactions were fair and equitable to, and presented an attractive valuation for, Times Mirror stockholders.

The Times Mirror board additionally considered potential detriments involved in the tender offer and the merger, which include, but are not limited to, the following:

- Provisions of Times Mirror's charter discussed above under the caption "Background or the Merger" relating to and affected by the conversion or shares of Times Mirror series C common stock into shares of Times Mirror series A common stock in conjunction with the merger and the views of the Chandler Trusts with respect to such conversion.

- The conditions imposed during the negotiation of the merger and the terms of the merger agreement limiting Times Mirror's ability to consider other proposals by third parties and requiring Times Mirror to pay a $250 million termination fee under certain circumstances, which make it more difficult for Times Mirror to engage in a transaction superior to that contemplated by the merger agreement.

The Times Mirror board, however, determined that the foregoing detriments were outweighed by the potential benefits of the transactions described above.

The foregoing discussion of the information and factors considered and given weight by the Times Mirror board of directors is not intended to be exhaustive. In view of the variety of factors considered in connection with its evaluation and approval of the tender offer, the merger, the merger agreement and the transactions contemplated thereby, the Times Mirror board did not find it practicable to, and did not, quantify or otherwise assign relative weights to the specific factors considered in reaching its determination. In addition, individual members of the Times Mirror board may have assigned different weights to different factors.

DEAL TERMS

The deal was announced on March 13, 2000. Tribune agreed to pay about $6.4 billion in a combination of cash and stock. It planned to purchase up to 28 million Times Mirror shares for cash at $95 per share. Following that exchange, the remaining shares were to be exchanged for 2.5 shares of Tribune stock. The $95 offer was about twice the pre-announcement price per share of Times Mirror. The announcement of the merger caused Times Mirror stock to increase from $47.94 to $85.63 (+79%). Meanwhile, Tribune fell from $37.19 to $30.81 (−17%), although it recovered the next day. The $95 offer to Times Mirror shareholders was a 98% premium over the closing price of the day before. Although the premium was well over the market price, analysts noted that it was only about a 10.5 multiple on Times Mirror's expected 2000 EBITDA. Most newspaper deals had been in the 11X to 14X range.

VALUATION ANALYSIS

Cost of Capital

We begin our valuation analysis with the calculation of the cost of capital. We use CAPM to determine the cost of equity. We use a risk free rate of 6% and a market risk premium of 5%. Using Value Line beta estimates of 0.8 for Times Mirror and 1.05 for Tribune yields the following calculation:

Times Mirror: $.06 + .8*(.05) = 10\%$
Tribune: $.06 + 1.05*(.05) = 11.25\%$

We next proceed to calculate the weighted average cost of capital (WACC). We estimate the capital structure of Tribune to be 25% debt and that of Times Mirror to be 30% debt. The estimated tax rate for Tribune is 40% and that for Times Mirror is 41%. Because both firms are relatively healthy financially, we estimate an 8% cost of debt. These assumptions yield the following WACC calculation:

Times Mirror: $(.7*.10) + (.3*(1-.41)*.08) = 8.4\%$
Tribune: $(.75*.1125) + (.25*(1-.40)*.08) = 9.6\%$

Individual Companies

To determine if the merger will create value, it is first necessary to determine the value of the individual companies before the merger. Tables 3 and 4 illustrate pre-merger values of Tribune and Times Mirror. These are made using historical value driver patterns, the WACC calculated above, and certain judgments about the future based on the characteristics of the industry. Tribune had a higher operating margin, and we judged it to have more prospects for growth, thanks to its television possibilities. We judged Times Mirror (Table 4) to have relatively high margins, but little prospects for future growth, based on the nature of the newspaper industry. The prices per share that resulted from our assumptions in Tables 1 and 2 were close to the prices of the two firms before the merger was announced.

TABLE 1 Valuation of Tribune

R_0 = Initial year revenues	$3,222
n = Number of supernormal growth years	10
m = Net operating income margin	29.0%
T = Tax rate	40.0%
g_s = Supernormal growth period growth rate	8.0%
d_s = Supernormal growth period depreciation	0.7%
I_{ws} = Supernormal growth period working capital expenditures	0.6%
I_{fgs} = Supernormal growth period capital expenditures (gross)	0.9%
k_s = Supernormal growth period cost of capital	9.6%
g_c = Terminal period growth rate	3.0%
d_c = Terminal period depreciation	0.7%
I_{wc} = Terminal period working capital expenditures	0.6%
I_{fgc} = Terminal period capital expenditures	0.9%
k_c = Terminal period cost of capital	9.6%
h = calculation relationship = $[(1+g_s)/(1+k_s)]$	0.9854

$$V_0 = R_0[m(1-T)+d_s - I_{fgs} - I_{ws}] \sum_{t=1}^{n} \frac{(1+g_s)^t}{(1+k_s)^t} + \frac{R_0(1+g_s)^n[m(1-T)+d_c - I_{fgc} - I_{wc}]}{(1+k_s)^n} \times \frac{(1+g_c)}{(k_c - g_c)}$$

$$V_0 = R_0[m(1-T)+d_s - I_{fgs} - I_{ws}]h\left[\frac{h^n - 1}{h - 1}\right] + R_0[m(1-T)+d_c - I_{fgc} - I_{wc}]h^n \times \frac{(1+g_c)}{(k_c - g_c)}$$

V_0 = 3222.22[0.29(1-0.4)+0.007-0.009-0.006](0.9854)[((0.9854)^10-1)/(0.9854-1)]   <--present value of supernormal cash flows
+[3222.22(0.29(1-0.4)+0.007-0.009-0.006)(0.9854^10)][(1+0.03)/(0.096-0.03)]   <--present value of terminal value

= 3222.22(0.166)(0.9854)(9.368)   <--present value of supernormal cash flows
+[3222.22(0.166)(0.8632)]x[(1.03)/(0.096-0.03)]   <--present value of terminal value

= 4937.7+7205.9

= $12,144

Calculating Firm Value

Present value of supernormal cash flows	$4,938
Present value of terminal value	$7,206
Total present value of future cash flows	$12,144
Add: Marketable securities	0
Total value of the firm	$12,144
Less: Total interest bearing debt	2400
Equity value	$9,744
Number of shares	237
Value per share	$41.11

TABLE 2 Valuation of Times Mirror

R_0 = Initial year revenues	$3,190
n = Number of supernormal growth years	4
m = Net operating income margin	19.0%
T = Tax rate	41.0%
g_s = Supernormal growth period growth rate	5.0%
d_s = Supernormal growth period depreciation	0.4%
I_{ws} = Supernormal growth period working capital expenditures	0.4%
I_{fgs} = Supernormal growth period capital expenditures (gross)	0.6%
k_s = Supernormal growth period cost of capital	8.4%
g_c = Terminal period growth rate	0.0%
d_c = Terminal period depreciation	1.0%
I_{wc} = Terminal period working capital expenditures	0.0%
I_{fgc} = Terminal period capital expenditures	1.0%
k_c = Terminal period cost of capital	8.4%
h = calculation relationship = $[(1+g_s)/(1+k_s)]$	0.9686

$$V_0 = R_0[m(1-T) + d_s - I_{fgs} - I_{ws}]\sum_{i=1}^{n}\frac{(1+g_s)^i}{(1+k_s)^i} + \frac{R_0(1+g_s)^n[m(1-T) + d_c - I_{fgc} - I_{wc}]}{(1+k_s)^n} \times \frac{(1+g_c)}{(k_c - g_c)}$$

$$V_0 = R_0[m(1-T) + d_s - I_{fgs} - I_{ws}]h\left[\frac{h^n-1}{h-1}\right] + R_0[m(1-T) + d_c - I_{fgc} - I_{wc}]h^n \times \frac{(1+g_c)}{(k_c - g_c)}$$

V_0 = 3190.48[0.19(1-0.41)+0.004-0.006-0.004](0.9686)[((0.9686)^4-1)/(0.9686-1)]   <–present value of supernormal cash flows
    +[3190.48(0.19(1-0.41)+0.01-0.01-0)(0.9686^4)][(1+0)/(0.084-0)]   <--present value of terminal value

= 3190.48(0.1061)(0.9686)(3.8157)   <–present value of supernormal cash flows
    +[3190.48(0.1121)(0.8803)]x[(1)/(0.084-0)]   <--present value of terminal value

= 1251.1+3748.2

= $4,999

Calculating Firm Value

Present value of supernormal cash flows	$1,251
Present value of terminal value	$3,748
Total present value of future cash flows	$4,999
Add: Marketable securities	0
Total value of the firm	$4,999
Less: Total interest bearing debt	1300
Equity value	$3,699
Number of shares	72
Value per share	$51.38

Event Returns

Figure 1 shows the stock prices of Tribune and Times Mirror ten days before and after the announcement of the merger. Times Mirror experienced about an 80% increase, which is to be expected with the large premium that was offered by Tribune. After a sharp dip for Tribune immediately following the announcement, the market rebounded to about the same levels as before the merger.

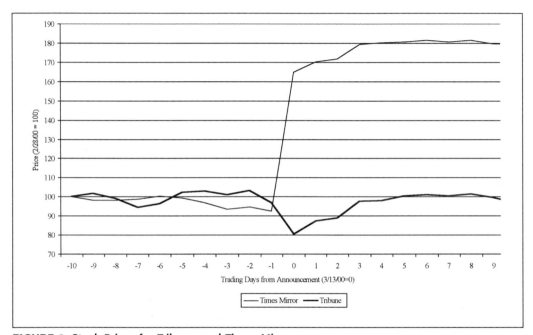

FIGURE 1 Stock Prices for Tribune and Times Mirror

IMPACT ON COMPETITORS

The merger between Tribune and Times Mirror will eventually lead to a direct challenge of the FCC prohibition of newspapers from owning broadcast media. The opponents of the regulation point out that it was brought into being by the Nixon Administration as a revenge for tough media coverage of the Vietnam War and Watergate. Opponents point out that cable and satellite TV, the Internet, and other new information sources have made the fears of one company controlling media in a market obsolete.

Tribune is at the forefront of the argument. Tribune's strategy of owning multiple media outlets in large markets is contingent on the FCC overturning its earlier decision. The Times Mirror acquisition gives Tribune newspapers in two markets where it already has broadcast television stations. However, barring a rule change, it will be allowed to hold the stations until their licenses come up for renewal (which will be in 2006 at the earliest). This gives Tribune years to continue lobbying for the FCC to change its rules. Some analysts believe that the outcome could be as simple as which candidate wins the 2000 Presidential election; while Gore has said he supports the rule, Bush has many advisors who are against it.

If the FCC regulations are discontinued, Tribune may be at the cutting edge of media consolidation. If there are true synergies to be had from owning newspapers as well as broadcast and internet media, other firms will have to reassess their strategies to maximize value.

QUESTIONS

1. Why was Robert Erburu, the CEO of Times Mirror from 1980 through part of 1995, replaced by an executive whose mission was to improve the performance of Times Mirror?

2. Evaluate the performance of Mark H. Willes as chief executive officer of Times Mirror from 1995 through the merger announcement with the Tribune on March 13, 2000.

3. Why was the Tribune interested in acquiring Times Mirror?

4. Why did the Chandler's agree to the sale of Times Mirror to the Tribune?

5. Estimate the value of the combined companies under optimistic and less optimistic judgments. Include the basis for the alternative judgments.

6. Discuss the division of gains from the merger to the shareholders of the Tribune and Times Mirror, respectively under the two alternative assumptions.

Case 24

AT&T's Renewal

AT&T is among the world's communications leaders, providing voice, data, and video telecommunications to large and small businesses, consumers, and government entities. AT&T and its subsidiaries furnish regional, domestic, international, local, and Internet communication transmission services, including cellular telephone and other wireless services. AT&T also provides billing, directory, and calling card services to support its communications business.

BACKGROUND HISTORY

AT&T has historically been the premier telecommunications company in the United States. Prior to 1984, it operated a virtual monopoly over U.S. telephone services. AT&T was incorporated in 1885 and had an early lead in the telephone market because it controlled the patents of Alexander Graham Bell, the telephone's inventor. Beginning in 1913, AT&T and the United States government agreed that AT&T would become a regulated monopoly. This relationship was at times contentious.

The U.S. government began an antitrust action against AT&T in 1949. This action was settled by a consent decree in 1956. AT&T was restricted from certain activities. The most notable was computers. The logic of the decree was that AT&T would be able to use revenues from its telephone monopoly to subsidize its ventures in other industries. While AT&T's Western Electric equipment company could sell computing equipment within AT&T, it was forbidden from selling to independent firms.

By the late 1970s, new technologies had emerged in the telecommunications industry. Microwaves and fiber optics began to lower the costs of entry to the industry. It was becoming more feasible for rival firms to build a network to rival AT&T's. However, as long as AT&T was protected by the government, serious rivals could not challenge AT&T. In recognition of the realities of new competition, AT&T was forced to break itself up.

On January 1, 1984, AT&T entered a new phase in its history. Its monopoly of local and long distance telecommunications was officially broken up. In place of the monolithic "Ma Bell" telephone company were the seven "Baby Bells" or regional Bell operating companies (RBOCs) and a "new" AT&T. AT&T saw significant changes in its structure. Its assets decreased from $149.5 billion to $34 billion. It only retained 373,000 of its close to 1 million employees from before the breakup. However, the hope was that the new, smaller company would be able to more effectively serve its customers and keep abreast of the changing technology of the telecommunications industry.

The breakup of the government sanctioned and regulated monopoly created a more dynamic telecommunications industry. The RBOCs still had few legitimate competitors. Because they operated the physical lines into people's homes, it was generally not feasible for companies to lay down their own lines to compete with a strong established firm.

However, in long distance, many new firms arose to challenge AT&T. MCI had long lobbied against AT&T's protection by the government. Once the firm was broken up, MCI became AT&T's most serious competitor. Another major competitor was Sprint. These new firms were able to compete by utilizing new technologies. Developments such as fiber optics allowed new competitors with established networks to match the capacity AT&T's older system at one-tenth of the cost. Because the bulk of AT&T's revenues were from long distance, the emergence of new rivals threatened the existence of the firm.

The telecommunications industry underwent even further transformation in the 1990s (for a more detailed assessment of the industry, see the WorldCom/Sprint case). Long distance prices eroded even further. By the end of the decade, firms were moving toward providing "all distance" service, which essentially would eliminate the surcharge for long distance. This resulted from the emergence of many competitors, which caused long distance prices to fall to the point where some analysts were calling them a commodity.

The Telecommunications Act of 1996 also increased the number of potential competitors. The Act was designed to increase competition throughout the industry. Local phone companies were opened up to the threat of increased competition. But AT&T's threat came from the RBOCs, the same firms that had been broken off from the company in 1984. These firms would be allowed to offer long distance service to their local customers provided they could show that sufficient local competition existed in their home markets. This meant that AT&T would be faced with additional large rivals in long distance.

Thus, AT&T's core business following the 1984 breakup was essentially in jeopardy. AT&T was faced with a unique strategic challenge. It had to reinvent itself so that its revenue sources were not locked into a dying industry.

AT&T'S M&A ACTIVITY

Computers

AT&T had a long history with computers. Even though Western Electric had been prohibited from selling equipment by the 1956 consent decree, it continued to make computing equipment for AT&T. Much of telephone switching equipment had been essentially specialized computing equipment.

However by the late 1980s, AT&T's computer segment was consistently losing money. This was particularly disturbing to the firm because statistics and projections at that time were already showing the potential explosive growth of data networking. AT&T recognized that computers transmitting data were likely to be a major source of economic growth in the United States. Thus, AT&T decided to expand its computer business.

In 1990, AT&T began an attempt to take over NCR. The hope was that AT&T would gain valuable expertise in the computer business. On December 3, 1990, AT&T made an unsolicited offer of $90 per share for NCR, which NCR called "grossly inadequate." This original bid would have represented a deal size of $6 billion. The market responded to the announcement by a 6.3% drop in AT&T's stock value, a market value of more than $2 billion. In the subsequent 6 months of bidding, AT&T raised its bid to $7.5 billion. During the bidding, AT&T's market value fell by between $3.9 billion and $6.5 billion. The shareholders of NCR finally approved the deal on September 13, 1991.

In the early 1990s, the computer industry underwent massive upheaval. The old-line computer firms, such as IBM and NCR were struggling as more competitors emerged and the industry continued to become decentralized. New competitors in the personal computer (PC) market, such as Hewlett Packard, Dell, Compaq, and others, eroded profit margins, forcing PC prices to the sub-$1,000 level before the end of the decade. New competitors were also emerging and having similar effects on the market for more sophisticated computers.

The condition of the computer industry indicates that NCR would likely have struggled as an independent company, let alone as a savior for AT&T's troubled computer business. Rather than leading AT&T to the forefront of the data networking and computer fields, NCR became a multi-billion dollar sinkhole for AT&T. AT&T's acquisition of NCR is regularly held up by journalists as a prime example of a failed merger.

While AT&T's computer business suffered, its equipment segment performed well. The equipment segment had originated as Western Electric in the old AT&T structure. It was on the cutting edge of new technologies, and provided crucial devices to AT&T's massive network. In fact, AT&T was worried that competitors, such as MCI and Sprint, were avoiding buying equipment from the division for fear of subsidizing AT&T, a competitor.

Restructuring

On September 20, 1995, AT&T announced a plan of restructuring. The core Communications Services division would become the focus of the company. The computer and equipment businesses would be spun off. Other businesses, such as AT&T Capital, would be sold off. The plan would become the largest voluntary breakup in U.S. history. The ultimate goal was to reorient AT&T on its core business of communications, and away from other businesses where it may have been lacking in the necessary competencies.

As may have been predicted, the computer and equipment divisions followed vastly different paths after the spin-offs. The equipment division, which became Lucent Technologies, became a "high flyer" on Wall Street. It benefited from the late 1990s frenzy for tech stocks. Lucent became identified as a key equipment maker, alongside Cisco and Nortel. It benefited from being out from under the AT&T umbrella. Meanwhile, the computer division, which was once again named NCR, has maintained a relatively flat stock price since being spun-off.

Wireless

AT&T's Bell Laboratories was among the leading sources of the wireless technology that led to cellular phones. However, AT&T felt that the market for wireless communications would remain limited. Company projections at the time of the breakup in 1984 estimated that only 900,000 cellular phones would be in use in the United States in 1995. These figures vastly miscalculated the popularity of wireless telephony. In December 1995, there were approximately 33.8 million cellular phone users in the U.S. As a result of its miscalculations concerning the market for wireless, AT&T elected not to pursue the wireless market in the 1980s. (For more information on the wireless telecom industry, see the Vodafone or WorldCom/Sprint cases.)

By the early 1990s, it became clear that AT&T had made an error in projecting the possibilities of wireless communications. The company felt that wireless would be critical to its ability to offer customers a full range of telecom services. While the firm had the resources to potentially build out its own wireless system, it was starting far behind the leading competitors, which were primarily the "Baby Bells." Thus, AT&T felt the necessity to seek out a merger partner that was established in the wireless industry. The firm that it eventually settled on was McCaw Cellular. It was acquired in 1993 for $12.6 billion. It gave AT&T a market presence in most of the major markets in the western and southern states. One complication in the combination was the concern of the Department of Justice and Federal Communications Commission about the re-expanding market power of AT&T. The firm was prohibited from giving its name to its wireless properties for a year. In addition, AT&T was forced to offer other long distance providers to its wireless customers, even though McCaw had previously had an exclusive contract with AT&T to provide long distance.

The McCaw acquisition gave AT&T an adequate start from which it could build a nationwide cellular network. This was accomplished through a combination of internal growth and acquisitions of local firms. AT&T was the first firm to build a substantially nationwide cellular network. This strategy was further strengthened in May 1998 when AT&T began its "Digital One Rate" program, which offered digital subscribers the same price for calls throughout the nation, without roaming or long distance surcharges. This program helped AT&T become one of the wireless leaders.

Despite its innovative pricing and national coverage, AT&T's wireless division was still competing in a difficult marketplace. Sprint's PCS wireless division had the advantage of being the first entirely digital nationwide system. Meanwhile, in September 1999, Bell Atlantic, GTE, and Vodafone Airtouch reached an agreement to combine their United States wireless holdings to form Verizon Wireless. This joint venture became the leading wireless provider in the United States. In addition, the combined resources and assets of the firms gave Verizon the ability to offer a pricing plan and nationwide coverage to rival AT&T. Another implication of the Verizon joint venture was the possibility that it could form a global network by coordinating with Vodafone's international wireless holdings. In response, AT&T reached a strategic alliance with British Telecom (BT) in which the firms agreed to work together to establish a global wireless system. AT&T and BT already were working together in Concert, a joint venture to offer international telecom services to businesses.

After establishing one of the leading U.S. wireless networks, AT&T recognized that significant improvements would be needed to retain that position. By the end of 1999, the firm realized that its system would need significant capital investments. AT&T needed to increase the capacity and capabilities of its wireless network. With the coming third generation (3G) wireless systems, AT&T needed to upgrade some of its infrastructure. To raise some of this needed capital, the company decided to establish a tracking stock for the AT&T Wireless division. AT&T offered 15% in an IPO in April 2000, raising over $10 billion for the unit. The rest of the stock was to be distributed to AT&T shareholders.

Local Phone Service

The Telecom Act of 1996 opened the door for AT&T to offer local telephone service. So long as AT&T could demonstrate that long distance was competitive, it could offer local phone service. In the summer of 1997, AT&T engaged in talks with SBC, a "Baby Bell," about a possible combination. This would create a combination of one of the leading local phone providers with the leading long distance firm. The FCC made an unusual move and condemned the possible combination before it was announced. Regulators were concerned that it would lead to a recombination of the anti-competitive Bell system. This set the precedent that AT&T would not be allowed to provide local phone service through the conventional RBOC system.

On January 8, 1998, AT&T announced a merger with Teleport. Teleport was a leading competing local exchange carrier (CLEC). The CLEC's had emerged following the Telecom Act as competitors to the RBOCs. The deal with Teleport was valued at $11.5 billion and gave AT&T access to local customers in many major markets, most notably New York City. This was AT&T's first major move toward becoming a major local competitor. However, the drawbacks of AT&T entering the CLEC market were that the CLEC's did not have large established customer bases and had not become sufficiently large to easily compete with the RBOCs. AT&T believed that a larger move would be necessary to become a serious local competitor.

AT&T's decision regarding local phone service was revealed on June 24, 1998 when the company announced a combination with Telecommunications, Inc. (TCI). The deal was valued at $44 billion. TCI was a leading provider of cable television, holding approximately 20% of the market. By acquiring it, AT&T gained access to potentially millions of customers via the established television cable lines. Cable offered the possibility to offer television, phone, and broadband Internet access via the same "pipeline" into the home. With the growing importance of the Internet and computer data traffic, this was seen as an important addition of capabilities.

The complication to AT&T's cable move was that the technology to offer telephone service over cable lines was still relatively undeveloped. This is a crucial problem because people depend on their phone lines to be working. The boxes that were required to distribute the television, phone, and Internet services were prone to problems. Investment in research became a critical new cost for AT&T, which needed to get the system to become reliable and easy to implement. The other difficulty was the archaic and patchwork nature of TCI's cable holdings. TCI did not have a standard system, but rather was a conglomeration of many formerly independent cable operators. These systems were often not technologically capable of offering all the services that AT&T aspired to offer. Hence, additional investments were required to upgrade these cable systems.

On April 22, 1999, AT&T made a move to increase the scale of its cable operations. It launched a hostile bid for MediaOne, which valued MediaOne in the neighborhood of $60 billion. MediaOne had already entered into an agreement to merge with Comcast, another cable firm. The deal created a stir in the telecom, television, and Internet industries. It showed rival telecom firms that AT&T was serious about its cable venture. Rival cable firms were concerned about AT&T's growing market share. The combined TCI and MediaOne networks would make AT&T the largest cable television provider in the United States. Internet firms, such as AOL, were concerned that AT&T would be able to use its control of cable lines to prevent customers from choosing an Internet service provider (ISP).

AT&T recognized that these firms could pose a serious challenge to its MediaOne bid in the form of potential rival bidders. This led to a series of complicated arrangements. AT&T arranged a swap of customers on a geographic basis with Comcast in order to get the firm to drop its competing bid for MediaOne. Comcast would also have an option to purchase up to 1.25 million additional subscribers in the future. AT&T also made a deal with Microsoft. Microsoft was concerned about the possibility of AT&T becoming an Internet leader and having the power to wring concessions out of Microsoft. The deal involved Microsoft's making an investment of $5 billion in AT&T convertible bonds. In exchange, AT&T agreed to use Microsoft software in the set-top boxes in at least 5 million households.

Regulators reviewed the merger for over a year before the merger was approved, with conditions. One of the main concerns was that AT&T would be in control of too large a percentage of the U.S. cable industry. This would violate a law that restricted the holdings of cable companies to 30% of the market. To resolve this conflict, AT&T was required to restructure its relationship with Time Warner Entertainment, of which MediaOne owned 25.5%. Further FCC commentary on the merger follows, as the FCC released on the FCC Web site:

> The FCC found that the combination of AT&T and MediaOne's cable and telephony assets and experience will help to increase local telephony and Internet access competition through the cable systems. The FCC noted that local telephony competition is an important goal of the Telecommunications Act of 1996, and it concluded that the merger would enable AT&T and MediaOne to compete in providing these new services more successfully than either company could independently or through joint ventures. In 1996, competitors to the incumbent phone companies had one percent of the local market. In the second quarter of 1999, competitors reached six percent of the market.
>
> In the broadband area, the FCC noted that it expects AT&T to fulfill its voluntary commitments to give unaffiliated Internet service providers (ISPs) access to its cable systems to provide broadband services to consumers. The FCC also noted that AT&T has entered a proposed consent decree with the U.S. Department of Justice, which requires the merged firm to divest its interest in the cable broadband ISP Road Runner and to obtain Justice Department approval prior to entering certain types of broadband arrangements with Time Warner and America Online. Given the nascency of broadband Internet services and growing competition from alternative broadband access providers, the FCC declined to impose additional conditions in this regard. The FCC emphasized, however, that it will scrutinize broadband developments closely and will review its policies if competition fails to grow as expected, especially if the merged firm fails to fulfill its commitment to open its cable systems or otherwise threatens the openness and diversity of the Internet.

AT&T'S FUTURE PROSPECTS

By late summer 2000, AT&T was trading at about $30, after reaching as high as $63 in February 1999. The low price has been attributed to a variety of factors. AT&T's cable bet still faces considerable uncertainty. It is unclear if consumers will move toward cable phone lines. AT&T's plan of bundling a variety of telecom services is very dependent on finding the technology to make a cable phone as effective and reliable as conventional phones. AT&T also must deal with many effective competitors. AT&T's long distance business has deteriorated under competition. The move to cable has created an entirely new set of rivals for AT&T to deal with.

A more fundament problem with AT&T's stock price has been the company's declining earnings projections. While analysts and the market recognized the decline of consumer long distance, AT&T has been consistently disappointing with its business services division's earnings. A *Wall Street Journal* article of August 4, 2000 analyzed the problems. The core problems centered around the slower than anticipated growth of business services. AT&T had anticipated that growth in this segment could be used to fund the necessary investments to cable, wireless, and other parts of AT&T's infrastructure. However, shortfalls in the business division became a serious concern of analysts. The *WSJ* article attributed some of the problems to a cost-cutting retirement program that AT&T implemented to encourage certain middle managers to retire. The program was so popular that it had to be stopped a year early. It had the side effect of encouraging some managers in business services with established relationships to retire. The loss of these relationships was often cited by firms as their reason for changing companies away from AT&T.

The languishing stock price led many to begin speculating that AT&T may be best suited to be split-up again. Some analysts project that the separate pieces of AT&T could trade as high as $73 a share after being spun off or broken into tracking stock of wireless, cable, consumer telecommunications, and business services.

QUESTIONS

1. What approaches has AT&T taken to deal with the decline of its long distance business? Have these approaches been successful?

2. How have regulatory agencies affected AT&T's strategic options?

3. In what ways has financial engineering (spin-offs, tracking stock, etc.) played a role in AT&T's renewal?